ROYAL
WORCESTER
PORCELAIN

By the same author
Illustrated Guide to Worcester Porcelain 1751 to 1793

Frontispiece, 6 pieces by later painters; from right, top row, plate embossed and pierced, decorated in old ivory and painted with 'The Guitar Player', after Meissonier and panels of flowers by Hawkins in 1893; centre, fish subject by Salter on a Rose du Barry one coat ground; left, Australian birds painted by R. Austin in 1915, surrounded by an acid etched 'Tooled Leather' border; bottom row, landscape in Corot style by G. H. Evans in 1932, with royal blue ground and rich enamel border, signed by T. Morton; dessert dish, pattern C55 fruit centre painted by Sebright; left, 'Bluebells in Kew Gardens' by R. Rushton in 1935.

ROYAL WORCESTER PORCELAIN

from 1862 to the Present Day

HENRY SANDON

Curator of the Dyson Perrins Museum
and The Worcester Royal Porcelain Co. Ltd.

Photographs by John and Joan Beckerley

 Clarkson N. Potter, Inc./Publisher   NEW YORK

DISTRIBUTED BY CROWN PUBLISHERS, INC.

Contents

List of Plates

COLOUR PLATES

MONOCHROME PLATES

All between pages 18 and 19

MONOCHROME PLATES

All between pages 34 and 35

MONOCHROME PLATES

All between pages 82 and 83

MONOCHROME PLATES

All between pages 98 and 99

MONOCHROME PLATES

All between pages 146 and 147

MONOCHROME PLATES

All between pages 194 and 195

MONOCHROME PLATES

All between pages 242 and 243

Foreword

The wide coverage of this book unfolds in a clear and interesting manner the history of the Royal Worcester Company from its formation in 1862 to the present time.

The story is unfolded with the help of factory records and documents and Mr. Sandon has rightly laid emphasis on the personal aspect, giving interesting details of the work and lives of the talented artists, designers and modellers who made the Royal Worcester name famous throughout the world for quality of design and finish.

This richly illustrated work is unique in the field of ceramic reference books and is unlikely ever to be superseded—so thoroughly has the Curator of the Dyson Perrins Museum at the Royal Worcester Works researched the many available records. The visual attractions of these varied pieces are plainly seen. This book ably fills in their historical background and tells the story of the men and women who produced such highly collectable and decorative objects.

GEOFFREY A. GODDEN

Author's Preface

This book deals with the production of china and porcelain at Worcester from 1862 to the beginning of 1972 and covers the factories involved: the Worcester Royal Porcelain Company, Grainger's, and Hadley's, all of whom amalgamated, and Locke's which did not join the main factory.

All these wares, with the exception of those of Locke's factory, are generally known today as Royal Worcester and it may be asked why a book is needed dealing with wares that are relatively recent in date. However, there is now as much interest in the fine wares of the Worcester factories of this time as in those of the Dr. Wall (or first) period and with some of the limited edition subjects appearing in the world's major auction rooms while still in current production in the factory it can be appreciated that it is difficult to draw a line as to what is collectable and what is not. Today, rightly, we are not so much concerned with the age of a piece as its quality and beauty.

The book concerns itself in detail with the personalities involved in the factory, especially with the artists and craftsmen, as it is my firm belief that a knowledge of the personality of the man or woman who made or decorated a particular work of art gives a greater understanding of its qualities. I have been most fortunate in being privileged to work among so many of the characters involved in the recent history, and in being able to obtain details of those who are no longer there from their colleagues.

I also feel that a knowledge of how particular shapes or decorations are produced is very important in appreciating the qualities of an item. In fact the sections dealing with processes and artists are, I think, among the most important parts of the book.

Also important is the complete list of all the shapes produced during the years from 1862. This incredible list of shapes will enable the reader to ascertain what figures were issued as sets or groups, the different sizes of each shape produced, whether a vase should have a cover to be complete, and if it is rare or common.

Acknowledgments

The writing of this book would not have been possible but for the ready assistance and kind help given by a great number of people. In particular my grateful thanks are due to the Trustees of the Dyson Perrins Museum for allowing me to photograph and illustrate a great number of pieces from their superb collection of Worcester china; to the Directors of the Worcester Royal Porcelain Company Limited for allowing me to photograph examples of pieces of recent production, for granting access to records and pattern books and for guidance and help at all stages; to the Worcester staff, artists and craftsmen, who have ungrudgingly provided information about processes, skills and old colleagues. I have had great help from Cyril Shingler, the previous Curator of the Dyson Perrins Museum; from Robert Stones who for a year assisted in the Museum and obtained a great deal of information from the older workmen; from the many thousands of correspondents who have provided information about their pieces that have built up into our present full knowledge about the wares.

Many people have kindly allowed me to photograph interesting and rare pieces not represented in the Museum Collection, or provided information which has proved helpful, and a few photographs have been provided. These include: Her Majesty the Queen, Messrs. Allen & Bott, Mr. V. Baldwin, Mr. R. Baldwyn, Mr. E. Benton-Evans, Berrows Newspapers Limited, Mr. J. Broad, Mr. D. Bullock, Mr. R. Bullock, Mr. R. Checketts, Mrs. J. Child, Mr. G. T. Clark, Mr. E. F. E. Collins, Mr. A. B. Demaus, Dolphin Antiques, Miss F. G. Doughty, Mr. M. Dowty, Miss Farmer, Miss M. Fildes, Mr. L. Furnival, Mr. G. A. Godden, Messrs. Godden of Worthing Ltd., Mrs. M. Haig, Miss N. Halliwell, Mrs. Harrison, Mrs. Harvey, Mrs. B. Heirs, Mrs. M. Hewitt, Mr. A. H. Hipkiss, Mr. E. M. Holdstock, Miss J. C. Hoskins, Mrs. D. Howell, Mr. J. Hughes, Mr. J. Lance, Messrs. Lees Brothers, Mrs. Lester, Mrs. M. MacGeoch, Miss D. Rea, Mr. G. H. Robertson of A. C. Cooper Limited, the Misses Sievers, Mrs. D. Silvester, Miss D. Smith, Miss F. Stevens, Mr. C. S. Titman and Mr. C. W. Ward. The uncredited illustrations are of examples from the Works collection or from the Dyson Perrins collection now displayed in the Dyson Perrins Museum at the Worcester Royal Porcelain Company.

Special thanks are due to John and Joan Beckerley who, with very few

B

exceptions, have taken all the splendid photographs that are such an important part of this book.

My thanks are also due to Mr. Geoffrey de Bellaigue of the Lord Chamberlain's Office and to the staff of the Royal Palaces.

Introduction

Although this book is about production of porcelain and china at Worcester from the year 1862, it will surely help the majority of readers to a greater understanding of this period if a brief account of the earlier years is given. Worcester's history is so long and has become so complicated by the different factories and divided periods that the family tree printed on page xxi will help to explain this at a glance.

The first production of porcelain in Worcester was in Warmstry House, on the banks of the River Severn, to the north of the Cathedral, where the part of the Technical College beside the Bishop's Palace now stands. In June 1751 the Worcester Porcelain Company with fifteen partners, headed by Dr. John Wall and William Davis, was established. Early in the following year the short-lived factory of Miller & Lund in Bristol was acquired and the moulds and some of the workmen brought to Worcester, where a similar soft paste was made; an artificial porcelain body, the main ingredient of which was soapstone from The Lizard in Cornwall. One advantage of vessels made from this body was that they did not crack nor craze when boiling water was put in, unlike the wares of some of the other English factories. So the concentration was on the making of superb useful wares, principally tea and dessert wares, and very little purely ornamental ware was made, such as figures. Great quantities of underglaze blue and white and onglaze enamel decorated wares were made, finely painted in an Oriental or Chinoiserie style. From about 1755 or so the application of transfer printing to porcelain was extensively used, at first onglaze and then underglaze from about 1760. Fine ground colours—yellow, green, turquoise and claret—began to be used after about 1760 but most of the best quality wares had the typical Worcester deep blue cobalt underglaze ground, the blue either solid or painted with scales, reserving panels in which were painted such subjects as fabulous birds, flowers and insects.

The period from 1751 until Dr. Wall died in 1776 is known as the Dr. Wall period. The principal marks used were crescents on blue and white wares and fretted squares on blue grounds with onglaze enamels, but many pieces were unmarked and some bore copies of Meissen, Sèvres and other factory marks. The factory was run by William Davis until his death in 1783 and then was bought by Thomas Flight. The years from 1776 to 1793 are known as the

Davis/Flight period, when patterns became more simple, often just gold and white, and a great quantity of printing in a Nankin style in a violet-toned blue was made. The marks were either a very small crescent or the so-called disguised Chinese numerals.

In 1793 Thomas Flight and his sons were joined by Martin Barr and the period to 1807 is known as the Flight & Barr period. The marks are either an extremely small crescent or a B scratched into the base. Patterns continued to be rather plain. A family change in 1807 resulted in the firm being known as Barr Flight & Barr until 1813. The mark was either the words Barr Flight & Barr in various forms or the impressed letters B F B under a crown—the Company having had its first Royal Warrant from George the Third in 1789. Styles of decoration were very flamboyant, such as shells and feathers or the splendid colours of the Japan patterns. In 1813 another change of name occurred and the factory was known as Flight Barr & Barr until 1840, the mark being the name or the impressed letters F B B under a crown. Patterns continued to be very colourful, finely painted and gilded and many services continued to be made for Royalty and great families in this country and abroad. In 1840 Flight Barr & Barr amalgamated with Chamberlain.

Robert Chamberlain had set up a decorating establishment and retail shop at Diglis in about 1786 mainly buying ware in the white or with underglaze blue from Caughley in Shropshire and a smaller amount from Flight. Gold and some onglaze decoration would be added to these pieces and then they would be sold—'Chamberlain's Worcester' being marked on a few of the pieces. By the mid 1790s Chamberlain was making his own wares and he followed a stylistic development similar to Flight. In 1840 the two factories amalgamated—Mr. R. W. Binns calling this 'a Marriage of Convenience and not of love'—and Chamberlain being the dominant firm, Flights moved over to Diglis, the old Warmstry House factory being used for the production of tiles made in the Medieval style. There was more room available at Diglis and the Company, now called Chamberlain & Co., enlarged the factory. Quality of production tended to decline and by the time of the Great Exhibition of 1851 it had reached a low ebb.

In 1852 the firm was bought by W. H. Kerr and R. W. Binns and the years until 1862 are known as the Kerr & Binns period. A great artistic recovery is seen, from the exciting Shakespeare or Dublin service of 1853 to the beautiful service made for Queen Victoria in 1861. When in 1862 Mr. Kerr retired, Mr. Binns formed the joint stock company that is the subject of this book.

Another important factory in Worcester was Grainger's, in the Blockhouse area of the City, on the corner of St. Martin's Gate and Pheasant Street. This was founded by Thomas Grainger, who had married Robert Chamberlain's daughter, in 1801. From 1801 to 1812 the firm was known as Grainger Wood & Company; some of the ware being bought in the white and decorated. From 1812 to 1839 the firm was Grainger Lee & Company, and they were manufacturing their own china. After the death of Thomas Grainger, his son George continued the business under the name of George Grainger &

Company until it was taken over by the Worcester Royal Porcelain Company in 1889, although production continued at the St. Martin's Gate factory until 1902.

Two other factories in Worcester were James Hadley and Sons, near the main Diglis factory, which ran from 1896 to 1905 and was bought by the main Company, and Locke & Company's factory, under the arches of Shrub Hill railway station, from 1895 to 1904, which was not taken over and whose wares do not count as Royal Worcester.

A family tree can be expressed as follows:

ST. MARTIN'S GATE FACTORY

Grainger Wood	Grainger Lee	Grainger and Company		Royal China Works	
1801	1812	1839		1889	1902

DIGLIS FACTORY

Chamberlain			Chamberlain and Co.	Kerr and Binns	Worcester Royal Porcelain Company →	
Circa 1786			1840	1852	1862	1905

WARMSTRY HOUSE FACTORY

Dr. Wall Period	Davis/ Flight	Flight and Barr	Barr Flight and Barr	Flight Barr and Barr		DIGLIS ROAD
						James Hadley and Sons
1751	1776	1793	1807	1813		1896

SHRUB HILL WORKS

Locke and Company

1895   1904

Glossary

Before progressing to the story of the Worcester Royal Porcelain Company and the review of its very varied products it would be as well for non-technical readers to understand the various terms that are employed, which are therefore contained in this brief glossary.

Bodies

Barr's porcelain An experimental body made in the 1890s marked with a mark incorporating the words 'Barr's Porcelain'.

Bone china A light, white, strong, translucent body, the Worcester recipe being 50 per cent ox bone, 25 per cent china stone (feldspar) and 25 per cent china clay, in its finest form, firing at about 1250° C.

Crown ware A high-fired earthenware, a form of semi-porcelain, with a large proportion of clay, that is heavy and opaque.

Faience or majolica, names derived from Faenza and Majorca; the body does not consist of clay only, but contains sand and fluxes; it is always glazed.

Ivory A form of glazed Parian, used from the 1850s.

Majolica Like faience, generally has a porous body coloured with a white, opaque tin-glaze.

Parian Named after the island of Paros, another title being statuary porcelain, as the body imitated Greek marble statues so well. An unusually high amount of feldspar—about 70 per cent—forms the body, plus nearly 30 per cent china clay and a small amount of cullet (scrap glass). The body does not need glaze, but it can be glazed, and Parian was invariably slip-cast as it was not a very plastic body, used mainly for ornamental wares but also for many useful wares at Worcester. Firing temperature about 1200–1250° C.

Porcelain Technically the only true porcelain is hard porcelain of the type made in China for many hundreds of years, the body comprising *kaolin* and *pe-tun-se*—china clay and china stone. The firing sequences are different from most other ceramic bodies, in that the first firing is merely a hardening at about 900–1000° C then, after glazing, the main firing is done in a reducing atmosphere of over 1400° C.

Semi-porcelain A high feldspar content body, low fired and slightly porous, basically opaque but possibly having slight translucence in the thinnest parts.

Terracotta A common, red, unglazed pottery, made by James Hadley in the 1894–6 period before he started his main factory. Popular at several nineteenth-century factories.

Vitreous ware A difficult term, as it is now used so vaguely. Basically it is a highly vitrified body containing clay, quartz and feldspar, matured at a rather low temperature (under 1200° C), the glaze fired at under 1100° C. It is mechanically very strong, but very heavy and opaque.

Wall body A twentieth-century china body which has a green translucency when held up to the light, like the wares of the Dr. Wall period.

Colours

Dry colours Matt or dry enamels, fired lower than they should be, and so underfired. While this is basically a fault, improved by an increase in the flux used, the effect can be very attractive when deliberately used. These are low flux colours.

Enamels Oxides of enamel, mixed with fat oil and turpentine or aniseed, are used as most onglaze colours. These are high flux colours.

High kiln colours These are mostly ground laid, high temperature fired over 810° C, such as sage green, ruby, yellow, pink and black, medium flux colours.

Coral ware A pretty blush colour pink.

Nickled Raised colour is allowed to dry to a hard paste, indents are then pushed into the centre with a domed stick, indenting the raised colour.

Prismatic Used at Worcester from the 1890s, beautiful rainbow effects.

Raised Nicks and niches cut into the raised colour near the edges.

Raphaelesque Capo di Monte-style colours, purples predominating, used on a glazed Parian (ivory) body.

Satin An early form of shot enamel done by pencilling or aerographing.

Shaded blush pink From early 1898s, the successor to stained ivory.

Shot calabash A speckled form of calabash colour, produced by spraying, then flicking petrol on a brush onto the colour; the two break away on the surface, leaving the mottled effect.

Shot enamel From 1894, a very beautiful varying effect, could be used in a Harlequin way in a service.

Shot silks Similar to the above, with a satin finish.

Decorating Processes

Aerographing Spraying on of colour by means of an aerograph pencil; this is not a mechanical process but a legitimate way of producing certain sprayed and variable effects.

Fruit Worcester traditional painted fruit style has two firings. First the large pink fruits are painted (apples, peaches, etc.) in yellow, orange and just a touch of pink; the orange is not the colour of an actual orange but a very deep yellow; the pink in the first firing is really just shading to indicate the dark sides of the fruit. This is then fired on in the kiln. The piece returns to the painter for the second fire colours; a coat of pink is applied very thinly and allowed to dry, in a second coat of pink the artist uses more fat oil in the brush, applied on top of the first dry coat, which calls for considerable skill and many years of practice, as it is only too easy to pull the first coat off; the reason for this sequence is to give the great depth of colour that is typical of the Worcester style. The pieces then have their second kiln firing.

Ivories See page xxvi.

Limoges enamels The long and complicated building up of onglaze translucent white enamels over a deep underglaze cobalt blue ground. The finest work in this field was done by Thomas Bott, almost equalled by the work of his son T. J. Bott. The depth of the heaviest built-up parts is quite considerable and the work could take a long time.

Pâte-sur-pâte A difficult process involving the building up of thicknesses of slip painting on the biscuit body, which is then glazed over; done with skill, the translucent slip allows the body to show through giving great depth to the effects. The onglaze equivalent was Limoges enamels.

Pencilled A strange term; colouring is not done with a pencil but painted on by brush, or a domed hair brush called a 'mop'.

Prickwork A piece of tracing paper is placed over a pattern and pricked through to obtain the main outline of the pattern. The paper is then laid on the vessel to be decorated, colour is sprinkled on which leaves a tiny dotted outline, used as the basis of completing the painting by hand. This dotted outline may be seen with careful scrutiny.

Onglaze Colours put on after the glaze has been fired are termed onglaze; they have to be fired into the glaze at lower temperatures than the glaze is fired at. No glaze is put on the top of onglaze colours, as the temperature needed for firing the glaze would burn away the enamels. The colours change in the firing, often quite considerably, and great knowledge and skill is needed to learn and use these changes correctly. Most paintings require two or more onglaze firings to build up the final colours necessary.

Reserves Panels left white, surrounded by coloured grounds, are termed reserves and in these are put scenes in onglaze enamels. The reserves can be left white by masking them with paper cutouts or by the use of resist.

Resist Parts to be left free from colour are painted with a resist, such as sugar and water, which resists the overall application of the colour.

Sabrina This beautiful colour effect was done on a Parian body. The vases were first fired in a temperature high enough to allow them to be handled but at the same time remaining porous. Decoration was then painted on using black resist, in the same way as resist is used in blacking out in acid patterns, more or less of the resist being used according to whether the subject is to stand out in white on the surface or in gradations of tone merging into the blues and greens of the staining in the colour impregnating process. The vases were then impregnated with solutions of metallic salts, chiefly cobalt, chrome green and copper green, with sulphuric acid and water that make the solution. The impregnation had to be done by someone with artistic taste and imagination and each piece was treated separately. When they had absorbed a sufficient quantity of the solution the pieces were placed in hot drying cupboards and when dry were biscuit-fired. During firing the various mineral salts crystallised and often produced starry points and luminous clouding. Every piece was unique, as its final effect could not be foreseen nor controlled. Many of the best painters worked on Sabrina ware.

Shot silks Types of satin finishes that shimmer with various greens and bronzes that could be pencilled or aerographed.

Sgraffito Designs incised into the raw clay or through a different slip to expose the body.

Underglaze Colours put onto the biscuit so that the fired glaze covers and protects them. Because of the necessity of firing temperatures higher than that of the glaze, the colour possibilities are limited, the main one being cobalt.

Glazing

Crazing The breaking out on the surface of fine hair cracks caused by the glaze shrinking more than the body during the cooling. Strictly a fault, but it can be turned into a virtue by being deliberately induced.

Glaze The skin of glass that covers the surface of the body and is fired on in what is called the glost kiln. Its composition varies according to the body. In glazes for china and vitreous ware the main ingredient is silica, and boric oxide is mainly used; a lead oxide gives greater brilliance to the glaze and was used in the early days, but was dangerous because of the lead content. A form is now used which is not dangerous. From the 1890s the words 'Leadless Glaze' with the Worcester mark indicate the fact that its use had stopped.

Matt glazes These are opaque, the crystals being very small and evenly dispersed; the glaze has a smooth and velvety surface.

Golds

Acid Gold A piece is printed with an acid resist pattern, then the other areas are blacked out with acid resist. A etched pattern is bitten into a plate by immersing it in a bath of hydrofluoric acid and the raised part is then gilded by hand.

Chasing The scratching of patterns into the gold with agate.

Cut up black, or red Gold first, then the colour is painted on by brush. This can be done by a gold print. The gold is usually a flat gold and not raised.

Dead gold Precipitated gold used mostly on vases or very rich services, it is best gold, requiring two firings, the gold coming out dead or dull from the kiln, showing it was in good order for chasing and burnishing.

G.E. way (i.e. 'gold edge way') A term used by gilders to indicate that whatever shape you are working on—round edge, gadroon etc.—you follow it round according to its natural edge.

Dragged gold Generally done on modelled edges, the brush dragged down in strokes to leave an ill-defined, messy ending.

Gold Many different qualities of gold are used, ranging up to the finest 24 carat gold. The gold is generally powdered and mixed with a medium to make it flow, the medium burning away in the kiln firing to leave the precipitated gold, which has to be burnished with fine silver sand, bloodstone or agate to bring up its bright, shining appearance.

Jewelling The application of droplets of gold or enamel onto the surface, to imitate jewels, a fine example being the Countess of Dudley déjeuner service, see Plate 27.

Lustre Solutions or suspensions of metallic resinates mainly applied by brushing; carbon dioxide is produced during firing which produces the lustrous effect.

Raised gold Pattern traced in raised colour, which stands up proud of the piece. After it is fired, the raised colour is gilded by hand with best gold and fired again and then burnished.

Ground Colours

B. Blue Term used in the industry for underglaze cobalt-blue.

Colours Used as ground colours are such as celadon, cobalt, gold, maroon, rose du Barry, turquoise.

Ground laying A coat of ground laying oil is evenly applied, carefully 'bossed' with a fine silk pad packed with cotton wool to remove brush marks. The ceramic powdered colour is applied by means of a cotton wool pad and worked into the ground laying oil. This highly skilled operation, at its best, can produce beautifully smooth and even ground colours.

Powder A broken, speckled ground is produced by blowing or dusting powdered colour onto an oiled layer. The usual colour is blue but other powdered colours can be used.

Scale blue The painting or printing of scaled blue patterns underglaze in the style of eighteenth-century Worcester.

Ivory Colours

Blush ivory Later version of stained ivory, a pinkish colour often used under flower paintings and often *incorrectly* referred to as 'biscuit' ware.

Cream ivory A lighter form of the colour.

Dry ivory A matt effect.

Ivory decoration Most forms were put on with a domed hair brush called a mop, or they could be done by ground laying, aerographing, or with a sponge, all giving different textures.

Old ivory One colour only with no shading, looking like the colour of an elephant's tusk.

Pencilled Put on with a brush.

Stained ivory Put on in two shades—a deeper yellow base and a brown, shaded, veneted surface.

Making Processes

Biscuit The term given to the once-fired body, before it is 'glazed'; the kiln in which the raw clay pieces are fired is called the biscuit kiln. The term should not be applied to stained or blush ivory decorated wares.

Casting Process of pouring slip (liquid clay) into porous plaster of Paris moulds. The water is absorbed by the plaster and when sufficient thickness of body has built up around the edge of the mould the surplus slip is poured away, leaving the resultant shape hollow, and when it has contracted it can be removed from its mould. Any pattern incised in the mould will come out embossed on the piece and a pattern embossed in the mould will emerge impressed on the piece.

Jiggering Producing flat ware—saucers, plates, dishes—is done by pressing a bat of clay over a revolving mould using a shaped template or profile to produce the shape of the underside of the plate.

Jollying Hollow wares—cup, bowls, casseroles—are made by an inside-out version of jiggering, in that the clay is pressed into a hollow, revolving mould. Both these processes can be done mechanically, or semi-mechanically.

Moulds Made from plaster of Paris, an original model being made from which by alternating series of positive and negative moulds is made the master mould, from which working moulds are made. The positive mould is called a case and the negative mould a block.

Reticulating The term used for piercing; holes have to be cut in the raw clay while it is in the 'green', or leather hard stage, before it has fully dried out.

Throwing The ancient process of making pots by hand on a revolving wheel head. A lump of clay is centred on the revolving wheel, opened up in the centre and, with water as a lubricant, right and left hand squeeze and pull the sides upwards, shaping the vessel by pressure. The method is not now used to a great extent in the china or porcelain industry as the body is not very plastic and lends itself much more to casting, jiggering or jollying.

Marks

Impressed marks Pushed into the raw body with a die.

Incised marks Scratched into the raw clay when it has dried, but before it is fired. Many early Royal Worcester shape numbers are incised, as are workmen's marks.

Moulded marks Produced on a pad raised above the surface of the base. Some early Royal Worcester Trade Marks (Mark 1) and diamond-shape registration marks are put on in this way.

Printed marks Put on over the glaze and comprise factory marks, shape and registration numbers and other marks such as names of dealers.

Registration marks Two kinds, both referring to registrations of shape and pattern at the Patent Office. The earliest form was a diamond shape which by its code of letters and numbers in the corners shows the date of registration. It does *not* indicate the date of making of the actual piece, which would be made after that date. The later method of registration was in the form of a number. Neither the diamond shape, nor the number, show directly the factory that produced the piece.

Printing

Cover coat Modern method of litho transfers, sometimes called 'slide-off' transfers. The transfer is printed onto simplex litho paper by silk screen process and overprinted with a clear coat which acts as a support of the transfer in place of a backing. The transfer is soaked in water, which releases the paper and it is then placed on the ware and sponged on. It is an easier method to use than the size down process and, if well done, produces splendid colour densities.

Lithographic transfers Now used widely for colour printing, were originally of size down and now are cover coat type.

Register Transfer printing done for one colour at a time, the pattern being slowly and skilfully built up by registering it on the pieces. This can be done by gold printing and for crests, but if work is done by hand it is not called registering.

Size down The description of the old method of litho transferring in which the patterns were cut up and pressed onto the pieces which had previously been painted with a thin layer of varnish. It was not possible to slide the lithos around to get them into the correct position, as can be done with the cover coat versions, so it was a much more skilled job.

Transfer The great traditional method of printing by taking pulls on thin paper from an engraved copper plate. The process has been in force at Worcester for over two hundred years in virtually an unchanged form. The method is that a heated oil-based engraved copper plate has a single enamel colour or gold rubbed hard into the incised lines, the surface is cleaned off with a spatula and polished with a tow-filled boss so that the colour is now only in the incised lines. A sheet of toughened tissue paper is wetted with soapy water, spread onto the still hot copper, to which it sticks and it is pressed through a roller press, rather like a Victorian mangle. The rollers are reversed and the copper is put back upon the hot back-plate. The paper tissue is very carefully peeled off, leaving the pattern printed on the paper in reverse image. The vessel to be printed has meanwhile been warmed and covered with a sticky varnish and the print is cut up by the team of girls working with the printer, carefully placed upside down on the piece and rubbed hard on. It is impossible to slide the print around, of course, and great skill is needed in laying down the more complicated patterns and especially borders so that they join without gaps or overlaps. When dry, the paper is washed away, the pattern carefully checked for any small missing parts which are carefully 'mended' by hand and then the piece is fired. A fresh print has to be pulled each time, so it will be appreciated that it is not a quick, mass-production method of decoration but it is, at its best, superb.

Chapter I

The 1860s and 70s

On the 24th day of June 1862 the new Articles of Association of The Worcester Royal Porcelain Company Limited were drawn up. This new Company, incorporated under the Joint Stock Companies Acts, was the direct successor of the original Worcester Porcelain Company whose articles were drawn up in 1751.

The short wording of the Memorandum of Association is worth quoting in full:

The name of the Company is 'The Worcester Royal Porcelain Company Limited'.

The registered office of the Company is to be established in England.

The objects for which the Company is established are to carry on the business of Manufacturers of and Dealers in Porcelain Parian Earthenware Stoneware and other Ceramic Wares Terra Cotta Tiles and Glass and to carry on any branches of any such business and to purchase and sell any of the products of any such business or of any branch thereof and to do all such other things as are incidental or conducive to the attainment of the above objects.

The liability of the Shareholders is limited.

The nominal capital of the Company is Forty thousand pounds divided into Eighty Shares of Five hundred pounds each.*

We the several persons whose names and addresses are subscribed are desirous of being formed into a Company in pursuance of this memorandum of Association and we respectively agree to take the number of Shares in the capital of the Company set opposite our respective names:

Edward Phillips of Hanley, in the County of
Stafford, Porcelain and Glass Manufacturer.   Twenty shares

William Litherland of Bold Street, Liverpool,
Glass and China Merchant.   Four shares

---

* This paragraph was subsequently altered by Special resolution passed 10th October 1864 to read that the nominal capital is £70,000 divided into eighty shares of £500, to be known as A shares and 3,000 shares of £10 each to be known as B shares.

Martin Abell of Foregate Street in the City of Worcester, Banker.	Two shares
Peter Hardy of The Grange in the Parish of Claines in the County of Worcester, Iron Founder.	Two shares
Alexander Clunes Sherriff of Shrubb Hill in the City of Worcester, Esquire.	Two shares
William Thompson Adcock of Lansdowne Crescent in the City of Worcester, Gentleman.	Two shares
Richard Padmore of Henwick Hall in the County of Worcester, Iron Founder.	Two shares
Thomas Southall of the London Road in the City of Worcester, Solicitor.	Two shares

The occupations of the eight subscribers read not unlike the fifteen in the 1751 Articles, even though the provincially rural aspect has moved towards an industrial climate and the new group has a practical potter and a ceramic dealer among them, an advantage not shared by the early pioneers.

Factory production was in the capable hands of Edward Phillips, a practical potter from Staffordshire who threw in his lot with Worcester until he resigned in 1875, subsequently going to Derby to refound the porcelain industry there. Artistic production was under the control of Richard William Binns, invariably known as R. W. Binns, who had been the partner of W. H. Kerr, having previously been Art Director at the Falcon Glass Works of Messrs. Apsley Pellat and was to be the mainstay of the Company for the remainder of the century.

Edward Phillips and R. W. Binns were appointed directors together with five others—Martin Abell, James Gully, Peter Hardy, Thomas Hill and Alexander Sherriff—and upon these seven fell the task of steering the Company through the difficult early days. Although the ten years of the Kerr & Binns period had done a lot to improve the quality of the Worcester products after the low state to which the factory had descended in the last years of the Chamberlain period, there was still a long way to go, artistically and financially.

In fact, the first Company report in 1863 makes depressing reading. The factory was reported to be in a very poor state, needing over £1,000 to put it in order; a profit of only £642 2s. 4d. was made and no dividend could be declared. By the following year, although the Company was able to report that business had increased by 20 per cent, £400 had to be drawn out of the reserve funds, leaving assets of only £759. From 1865 slow, steady progress can be seen; in 1867 the Company gave Messrs. Binns & Phillips £100 each, for services rendered and a profit of £2,400 is recorded; in 1871 repairs and additions to the factory cost £1,500 and profits of £3,527 were made. The following year saw more additions to the works, 6 per cent debenture shares for £3,000 were issued and a 10 per cent dividend was declared.

In 1874 a Special General Meeting was held on 10th July to discuss 'considerable extensions' and by the time of the next Annual General Meeting on

5th August 1875 the Company had consolidated their mortgage arrangements on the basis of the major improvements, a fresh mortgage of £14,000 had been arranged and a 10 per cent dividend and profits of £5,273 declared. (This mortgage was later to be in the sole name of the Worcester-born artist Benjamin Williams Leader and was finally redeemed in 1878.) The extensions were only half finished in 1878, due to lack of funds and an issue of £9,000 Preference Shares was arranged, £6,000 to be put on offer at once.

Not a very healthy state of affairs, to be sure, although little hint is given of these difficulties in R. W. Binns' *Worcester China*, and he continued to put on a bold face. It certainly reflects the extreme financial problems of fine china making in this country, where even Companies with the prestige of Worcester had to struggle for survival, without the support of state or Royal financial patronage.

A number of talented artists and craftsmen were still left of those who had assisted in the Kerr & Binns revival. The most important of these were the modellers W. Boyton Kirk, E. J. Jones and C. Toft, painters David Bates (Flowers and Birkett Foster subjects), Stephen Lawton (enamel decorations), Robert Perling (Landseer subjects), Josiah Rushton (human figures), William Taylor (floral subjects) and Luke Wells (animal and other subjects) and Josiah Davis, the gilder.

The new Company took over the following painting apprentices who had been bound to William Henry Kerr & Company (Kerr & Binns)—William Ball (apprenticed 3rd February 1857), James Bevington (25th October 1859), Robert Booth (26th October 1859), Thomas Sanday (26th October 1859) and Walter Willoughby (27th October 1859). Other apprentices taken over included Thomas Brock (later Sir Thomas Brock, the famous modeller). These were to be joined shortly by an important group of painters: the Callowhill brothers, John Hopewell, James Sherriff junior, George Hundley and Joseph Williams; also by James Hadley the modeller and designer and Samuel Ranford and George Gibbs the gilders who were to consolidate the growing artistic promise.

The main Kerr & Binns factory mark of a circle was retained as the mark of the new Company, with the addition of a crown above it. This mark has changed but little in the years since then, the only major change being in the shape of the crown, which altered in 1876 to sit down tight around the circle (Mark 5 on page of marks) and to pearls instead of thorns at the top in 1891 (Mark 6). The earliest form (Mark 1) will frequently indicate the year of manufacture either by the last two numbers of the year or a code mark letter under the circle, for example '67' or 'A'. Both these code marks represent the year 1867, the year in which code marks begin to be used commonly (see Appendix II). It ought to be clearly understood that the year mark only appears when the mark is printed in colour and does not appear when the mark is impressed into the body. There is no significance in the colour in which the trade mark is printed. Many people, especially in the United States, have the idea that the colour represents a period and a quality, referring to 'the rare or valuable purple mark', or some such statement, as if it were an early Derby mark. This is quite incorrect and although the pattern books very occasionally mention the colour of the mark to be used, generally gold, it has no deep significance, merely being the handiest colour available to the printer or painter and will usually be found to be the colour mainly represented in the pattern.

It is, however, true that after about 1942 the mark is generally in black, except on acid gold patterns which have a gold stamp, as do plates with a gold foot, or special pieces. For some years before 1942 the usual mark on china was purple, and blue on 'Wall Body'.

The various symbols inside the circle often cause confusion but are quite simple and full of meaning. The four script W's around the inside of the circle are marks used in the Dr. Wall period, as is the crescent in the centre (although between the years 1862 and 1875 this crescent changed to a C) and the 51 is an abbreviation of 1751, the year of foundation of the Worcester Porcelain Company, and has no connection with the Great Exhibition of 1851. From 1862 it is usual to find the shape number on ornamental pieces and the pattern number on useful wares put on the base and these are dealt with later. These numbers, likewise the Design Registration numbers, should not be thought to be the year of manufacture—a common error—which is indicated by the year mark codes, as explained.

These trade marks could be printed on top of the glaze, or impressed into the body under the glaze, in which case they are often very difficult to see. The impressed mark of the crown and circle can have the word Worcester under and around the circle (Mark 4).

Not infrequently seen are large earthenware round plaques with impressed Worcester (or other Companies') marks bought in the white by amateurs and exhibited by Howell & James in London at annual exhibitions from 1876 for some years. These are generally signed by the artist and often have the exhibition label and sale price on the back. These pieces do not, of course, count as Royal Worcester productions. Neither do the productions of Callowhill & Co., a written mark often found on tea-wares of the 1870s to 80s, put on wares that the Callowhill brothers bought in the white, generally from Staffordshire from such firms as Moore, and decorated at home. Yet another outside group in Worcester made pieces sold by James Lane, a Worcester dealer, typical pieces being marked with an incised inscription recording the names of the makers—'Thrown by W. Radford, turned by W. Morris, fired by T. Hayes'. It would appear that R. W. Binns turned a blind eye on such outside work, no doubt done as a means of earning a bit of extra money.

The success of the 1851 Crystal Palace Exhibition led to another being held in London in 1862. The Company were able to exhibit the fantastic new dessert service made for Queen Victoria (see Colour Plate 1 and Plate 1), the last flowering of the Kerr & Binns era in which a classical quality was linked to a forward looking approach, the turquoise grounds, piercing, difficult modelling and firing and the fine enamelling having laid a great strain upon the growing talents of the factory. This fantastic service, still preserved at Buckingham Palace in its entirety, has subjects based upon Raphael's designs in the loggia of the Vatican, painted in shaded enamels.

Although this service must have been the high spot of Worcester's showing at the Exhibition the opportunity was taken of presenting in public a type of porcelain body, named Ivory Porcelain, of a soft creamy tone, many of the pieces decorated with soft enamel colours, particularly purple, in the style of Capo di Monte, the particular finish being called Raphaelesque and the shapes owing something to an Italian influence. This had been introduced in the last years of the Kerr & Binns period and was to reach its peak of popularity around 1865.

R. W. Binns was delighted with the effect that this Ivory Porcelain, which was a glazed Parian ware, had upon the public and its success was most encouraging. Photographs cannot do justice to the luscious appearance of the glaze and enamel and the feel of it has the most sensuous effect. Mr. Binns used the ivory body in many different ways, including the application of oxidised silver, a process developed in Paris by M. Rudolphi.

But by far the greater number of figure groups and busts were made in the very popular unglazed Parian body that so closely resembled marble. The Company started different classes of shapes, all recorded in the ornamental stock book (see page 159) and it is interesting that the first two classes were devoted to Parian, Class 1 being busts and Class 2 figures over 8 inches in height. The honour of the first number in the first class of this new Company was accorded to the fine bust of Queen Victoria, noted on the busts by incising 1/1 on the base; 1/2 was Prince Albert, the modeller of these being E. J. Jones. Many of the early Class 1 busts and Class 2 figures were modelled by W. B. Kirk and C. Toft and some of these have the modeller's name moulded into the body.

With regard to the moulded names of the modeller it should be clearly appreciated that the actual Company figure was not made by the modeller himself; he merely signed his name in the original plasticine or clay model and when the moulds were made from the model they carried the name embossed, which would turn into an impressed name on the finished figure. Many Worcester figures are found with the name of Hadley impressed in the body (see Plate 79) but he, of course, only made the original model. Many of the Class 1 busts were of popular people of the time, although some had a classical origin, as befitted the original conception of Parian in depicting Greek and Roman marbles. These busts are generally of superb quality, finely modelled and potted, in a Parian body which is usually of a slightly greasy-looking greyish tone of colour, much more grey than Minton and slightly more grey than Copeland Parian.

Class 2 figures were mainly in the classical or literary taste and many pairs were produced. It is worth stating how much more attractive a pair of figures are than just an odd one, as they were designed to complement each other. Some of the Class 2 figures became very popular and had a long run, such as Morning and Evening Dew; some went on being made for fifty or more years, such as Joy and Sorrow and Liberty and Captivity which continued into the twentieth century. After the 1860s it was more common for the larger figures to be made in china, although Parian continued to be used for many small figures and for great quantities of small useful ware and vases.

Plate 9 shows a superb example of one of the Class 2 groups—2/46, which is called Paul and Virginia. In the glazed Parian Ivory body and decorated with beautiful Raphaelesque colours, the group is based upon the novel *Paul et Virginie* by Bernardin de Saint-Pierre (1737–1814) which must have been popular reading at Worcester, as a card tray painted with a scene from the book was made in the Flight Barr & Barr period. Paul and Virginia were children brought up together in the tropical paradise of the Île de France. Paul's hat is filled with flowers, Virginia's dress is holding pineapples and other fruits, and the figures are supported from sagging in the kiln by a palm tree stump at their back and pineapple leaves by Paul's side. The young lovers were also made separately as 2/103 and 2/104 as a pair of figures.

Many of the early Class 1 and Class 2 busts and figures were first made in the Kerr & Binns period and continued after 1862. For instance, group 2/44—'Uncle Tom and Eva' was first made in 1853 as is indicated by a letter from Charles Beecher on behalf of Harriet Beecher Stowe, the author of *Uncle Tom's Cabin*. In the letter, dated 13th May 1853, he wrote

> Mrs. Stowe, being unable to write herself, requests me to acknowledge the receipt of the porcelain group of U. T. & Eva. She is very much gratified with the conception and execution of the work, and requests me to say that the artist has succeeded in giving the best realisation of her little Eva she has yet seen. In this regard she feels doubly grateful, both for the present to herself, and for the work of art viewed as a tribute to the cause of the oppressed. Very respectfully yours, Charles Beecher.

The figure group was later re-numbered 1604 in the year 1892, showing the long surviving interest in the subject and the book.

Some shapes continued from an even earlier period, for example the ink pot or casket in the shape of King John's tomb in Worcester Cathedral, first made in the last years of Chamberlain & Company, in about 1850, and later produced as Class 10 numbers 1 and 2. There were at first ten separate classes for wares, but this must have been found cumbersome and Class 6 became the only one used, but leaving out the 6 prefix, and the series continues to this day, now nearing the four thousand mark.

In 1863 the Corporation of Worcester turned to the new Company for a suitable presentation service for the marriage of the Prince of Wales to Princess Alexandra of Denmark. For this was produced a tête-à-tête tea equipage. The plateau upon which the pieces were set had rose-coloured panels with a centre taken from 'The Marriage of Cupid and Psyche' by Triphonis, around the borders portraits of the Queen and the late Prince Consort, and the parents of the bride. The other pieces of the service had ornaments of elephants' heads, as a reference to the Danish order, which have the effect of making the pieces look rather like the later Japanesque, with decorations based on Correggio's designs in the Church of St. Paul at Parma, scenes of amorini. This service was presented to Her Royal Highness at Marlborough House in London by a deputation comprising the Mayor of Worcester, Mr. A. C. Sherriff, Mr. J. D. Perrins, the Sherriff, Mr. R. Wolf, Deputy Town Clerk and Mr. R. W. Binns. It will be remembered that Mr. Sherriff was one of the original Subscribers.

Within a few years, in 1865, another fine presentation service was ordered, the magnificent 'jewelled' service made as a wedding present for the Countess of Dudley. This déjeuner service comprised a plateau with a teapot, sugar, cream, cup and saucer, the surface overlaid with gold on which were placed droplets of turquoise enamel and tiny droplets of gold, all in graduated size. These 'jewels' all applied by hand by Ranford, surrounded reserve panels in which were painted classical heads by T. S. Callowhill. On the plateau were put the Worcester, the Dudley and the Moncreiffe Arms. Duplicate pieces of the service were later produced and can be seen in Plate 28 and the original service, Plate 27, was exhibited in Paris in 1867 by permission of the Earl and Countess and attracted much attention, being very much in the French style.

Another important service was made in 1866, as noted in the memoirs of Martha A. Howlett who visited the factory that year and described her experiences.

> On the day of my visit, a number of women were engaged in burnishing the gold on a set of plates ordered by the Lord Mayor of London, for use at a banquet to be given to the Prince of Wales on his return from India. The rims bore bands of dark green and gold, and the City arms were emblazoned in the middle of each plate. The burnishing was being done with pointed agates set in handles. I think the order was for a hundred dozen of these plates, which were to match others already in use. I laughed to myself while looking at the putting together of the biscuit china statuettes. The workman held a torso, and in front of him on his bench, were groups of heads, legs and arms, ready for application.

A Royal dessert service, made in 1875 for the Prince of Wales, is still in use at Sandringham and has a beautiful decoration with the initials AE (Albert Edward) and crest that is depicted in Sandringham, which had been enlarged by the Prince in 1870. A few pieces of this service are also exhibited at Windsor Castle.

These services were important in that they put Worcester back into the social swim but of much greater potential importance was Worcester's participation in the two important European Art Fairs that followed the 1862 London Exhibition—Paris in 1867 and Vienna in 1873. These were not only important in putting Worcester's artistic qualities to the test of critical appraisal but they also brought Mr. Binns in contact with the ceramic arts of other countries, both ancient and modern.

The effect of this contact made itself felt in a spate of shapes and styles of decoration based on Medieval Italian, French, German and Persian vessels, both ceramic and metal. But the foreign style that had the greatest influence on Mr. Binns was that of Japan.

Japanese arts had been kept away from Western eyes until they burst upon an astonished audience at the 1862 and 1867 Exhibitions. Mr. Binns was swept overboard by these pieces and quickly built up a huge collection of Eastern ceramics, principally Japanese, Chinese and Korean, and these pieces were shown to the factory workers to inspire them. The great collection of some 10,000 pieces were sold off after Mr. Binns' death and every so often one of these pieces turns up to cause confusion and worry because of the Royal Porcelain Works Museum label underneath, the owner fearing that the piece has been stolen from the Museum.

Mr. Binns found a ready assistant in his new modeller, James Hadley, and Japanesque wares began to flow from the factory, very few of them being direct copying, but with the spirit of the Japanese prototypes in them, and these rapidly superseded the Henri Deux and Capo di Monte styles with their majolica and Raphaelesque colours, faience and earthenwares. By 1876 the Japanesque style had been absorbed and perfected sufficiently to be shown at the Albert Hall Galleries in London, to great acclaim, and the Company was put to the test in November of that year when they received a visit from a Japanese Mission visiting the country. This party included the Junior Prime Minister, the Minister of Finance and the Assistant Minister of Foreign Affairs. After visiting Cotheridge Court to see the Worcestershire Hounds throw off, presumably to give them a taste of traditional English country life, the party was conducted round the factory by Mr. Binns himself. He found the Japanese visitors deeply interested in all they saw and realised that they were taking careful notes of the processes when he asked if he would 'speak a little slower as the Secretary could not write the description given.'

By the time of the Vienna Exhibition of 1873, Mr. Binns felt that Worcester had improved so far over their bad showing in 1851 that a splendid display must be made and to his great joy Worcester was granted first prize jointly with Minton's. This accolade brought the reputation of Worcester once more to the forefront and the wares shown made a great impression on the visitors.

The centre pieces of Worcester's display were the Norman Conquest vases painted in Limoges-style enamels by Thomas Bott and although Bott had died tragically young in 1870 the Limoges style was continued by Thomas John Bott, his son, and by Thomas Scott Callowhill. Also shown were vases in the Japanesque style, decorations in the old ivory finishes, double pierced vessels (long survivors from the 1851 Exhibition) and many pieces in the Persian and Italian Renaissance style.

The Worcester Japanesque pieces were so admired that a number of European potters extensively copied them and the extraordinary position was reached, within a few years, that Worcester's copies of Japanese arts were even copied by the Japanese themselves. Multitudes of Japanesque shapes poured from Worcester—spill vases, tea-wares, flat vases with pierced panels—many looking more Japanese than their prototypes. Many Japanese patterns were used, especially storks in raised gold, a decorative speciality of the Callowhill brothers, and curious Japanese symbols scattered over the pieces. One great characteristic of the Japanesque style of decoration was its asymmetry, with the pattern off centre or unbalanced (Plate 93).

Also very popular were the Persian, Indian and Italian Renaissance styles. The Persian-shaped vessels often had embossed panels with scenes from such books as Thomas Moore's 'Lallah Rookh', published in 1817; Indian vessels could depict modelled scenes of ancient potters; Italian vases could be in the shape of Renaissance silver and gold vessels, supporting shells.

Useful wares could be made either in a Parian body or bone china. The Parian body could have a lustrously iridescent glaze very similar to that of Belleek. The glaze on Worcester bone china made about 1870 had a tendency to craze, smaller flat wares sometimes showing this to a great degree, and about this date they brought out Crownware, or, as it became known, Vitreous ware, a heavy earthenware found to be extremely durable and made from about 1870 until 1930 for hotel and domestic ware. This ware, of course, is opaque and not translucent. Printing in gold was also introduced in about 1870, as is noted by its first mention in the pattern books in pattern number 7926.

Even though gold printing enabled more simple patterns to be produced semi-mechanically, fine hand gilding still continued, in the capable hands of Josiah Davis, Stephen Lawton, Tom Morton senior and Sam Ranford. Possibly the finest gold work was done by Béjot, who first from his Paris studio and later at Worcester did highly original work in chased gold. Raised gold paste work was introduced by Leonard Burgess in the late 1870s.

An impressively fine group of painters was the pride and joy of Mr. Binns and a list of the principal artists of the 1860s and 70s reads almost like a Who's Who of mid-Victorian china painters. Their details are given in Chapter 7 but briefly, in alphabetical order, with their main subjects they are:

David Bates, flowers
Thomas Bott, senior, Limoges enamels and portraits
Thomas John Bott, Limoges enamels
James Bradley, senior and junior, landscape subjects and dogs
James Callowhill, figure subjects, heads and raised gold storks
Thomas Scott Callowhill, figure subjects, raised gold storks and Limoges
   enamels
Octar H. Copson, fruit, birds, etc.
Albert Gyngell, landscapes and grasses
Albert Hill, birds
John Hopewell, birds
George Hundley, flowers and plants
Charles Palmere, figure subjects and Tenniers style
Robert Perling, landscapes, especially Landseer subjects
Po-Hing, a Cantonese, who did Canton enamel work, often wrongly
   believed to have been done in China on Worcester blanks

Edward Raby, senior, hand-modelled flowers on plates
Edward Raby, junior, floral subjects
Robert Rea, butterflies and feathers
Josiah Rushton, figure subjects and heads
James Sherriff, senior and junior, flowers, butterflies, grasses
William Taylor, floral subjects, especially Australian heathers
James Weaver, grass and flies
Luke Wells, senior and junior, dogs and Watteau subjects

Mr. Binns was not only very proud of his workers but he also looked after their education and well-being. Many of the young artists and craftsmen were sent to the Worcester Government School of Design to study and to develop and be rewarded for their skills. This school was founded in 1851 and among the prizewinners in the first year are to be found Joseph Brecknell, Josiah Rushton, Jabez Bly, John Hopewell, James Callowhill and Benjamin Leader Williams, who was later to change his name to Benjamin Williams Leader and become one of England's foremost landscape painters. In the 1880s the Worcester Royal Porcelain Company was to be mortgaged to him under a trust fund for his daughter and in 1914 he became a Freeman of Worcester (a privilege bestowed on such famous people as Admiral Nelson, Sir Edward Elgar, Sir Thomas Brock, Lord Nuffield, Mr. Dyson Perrins and Sir Winston Churchill).

The Sick Club worked on a sliding scale of small weekly contributions from the members and was reorganised on a permanent basis in 1874 and the Company established a Benefit Fund in 1879, both of these funds being chiefly the work of Mr. E. P. Evans, who became the Company Secretary in 1867 and later Managing Director. Edward Probert Evans became a well-loved man and Mr. Binns said of him that 'if he had to dock a man's wages he could do it in such a way that he seemed to be conferring a favour'. His kindliness could sometimes cover a more stern appearance and many an older workman has said that you could tell in what mood he was by the position of his top hat when he arrived in the morning. If it was on the back of his head he was in a sunny mood and there were very few occasions when the hat was in a more stern, frontal position.

In 1879 Mr. R. W. Binns opened the Company Museum which was intended to benefit the staff as much as to interest the visitors. The fine large building in which the Company's collection of historical pieces were to be shown was next door to Mr. Binns' office and he wished the employees to receive inspiration from great works of the past, the paintings of Baxter and Bott, whose work was arranged around the walls alongside older and more modern pieces and the Japanese collection. As Mr. Binns saw it, the Museum was to be:

at once a source of emulation and a means of advancement, for it is possible for the craftsmen to examine on the one hand what has already been done at Worcester, with the inevitable result that their pride in the establishment shall be fostered and developed, so they may upon the other study and criticise the achievements of their competitors, equipping themselves for further progress and preparing for the still keener struggle through which they must inevitably pass.

But Mr. Binns had one great failure. He had hoped to move the factory from Diglis to a site known as The Arboretum Gardens, just over a mile away to the North of the centre of Worcester and to build there a brand new garden factory. As *The Builder* of 22nd April 1865 noted:

> The Arboretum Gardens, Worcester have been acquired by the Royal Porcelain Company and plans for new porcelain works are in the hands of Messrs. Scrivener & Sons of the Potteries—designers of large establishments of china and pottery works.

The splendid conception, shown in Plate 25, collapsed from lack of finance but its memory was kept alive by the Severn Street frontage of Chamberlain's old Diglis factory being remodelled to use the proposed new design. Of interest, the small lodge shown in the plan is still in existence and where the main entrance is shown leading to the factory was built Arboretum Road, where C. H. C. Baldwyn, the painter, was to live.

In November 1874 there was to arrive at the factory a curious letter which rekindled the long past battle between the Worcester factory of Flight & Barr and William Billingsley and his son-in-law Samuel Walker, who had been engaged to develop a new frit porcelain but left to produce the ware at Nantgarw and Swansea. The letter, dated 12th November 1874 from New Troy, in the State of New York, U.S.A., was from Samuel Walker who had established the Temperance Hill Pottery at West Troy, and reads:

> Gentlemen, Please to excus this liberty I have been makeing experiments this last 20 years in the arts of Potting and China Makeing. I have made several discoveries valuable to Potters and China Manufacturer; I have discovered a machine for printing on clay ware unburnt without difficulty or damage, I make flower pots hang ups, they look well and sell well here. I make them square and octagons, they print easy and the commonest hands can do the work Prentics cheap and easely. One firing will do for the printing of the ware, print in all colours, the printing must be semevetrefy'd or quiet glossy to suit the ware, (flower pots will do in biskt. state). Lades say flowers look best in Biskt. pots you can print them different patterns and Chequer work to suit your ware, handsom yours can be made, for suggar, Tea, butter, Jelley cups and If this thing suits your consideration and pattronage, I shall be glad to hear from you soon as convenient. I will let you have the thing cheap, say £5, you can make the Machinery yourself, your Moddler or Carpinter can do it, its so plain and easey to be don, wont cost you a £1 note—I have a number of new things in Bodies, Glazes, Colours etc. I have a nice Green Oxide of Chrome for Bodies, Glazes and Colours etc. thes will make fine printing colours—for the flower pots etc. I have another little Instrument that

will print on clay, pattrons much like the Scotch Plaid cloth thing etc, this is handsom. I will let you have the receipts of thes colours for £5 each—you can make these things without any difficulty. I have a handsom mode of marbleing ware beauifulley in all colours on the same piece of ware. I will let you have this receipt for £10—please to excuse this Rhapsadde on potting. In hopes of hearing from you direct

I Rn.

Sir Yours Respectfully

Sam¹ Walker

I can make Beautifull China without clay in the Composition heres a discovery for valuable fancy work—never been done before, wither on France, Paris or Pekin on China.

I can make the Dresden China the finest and best ever made you shall have the receipt for 5£

I was employed by Mess⁵ Flight & Barr 50 years ago makeing experiments.

I made them a fine China Mr. Barr gave a £100 for it

There is no record of Mr. Binns' reply, unfortunately, but it is doubtful if any notice was taken of the great inventions claimed. The factory had plenty of work in hand without exploring the experiments of Samuel Walker and a study of the shape book records and patterns of the 1870s shows a bewildering range in both quantity and variation.

A large number of the shapes were based on the Japanesque, but there were many that had an English origin. Many charming figures were produced ranging from small figures used for holding menus, one set being based on London down and out characters who might have been seen carrying sandwich boards around the streets (the menu cards would be slung sandwich-board-like over the shoulders), and another set on popular (or unpopular) politicians of the day (Plates 94 and 95) the Politician set is very rare; exquisite candle extinguishers, hollow underneath and used for dowsing the candle, some of which can be seen in Plate 83, and a good idea of the great characterisation that went into such little pieces will be obtained from this photograph. For instance, observe the characters of the participants in the great Tichborne trial where Arthur Orton, a butcher, claimed that he was the long lost heir believed drowned at sea. His claim was defeated by the brilliant advocacy of the Attorney, Coleridge, and Orton was sent to prison for perjury. Orton is shown on his butcher's block and he can be taken off and used as an extinguisher, but Coleridge is made to fit over the top of Orton, thus extinguishing his claim! Many people do not realise that there can be tremendous touches of humour in Victorian ceramics but these candle extinguishers are full of quiet fun; observe Mr. Caudle being nagged in bed by his wife so that the poor man has to put his sleeping cap over his ears in the hope of sleeping; the two versions of Jenny Lind, the great soprano known as the 'Swedish Nightingale' are called 'Diffidence' (eyes demurely cast down) and 'Confidence' (boldly looking up, singing like a bird); Budge and Toddie the children from 'Helen's

Babies' by John Habberton, are dressed in Uncle Harry's clothes that are much too big for them.

Many other unusual objects are shown in Plates 19 and 100, the top of the little dog's head lifts off to form a match box, the matches being struck on the corrugated base; the teapot is a skit upon the Aesthetic Movement of Oscar Wilde, the tea pouring out of the hand, the arm being the handle and the head (male on one side and female on the other)—lifting off to act as the cover, all decorated in the 'greenery-yallery' colours referred to in Gilbert and Sullivan's *Patience*; a great curiosity, discovered in an ancient Phoenician tomb caused Mr. Binns, a keen antiquarian, to make an ink pot from it. Many of the shapes can have a very humorous content, such as those in Class 7— number 39, 'Don Catsquali', a skit on the opera *Don Pasquale* showing a cat playing a guitar; the match boxes numbered 63 to 66 and 82, 'Canaryensis bottle', i.e. Canary inside a bottle. Other very popular shapes were 'violets' (small vases for holding violets), groups of amphora stacked up in piles (up to as many as ten) wall brackets and wall pockets, the latter often in the form of birds' nests with birds, possibly used as hair tidies. A curious pair of Mansion House Dwarfs, shape 602, were made in the style of old Derby.

It will be claimed that not everything that Worcester made at that period was of great artistic merit and I do not think that a number of the pieces just mentioned were intended to be thought of in the same way as the finest shapes. Not all the patterns produced at the time were meant to be put on the same plane as those shown in this book, which tend to be of the finer sort. Great quantities of ordinary wares for ordinary people were made, and such pieces, cheap blue printed wares, say, should not be thought grander than they are merely because they bear the Worcester trade mark. However, the wares are invariably good of their kind, in the class for which they were being made. The one bad feature that is to be found around the year 1870 is the fault of crazing, a breaking out of a cobweb of lines on the glaze that disfigures the surface, possibly caused by a change in raw materials. It is advisable to treat such crazed wares of the 1870s with great care, preventing them from getting damp and keeping them at an even, warm temperature, but not wrapping them up in newspaper or tissue, which, if it gets damp and sticks to the glaze, can cause great damage.

However, the 1870s were to end in a blaze of triumph for Worcester with the Paris Exhibition of 1878. After gaining joint first place at Vienna in 1873, Worcester was riding the crest of the wave, but a visit by Mr. Binns to the Centennial Exhibition at Philadelphia, at which a pair of vases was presented to George Washington, reminded him of the great qualities of the Japanese ceramic arts and he ended up by buying great quantities of Japanese pieces to be shipped back to Worcester. These arrived in early 1877 and were shown at an Exhibition in the Worcester Public Hall, first at a *conversazione* for the citizens, who were given a chance of comparing them with Worcester wares and, on the following evening, they were shown to the factory employees. On the latter occasion Mr. Binns was pleasantly surprised to be presented with a suite of plate—a pair of salvers and a ewer in electro-art silver—and an address, illustrated by the Callowhill brothers, to mark Mr. Binns' twenty-five years at Worcester. The presentation was made by the Chairman of the Board of Directors, Mr. A. C. Sherriff, and the address was read out by James Sherriff, senior foreman of the men's painters. The wording, (quoted in *Worcester China*) although sounding rather fulsome to our ears, showed the great affection in which he was held by all the workers. In reply, Mr. Binns reminded everyone that twenty-five years before he had set before them a motto of two words—'aim high'; his new motto now was to be of two letters only; 'X L'.

Worcester certainly intended to excel at the Paris Exhibition. They put on a large general display, a great deal of space being devoted to Japanesque wares and ivory porcelain and two experimental wares were shown—a marbled faience similar to Japanese Namako ware and a dark green porcelain with dramatically contrasting gilding. A special display of a rich dessert service for twenty-four persons reproducing the Dr. Wall period 'fabulous birds' on a deep cobalt ground caused great interest. The pieces which made the most effect were a fantastic pair of vases in the style of the Italian Renaissance, the subjects, deeply placed in sunken panels (alto relievo), were suggested by drawings in the famous work of the Cavaliere Picolpasso and depicted scenes of sixteenth-century Italian pottery making, with portrait busts of Luca della Robbia, Maestro Georgio, Michaelangelo and Raphael. These large and impressive vases, 29 inches high and decorated in Raphaelesque colours on ivory porcelain were worked on by James Hadley, who was the designer and modeller, W. Farringdon and G. Radford, potters, J. and T. Callowhill, J. Davis, T. Stephenson and W. Jones, painters and decorators, E. Blake, biscuit fireman, T. Goodwin, glaze fireman, and J. Goodwin, enamel fireman (Plate 74). The vases attracted much attention, and for their overall exhibition Worcester was awarded the Gold Medal and Mr. Binns was invested with the Cross of the Legion of Honour.

Needless to say, Mr. Binns was highly delighted at this success but he had even greater pleasure over the reports of a special National Commission appointed to report on the ceramic exhibits for the benefit of the Royal Manufactory of Sèvres. The President of the Commission was the Director General of Fine Arts and the members included such well-known people as Berthelot, Gallard, Lamière and Mazerolle and a section of their report was proudly read by Mr. Binns.

Having finished a brief review of the French ceramic section, we enter the midst of the foreign productions on the north-west side of the Exhibition and commence our comparative examination with England. We must place here highest in rank the productions of the Worcester Manufactory. They are distinguished from all others by skill and accurate judgment in the ceramic art, and by great perfection in the execution. The bisque Parian, which reminds us rather of ivory than of marble, invites attention by its creamy tones, upon which foliage and fantastic animals in coloured golds combine happily with the ground which they decorate. We must also notice services of simple outlines cleverly pierced, and equally large gourd-shaped vases with birds in gold and foliage of happy arrangement. We cannot speak too highly of the charm contained in each of the thousand pieces—vases, table, dessert and tea services—where the ornament is always in harmony with the object decorated.

Worcester had arrived!

Chapter II

The 1880s and 90s

The two most important events of the last twenty years of the nineteenth century at Worcester were the taking over of Grainger's factory by the Worcester Royal Porcelain Company in 1889 and the founding of James Hadley's own factory in 1896.

Grainger & Company

This factory, started by Thomas Grainger in 1801, was in the St. Martin's Gate area of the City, on the corner of St. Martin's Gate and Pheasant Street. Two early partnerships of Grainger Wood & Co.—1801–12—and Grainger Lee & Co.—1812–39 ended with Thomas Grainger's death and the business was continued by his son George as George Grainger & Company.

The firm did well at the Great Exhibition in 1851, specialising in semi-porcelain and pierced china. Grainger was very proud of his semi-porcelain—an opaque body—and a testimonial from William Herapath, dated 'Bristol, Dec. 1st 1849' reads:

> Sir,—I have now worked for some months with your Semi Porcelain Ware in my Analytical Laboratory, subjecting it not only to the ordinary usage of the place, but to very severe trials, with the view of learning the extent of its qualities, and I feel pleasure in certifying that, for Chemical purposes, it is superior to every article of English manufacture I have hitherto had in use.

This testimonial was reproduced on a semi-porcelain plaque by George Grainger. In 1862 the Midland Counties Herald was able to say of the Exhibition displays:

> Messrs. George Grainger & Co. Worcester, have one of the most tasteful and charming displays in the whole ceramic department. The dinner-service of semi-porcelain, decorated in *rose du Barry* or rather *rose du Pompadour* as it ought to be called and gold, is at once tasteful and rich

16

in its effect. The ornamentation is classic in detail, but skilfully adapted to the purpose. The great novelty, however, of Messrs. Graingers' exhibit is the perforated parian. These are most ingeniously and skilfully designed and modelled for the object intended to be achieved. The forms are in themselves elegant, and in combination with the perforated ornament add materially to the result. The enrichments of gold are very effective and we should like to see the effect of a few spots of colour. . . . The two vases in the Italo-Romanesque style are very cleverly modelled, and give a charming variation to the display by their forms and the quiet olive-green tint of the surface.

Many different articles for chemical use were made in semi-porcelain, including funnels, pestles and mortars, spoons, galvanic jars and photographic dishes.

The local paper—'Berrow's Worcester Journal'—on 22nd December 1866 devoted an article to Grainger's factory and described semi-porcelain as:

a semi-vitreous body, free from lime, and whilst stoutly resisting the action of acids will bear sudden changes of heat and cold without cracking. The glaze upon it is free from lead—another very important feature.

The article speaks with pride of the perforated porcelain, which was to become a great speciality of Grainger and although the pieces are never of the outstanding quality of those pierced by George Owen, they compare well with the ordinary pierced wares of the main factory.

Another invention of George Grainger was a patent drawing-room flower pot, which he advertised as follows:

George Grainger begs most respectfully to invite the attention of the Nobility, Clergy, Gentry, and the Public, to his newly invented Drawing-Room Flower Pot (registered in the Office for patents); and to state that he has consulted many eminent Florists upon the subject, whose opinions of the invention have been most favourable; he therefore confidently recommends the article to the use of the cultivators of choice plants, and Florists generally, and submits to their notice a description of its merits and advantages.

The Patent Flower pot consists of two cases; the outer one of which, being of glazed Porcelain, may be ornamented in any style, or made to correspond with the Dinner or Dessert Service. The inner case, in which the plant is to be grown, is composed of a porous White Clay, and is as well calculated to preserve the roots in a healthy state as the common and unsightly Pots now in use; and, as the inner case may be removed from the outer or ornamental one at pleasure, Hot-house or other Plants may be grown in their proper temperature, and introduced into the Dining or Drawing Room by replacing the porous Pot in the outer case. An opportunity is thus afforded of exhibiting a succession of the choicest Plants in full bloom, for the decoration of the *Boudoir*, the Drawing Room,

or the *Salon à Manger*, without destroying the beauty of the plants by
cutting off their blooms.

If it should be desired that Plants should be grown continually in the
ornamental part of the invention, provision is made between the outer
and inner cases for the free circulation of air and an ample supply of
water; and this is afforded in such a manner that the Pots may be placed
upon the most delicately polished tables or other surfaces, without the
slightest risk of soiling or wetting.

I have not seen any examples of these flower pots.

Favourite Grainger shapes were eagles or dolphins supporting vases,
pilgrim flasks, spill vases, flower vases in the forms of flowers and wall
pockets in such shapes as orchids.

George Grainger opened a retail shop in the 1850s at 39 Foregate Street,
Worcester (now the premises of W. H. Smith & Sons Ltd.) and an illustration
of the shop front can be seen in Plate 108 with George himself standing
proudly in the doorway with a fine array of the firm's wares displayed in the
windows. All around the shop front are set small square wall tiles, a speciality
of the firm. The principal artists who worked for Grainger were John Stinton
senior, his sons John, James and Walter Stinton, George Cole and Edward
Locke and his sons. The younger John and James Stinton and Cole were to
move over to Royal Worcester after the amalgamation and Walter Stinton
was to join Edward Locke and his sons in the short-lived Locke china factory,
which is dealt with later.

As well as pierced Parian wares, the factory specialised in the production
of door furniture, green and white Parian ornamental wares, pâte-sur-pâte
decoration of fine quality and reproductions of old Dr. Wall-style decorations,
especially scale blue and fabulous birds. The mark for the latter wares was
often a square mark, like the Dr. Wall one, with 'Grainger & Co. Worcester'
underneath (Mark 12) but the general mark used on other wares was a shield
mark with 'G & Co. W' inside and the three black pears from the City of
Worcester coat of arms in the left-hand quarter (Mark 10).

In 1889 this shield mark changed (Mark 11) when Grainger's was bought
up by the Worcester Royal Porcelain Company. The valuation of the stock
in trade at the St. Martin's Gate factory and at Grainger's grinding mill at
Powick, near Worcester, was £2,700. Mr. E. P. Evans drew up a list of the
employees taken over and their wages, headed by the foreman Brock (44s.
per week), Cole (flower painter) and Stinton, senior (view painter on piece-
work), Stinton, a boy, who was presumably John Stinton junior (3s. per week).
One of the highest paid workers was Gale senior, the thrower, who was
getting 47s. per week, but E. Locke was earning £160 per annum, which
possibly included wages for other members of his family. This move brought
the two Companies under one control although production went on at the
St. Martin's Gate factory until 1902, and on the 11th March 1903 the site
was sold in two lots—a total area of 3,930 square yards. Many of the early
nineteenth-century Grainger buildings are still standing, including part of one

1. Combined dessert stand and flower tube with 2 plates from the dessert service made for Queen Victoria in 1861. Decorated by Thomas Bott with white enamel classical and trophy motifs on a turquoise ground. Special mark as shown in Godden's *Encyclopaedia of British Pottery and Porcelain Marks*, Plate 4. Height of flower tube 20½ inches. See page 4.

2. Three Class 1 busts of c. 1862–5. Above, Queen Victoria, shape 1/1, 13½ inches. Below, the Prince of Wales, 1/10, 13½ inches, and Princess of Wales, 1/11, 13 inches. The busts are in unglazed Parian, modelled by E. J. Jones. The Queen has a W. H. Kerr & Co. mark, the Prince and Princess a printed mark of 'Worcester Royal Porcelain Works' under the Royal Coat of Arms. *The latter in the collection of Mr. C. S. Titman.*

3. Bust of Peace, shape 1/32, bust of Shakespeare, shape 1/22, and statuette of Dr. Hahnemann, shape 2/23, height 11 inches, all in unglazed Parian and from the 1860s.

4. Busts of Mr. and Mrs. R. W. Binns, dressed in Roman style, height 6 inches, c. 1862–4, unglazed Parian, From Mrs. Coad, grand-daughter of R. W. Binns.

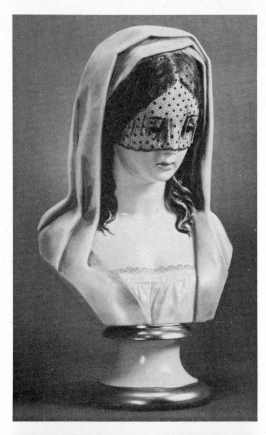

5. Bust of Charity, shape 1/15, the effect of a veil cleverly suggested by fine modelling and decorating, height 11 inches. Parian body.

6. Statuette of King Lear, impressed quotation on the base 'Ay, every inch a King', shape 2/9, height 17 inches, unglazed Parian, 1860s.

7. Statuettes of Tragedy and Comedy, shapes 2/13 and 2/12, heights $17\frac{1}{4}$ inches and $17\frac{1}{2}$ inches, modelled by Kirk, in the background Lady Macbeth shape 2/15, $14\frac{1}{2}$ inches in height, unglazed Parian, 1860s.

8. Charles I (left) and Oliver Cromwell, shapes 2/6 and 2/7, height 18 inches, unglazed Parian, 1860s. These are typical of the superb quality of the modelling of the fine Worcester Parian.

9. Magnificent group of Paul and Virginia, shape 2/46, in glazed Parian (Ivory Porcelain), decorated in subtle Raphaelesque colours of purples, pinks and pale pastel colours. Height 10 inches, width $13\frac{3}{4}$ inches, mark number 1 impressed, c. 1865. *In the collection of Mr. A. H. Hipkiss.* See page 6.

10. Four popular and long-running Class 2 pairs. Centre, Joy and Sorrow, shapes 2/57 and 2/58, set on fluted pedestals, shape 5/15, and decorated in Raphaelesque colours on a glazed Parian body; left, Liberty, 2/116; right, Captivity, 2/117, set with flower tubes at the rear, decorated in shot enamel colours of the 1890s; Joy and Sorrow being of the 1860s. *Joy and Sorrow from the collection of Mr. J. Broad.*

11. A pair of Spring (with harp) and Autumn (with fruit), shapes 2/33 and 2/34, faience body coloured by E. Béjot and gilt, c. 1870, and a pair of Iris (left, with hands above her head) and Venus, shapes 2/98 and 2/97, decorated with pencilled ivory and gilt.

12. Two groups of lovers. Left, Faust and Margaret, shape 2/42; right, Henda and Hafed, 2/40. The former is 12 inches in height in Parian covered with an iridescent lustre glaze, the latter is $13\frac{1}{2}$ inches in height and is in unglazed Parian. The third group in the series of lovers is Romeo and Juliet, shape 2/41, height $13\frac{1}{2}$ inches.

13. Canova's Venus, after the marble in the Villa Borghese, said to have been modelled on Pauline Bonaparte, unglazed Parian, 22 inches by 11 inches, shape 2/91. Also shown are 18 Class 2 subjects from one of the Company's photographic shape books. Above, left to right, 53, 54, 57, 97, 98, 99; centre, 55, 56, 71, 100, 101, 102; below, 72, 73, 95, 110, 111 and 113.

14. From left to right, Sabrina, shape 2/71, $18\frac{1}{2}$ inches high; Evening Dew, 2/36, Morning Dew, 2/35, and Psyche, 2/14, height 14 inches, all in glazed Parian.

15. Left, Plenty bestowing her gifts, shape 2/48, 11 inches high, in unglazed Parian. Above, right, Uncle Tom and Eva, shape 1664, in glazed Parian (also shape 2/44).

16. Pair of Water Carriers, in old Grecian style, shapes 6/46 and 6/47, in glazed Parian with tinted hair and features and gilding, height 7 inches.

17. Class 3 candlesticks.
Left, 3/40, Japanese
Juggler, height 14 inches,
decorated. Above, 3/6,
male and female in style of
Louis XV, 10¾ inches,
glazed Parian, coloured
and gilded. Below, 3/9,
Egyptian candlesticks,
glazed Parian with slight
gilding, height 7¼ inches.
*The Egyptian candlesticks
from the collection of Miss
N. Halliwell.*

18. Grape Wagon, shape 4/100, used for passing grapes along the
table, in green and white glazed Parian.

19. Above, left to right, Cock and Rat salt, shape 7/24, faience decorated with majolica colours; Helmet ink, 10/8, with naturalistic colours and gold; Dog's Head match-box with removable head, faience with majolica colouring, 7/98. Below, left to right, Puck salt, 4/51, in unglazed Parian; fountain and amphora with iridescent lustre glaze; Trident, Triple Shell and Dolphin salt, 6/95, in unglazed Parian. See page 13.

20. Above, left, The Ariosto Ink, class 10/3, unglazed Parian with gilding, 6 inches; right, Grecian flower bowl, glazed Parian, with tinting, shape 6/495, $8\frac{1}{2}$ inches. Below, left, King John's Tomb in Worcester Cathedral, as an ink, 10/1, 8 inches in length, unglazed Parian; right, small low font, 10/16, Parian, glazed inside. See page 6.

21. Faience plaques, with Claude Michel Clodion subjects in relief, decorated with majolica colours. Above, 5/9. Below, left, 5/11; right, 5/10. 11 inches and 9 inches. Mark 1 impressed, c. 1865.

22. Magnificent pair of Japanese lady and gentleman, shape 2/123, finely decorated, height 16 inches. Glazed Parian.

23. Beautiful model of a boy and dolphin, shape 3/45, for use as a candlestick, height 12 inches. *From the collection of Mr. E. M. Holdstock.*

24. Angel bracket, class 5, numbers 4 and 23, in green and white Parian. Left, Winter; right, Autumn, from the Four Seasons wall brackets, 5/2 and 5/34, with iridescent pearl lustre glaze and tinting, and above them a pair of vases with modelled reeds, class 10/28, with iridescent pearl lustre glazes on ivory body.

25. Plan of the proposed new garden factory to be built in the Arboretum Pleasure Gardens in Worcester in 1865. The plan fell through because of lack of finance. See page 11.

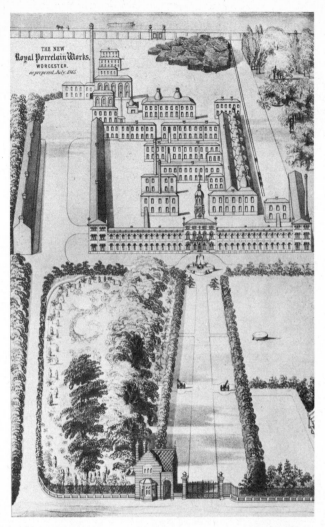

26. Drawing by James Callowhill of the fully developed and rebuilt Diglis factory, as it was in the 1870s. The showroom, now the Company Reject Shop in front of which the group photographs in the book were taken, faces the gate; the canal still lies at the rear of the factory, but the great bottle kilns are no longer there. The original Chamberlain buildings of the late eighteenth century may be seen in the courtyard to the right of the showroom, in front of the left-hand set of bottle kilns. See page 11.

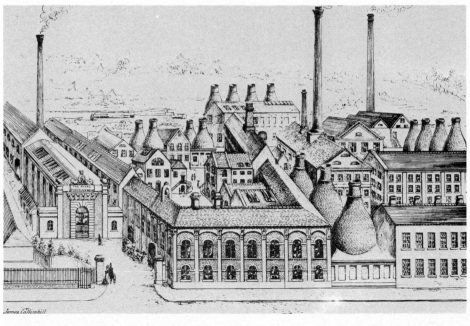

27.   The original photograph of the magnificent déjeuner service made for the wedding of the Countess of Dudley in 1865. See page 7.

28.   Duplicates of the Countess of Dudley déjeuner service, made by the Company between 1875 and 1877 with classical heads painted by T. S. Callowhill on a gold ground, with droplets of turquoise enamels around the rim, gilding by Samuel Ranford, height of teapot 5½ inches.

29. Two superb large figures. Left, 'The Bather Surprised', 486, modelled by Sir Thomas Brock, ivory and shot silk, height 26 inches, the largest of 3 sizes, decorated with pencilling and gold; right, Roman female in unglazed Parian, 487, height 28 inches. The Bather Surprised was made in 1902 and the Roman figure in the late 1860s.

30. Groups of small figures. Left, in front, Bacchus and companion, class 7, numbers 5 and 6, Bacchus decorated in lapis lazuli and gold, companion with pencilled ivory, no mark; right, in front, St. John and infant Christ, class 7, numbers 8 and 9, decorated with oxidised silver, $4\frac{1}{2}$ inches; centre, Mermaid taper, class 3/34 (this one marked with Kerr & Binns shield mark), decorated with oxidised silver, turquoise and gold; behind these, pair of boy and torch candlestick and boy and taper companion, class 3/13, decorated with pencilled ivory and gold and oxidised silver, height $19\frac{1}{2}$ inches.

of the large bottle kilns, the only one remaining in Worcester. So the amalgamation did not change ceramic life in Worcester all that much, not as much as the starting up of James Hadley's factory did.

James Hadley & Sons

James Hadley, whom many regard as the finest ceramic modeller of the nineteenth century, had been the chief modeller of the factory from the early days of Royal Worcester, being responsible for the greater majority of figures and vases from the mid 1860s.

In 1875 he left the employment of the Company to become a freelance modeller and designer at 95, High Street, Worcester, virtually all his work being bought by Royal Worcester, and it was from these premises that he produced the fine exhibition vases for Paris in 1878 and Chicago in 1893. Many of the large Hadley figures or groups made for Royal Worcester can have the word Hadley at the side or rear of the figures and it is worth mentioning again that this is not a signature put on the individual piece of china, nor is the piece made by Hadley. It merely means that Hadley signed the original clay or plaster model and the moulds made from that model by the Company would produce a finished piece having the name impressed on it.

James Hadley decided to start his own manufactory in 1896 on a site in Diglis Road, only a hundred yards from the back gates of the main factory. He did not attempt to compete with Royal Worcester and he concentrated on producing a highly original ornamental art pottery. In fact the *Pottery Gazette* was able to say in his obituary notice:

> He had made a name, and a famous one, by decorative treatments executed for the firm which tutored him. These treatments had helped to maintain the reputation of the famous Worcester china. To his lasting credit he does not seem to have done anything to discount that reputation, by producing in his own name (as he would have been justified in doing) the main features which characterised his work for the Royal Porcelain Works. How original he was, is seen in the diversity which exists between his productions as an employee and those on his own account.

A number of workmen left the Worcester Royal Porcelain Company to join him, especially a number of the Blake family, one in particular—Roland Blake—becoming the jack of all trades.

James Hadley was assisted by three of his sons—Howard, Louis (or Lou) and Frank and the working staff was never to grow very large. Five distinct periods of development can be traced and they have been well summed up by John Haywood, one-time curator of Royal Worcester, as follows:

1. A period before the factory started, comprising unglazed terra cottas produced at the High Street shop, the mark being 'James Hadley & Sons, Art Pottery' or 'Hadley's Fine Art Terra cottas', impressed in the clay.

D

2. An experimental period in 1896, the mark being just the monogram J H & S mark (mark number 13 without the words 'Hadley's Worcester England'), either painted or stamped with rubber. Opaque faience was made, the mounts being in coloured clays, thinly glazed.

3. From February 1897 to June 1900, the more elaborate monogram mark with FAIENCE in a scroll (mark 14), glazed faience bodies with coloured clay mounts, conventional decorations chiefly in monochrome.

4. From June 1900 to August 1902, mark number 13, glazed faience body, coloured clay mounts, with a more realistic treatment of subjects.

5. From August 1902 to June 30th 1905, mark number 15, glazed faience body, mounts treated with or without coloured clays, in various ways, further development of the realistic treatment of subjects, some figures and figure groups being made.

From July 1905 the Hadley firm was amalgamated with the Royal Worcester Company but for many years Hadley-style wares continued in production. It goes without saying that the wares of James Hadley & Sons were well designed, but the firm's chief claim to originality is in the ingenious mounts in different coloured clays that were produced, the colours being through clay ones and not requiring enamel painting. An interesting account of a visit to the factory is given in the *Magazine of Art* for October 1898 and the writer gives a very full and accurate description of the method of producing these coloured embellishments.

> I have had the honour of being the first visitor to a little manufactory of pottery where unknown to the general public, very notable results indeed are being obtained. . . .

> Take a large dish with raised scroll ornament in coloured clay on a white ground as an example of the method of 'making'. Into the 'intaglio' hollows of the mould, which, of course, produces a counterpart in relief, the watery blue clay of the ornament is first carefully painted. So plastic is it, so admirably adapted to its purpose, that it fills every angle and curve with equal ease and consistency. Then when the hollows are full to the brim, the edges being kept carefully cleaned of superfluous blue clay, after a short interval of partial drying, the white ground of the dish is laid over all. The two different clays adhere, superfluous moisture sinks into the porous plaster of the mould, and after a time there emerges a dish with raised ornament for the firing. This is no mere dull earthenware production with only a surface glaze of colour, but a work of art in which body and ornament alike are formed of clays each of a uniform and homogeneous 'through-colour'. . . . It will be seen at once that the body of this ware, or 'faience' as Mr. Hadley names it, is an absolute novelty and superior in colour and texture to that of any former earthenware.

It will be seen that the ware of Mr. Hadley and his three sons, each of whom has a complete knowledge and direction of his special branch, shows nothing of the amateurism often characteristic of new ventures. It has found its way to appreciation without advertisement of any kind. Very few people have seen the examples in the tiny showroom in Worcester High Street, but their inherent merits of design and modelling, and originality of colour and material, have opened up in the short space of a year and a half the prospect of a successful future.

Production up to June 1900 did not involve the use of fine free-hand painters and it was not until after that date that James Hadley brought in such fine artists as Bill Jarman, Arthur Lewis and Walter Powell, but these will be dealt with in the next chapter.

An elaborate system of numbers was drawn up to indicate the mount and the painting subject and these numbers were written on the base of most Hadley wares and also on Royal Worcester pieces made in the Hadley style after 1905. This generally comprised two numbers divided by a dot, the first one indicating the painted subject and the second the type of mount. This numbering system continued to be used by the 'Hadley painters', as they were called, who moved over to Royal Worcester in 1905 and by the painters they trained in the Hadley style.

The principal numbers were as follows:

Mounts	38	—Clays, green, blue and buff
	49	—Clays, blue, green and pink
	54	—Bronze
	67	—Green and gold
	70	—Yellow and gold
	74	—Bronze and ivory
	76	—Mauve
	78	—Satin
	80	—Green (same as for satin but without the gold) (*after 1923*)
	15a	—Rose, pink and red
	20a	—Pink, white and red
Subjects	10	—Roses, pink and yellow
	10a	—Roses, white and yellow
	10b	—Roses, white and pink
	15	—Roses, pink and red
	15b	—Roses, deep red
	127	—Roses, Gloire de Dijon
	128	—Roses, La France
	20	—Roses, Pink, red and white (from 1923)
	30	—Violets, purple and white
	33	—Chrysanthemums
	40	—Violets, purple
	50	—Peacocks

50a—Peacocks
79 —Swans
85 —Storks
99 —Sweet peas, mixed colours
99b—Sweet peas, mauve and white
101 —Daffodils and violets
102 —Roses and forget-me-nots
145 —Dry blue and storks (Powell)
146 —Yachts
151 —Dry blue and flamingoes (Powell)
156 —Rose and lily

A further shape-number can appear under the base, usually on top of the pattern and mount numbers, and a full Hadley number reference gives a great deal of information generally expressed in a fractional form. For example, the jardinière painted with storks, shown in Plate 117, has 2498, 145.74. 2498 is the shape number, 145 refers to storks subjects and 74 to the bronze and ivory mounts.

The early terra-cottas are charming pieces, many designed as pictures in frames; such subjects as 'Where are you going to my pretty maid?' and 'I'm going a-milking sir she said' being handled with great subtlety. The conventional monochrome decorations of the 1897–9 years are always sensitively and beautifully drawn and are found on small, classical shaped vases or candlesticks, many of the decorations having the sinuously arabesque movement of the Pre-Raphaelites, or even Art Nouveau. These pieces are always of superb quality and although apparently not yet regarded as being 'highly collectable' they should be appreciated much more than they are. The crowning glory of the factory was the splendid vases and jardinières with the typical Hadley-style flowers, the style typified by the roses with boisterous colourings that almost make me think of the term 'blowsy', not in a derogatory sense, but giving the impression that the rose is just past its full bloom with the petals ready to drop off at any moment. This style was so different from the quieter style of flower painting practised at the main factory, that when the Hadley painters were to move over to Royal Worcester their different type of painting made a separate department a necessity. The 'Hadley' and the 'Royal' painters were to continue to lead a separate existence for quite a while and the division of styles still persists in the minds and work of many of the older paintresses, such as Daisy Rea, who were trained as Hadley painters by Walter Sedgley. The method of painting was that the colour background was put on roughly, then badgered with a large badger brush, breathed on and then the lights picked out.

The wares of both Grainger's and Hadley's factories, of course, technically count as 'Royal Worcester', as both firms were taken over by the main Company and this infusion of talent, not only from the craftsmen and artists who moved across but also from the shapes and patterns now made available, was gladly welcomed. One outside factory however, was not taken over by the main Company—the factory of Locke—and its wares do not count as Royal Worcester but it is as well to mention them here.

Locke & Company Limited

This firm was started in 1895 by Edward Locke, a decorator at Grainger's factory, and several of his sons. It was a small factory, built under some of the arches of Shrub Hill railway station, and the wares were rather poor imitations of Grainger and Royal Worcester pieces. They suffer from a generally poor quality of potting and decoration but, in particular, from a body which was very inferior to that of the main factories. The pieces are generally small, seldom more than a few inches in height or length, often decorated with a pinkish aerographed colour in imitation of Royal Worcester and sometimes with small birds or scenes in a poorish version of the main Stinton style, done by the Lockes, Walter Stinton, H. Wall and Greatbach.

Not a lot for Royal Worcester to get worried about, you may think; certainly not enough for them to want to take Locke to the High Courts in 1902. However, Locke's firm was a painful thorn in the flesh as the wares had such a similarity of style in the eyes of a non-discerning public, especially on the continent of Europe, and the factory trade mark of a globe of the world with the word Worcester was too uncomfortably like the circle mark of the main Company to be allowed to exist without a fight. The final straw came when Royal Worcester found china shops stocked with Locke pieces in the window with a trade card reading 'WORCESTER CHINA' in large letters and in very small letters at the bottom 'From Locke and Company', the card being so placed that the lower half was hidden by the china.

The action before Mr. Justice Byrne lasted for three days, Royal Worcester producing photographs of the shop windows in evidence (Plate 121) and also a huge quantity of photographs of their own production ranging from the Dr. Wall to the current periods, which were arranged on a great scroll so that they could be unrolled in court to give an idea of the quality of production over the years. To the main Company's great delight their plea was upheld and an injunction in perpetuity granted to the effect that the words 'Worcester' and 'Royal Worcester' were to be regarded as Trade Marks and only used by the Worcester Royal Porcelain Company. No longer able to use the word Worcester, Locke's wares would not sell and the firm quickly folded. This injunction, of course, still stands and has had to be pointed out to a number of firms, ranging from china to corset manufacturers.

The Worcester Royal Porcelain Company

Through all these changes and chances the Worcester Royal Porcelain Company continued its steady progress to financially better times. Martin Abell had taken over as Chairman after the death of Mr. A. C. Sherriff, but in 1884 Mr. Abell died, and was succeeded by Mr. G. W. Hastings. In 1892 Mr. C. W. Dyson Perrins, later to be such a key figure in the Company's history, joined the board. The Directors were able to announce the first five-figure profits—£12,700 in 1888—and a considerable amount of money was being spent on improvements and extensions to both the main factory and the Royal China Works (the name given to Grainger's factory from 1889).

The comfort and well being of the employees were ever at the forefront of Mr. Binns' mind. In 1884 the Company purchased some property in Severn Street, opposite the main gates of the factory, for the provision of a Works Institute, to provide messing and recreational facilities for the staff. Nowadays these things are taken for granted, but in the mid-Victorian period they were provided by very few industrial factories. To mark the event an address, illuminated by Charles F. Binns with lettering by Eli Haywood was presented by the employees to the Chairman and Directors of the Company. The Educational and Entertainments Committee, under the Chairmanship of Charles Binns, included R. W. and W. M. Binns, James Bradley, George Evans, William Hawkins, Edward Evans, Sam Ranford, Thomas Sanday and F. H. Thorpe and a list of the activities for the Winter season of 1884–5 makes interesting reading:

TUESDAY: In connection with the South Kensington Science and Art Department a class for the study of Botany will be held from 7.0 to 8.0 o'clock, teacher Mr. A. R. Edgington (an examination was to be held in May and Government certificates or prizes awarded to the successful students).

TUESDAY: A class for improvement in Reading, Elocution and the Elements of Music at 7.30 o'clock, conductor Mr. George Roberts.

WEDNESDAY: A series of familiar Art Lectures, open to all the Apprentices on the works at 7.30 o'clock, delivered by Mr. James Bradley on Birds, Mr. F. H. Thorpe on Foliage and Mr. Charles Binns (to Apprentice Girls) on Elementary Drawing.

THURSDAY: A practical class for girls, conducted by a committee of ladies, at 7.30 o'clock.

THURSDAY: Mr. Charles Binns will conduct a Conversational Bible Class (open to both sexes) at 7.30 o'clock.

FRIDAY: The Society of St. John of Jerusalem have kindly arranged for a 'First Aid to the Injured' class at 8.0 o'clock, lecturer J. Randle Buck Esq.

Some high spots of the twenty-year period were the gaining by the Company of the Gold Medal at Melbourne in 1881 and considerable success and praise in the Royal Jubilee Exhibition at Manchester in 1887 and the World Fair in Chicago in 1893. For wares sent to the latter exhibition special marks were used, either words referring to the Fair or a very large letter 'C' below the Trade Mark. The Prince and Princess of Wales visited the factory in September 1884, while staying at nearby Witley Court, where Queen Adelaide had frequently stayed (scenes of Witley Court were frequently done on non-Worcester pieces by George Sparkes—the Worcester outside decorator and dealer).

Many popular styles of shape and pattern continued over from the 1870s, especially Indian, Persian and Japanesque. A pair of large Indian-style vases, shape 979, were presented to Queen Victoria at her Jubilee in 1887. Shapes 850, 854, 931 and 943 could have actual Persian script put on in platinum or metals fused onto the body, in addition to splendidly rich decoration, a style in which the Callowhill brothers and Samuel Ranford played an important part. Large table centres or fern stands became popular, with tree trunks, fences and children or grown-up figures, typified by shape 828—'county courtship group' or '10 years after', in which the courting couple are shown by the old stile, balanced by a boy and girl squabbling at the other end of the fern stand who are obviously the lovers as children. (Plate 79.) Children studies, either on their own or set up as candlesticks or elaborate candelabra or holding baskets, were the most characteristic shapes of this period. Most of these pieces were modelled by James Hadley and it is generally thought that the children were modelled on his own children and the female faces on that of his wife. Certain it is that there always seems to be a family relationship about Hadley's faces, having seen one it is very easy to recognise others. Even if he is depicting Africans one can see clearly who has done the modelling (Colour Plate VI). The very popular hand-vases—various forms of a hand holding a vase—have a female hand that is said to be modelled on the hand of his wife; the old factory workers used to refer to it as 'Mrs.' Adleys' 'and' (Colour Plate IV).

Many different forms of water carriers were made, Arabian, Eastern, African, etc. and these were probably inspired by the growing knowledge of and interest in these lands, both with the opening up of Africa and the increasing use of the Suez Canal. Indian craftsmen, Countries of the World, historical figures, all were popular and commemorative pieces made for the Jubilee of Queen Victoria in 1887. The Australian market was opening up and an Aborigine figure comport was made (shape 1247). A number of bases for Clarke's Fairy lamps and Night Lights and Cricklites were made and menu cards for use on the table were produced in profusion (Plate 89). From the 1890s many vases or figures were produced intended for use as electric lamps and show the technical advances that were coming into middle class life, some of these lamps converted from earlier types of oil or gas lamps.

Possibly the most incredibly complicated group is shape 1580—the Russian table centre decoration. This comprises about two dozen pieces which could be grouped in different arrangements on the table while you ate your new-style Russian dinner, a less formalised meal than the old English dinner, in which the course was served complete on a plate direct to the guest at the table. Salad sets were also very popular (e.g. shape 1681) and could come complete with cutlery; also popular were déjeuner sets on a tray, berry sets (shape 1780) and condiment sets with a unified shape, such as a potato (shape 1863). Many of the popular figures, even those continuing to be popular since the 1860s such as Joy and Sorrow, were used in all sorts of different ways—as flower tubes, comports and lamps, and this might be held to herald the drop in quantity of new fine shapes when James Hadley stopped modelling for Royal Worcester in 1894. The taking over of Grainger's factory, however, brought an influx of new shapes to Royal Worcester and many shapes based on the Flight Barr & Barr period were made.

However, the piece that sums up the whole twenty years is the fabulous Chicago vase, the great centre piece of Worcester's display at the World's Fair of 1893. No one outside the ceramic industry can really appreciate the enormous difficulties that the production of such a huge pot can pose in the making and firing and it says a lot for the wonderful design that it came through all trials by fire unscathed. Of tremendous weight (it took eight strong men to carry it in a crate from the old Museum to the new building), it has a double body, the outside of Parian and the inner of china. Whenever I look at this four-and-a-half foot high vessel I marvel at how it was taken all the way to Chicago and back without coming to harm. In 1970, the last person who was closely connected with the vase, Mrs. Gegg, who in 1893 was personal assistant to Mr. Binns, died in Worcester. She was offered the marvellous chance for a girl in those days of going to Chicago to represent the Company but preferred to leave to get married. Her very last job, on the day she left the factory, was to dust and clean the vase before it was packed into its crate for the journey to America. A very lively lady, she always spoke vividly about life in the factory in the 1880s and remembered the warm welcome that was given by the girls to the Company sales travellers on their infrequent returns to the factory, generally while hidden behind the stillages of ware.

Styles of decoration through the twenty years ranged from stained ivory, popular as the period began, to more daring colour effects as the years passed. Also made was coral ware, a beautiful blushing colour, marked underneath 'Coral Ware', in 1893; 'Shot Enamels' from 1894, the title again put underneath, the colours glowing iridescent; 'prismatic colours' from 1894, again marked, a kaleidoscope of colour; colours which are similar to those found on Tiffany glass of the time; 'shaded pink', the real successor of stained ivory, with colour effects produced by aerograph spraying and 'Sabrina Ware', a beautifully subtle decoration caused by the effects of metallic salts, which started in 1894 and ran on to 1930. The various forms of ivory decoration should not be called 'biscuit', a term which should be retained for unglazed wares, but the term 'biscuit' has been extensively used in describing stained ivories. An experimental body was produced in 1896 called, without any apparent reason, 'Barr's Porcelain'. The body is not as translucent as Parian or bone china, and a special mark was used for this having the words 'BARR PORCELAIN' in a scroll under a monogram. The mark is very rarely seen and it is likely that very little of this ware was produced. One of the most important forms of decoration were the lithographic transfers which started about 1890 and were used on many cheaper printed services, instead of copper-plate transfer prints which had then to be enamelled by hand to produce coloured patterns. Lithos would give a simple coloured pattern without effort, but they were much harder to put on, being of the size-down type, rather than the present-day cover-coat versions. One of the early commemorative plates that was made in 1896 had litho portraits, drawn by E. Raby, of Earl Beauchamp and Lady Mary Lygon, his sister, the Mayor and Mayoress of Worcester of that year. The Earl presented all the children of Worcester's church schools with a plate and arranged a splendid fête for them in the grounds of Madresfield Court, his home near Malvern. Many elderly residents of Worcester still remember travelling in horse-drawn wagonettes to Madresfield, where they consumed huge quantities of tea and buns and enjoyed all the fun of the fair on swing boats and roundabouts (Plate 159). Some of the plates might have been made in the experimental Barr's porcelain.

For the Diamond Jubilee of Queen Victoria in 1897 the Company made twelve special large saucer dishes for presents to the Robinson and Joicey families and others. The work was done by the leading decorators. Some of the saucers had raised gold designs, and turquoise on gold grounds, some had rose du Barry or B. Blue (underglaze cobalt-blue) grounds painted with birds, and others had painted cupids on gold or maroon grounds. One was jewelled and had painted cattle, and one had a sea view and raised gold border. In the centre of each was the Royal Coat of Arms surrounded by the words 'Victoria Diamond Jubilee 1837–1897'. The saucer painted with cattle was done by one of the Grainger painters, John Stinton.

The stained ivory and shaded pink effects, decorated with flowers, were very popular in Europe and many Continental firms copied Worcester shapes and decorative effects very closely. Although these copies do not approach the quality of the originals they look very like Worcester from a distance. Even the Japanese started copying Worcester, a particularly favourite subject being C. H. C. Baldwyn's flying swans (Colour Plate XIV). Worcester finally had to register this and a number of other designs to discourage copying and later versions of the Baldwyn swans registered pattern could be printed in outline and coloured in.

The finest services and vases were, of course, still painted by hand by a splendid group of painters. During this period the principal artists and their subjects were:

Charles H. C. Baldwyn, swans, small birds and landscapes
Albert Binns, sgraffito decoration on earthenware plaques
Thomas John Bott, Limoges enamels, birds, etc.
J. & T. S. Callowhill, continued their gold decorating and also did a
    quantity of outside work on blanks; these were marked 'Callowhill
    & Co.'
Harry Chair, roses
George Cole, roses and other flowers
Octar H. Copson, fruit and other subjects
James Crook, gilt decorative motifs
Albert Gyngell, landscapes

William Hale, fruit, flowers and birds
William Hawkins, roses, interiors, copies of famous paintings
John Hopewell, birds
George Houghton, views
George Hundley, birds and plants
Harry Hundley, flowers
George Johnson, game, exotic birds and flamingoes
James Henry Lewis, landscapes
Thomas Morton, raised gold exotic sprays
Ernest Phillips, flowers, especially old Worcester style
Edward Powell, ferns and butterflies
Edward Raby junior, flowers
Samuel Radford, foreman painter
Robert Rea, butterflies and feathers
William Ricketts, flowers and fruit
Frank Roberts, fruit
Edward Salter, fish
Gustav Sievers, figures and Tenniers style
E. Stephan, orchids

Worcester lost T. J. Bott, the talented son of Thomas Bott, in either 1885
or 1886, but he continued to do some freelance work at the home of Charles
Baldwyn before going to the Staffordshire firm of Brown-Westhead, Moore
in 1889. He later became Art Director of Coalport. While not as fine a painter
as his father he produced a quantity of fine 'Limoges enamel' plaques and
also did a lot of work on fine quality dessert and dinner wares, sometimes in
association with Charles Baldwyn. While with Brown-Westhead, Moore he
applied to Mr. J. Bruff for the post at Coalport in two long letters and I quote
some of the sections relevant to his work at Worcester, by kind permission
of Geoffrey Godden:

26 Sheppard Street,
Stoke-on-Trent. March 4th 1889.
Dear Sir,
   In fulfilment of my promise to supply you with a statement of my
experience in the business and the duties I would undertake if taken
into your employment, I beg to submit the following for your consideration.
   I served my apprenticeship at the Worcester Royal Porcelain Works,
and was especially trained by the Director, Mr. R. W. Binns, for the
highest class of decoration they produced, to succeed my father, who
was the principal artist employed there. About two years after completing
my apprenticeship, I received an offer from Messrs. Brown-Westhead,
Moore & Co. to work for them at their London Studio and as they
offered me an increased salary and I was desirous of studying in London
to improve myself, I accepted it, and left Worcester, after having been
there about nine years.

About two years afterwards, Messrs. B. W. M. & Co. decided to close their London Studio, and they wished me, alone of the artists engaged there, to go down to their Works in the Potteries, and made me a very good offer if I would do so. But, not wishing to leave London until I was more satisfied with my progress, I refused, and remained there for some time afterwards, doing work for myself, which I disposed of to some of the chief West End dealers, and I also did something for the Worcester Works, again, until Mr. Binns wrote me, saying that he could dispose of all the work I could do, and it did not suit him for me to be working independently as well, so if I would say what I should require to come back to Worcester again, he would if terms were suitable, employ me entirely. As my friends were all in Worcester, I had not the same objection to going back there, that I entertained against going to the Potteries, I mentioned what I should expect to make, Mr. Binns agreed, and I returned to Worcester. While there, as, in all probability, I seemed likely to remain, about two years later I married and some few months afterwards, several of the artists had to submit to a reduction in their salaries, and the Manager, no doubt thinking, as I had just settled, I should not be desirous of moving, proposed that I should take a little less also; to this I did not feel inclined to agree, and preferred to start again for myself, with the result that I sold everything as fast as I could produce it to my former customers, the London dealers, Mr. Goode in particular, taking all I did for the first two years, and I made considerably more money.

. . . Regarding the decorative department, I could take charge of that completely, from designing the shapes for the modellers, and the new patterns for the decorators, and if desired, could instruct the latter how to obtain the novel effects which have lately been introduced at Worcester, in many cases cheap and attractive. . . . I can produce the Ivory stains, similar to those used at Worcester, and as I showed you, can obtain a representation of carved or modelled ivory in relief over-glaze, which is a mixture of my own, and is not so far as I am aware known either at Worcester or elsewhere. . . .

The second letter is dated 11th March 1889, and in it he sets out to prove that he is skilled in many other ceramic fields than purely decorative ones.

. . . I was pleased to hear that the pieces of my own work sent for inspection, met with your approval, although they were not what I should have selected, being only what I could obtain at a short notice; I have however now obtained several others, more fully shewing what I can do, as well as several specimens of decorative work that I could teach your men to do; but if entrusted by you with the appointment, my efforts would principally be conducted (if approved by your son) on the methods for cheapening production, now in use so profitably at Worcester, by using when possible girls and women labour, assisted by devices to make it appear as men's work, at least in effect and I have known buyers to purchase some thinking they had got all hand work especially as they had paid high prices for it, leaving very handsome profits for the firm. For the men's work, I should have in view an entirely new application of the jewel work, which I see is a characteristic of Coalport ware, and which as I understand Dark Blue ground and raised gold designs will be likely to be going this season. . . .

Two most interesting points arise from these letters that are not found in any other writings known to me; first, that a number of the major Worcester painters had a reduction in pay and second, that cheaper decorating techniques were brought in, probably referring to outline prints filled in by hand by girls. From a close perusal of the diary kept by Henry Baldwyn, the father of Charley Baldwyn the painter, it is obvious that work was very short for even such a magnificent painter as he was.

R. W. Binns' sons played an important part in the running of the Company but he suffered a sad loss with the death of his son Albert at the tragically early age of twenty in 1882. Albert showed great promise, specialising in doing sgraffito, or incised decoration, in the raw clay of round earthenware plaques (Plate 59). Another son, Charles, left to go to the United States in 1897.

In 1887 Mr. E. P. Evans was promoted to Manager, after twenty years service and a presentation was made to him in the Public Hall on 26th April when he received an address and a silver tea and coffee service. In an evening of music and speeches, the most important speech was inevitably given by R. W. Binns who said that when he had joined the Company there were between seventy and eighty employees; now there were about seven hundred and he quoted from a Continental correspondent saying that the Works and their productions were considered the first in the world. (Loud Applause.) He spoke of those things, he said, because Mr. Evans had been the means, during the last twenty-one years, of producing such perfect unanimity amongst the people and such confidence in one another, that they had been enabled thereby to raise their manufactures to the position they now occupied.

The presentation, on behalf of the employees, was made by Mr. George Gibbs, who was himself just completing fifty years of service with the Company. In reply, Mr. Evans spoke of what in his opinion were the major developments during his time as Secretary; these were that the freehold had been purchased, the works almost reconstructed, the number of persons employed more than doubled, and £600,000 paid in wages. (Applause.) He spoke of the Company's debt to Mr. Binns and referred to their motto which translated read 'Through difficulties to honours'. While tonight they had made the honours his, they could all say of Mr. Binns that he had reached —truly through difficulties—the high standard he laid down twenty-five years ago in adopting that motto. The illuminated address was written and drawn in a beautifully tooled and embossed book by W. Moore Binns, F. H. Thorpe and A. Turner. With it came an album containing all the signatures of the factory's employees, or in the case of those that could not write, their marks. The album ends by quoting an extract from the minutes of a meeting of the Directors held at the Royal Porcelain Works on 10th October 1887, at which were present: G. W. Hastings, M.P.—Chairman, B. W. Leader, R. Smith Carrington, Henry Willis, Joseph Rutland, George E. Abell and R. W. Binns. The extract reads:

> This being the twenty first year of the manager's connection with the Company, the Employees in April last presented him with a Silver Tea and Coffee Service and an address. The Directors then determined to supplement the Silver Service by presenting Mr. Evans with the necessary cups and saucers in porcelain to make it complete and requested him to select a pattern, the porcelain was today laid before the Board and handed to Mr. Evans with the kind congratulations of the Chairman and Directors.

E. P. Evans went to Chicago to represent the Company, met his future wife, a daughter of a Chicago banker, and faced a nine year engagement before returning to Chicago to marry.

Through all the difficulties that were besetting the Company the Staff remained very loyal, even though work was very short and pay small. Many of them turned to other ways of making money, for instance the Callowhill brothers doing outside decorating, Charley Baldwyn painting on canvasses or cards. George Owen experimented with incredibly fine piercing, most of the work done in his own time or when work was short and these he would hope the Company could sell to specialist collectors and then he would be paid. A lot of George Owen's finest wares could take months of slow, careful, skilful work. Reticulating (the technical name for piercing) had to be done before the biscuit firing and while the clay was still wet, a task made doubly difficult by the necessity of preventing the vessel from being pushed out of shape and the problems of drying out. Clay dries quite quickly and if the piercing was a long job of more than a few dozen holes, the pot would dry into too brittle a state on which to work. At that time the only method of keeping a pot in a 'green' state, the term used for clay which is workable and still has moisture in it, was to put it into a wet box. A wet box was metal lined and had damp rags in the bottom and slowly brought drying-out pieces put into it back into a green stage; meanwhile, other pieces would be worked on.

This meant that the length of time spent on one of these difficult 'pierced ivory' pieces, as they were termed, could be spread over some months and right up to the end there was no certainty that the work would be brought to a satisfactory conclusion. A momentary lapse of concentration and a slip of the knife could lead to two holes being cut into one and this would ruin the vessel, as a piece could not be replaced in the raw stage because it would inevitably come out again in the firing. In the kiln anything could go wrong with these fragile pieces and they could end up broken or distorted. So it was very difficult to arrange a sensible method of paying for the work of such craftsmen as George Owen and it was necessary for the Company to purchase some completed work at an agreed price.

George Owen's work was unique. I know that unique is an overworked word and its use can seldom be justified but there can be no doubt about its accuracy in this case. George had the ability to take a complete vase, without moulding or pattern on it, and, as he slowly revolved it on the turntable, he would cut out hole after hole, first the top row, then lower and lower down the vessel, fitting the last hole of each row into its correct place, varying the size in each row to graduate the holes. The incredible regularity of piercing is quite unbelievable and it is almost impossible to realise that the work was done by human means. One advantage over ordinary mortals that George possessed was that he was ambidextrous, enabling him to pierce as well with his left hand as with his right; this meant that he could pierce each side of the hole with equal and even pressure. Another advantage was that he had his vases cast extremely thinly by his son, a fine caster, and although this meant that the wares were more fragile, they could be pierced with greater precision.

The information that we have about his methods of work did not come from George himself, as he was an extremely canny craftsman who did not pass his secrets onto anyone, not even to his son, working behind a locked door. If you wished to see George, you had to knock on the door, wait while he put away his tools and the pieces on which he was working and then you would be allowed in. This secretive attitude seems very strange to those outside the industry but it was very general in the late nineteenth and early twentieth centuries for craftsmen and artists to guard their secrets very carefully. It should be realised that at a time when work was short, and you had a speciality that no-one else could do you would not be inclined to pass this on to all and sundry. Nowadays this attitude has changed and most potters are only too delighted to explain their particular methods, although you can still find great caution among many older people, even after they have retired. One special technique that George is said to have used was a method of preventing the small cut-out pieces from dropping inside the vessel, where they would have been difficult to remove, especially if the vessel had a narrow neck; his method was to dip the knives and saws in oil to which the cut-out piece would stick, enabling it to be pulled away.

All Owen's work was said to be signed, by incising his signature in the wet clay, generally under the base but sometimes on the side of the plinth. The usual signature was G Owen in written script and unless this signature appears it is a reasonable assumption that the piercing was done by some other reticulator, although I have seen some unsigned pieces which, because of their superb technique, would be reasonable to assign to Owen. George also did some rare flower modelling, applying the flowers to vases and pots, or making brooches, but most of this work was done privately for his own family or friends.

Although times were difficult for the workers there was enjoyment and fun to be had in their spare time. Many of them were ardent anglers but the most popular relaxation was the growing recreation of cycling. The Works Cycling Club was established in 1887 and the first minutes were recorded in the Cyclists' Year Book in the following year and I am grateful to Mr. A. B.

Demaus for providing the following information. The Secretary was G. H. Glover, the Club Captain William Hawkins and from 1892 to 1894 there were seventy-five members, yet the club became defunct by the following year. Like most other cycling clubs in Worcester the aims would have been social, with club runs and outings and there seems to have been little competitive element. Runs were organised for Saturday afternoons and sometimes for Thursday evenings. There were, however, closed competitive events and the Dyson Perrins Museum possesses the Championship Cup of 1893, painted with a scene of Tewkesbury Bridge by Edward Salter. The winner of the race to Tewkesbury was the artist himself, who was thus awarded his own painted work. A photograph of the Club is shown in Plate 99, taken on 2nd April 1887 and depicts a great variety of machines, embracing 'ordinaries' (or high bicycles, about that time beginning to be nicknamed 'penny-farthings'), seven front steering rear drive, and two rear steering tricycles and one 'safety' bicycle on the extreme right; all the machines have solid tyres. Uniform was optional, according to the Cyclists' Year Book, and as is evident from the photograph, but the club had a badge, which the majority of the members are shown wearing, together with a dark coloured cap, although some are wearing a light coloured cap and badge. It is interesting to see Mr. Evans, the Company Secretary, in the centre with the black beard, taking a convivial part, and Mr. Binns, the fifth person to his left, with the great white beard. The club was restarted in 1920 and ran for another five years.

The Company lost a well-loved figure when R. W. Binns retired in 1897. He had built up the firm on sound artistic and financial lines, taking the long term view and steering surely through many difficult years. As a mark of respect and obviously with sincere regrets at his retirement, the employees presented him with an illuminated address in book form, the wording written and designed by Mr. F. H. Thorpe, the designer from 1897. Four pages of wording were illuminated with paintings and scroll work by leading painters of both the main factory and the Royal China Works (Grainger's); John Stinton painted a beautiful scene of the City viewed by the river downstream from the factory, with cattle watering; Charley Baldwyn painted birds on branches; George Johnson—a pheasant in landscape and others flying, and Edward Salter painted boats beached by the sea coast. The wording reads:

To Richard William Binns, Esq. F.S.A. June 1897.
We the employes of the Worcester Royal Porcelain Company Limited, engaged at the Royal Porcelain Works and Royal China Works, have learned with much regret that by reason of failing health you feel it necessary to relinquish active participation in the management of the Works. Your resignation of the position of one of the Managers of the Company, after a connection with the Royal Porcelain Works extending over the long period of 45 years occurs at a time when the whole Nation is reviewing the progress made during Her Majesty the Queen's sixty years' reign; and in few departments of the National life has advancement been more marked than in the Art Manufacturers of the Country.

Among these, ceramic productions may justly be assigned an important place, and to your unwearied devotion, wide knowledge, and constant endeavours to obtain the highest standard of excellence, must be attributed, in a large measure, the splendid reputation which Worcester Porcelain has achieved and still enjoys. We are glad to hear that you will continue to be a Director of the Company and it is our sincere hope that you may be spared for years to come to assist the Board with your experience and advice. We do not, therefore, say 'Farewell' but, as you will not in future be brought into daily contact with us, we now ask your acceptance of this simple address as an expression of our affectionate respect and esteem.

A serious illness in 1891 from which, at the time, it was thought he could not possibly recover, had slowed him down physically. Almost up to the time that he died, on 28th December 1900, he used to visit the factory regularly, making the short but painful journey from his home, Diglis House, now the Diglis Hotel. Harry Davis used to recall how when Mr. Binns came through the department on the way to the Museum, the foreman would call 'Rise' and everyone would stand. After the great man had slowly shuffled through the far door, the order 'Sit' would be given and they would return to their work again.

R. W. Binns' final work of scholarship was his magnificent book *Worcester China, a record of the years 1851 to 1897*. He was succeeded as Art Director by his younger son William Moore Binns (his elder son Charles having already gone to the United States) and Mr. F. H. Thorpe was appointed Designer. A great change is to be seen in the shapes produced, many of the elaborate ornamental vases dropping out and being replaced by plainer shapes. From this time many small pieces were made for mounting in silver by Birmingham silversmith firms, often with the monogram mark of these firms put under the bases. Such shapes as biscuit barrels with silver rims, silver stands with porcelain insets and condiment sets in the forms of acorns and other shapes were popular. One curious vessel in the form of a cottage loaf which opens in half on hinged silver mounts was not entered in the Company records but was registered at the Patent Office by the Birmingham silver firm of Norton de White.

Also produced in the Parian body was the beautiful Sabrina Ware, which might almost be thought of as a kind of high class art pottery, the Worcester equivalent of the fine productions of Royal Lancastrian, Doulton and Bernard Moore of that time. Sabrina Ware, which had a run from about 1897 until 1930, can have a very attractive appearance, the decoration shimmering under the surface, almost unseen. One big change for Worcester was that the exact final effect could not be controlled and this was regarded as part of its great charm, as indeed it was, in the style of art pottery. The body of these wares becomes opaque, and they are almost invariably marked 'Sabrina' underneath.

The 1890s saw the replacement of R. W. Binns as the figurehead of the Company by Mr. Charles William Dyson Perrins, generally known as Dyson

31. Pair of fine figures of Africans, shapes 1665 and 1666. The negress (left) is in glazed Parian, the negro is in biscuit china. These have the words 'Protat' on the negro and 'H. Protat 1863' on the negress incised on the plinths and they must come from an earlier period than is suggested by their shape number. Height without lamp 28½ inches.

32. Three pairs of Water Carriers. Above, Eastern Water Carriers, 594. Below, left, miniature Eastern Water Carriers, 1206, 9 inches; right, miniature Cairo Water Carriers, 1250, 9 inches, all in glazed Parian.

33. Models by James Hadley decorated in Raphaelesque, or Capo di Monte style. Above, set of 4 dancing cupids, shape 466, mark 1 and date letter N for 1878. Centre, Mermaid and Nautilus shell decorated by Callowhill, mark 1 impressed, 15 inches, and pair of boys on dolphins, shape 541, mark 1 and year letter N, 7½ inches length.
See page 5.

34. Right, Squirrel in stump, 6/220, height 8 inches; left, Squirrel on stump vase, 490, both naturalistically coloured and gilded. *Collection of Mrs. D. Silvester.*

35. Pair of figures. Right, Satyr, 1440; left, female companion Bacchante with cymbals, 1441, glazed Parian.

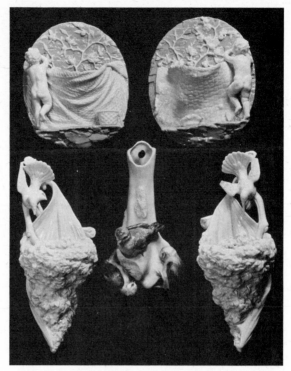

36. Large vase, one of a pair, earthenware with majolica colours and green pedestal, snake handles, painted by Josiah Rushton with figure subjects after Rubens, c. 1870, 30 inches high and unmarked.

38. Wall brackets and pockets, or hair tidies. Above, boy brackets, 662, in green and white glazed Parian. Below, left and right, humming bird brackets, 536, height 13 inches, glazed Parian; centre, 'The Christmas Dinner', depicting 3 tits on a bone (from the Grainger factory). *The latter the property of the Misses Sievers.* See page 13.

37. Five pieces of the late 1860s in glazed Parian. Top left, triple Carthage Violet, 6/49, painted birds probably by Hopewell; right group of 3 amphorae similarly painted. Bottom, left, elephant and howdah, one of a number of such subjects; centre, tri-rhyton vase, 6/20; right, cup and saucer with applied coloured flowers in the Belleek style. See page 13.

39. Above, 3 from the set of London Cries figures, height 7 inches. From left, Ye Brush Man, shape 1001, Ye Prison Basket, 1000 and Ye Watchman, 998, the latter could have a pike or a lantern. Below, left, pair of Sowers, 1480; right, Elizabeth and Raleigh, 786, height $6\frac{1}{2}$ inches.

40. Candlesticks. Above, boy and girl, shapes 938 and 939, fitted as candlesticks, height $7\frac{1}{2}$ inches; owl candlestick, 1043, $7\frac{1}{2}$ inches. Below, left, shape 1873, $12\frac{1}{2}$ inches; centre, shape 1478, 8 inches; right, shape 3/11, all glazed Parian.

41. Shells and a Grainger leaf, all coloured and bronzed, the tortoise and a mussel, shape 928; all glazed Parian. *From the collection of Mrs. D. Silvester.*

42. Clock (French movement) in clock case, shape 497, majolica colourings, 16 inches. A number of different clock cases were made.

43. One of a pair of large faience vases, coloured turquoise blue and bronze, painted with an artist's studio subject, 23 inches, mark 1 on a pad and printed letter N for 1878.

44. Left, Swan and Nautilus shell, class 6/9, Parian with lustre glaze face tinted; right, boy and swan, 532, glazed and tinted Parian. The reins are rope, but have been seen as a rope of modelled and coloured flowers; impressed mark 1, length 10 inches. *The property of Dolphin Antiques.*

45.   Royal Worcester and Grainger pierced vessels. Above, left, shape 1074, pierced vase, with inset vase, ivory finish and raised gold by Henry Bright in 1931; right, double pierced jug popular since Chamberlain period. Below, left, Grainger shape 1/3737, pink and gold lines and turquoise, raised gold spots, $11\frac{1}{2}$ inches, year 1892; centre, Grainger shape, pencilled ivory and pink raised spots; right, a Kerr & Binns shape, ivory ground and jewelling, $9\frac{1}{4}$ inches, 1884. See page 31.

46.   Pair of vases $14\frac{1}{2}$ inches and snake-handled vase (lacking cover, but see Plate 55) with fine floral subjects painted by David Bates in 1864 and 1866, mark 1.

47. Photograph of Thomas Bott, standing centre, with Josiah Davis on his right and William Turner on his left. Also examples of the work of the 3 specialists in Limoges enamel painting on dark blue ground. Above, right, by Thomas Bott senior, c. 1862; left, by Thomas John Bott, signed and dated under the base 'Worcester 1883'. Below, by Thomas Scott Callowhill, signed and dated under the base 'Worcester 1870', 8 inches by 5½ inches. See page 28.

48. Detail from the Norman Conquest ewer and basin shown in Colour Plate III, showing the 'Death of Harold' painted by Thomas Bott, gilding by Josiah Davis. This shows the remarkable quality of the detail and perspective in the translucent enamel.

49. Three fine china plaques. Above, by Luke Wells after a painting by Woodward, in 1865. Below, left, 'Angel of the Annunciation' by Josiah Rushton in 1871, after Carlo Dolci; right, after Andrea del Sarto, by Thomas Bott, c. 1868, the latter $14\frac{1}{2}$ inches by $11\frac{1}{2}$ inches.

50. Dessert plate, pierced turquoise and gold, 3 panels round rim with painted landscapes and cattle subject in centre painted by Robert Perling in 1870, 9 inches, mark 4 impressed. See page 9.

51. Plateau, green band and gold borders, painted with the '*Fighting Temeraire* tugged to her last berth' after J. M. W. Turner, by Joseph Williams in 1867, mark 3, 18½ inches.

52. Fine pair of vases with Landseer-type subjects painted by Robert Perling, on a rose du Barry ground.

53. Magnificent pair of vases, shape 6/173, pearls round rim, paintings on a pale celadon ground of parrots in bold enamel colours. Mark 1 moulded and raised, and 'T' in gold, height 10 inches; possibly painted by Thomas Shaw. *Collection of Miss N. Halliwell.*

54. Superb pair of vases topped by 4 dolphins, shape 6/131, rose du Barry ground, beautifully painted with continuous landscapes of farmyards, gypsy encampments, etc., possibly by James Bradley senior, Mark 1 and '68' under for 1868, height 14½ inches. *Collection of Miss N. Halliwell.*

55. Pair of vases, shape 519, b. blue (cobalt) ground, reserving panels painted with 'The Italian Mother' after Stanley of Munich (left), and 'The Young Mendicant' after Paul Delaroche, by Josiah Rushton, probably late 1860s, mark 1 and monogram JR, for Rushton.

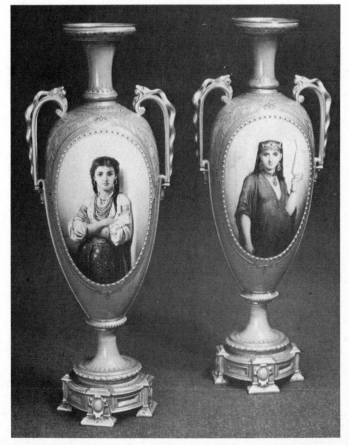

56. Pair of vases 'Royal' shape, serpent on handle, turquoise ground and fine gilding, reserving panels painted with figure subjects by Josiah Rushton, mark 1 impressed and printed.

57. Three pieces painted with 'Beauties of the Court of King Charles' by Josiah Rushton. Above, Jardinière with La Belle Hamilton (Countess de Gramont) and, on the reverse, with Catherine de Braganza; tazza with Elizabeth Countess of Northumberland; ewer with Angel handle with Mary, first Duchess of Devonshire. Flowers painted by David Bates, bronze and gold decoration by E. Béjot, Mark 1, 1869. See page 104.

58. Fine garniture, exhibited at 1867 Exhibition, royal blue ground richly gilt, painted figure subjects by Thomas Bott comprising Sibylla Libyca, Sibylla Cumana and Hellespontiaca, mark 1, date 1864, heights $17\frac{1}{2}$ inches and 22 inches.

59. Earthenware plaque, sgraffito decoration by Albert Binns, signed and dated 20/7/80, 1880, 12 inches. See page 30.

60. Pair vases in Japanese style, shape 562, embossed oblong panels with red ground and gilding, painted with Japanese patterns, 7 inches, mark 1 with 77 for 1877. See page 8.

61. Japanese style. Above, left, spill, modelled Japanese scene, decorated dry ivory colours and gilt; right, 6/212, stork spill, decorated in bronze and gold and coloured lustre. Below, left 6/217, stork spill and monkey, underglaze colours, gilt and bronze, height 7 inches; centre, dark green and red, with metallic storks; right, decorated violet green glaze, gold crackle and white enamel blossoms, $2\frac{1}{4}$ inches, date 1879.

62. Three Japanesque lotus candlesticks. Below, left, shape 1088, decorated pencilled ivory and metallic colours, $4\frac{1}{2}$ inches; right, shape 687, decorated old ivory and gilt, $7\frac{1}{4}$ inches. Above, shape 688.

63. Japanesque square shape tea-ware. Above, left, tea kettle, shape 254, embossed sprays and storks, coloured stippled aventurine, bronze lizard handle, $7\frac{1}{2}$ inches; right, milk jug from déjeuner service, shape 253, yellow ground, coloured and gilt, $5\frac{1}{2}$ inches. Below, teacup and saucer, underglaze storks and flies, year 1878. See page 8.

64. Japanesque spills and pots. Above, left, shape 329, pierced with animals and birds, blue enamelled and gilt; right, as shape 162 in brown clay, decorated with Japanese forms in gold. Below, left, shape 689; centre, 573, right, 499.

Perrins. Born in 1864 he built up a large fortune through the Worcester firm of Lea & Perrins, chemists, who were to achieve fame by producing a sauce with a secret recipe, said to have been acquired from a retired Indian Army officer. This fortune he used partly to build up superb collections of early illuminated manuscripts and eighteenth-century Worcester porcelain, but mainly to do many benevolent acts.

Dyson Perrins first became associated with the company when he was elected a Director on 12th December 1891. On 14th December 1898 growing financial pressures led him to loan the Company £20,000 on a first mortgage of the whole of the factory. In 1901 he was elected Deputy Chairman on 9th March and Chairman on 14th September and he was to guide and support the Company through the perilous years to come.

The nineteenth century was to end with the issue of the last form of indentures for a seven-year term to a painting apprentice, Harry Davis. This form of indenture had been in use in Worcester since the eighteenth century, with virtually no change and it is appropriate that young Harry Davis, who was to be the most important painter of the next century should sign the last indenture on 3rd November 1899. The wording of the indenture makes most interesting reading:

THIS INDENTURE WITNESSETH that Harry Davis with the consent and approbation of his father Alfred William Davis of No. 3 Jubilee Cottages, Portland Street, Worcester, Presser, doth put himself Apprentice to Edward Probert Evans of the City of Worcester, Porcelain Manufacturer, on behalf of The Worcester Royal Porcelain Company Limited as the Managing Director of the said Company and to the person or persons who shall for the time being be the Managing Director or Manager of the said Company to learn that branch of the Art or Trade of a Porcelain Manufacturer called 'Painting' and with him and them after the manner of an Apprentice to serve from sixth day of February 1899 unto the full end and term of seven years thence next following to be fully complete and ended During which term the said Apprentice his master faithfully shall serve, his secrets keep, his lawful commands everywhere gladly do. He shall do no damage to his said Master nor see to be done of others but to his power shall tell or forthwith give warning of the same. He shall not waste the goods of his said Master nor lend them unlawfully to any. He shall not contract Matrimony within the said term nor play at Cards, nor Dice-tables or any other unlawful games whereby his said Master may have any loss with their own goods or others during the said term without the licence of his said Master. He shall neither buy nor sell. He shall not haunt Taverns or playhouses nor absent himself from his said Master's service day or night unlawfully but in all things as a faithful apprentice he shall behave himself towards his Master and all theirs during the said term and shall during the said term be a constant student at a Government or other approved Art School and use his best endeavours to pass the second grade examination in Freehand and

E

Model drawing before the expiration of the fifth year of the said term and the second grade examination in Geometry and Perspective before the expiration of the sixth year of the said term And The said Edward Probert Evans for himself and for the person or persons who shall for the time being be the Managing Director or Manager of the said Company and in consideration of the service to be done and performed by the said Harry Davis the said apprentice in the said branch of the Art or Trade of a porcelain manufacturer called 'painting' which the said Company use by the best means that he and they can, shall teach and instruct or cause to be taught and instructed. And shall during the said term for such work as shall be done by the said apprentice pay unto him the sums following upon the amount which shall for the time being be paid by the said Company to experienced workmen for such work. That is to say—During the first five years the sum of sixpence in the shilling and during the remainder of the said term the sum of eightpence in the shilling. And for the true performance of all and any the said covenants and agreements either of the said parties bindeth himself unto the other by these presents.

In Witness whereof the parties to these Indentures interchangeably have put their hands and seals the third day of November 1899.

Signed sealed and delivered by the within named Harry Davis Alfred William Davis and Edward Probert Evans in the presence of F. Rogers.

Chapter III

The 1900s and 10s

The twentieth century was not long under way before financial difficulties began to make themselves felt. It was still possible to put a bold public face upon things, especially with the benevolent help of Mr. Dyson Perrins, but the reminiscences of old craftsmen, who were at the factory then, make a depressing story.

When Percy Lewis came to work at Worcester in 1905, the year that marked the taking over of Hadley's factory, he was already an accomplished all-round decorator, but chose to become a gilder rather than a painter, as work was so scarce for the painters. The men's painting department had shrunk to a dozen or so and it was necessary for the traveller, Albert C. Darling, to go out and obtain orders for the painter's particular type of subject. If the subject proved unpopular, no work came in, because a painter was not allowed to take on another's subject. The Stintons seemed to have a popular and lasting formula and were seldom without work, but such superb artists as Charley Baldwyn and Lucien Boullemier left for more re-munerative pastures. Albert Darling travelled the whole country by train, taking with him four or five huge hampers of samples, setting these out for several days at a time in the travellers' room in a hotel to which dealers would come.

There was relatively more work for a gilder to do, as nearly every vessel needed gilding, even the pieces with cheaper blue printing or the outline printed and coloured in flower subjects by the paintresses. In 1905 there were some sixty to seventy gilders and at times when work was short there was a curious system in force for its allocation. In the morning the work to be gilded was put out and the gilders would draw numbered tickets for ten shilling lots of work, the first ticket out of the hat allowing the recipient first choice, and so on down the line, until all the work was taken, those who had not been lucky having no work that day. This system continued on into the 1930s until most of the older gilders, such as Henry Bright, William Evans, Fred Lipscombe, 'Tubby' Morton and 'Dummy' Sheppard had died or left.

When special orders did come in, there were painters of great quality to execute them. Apart from Baldwyn and Boullemier, the principal painters in the period and their subjects, were as follows:

Reginald Austin, flowers, birds and fruit
Walter Austin, flowers, birds and fruit
Harry Chair, roses
George Cole, roses and other flowers
Harry Davis, landscapes, sheep, fish
George Evans, Corot subjects
William Hawkins, Foreman painter, interiors, still life, flowers
William Jarman, peacocks, flowers in Hadley style
George Johnson, old Worcester style birds
Ernest Phillips, flowers, especially old Worcester style
William Powell, English birds
William Ricketts, flowers and fruit
Frank Roberts, fruit
Richard Sebright, fruit
Walter Sedgley, roses and other flowers
Harry Stinton, cattle
James Stinton, gamebirds
John Stinton, cattle

Few young painters were taken on, until the arrival of the 'Terrible Seven' around 1919 and they are dealt with in the next Chapter. However, with all the difficulties, some magnificent large vases were produced and there can be few who will dispute that vases and plaques painted by Davis, Hawkins, Phillips, Ricketts, Roberts, Sebright and the Stintons must rank as among the finest ceramic paintings of the first twenty years of the twentieth century. These fine pieces cannot really be considered common and are probably more rare than equivalent fine pieces of the Dr. Wall period. As yet it is only the work of the Stintons and Davis that are being particularly sought, but the quality of the other Worcester painters can be judged from the photographs in this book.

Some of the loveliest services were made for the Australian market, in particular some beautiful reproductions of Australian flowers from paintings by the talented Australian artist Mrs. Ellis Rowan. These services, of such patterns as W9759, C546 and C547, were produced for the Australian dealers Prouds Ltd. and Flavelle Brothers and were painted by such painters as Sedgley and Phillips and the Austin brothers, the centres surrounded by an acid 'Quaker Grey' border. A magnificent series of plates painted with Birds of Paradise was done a little later from paintings which Mrs. Rowan made in 1916–18 when she went alone to New Guinea, while the island was still inhabited by cannibals and virtually unexplored. Ellis Rowan was then aged sixty-eight and, according to those who knew her, she was five feet tall and weighed only eighty pounds, but she took on the jungles of New Guinea and Queensland. Her biography is being written by fellow countrywoman Mrs. M. Hazard who quotes a letter in which Mrs. Rowan states:

Flavelle has almost all my designs, he is going to take home a set of Birds of Paradise plates that I designed for him. I believe the Worcester people are delighted with them and think it will be the finest piece of work they have produced.

These Birds of Paradise were copied by Sedgley and the subjects issued as pattern C2805, painted by R. H. Austin.

The most impressive piece produced during this period was the Imperial Coronation vase of 1902, shape 2219, of twenty-nine inches in height. The original cost in the white only was £30 but with full colours of scale cobalt blue ground and onglaze colours it cost £130, by far the most expensive piece produced for sale until the Doughty birds. The designer was F. Thorpe, modeller George Evans and the portraits were painted by Lucien Boullemier. A description of the vase, written at the time, gives a marvellous impression of Edwardian pomp and circumstance and Empire glory.

> The vase is emblematic and symbolic of Great Britain, and of the Empire beyond the Seas. The body is of Royal Blue Colour, 'scaled' after the manner of the Old Worcester China. It is supported upon a foot and plinth, the latter is surrounded by a Gold cable, which with the four supporting Dolphins signifies the Maritime supremacy of the Empire. The former, which also contains nautical emblems, shows the names of the four chief possessions beyond the Seas, India, Australia, Canada and South Africa. The Cup holding the body is decorated with the Oak Leaf and Acorn. The handles are each adorned with the Lion's Head, supporting in his mouth a wreath of Laurels, signifying power and fame. In the base of the neck there is a recurrence of the Oak and the Acorn motif, the neck itself bearing the National emblems—the Rose, the Shamrock, Thistle and Leek. The whole is surmounted by a cover, bearing the Tudor Rose and the Royal Crown. The body of the vase is adorned in the front with two framed panels, bearing portraits of the King and Queen in their Coronation Robes, (the portraits are from drawings made in Westminster Abbey by a celebrated London Artist who was present at the Coronation Ceremony). From between the panels hangs the 'George' in bold relief, while surmounting them is the head of 'Britannia' with steel and gold casque, and bearing upon her breast a Ruby Heart, signifying the love of the people for the Throne and for the King and Queen. Upon the back of the vase there is a frame, similar in design to the other panels in the front, but which contains the Royal Arms richly emblazoned. The whole of the decoration of the vase is carried out in dark blue and white and gold, and the effect, while exceedingly rich, is refined by the delicacy of the gilding. (Colour Plate XI.)

Other shapes of this period pale into insignificance compared with the Imperial Vase; although a few large vases were designed in this period, such as shape 2406, most of the important paintings were applied to shapes begun in the 1880s. Many versions of old Worcester shapes—Dr. Wall and Flight

Barr & Barr periods—were made and favoured forms of decoration were old Worcester (Dr. Wall) style flowers and fabulous birds, sometimes associated with scale blue ground. These shapes and styles were no doubt influenced by the great love of eighteenth-century Worcester by Mr. Dyson Perrins.

Most shapes, however, were smaller, insignificant items. Figures ranged from a set of six Boer War soldiers of 1900 (Plate 130), which are rather in the nineteenth-century Hadley style, to the small nude figures of 1919 (Plate 142) which point the way to the figures of the 1920s and 30s. Small shapes ranged from the vessels made for the Sabrina style of decoration to pieces made for silver mounting. The century started without a leading designer to take the place of James Hadley, the internal modellers on the works staff being Ernest, George and Sydney Evans and Bill Pointon, who were to be joined by Frederick Gertner in 1915. Within five years Gertner had produced a great number of figures, in particular the first of the Historical Figures that continue to this day, and were of a very different appearance from any that had been made before. Although Gertner's Historical series might now be thought rather stiff and formalised they point the way to the fine figures to come in the 1930s and the continuation of the skills in making the figures was an important factor in the artistic success of the Limited Editions of Doughty and Lindner; these arts and skills, once lost, are very hard to build up again.

Two important events in 1903 were the death of James Hadley and the successful High Court action resulting in the injunction preventing the use of the word 'Worcester' on any ceramics except by the Worcester Royal Porcelain Company.

In commemoration of the obtaining of the injunction the employees presented E. P. Evans with an illuminated address, designed and lettered by F. Thorpe and having four painted panels by leading artists—fruit by Hawkins, landscape by Johnson, birds by Baldwyn (shown in Colour Plate VIII), and orchids by Roberts.

The wording reads:

> We the undersigned, Members of the Company's Staff, desire to offer to you, and through you, to the Directors and Proprietors, our hearty congratulations upon the happy result of the recent Actions in the High Court of Justice, by which the Company's right to the exclusive use of the name 'Worcester', as applied to Ceramic Productions, has been maintained and confirmed. We believe that in securing this important decision the Company had the assistance of a most able Solicitor and Counsel, and the cordial co-operation of many friends of the Works, but we feel that to your great ability and unwearied exertions in preparing and presenting the Company's case must be attributed in largest measure the successful issue of the litigation.
>
> We avail ourselves of this opportunity to tender to you a renewed expression of our affection and respect, and it is our earnest hope that you may be spared in health and vigour to continue the eminent services

which you have rendered to the Worcester Royal Porcelain Works during the past thirty-five years.

January 1903

The death of James Hadley led to his three sons disposing of the business to Royal Worcester in 1905 and the latter's ranks were swelled by an influx of workers, who joined a Company which had already taken in a number of craftsmen and artists from Grainger's when that factory site was sold in 1902. The principal Grainger artists to make the half mile move from St. Martin's Gate to Diglis were John and James Stinton and George Cole and they were to find a greater amount of work available than at their old factory. Grainger's had fallen on difficult times and Walter Scrivens, later to be foreman printer, described how he was sent to Grainger's to work but found little to do. Most of the printers would wait in the more cheerful conditions of the local pub and when work came into the shop he would be sent to fetch them. Walter Scrivens, whose proud boast it was that he was never late nor absent once in sixty-eight years of work, began as a lodge boy, a lowly position but one that the Company has always used as a means of starting a lively lad on the right road for a more important job. One of his tasks as lodge boy, while W. Moore Binns was courting a Miss Isaacs of Boughton Park, some way out of the City, was to take billets doux to her and wait for an answer. This was a very pleasant task, as he was always regaled with a cup of tea and a large slice of cake.

The Hadley painters did not become easily absorbed into Royal Worcester and for many years there was a split between the 'Hadley' and the 'Royal' painters, each group having a separate room and continuing their styles of painting. As well as painters, the amalgamations brought a great number of the better shapes to join the existing Royal Worcester ones. The original Hadley shapes that continued were indicated by the use of the old F sequence of shape numbers or an H number or by putting a script H on the base; the Grainger shapes were noted by the addition of a G prefix.

The ordinary patterns of Royal Worcester which were very nineteenth-century in style in 1900, continued to be made in great quantity either in the vitreous body or bone china (ornamental wares continued to be made in a Parian body, except for pieces intended to be decorated with cobalt blue ground, which needed to be made in bone china). The favourite patterns of the first few years of the century were of coloured flower borders (usually prints coloured in) or blue and white transfer prints with three especial old time favourites—'willow pattern', 'royal lily' and 'Broseley dragon'. Many attractive ground colours were put on the basically simple shapes used around the time of the first World War. Plate 141 gives a good idea of the sort of ware made at that period, typically decorated in gold with conventional designs with enamel spots on top of such ground colours as Powder Blue, Maroon, Calabash, Celadon, Mottled Pink, Lavender and Purple. By 1920 these had changed to a modernistic style of black with red or green spots, rather pointing the way to the flappers of the Twenties. W. Moore Binns had been succeeded as Art Director in 1915 by J. Wadsworth, who joined Gilbert C. Solon, who, after being Works Manager for two years, had taken over as Managing Director from E. P. Evans. Mr. Evans had gone into honourable retirement, although he was to make a dramatic return at the time of the Company's great need in 1927.

Some finer quality decoration was done, which ranged from the beautiful Art Nouveau style to Sabrina ware which remained reasonably popular. The finest vases were decorated by a superb group of artists who seemed to keep faithful and cheerful during a long period of short time working. The Company made a brave show at the Franco-British Exhibition in Shepherd's Bush in 1908, where Royal Worcester's display was managed by Mr. John Haywood, who had followed his father Eli in looking after the retail showroom. On exhibition were large Hadley vases and figures, Owen pierced ware, apple-green ground services and still life by Hawkins.

The Company still strove hard to keep a forward-looking policy, constantly keeping abreast of the most modern scientific developments of the day. A fine new circular 'Climax' enamel decorating kiln was installed in 1902 and lasted until 1928 when it was replaced by an electric tunnel kiln. This was one of the first benefits of a laboratory and research department set up in 1900 under the direction of George Hancock who was replaced by F. E. Woolridge in 1913. The latter had made a special study of laboratory porcelain in Germany, the main producers of such ware, and he was the ideal person to conduct experiments in 1914 when the Company was asked to produce scientific porcelain for the war effort by the Government. This had to be a high fired, heat resistant body, capable of being heated to a red hot temperature and plunged into cold water without cracking.

The success that the Company made of this new venture was not only of great use to the country in replacing scientific porcelain no longer available from Germany but it gave Worcester confidence in their ability to conquer difficult ceramic problems. In fact, the production of this porcelain, which had to be fired in the hottest place of the 'stone Kiln' was the start of many years of slow and steady development which was to culminate in the fantastic success of porcelain production in the 1960s and the building of the new factory in 1970.

Another improvement of great importance was the use of electricity to replace coal as a means of firing the kilns following the building of the Corporation of Worcester's electricity generating station in 1908. In the same year the Company pensioned the magnificent old beam engine which was first installed in the 1870s. Just before the first World War a body called 'Wall body' (named after Dr. Wall), having a green translucence, was introduced and is still used.

At the end of the war, in 1918, production of the 'vitreous' earthenware body, long used for hotel and domestic ware, was given up. All workers who had served in the war were presented on their return with a covered vase (shape 2712) inscribed with their names, departments and war service in gold on a powder ground.

A number of curious marks are found on the bases of pieces produced at this period. One of the most interesting is a coloured Union Jack flag used in the years 1914–15 and probably meant as a patriotic flourish. Also frequently seen are the marks and names of the dealers for whom the wares were being made, such as the firm of Mather whose symbol was a Viking ship. Under the base of some pieces is found a bee printed in green, a mark used for Thomas Goode & Company. This should not be confused with a bee printed in mauve which is found under some wares of about 1891 and indicates a reject piece, or a seconds piece, one that did not reach the rigid requirement of 'best' ware before decorating. As a point of interest, the present day method of indicating a 'seconds' is to incise a diamond scratched X through the glaze under the base. Another interesting mark is a Cavalier and the words 'Fide et Fiducia', made for Woodwards and later for a number of wares going to America. Sometimes three blue dots are found on stained ivory ware of this period and this indicated some defect in the body, such as pinholes; these were known as 'Three Dot Ware'. A 2 beneath trade mark indicates seconds.

One of the finest vases made at this time was the presentation piece, shape 2569, to Henry Hawker, the foreman printer, to commemorate fifty years employment in 1916; painted with a superb panel of a Worcester scene by Harry Davis, and marked with the names of the designer—F. H. Thorpe— and the gilders A. Glover and W. Southall. The inscription reads:

> Presented to Henry Hawker, Foreman of Printing Department, in recognition of over 50 years faithful service with the Worcester Royal Porcelain Company Ltd. May 1916.

His son, William Hawker, became an engraver—printers and engravers worked very closely together—and was a colleague of Percy Burgess.

Percy, son of Leonard Burgess the decorator, joined the factory in July 1905 when only twelve years four months old, and when fourteen became a seven year term apprentice. His wages make interesting reading—first year 3s. per week, second 5s., third 8s., fourth 10s., fifth 12s., sixth 14s. and seventh 16s. per week. He did his first repair of an engraved copper plate—of the Rossetti lace pattern—in May 1906, that is, when only thirteen years of age. Even having to work as hard as these little lads did, there was still time to behave like children and in William Hawker's personal work books, kindly loaned to me by his son, are many examples. For instance, bets were laid for an even shilling on who would be a weight of ten stone ten pounds by a certain date or whose favourite football team—that of Hawker, Lewis or Burgess— would end up highest in the league.

It may be of interest to note here the composition of services, noted in a sales book dated 1912. Tea services could be of forty or twenty-two pieces, the full forty-piece service for twelve people comprised twelve cups and saucers, twelve 6¾ inch plates, two bread and butter plates, one slop basin and one cream jug. A twenty-two piece service had six cups, saucers and plates, plus two bread and butter plates, slop basin and cream jug. A teapot would be an extra piece, of course, but was not supplied except as an extra, as many people would have a silver pot. Breakfast services were of fifty-one or twenty-nine pieces, the full fifty-one piece service comprising twelve cups and saucers, twelve $7\frac{3}{4}$ inch plates, slop basin, sugar basin and milk jug, two bread and butter plates, one muffin dish and cover, six egg cups and two dishes of 10 and 12 inches. Dinner services could comprise fifty-two, sixty-seven, ninety-six or a hundred and one pieces, the full twelve-person hundred and one piece service being thirty-six meat plates, twelve soup plates, twenty-four pudding plates, ten dishes (two 9 inch, two 10 inch, two 12 inch, two 14 inch, one 16 inch and one 18 inch), a gravy well dish of 18 inches, soup tureen and stand, two sauce tureens and stands, four vegetable dishes and covers and a salad bowl. A dessert service would have twelve plates, four comports $2\frac{1}{2}$ inches high (or four low dishes) and two $4\frac{1}{2}$ inch high comports or else a set could comprise twelve plates and six low dishes. A full dressing table set would comprise up to fifteen pieces and include comb tray, pin tray, candlestick, tall puff box, small round box and ring stand. A full wash set would comprise ewer and basin, chamberpot, round and square soap dishes, brush box and brush vase.

These compositions have not changed very much to the present day, except that the tea service has lost one of its two bread and butter plates and each market and sometimes even each country has its own peculiarity in composition.

Through these first twenty years of the century Mr. Dyson Perrins continued to guide and help the Company, although the crisis years were yet to come. One of the many acts for which he is remembered by the staff of that time was his encouragement of a local school for physically handicapped children and many of these youngsters, deformed or deaf and dumb, came to work at the factory, which was given a special award for this encouragement.

Chapter IV

The 1920s and 30s

The Twenties began with few public hints of the troubles to come. The country itself was still in the grip of post-war enthusiasm—the Roaring Twenties—and there were few thoughts of the imminent slump and general strike. The British Empire was still a very real force to be reckoned with and a great British Industries Fair was mounted in 1920 and Worcester put on an exhibit. The return to the gold standard in 1925 and the lead that Britain still had in the field of the exporting of manufactured goods were comforting things but world trade was getting even more difficult. Unemployment was very high and although it was alleviated by insurance, which in 1920 covered about two-thirds of the population, benefits were not available for those who had not been in employment long enough to qualify and even to the qualified some form of additional relief was often necessary. Although world prosperity was very real, the wealthy were getting wealthier and the poor poorer and to keep up increased production various forms of hire purchase were introduced which could not for long conceal the fact that over production by the producers and lack of real purchasing power by the consumers would lead to the great crash of 1929, preceded in Britain by the general strike of 1926.

At Royal Worcester, the principal painters of the 20s and 30s (although many of these were to leave halfway through the period) were:

Reginald Austin, flowers, birds and fruit
Walter Austin, flowers, birds and fruit
Harry Ayrton, fish, fruit
William Bagnall, fruit and still life
Ernest Barker, flowers and sheep
William Bee, fruit
Kitty Blake, blackberries and flowers in Hadley style
Harry Davis, landscapes, sheep
George Evans, landscapes
John Freeman, flowers, fruit
William Hawkins, fruit, still life, flowers

George Johnson, old Worcester-style birds
Arthur Lewis, storks, irises
Thomas Lockyer, fruit
George Mosley, fruit and birds
Ernest Phillips, flowers
William Powell, birds
Horace Price, fruit, flowers
Daisy Rea, flowers
William Ricketts, flowers and fruit
Raymond Rushton, landscapes
Richard Sebright, fruit
Walter Sedgley, flowers, Italian garden scenes
Albert Shuck, fruit, flowers
Ethel Spilsbury, flowers
Jack Stanley, flowers and still life
Harry Stinton, cattle
James Stinton, gamebirds
John Stinton, cattle
Edward Townsend, fruit, fish
Charles Twilton, fruit

A fine bunch of painters indeed, without doubt unexcelled in any other china works, and an interesting blend of age and youth, as Plate 149 will show. This photograph, taken in 1928, to commemorate the retirement of William Hawkins, the foreman, shows his department plus a few of the paintresses. Just before 1920 there had been an influx of a number of youngsters—the last such major influx until the 1950s, and as most of them are still alive, and three of them still painting at the factory, it has been possible to piece together a great amount of information about their life at that time.

Young painters were always put to one of the seniors to be guided and trained by him but in addition they went to the Victoria Institute in the town to have more formal training in drawing and art appreciation. To a particular group of seven youngsters, who all joined about the same time, this formal continuation of what must have seemed like school work into apparent adulthood occasionally was very irksome. These seven, who were generally known as the 'Terrible Seven', were Tim Ayrton, Bill Bagnall, Bill Bee, George Mosley, Jack Stanley, Ted Townsend and Charlie Twilton and their favourite alternative to the Institute lectures was a game of football in a nearby school playground. One afternoon, in the middle of an enthusiastic game a policeman's helmeted head popped over the wall and a great voice boomed out 'Got yer!' The seven ran back in fear and trembling all the way to the factory, hiding in dread from the vengeance to come. But although everything that went wrong in the factory was blamed on them, usually with justification, they seemed to get away with it. One day, while playing cricket down the length of the painting shop a big hit knocked for six a fine vase but they were still able to convince Mr. Hawkins when he returned to the room that something had accidentally fallen on it.

As a foreman William Hawkins can have had few equals. Not only a magnificent painter himself, he was a fine teacher, held the respect of all his painters and saw that the available work was apportioned as fairly as possible. After a young painter had left the support of his master, who was getting paid for teaching him a particular subject, it was much harder for him to get work, especially any large pieces, to paint. Thus Ernest Barker's sheep subjects are generally found on only very small pieces whereas Harry Davis would automatically attract the orders for large vases painted with that subject. John Stinton produced relatively large quantities of big pieces, leaving Harry Stinton only smaller pieces for many years. It was said by some that Harry grew so accustomed to painting Highland Cattle subjects on small vases that when he was finally able to have large pieces on which to paint he could no longer raise his sights; so if you find a large Worcester vase with a small frieze of diminutive Highland Cattle marching around it you will know it to be a Harry Stinton. This is not really true, of course, although there is a grain of truth in the idea.

The young painters were not the only live wires around the factory, some of the paintresses bidding fair to rival the reputation of the Terrible Seven. A group of them were known as the Saucy Six, five of them from the factory —Kitty Blake, Edith Bradley, Ethel Spilsbury, Gertie Taunt and Daisy Rea —and Daisy's older sister, Nell. These young ladies were very lively, both outside the factory where they would round off a picnic by descending on a village inn and giving an impromptu concert gathered round the piano, and in the factory where anyone who offended the paintresses was liable to be put on their 'Murder list', a list put up in their room for all and sundry to read, although the names were disguised so that the person himself would not know. The one at the top of the list would have his life made hell by the girls.

Times remained very hard for these painters and grew steadily harder as the twenties unfolded. Many of them used the time when they had nothing to do, in painting water colours for sale on all sorts of materials from canvas, if they could afford it, to pieces of plywood, cardboard, or paper. These paintings they would then take around the town in the hope of selling them to an antique dealer or art shop at prices which were often as low as sixpence. Many thousands of such paintings were done, following the tradition of Charley Baldwyn and Harry Stinton, and the leading exponents of this were the Austin brothers, Barker, Davis, J. H. Lewis, Sebright and Shuck.

When work was particularly short there were a number of things that you could do to pass the day. The cycling club was resurrected and a day trip would be arranged. If you had not got a cycle a group would disperse to their homes to collect a bit of bread and cheese, meet again and go for a long hike. The paintresses would club together all the money they had to hire a rowing boat and row up and down the river, landing back at Diglis as twilight was descending. The gilders preferred to stay in their own work rooms and find something to occupy their mind; Fred Lipscombe would read the whole of his morning paper, out loud, beginning at the top of the first page and not stopping until he came to the bottom of the last, if a statement such as 'turn to page . . .' was reached even that would be read out as well.

The gilders were a law to themselves, some of them having an alternative means of employment. Some worked on the turnstiles for the local and nearby race courses; some would be available to take visitors for guided tours around the factory. Many are the tales of the ruses they used to get over the Company's prominently displayed notices to the effect that gratuities were not to be given to the guides. Harry Lewis would always take off his hat and put it in front of him so that it covered up the notice; if Fred Lipscombe saw a woman looking at the notice he would say 'Oh, Madam, don't you take any notice of that; a visitor was looking up at it last week and he fell down and broke his leg'.

Through these steadily worsening conditions, Mr. Dyson Perrins was making up the wages of the workers to a decent amount out of his own pocket, for at a rate of sixpence for a plate centre, which was all the Company could afford to pay a painter, there was not much money to be earned.

However, the Company was doing its best to sell fine quality wares in a world market that had less and less money to spend on such things and it is not to be wondered at that attempts were made to produce ware that would sell, sometimes at the expense of quality and the great traditions of the past. Around 1924, lustre wares were produced, no doubt inspired by Wedgwood's dragon and fairyland lustres (Plate 145). Vases and bowls in Crownware were painted underglaze with scenes of castles on islands, or ships, mottled with stippled green near and under the base; on top of the glaze the pieces were lustred in pearl and gold. Inside the vases sometimes was stippled a gorgeous orange vermilion lustre, not unlike some of the beautiful effects to be seen on Royal Lancastrian high temperature lustre glazes. The painting and lustre was taught by Daisy Rea to her sister and to Elsie Gibbons, who claim that they produced a considerable quantity although I must admit to having seen very few pieces. One vase is known on which an unscrupulous person has perpetrated a forgery by grinding off the Worcester Crownware trade mark and replacing it with a crude Wedgwood Portland Vase mark.

Up to 1928 this disastrous flirting with the earthenware 'Crownware' body produced small powder bowls, Toby jugs (Plate 150) and small nude female figures (Plate 142). One of the reasons for the failure of these pieces was that the colours and patterns were onglaze, lightly fired and soon wore off in use. They are marked under the base with 'CW' and their shape number in the special Crownware shape book, although some of the shapes had been used before or would be again, in the china body. John Haywood claimed that a father and son named Grice managed the making of this earthenware body.

The Company was still looking towards the future, however, and in 1928 installed an electric tunnel decorating kiln. A tunnel kiln is one in which trucks carry the ware very slowly through a tunnel in which the temperature rises at the centre to the required amount and then falls so that the ware emerges at the other end of the tunnel ready to be taken off the trucks. This was a great improvement over previous methods of firing decorated ware and enabled the Company to produce china of a standard unrivalled anywhere in the world.

Without doubt the finest services produced at that time were those for Ranjitsinji, the great cricketer, who, although a fabulously rich Indian Prince, was qualified to play cricket for England by residence in this country. In 1925 the Company received an order for two separate dessert services, one to be used in his Indian palaces and to depict scenes of his English country home in Sussex and the other to depict his Indian palaces for use in England. To Harry Davis was entrusted the painting of the whole of the work and right royally was it carried out. Sketches of the English scenes were done by Harry in Sussex but he painted the Indian palaces from photographs which were supplied. When looking at examples it is hard to realise that the artist had not painted his scene while sitting in front with the plate on an easel, so fantastically life-like are the paintings, the palaces shimmering in a heat haze with turbaned servants hastening about their tasks, the Sussex home, by contrast, the very epitome of soft-coloured Downland landscape.

Shortly after this Harry Davis was sent to London to do some sketches for London scenes and the results that flowed from his brush on his return can be summed up in the breathtakingly beautiful coffee service shown in Colour Plate XIII. This service, to my mind, and in the opinion of many others, represents one of the highest ceramic achievements, superb potting, firing, decorating and gilding. The paintings have an extraordinary atmosphere of London in the 20s, a yellowish smoggy haze tinting the buildings and figures with a magic that almost makes one long for a return to the days of one's youth, able to see again the little boy with hand gripped in that of his mother as he gazes with wonderment, and a cricked neck at Nelson's Column. Harry confided to me that of all his work he remembered the Trafalgar Square subject on saucers to be the most difficult: 'I had to bend the column to get it straight', he would say and I would try to understand what he meant while marvelling all the while that he remembered painting several dozen coffee services and many other pieces with these London scenes. The owner of the illustrated service, when he brought it to the factory, was sad that on two of the pieces the artist had forgotten to put his signature, the last thing to go on, but Harry, then eighty-three years old, took great delight in signing them. Although he commented ruefully that the time it took him to mix up the right colour and to practise his signature in the style of so many years ago was longer than it would have taken him to paint the original cup and saucer.

Lest it be thought that Harry Davis was the only fine painter of that time it is only necessary to look at the other illustrations in this book to realise that this is not so. Some of the finest work was being done by the Austin brothers, especially a magnificent series of paintings of Australasian flowers, and birds of paradise, for Australia, then, as now, one of Worcester's most important markets. The Austin brothers not only had a fine technique but also were great naturalists, having won a number of important prizes in their youth for plant and bird drawing. Walter Austin once spent a whole year studying the structure of a delphinium before he ventured to paint one, but once the subject was absorbed to as great a degree as that the artist could then paint with his mind's eye, not requiring the subject in front of him. This idea often puzzles those who see a china artist painting scenes of fruit, say, or flowers, every one different and all apparently being made up on the spot. It is harder still to credit that the three Worcester artists who specialised in Scottish Highland subjects—John and Harry Stinton and Harry Davis—never went to Scotland in their life and yet one can almost breathe the heather in their paintings.

In 1928 William Hawkins, the popular foreman of the men's painting department, retired and the occasion was marked by the taking of a photograph (Plate 149) and the presentation of an illuminated address and a clock. He was succeeded as foreman by Harry Davis.

It is true to say that china painting has a considerable element of copying in it and that highly original creations of art are few in the medium, but this element was necessarily built in by training methods and financial necessity, and within its limits, and in its finest standard, it can justly claim to be regarded as an art form. In fact, this growing realisation is what has brought such a book as this into being. What is especially interesting at the present time is that there is a greater awareness of the great quality of the best work of the last hundred years and the snobbish attitude that nothing of any quality was made after the year 1800 has been shown up for what it was by the extraordinary rise in values of relatively recent Worcester, not that financial value is necessarily a true judgement on a piece of art but it does indicate the way that the thoughts of people are moving.

Some of the most exquisite work done at this time were the miniature vases in the Dr. Wall style made for Queen Mary's dolls' house. Two pairs of these fantastic reproductions of hexgonal vases and covers, hand-painted with blue scales and fabulous birds, with exquisite gilding and yet only just over an inch in height, can be seen on mantle pieces in the dolls' house in Windsor Castle (Plate 160). The painter of them was George Johnson, who specialised in reproducing Dr. Wall style fabulous birds. The painting of such subjects, as also Dr. Wall style flowers, was still encouraged by Mr. Dyson Perrins. He is said to have tried to persuade the Company to drop the Worcester fruit painting, but as this was a reasonably good selling line, especially to the gypsies who, then as now, were avid purchasers of plates and vases decorated with fruit with which they adorned their caravans, this request was resisted.

These few financial and artistic successes were not sufficient, however, to hold off the growing crisis. Money was getting very short and, as a means of injecting capital into the Company, Mr. C. W. Dyson Perrins undertook to purchase the whole of the Museum Collection on 9th September 1926 for £15,000 on the assurance that the value was far below that sum and on the understanding that it would remain in the Museum for the remainder of his life. This was a typically benevolent gesture on his part, as most of the collection was Victorian and early twentieth century, a period for which he

1. Magnificent table centre from the dessert service made for Queen Victoria in 1861 and exhibited in the 1862 Exhibition; decorated by Thomas Bott with classical subjects and trophies in white enamel on a turquoise ground and finely gilded. Marked with the specially elaborate mark of this service and reproduced by gracious permission of Her Majesty the Queen.

11. Large faience vase painted with figure subjects in embossed panels in Majolica colourings by E. Bejot and others; 27 inches high, circa 1870, mark number 1.

did not care as he did for his beloved Dr. Wall period. This money was paid over to the Company on 9th April 1927 but by then the crisis had already come to a head.

On 4th February 1927 Mr. Dyson Perrins was advised by the Company solicitors to give notice regarding repayment of the mortgage that he had granted in 1891 and that a receiver should be appointed by the debenture holders. This drastic step was viewed as the only hope of stabilising the Company's finances and Mr. Perrins agreed, helping in his typically generous way by advancing £2,000 to meet current requirements, pending new arrangements. This was on 12th February and a month later, on 14th March, Mr. Solon left.

Mr. E. P. Evans, the gallant old war horse, dramatically returned in March to take up the reins of Managing Director again, but the strain was too great and he left in October, dying in the following year, on 2nd December. He was succeeded by Major Bernard Moore, son of the great Staffordshire potter, on 3rd October but little could be done and when, on 24th July 1930, receivers were placed in the works, Major Moore left and the works were shut on the following day.

These terrible times were resolved when Mr. J. Harrison bought the works on 8th August 1930 and Mr. Wadsworth was put in charge by the receiver. The factory was re-opened on 12th August and slowly work re-started, under the guidance of Joseph Gimson who was made Works Manager on 14th August. Every effort was made by him to get the factory running smoothly again but this was not an easy task and the engravers' department did not restart work until October.

Mr. Wadsworth left in August 1930, going to the United States firm of Maddox, but returned in February 1933, leaving again in May 1935 to go to Mintons as Art Director. He was succeeded as Worcester Art Director by Mr. C. B. Simmonds and by that time the Company was at least out of the hands of the receivers, Mr. Dyson Perrins having bought the factory and forming a new Company, becoming its chairman on 13th June 1934. The other directors were Mrs. Freda Perrins, Mr. J. F. Gimson and Major W. Kendall, the financial adviser to Mr. Dyson Perrins.

A difficult struggle had been successfully surmounted, with the help of Mr. Dyson Perrins but some major changes had to be made. Mr. Gimson, who had been promoted to Managing Director, took the bold step of dropping the production of all forms of earthenware in 1931 in favour of fireproof cooking porcelain, the domestic successor of the laboratory ware which was still continued. This body, made from china stone and china clay, was a very difficult one to produce and especially to fire, as it required a reducing atmosphere only successfully produced in a tunnel kiln. Fireproof porcelain, at that time only produced on the Continent, was a quiet success and was made in a complete range for domestic and hotel ware, with many special additions for special purposes. The Company was favoured with the complete outfitting of the *Queen Mary* liner and the ware made for this fine ship was typified by 'crust ware', the decoration giving the effect of slightly browned pie crust. A later development was gold and silver lustre decoration, which has a very attractive appearance and is still a considerable seller. The chief research chemist for the early years was Dr. T. White, who joined the Company in 1920 shortly before F. E. Woolridge left, and made a special study of laboratory porcelain and published an important paper on it in 1922, but he left the factory in 1923 or a little later.

In 1931 the Company put on an exhibition at the Beaux Arts Gallery in London to bring before the public the figurines that it was decided to launch. As well as a range of historical, naval and military figures by Fred Gertner, who was the Company modeller, the remaining figures were all by a new group of female freelance modellers—Margaret Cane, Stella Crofts, Jessamine Bray and Sybil Williams, Freda Doughty, Doris Lindner and Phoebe Stabler. Apart from the models of Freda Doughty, which were of a traditional sort, rather like twentieth-century versions of Hadley figures, the other figures were very modern and untraditional. They were probably too advanced for the time in which they were made, or possibly they did not resemble what people imagined Worcester figures to be, because the vast majority of them failed to sell. All sorts of attempts were made to push them, the Victorian Musicians of Ethelwyn Baker (2898/9 and 2901/2) were used as the basis of charming lamps adapted by Charles Selz of New Cavendish Street, London, but even this could not shift them (Plate 157). Some of these figures of the early 1930s must rank as the rarest Worcester pieces ever produced, rarer than Dr. Wall pieces, or even the Limited Editions that were to follow, some of them only selling half a dozen or so. Even some of the early Doris Lindner figures were unsuccessful, although some, such as the sitting up fox and hound (2993/4) were later resurrected when the modeller's work became famous following the success of the horse subjects in the 1960s.

The only modeller consistently to produce what the public seemed to require was Freda Doughty and the steady sale of her charming small children figure subjects was one of the few bright spots in sales and many of these subjects have continued in popularity. Freda Doughty had a great way with children, her house in which she lived with her sister Dorothy always being full of children so that she was able to observe them in play. One visitor commented 'what a happy lot of grandchildren you have', a remark which greatly pleased Miss Doughty. Many series were created, the most popular being a child representing each month of the year and the days of the week— the latter illustrating the old rhyme 'Monday's child is fair of face, Tuesday's child is full of grace, Wednesday's child is full of woe, Thursday's child has far to go, Friday's child is loving and giving, Saturday's child works hard for its living, but the child that's born on the Sabbath day, is fair and wise and good and gay'. Each day is represented by a boy and a girl and over the forty odd years that have passed since they started there have been a few changes. For instance the verse for Wednesday's child has been altered to 'knows no woe' and the figure has been changed from a crying child to a happy one, as purchasers who were born on a Wednesday seemed to prefer a cheerful replica of themselves. Add to all these a large number of Nursery Rhymes from

Mother Goose, children of different countries (Burma, India and China are still produced) and such enormously popular figures as 'Grandmother's Dress' and 'Boy with Parakeet', many of the figures appearing under different titles when painted in different colours, and it may be realised that hundreds of thousands of Freda Doughty figures have been made.

The painters of the greater number of the early children figures were Daisy Rea and her sister. The rate of pay was not very high for the painting of these figures and Daisy remembered getting 6d. for each figure and it was only possible to paint six in two days work. For painting the small dogs, which were modelled by Doris Lindner, the men painters were getting even less—3d. per dog for two firings.

In an attempt to bring in money the Company converted some of the oldest buildings on the factory into an olde world restaurant to cater for visitors to the factory and the Chamberlain Tea Rooms, as this was called, was opened on 6th April 1931. Many years later Mr. Gimson was very fond of saying that the Company made more money from the tea rooms than they did from the sales of china, and the arched rooms were a great favourite with visitors, presenting a charming appearance with small tables, the cloth laid with Worcester china decorated with the Broseley Blue Dragon pattern. The prices make interesting reading in these days, and the customer's choice could range from a single cup to a special set tea, which went under special names. The 'Chamberlain' tea comprised a pot of tea, assorted sandwiches and a slice of fruit cake and cost a shilling; for the same price you could have a 'Clifton' —a pot of tea, tomatoes or beans on toast and cake; for an extra 6d. the 'Devon' provided pot of tea, fruit salad and cream, bread and butter and cake or the 'Savoy', also at one and sixpence, gave you egg mayonnaise, brown and white bread and butter and cake, as well as the inevitable pot of tea. Light lunches could also be obtained, from beans on toast at 8d. to lobster mayonnaise at 1s. 6d. and the tea rooms were open from nine till six p.m. daily (on Saturdays, nine till one p.m.) On wall brackets were displayed the sculptured figure lamps and shades, which could be bought, as also could antique furniture and antique and modern Worcester china.

An important event of the year 1932 was the visit to Worcester of the Prince of Wales, who spent some time at the factory, where his cheerful presence struck a hopeful note.

One of the most colourful characters at this time was a Maltese named Antonio Vassalo, who specialised in making small flowers by hand and applying them to small ash trays and boxes, thus continuing a Worcester tradition of flower making from the 1760s, although there had been a few breaks. The last Worcester flower maker had been Edward Raby senior, who flowered plates and large plaques, although George Owen produced some exquisite flowers in the form of brooches and baskets of flowers, most of these for his own pleasure in his own time. Antonio, as he was generally known, was to have an important part to play in the early Doughty Birds of the late 1930s.

The Company had been keeping a careful watch on the prospects of improvement in the United States market and Mr. Gimson made a number of trips to that country. By 1934 Roosevelt's 'New Deal' had got the wheels turning again and Mr. Gimson arranged with Mr. Alex Dickins, the fine art publisher of London and New York, to issue a limited series of service plates painted with birds taken from Audubon's *Birds of America*, as a collector's centenary edition. Service plates had been produced for a long time. They are very richly decorated plates that are intended as place settings before a meal to provide the guests with beauty and a talking point, then they are removed and replaced with the actual food plates. These plates can also, of course, be cabinet pieces, or used as wall plaques.

This was the first time that the Company had produced limited editions, which are particular items produced in a certain limited number. When this number has been reached their production is stopped and the moulds, if any, from which they are made are destroyed, so that no more can be produced. The Audubon Bird paintings were produced on octagonal modelled plates, with coloured grounds of two shades of green with rich raised gilding. The birds were painted in the centre, by different bird painters and as a first set of twelve proved so popular a second set was made, the whole work taking several years to complete. The first set of bird paintings comprised:

> Chestnut Titmouse, Louisiana Tanager, Robin, Whitebreasted Nuthatch, Barn Swallow, Blue Jay, Crow, Redstart, Ruby-Throated Humming Bird, White-Throated Sparrow, Hermit Thrush.

and the second edition comprised:

> Audubon Warbler, Black-Throated Blue Warbler, Cardinal Grosbeak, Catbird, Goldfinch, Pigeon Hawk, Le Petit Caporal, Orchard Oriole, Great American Shrike, Yellow-Bellied Woodpecker, Rice Bunting, Downy Woodpecker.

The first limited edition figure subjects were the Statuettes of King George V and Queen Mary (Plate 152), the King shown in Naval Uniform and holding a map of the world, the Queen in Garter Robes, to commemorate the Silver Jubilee of 1935, modelled by Gwendolen Parnell. Originally an edition of two hundred and fifty pairs was projected, at a cost of up to eight guineas a pair, including plinth, but the death of the king had an effect upon the sales, which went well at first but struggled on for several years until after seventy-two pairs had been sold the edition appears to have been withdrawn. The figures look very stiff and formal compared with the liveliness and movement of the figures of the 1960s. All the seventy-two pairs were painted by Daisy Rea and her sister and Daisy recalls doing the colouring from photographs. The first pair was sent to the Queen, the second to the Princess Royal, the third to the Duchess of York and the Company received a request from Buckingham Palace that the King's hair should not be shown so silvery white, so Daisy darkened the hair of the subsequent statuettes. Some of these went to such well-known dealers in England as Asprey and Maple of London and Stonier of Liverpool, and a number went abroad, principally to Heath of Sydney and Gilpin of Winchester in the United States.

The Company also produced a number of the busts of the King and Queen as little miniatures on plinths, shapes 3091/2, but very few of these were sold. In the same year (1935) the Doris Lindner horse group models were started —'At the Meet', 'Over the sticks', 'Cantering to the Post', and 'Huntsmen and hounds', which have been produced to the present day. Also produced in that year were the first of the Doughty Birds, the figures that were to become a watershed in the modern history of the Company. The development of the American market was the particular concern of Mr. J. D. Milne, who was appointed Sales Director in 1936.

The artistic and financial success of the Audubon Bird series prompted Alex Dickins to ask for a follow-up. The Company had been making small models of English Birds, modelled by Eva L. Soper and Fred Gertner, in unlimited numbers as early as 1933 and Mr. Dickins suggested a limited edition of full size naturalistic birds on foliage, indigenous to the United States, for sale in that country. One point upon which he was insistent was that the birds should not have a shiny glaze, to avoid them looking like china figures. Mr. Gimson recalled a fine model of a pug dog, full size with a matt glaze that had been made about thirty years before and was in the Museum Collection (Plate 129), and he told Mr. Dickins that it could be done.

A very full account of the making of the Doughty Birds is given in the magnificent book *The American Birds of Dorothy Doughty*, by George Savage and published in 1962 by the Worcester Royal Porcelain Company. This was a fine book, superbly illustrated with coloured photographs of all the American series and with Dorothy Doughty's own reminiscences about the particular birds. It is, however, very difficult to obtain as it was itself a 'Limited Edition' limited to 1,500 copies, so a brief account is necessary in this book.

In seeking someone to make the basic model of one or two birds the Company first approached Freda Doughty, who could be regarded as their most successful modeller at that time and who was living at Sissinghurst in Kent with her sister Dorothy. Freda suggested that her sister would be an ideal person for this work, having been well trained in drawing and painting by their mother, a talented watercolourist and, moreover, she was an expert ornithologist.

Her first model was a pair of American Redstarts on Hemlock which had to be modelled from photographs as there were no living specimens available in this country. All the parts of the cock and hen birds and the stump and leaves were slip-cast and the resultant effect was really no artistic nor ceramic advance upon the work that could have been done by any good modeller of the day who was also a lover of birds. In fact, there is really something of an eighteenth-century quality about the American Redstarts in the way of a Bow bird on a stump. Freda had shown her sister how her own children figurines were cut up, the parts turned into plaster moulds, and the resultant slip-cast pieces assembled; but in Dorothy's next pair of birds—the American Gold-finches and thistle—one has the feeling that, although produced by exactly the same method of slip-casting, her keen mind was seeking an alternative system of making the leaves and flowers to give an even more natural and lively appearance. Sixty-six pairs of the Redstarts and two hundred and fifty pairs of the Goldfinches were produced and both Mr. Dickins and the Company were emboldened to go further ahead.

At this point, in 1936, Dorothy paid another visit to the factory, to discuss a new group of models. She was shown around some of the different departments by Mr. Gimson and what she saw can best be put in her own words:

> I caught sight of an old man in a corner, surrounded by the cigarette stumps from endless chain-smoking, busily modelling little fine flowers by hand, which he put onto small pin trays. I said, 'Who's that?' Mr. Gimson said, 'Oh that's Antonio. He's Maltese and he makes those flowers quite beautifully. No one else can do it'. I thought for a long time about that and finally said to him: 'If I designed the next American Bird Models with handmade flowers, would you give me Antonio to do them?' Mr. Gimson stood still and stared at me. 'Good gracious,' he said, 'how could I? He is the only person who can flower the trays, and we have more orders for them than we can carry out. You ask me the impossible.' But the next morning he sent for me, 'I have thought it over', he said, 'and I have changed my mind. You can have Antonio.' So the Bluebirds were born, for now I knew Apple Blossom could be made.

Dorothy managed to find a pair of these beautiful birds in an aviary but the modelling was slow work and Spring had gone, and with it apple blossom, before she was able to get down to the flowers. But her mother found an apple tree in full bloom—in July—and this stroke of luck seemed to inspire her to produce what might be called the first true Doughty Birds, that is birds which are not only absolutely correct in their own size and colours but also the foliage on which they are found is correct in every minute detail. In addition the figures have that incredible sense of movement that makes one feel that they will fly away if approached too closely and they also have an extraordinary sense of balance and proportion, the pair of birds being designed to complement each other in a perfect grouping. Dorothy was the first to admit that she owed a tremendous amount to the patient guidance that the factory craftsmen gave her. She would sit for hours by the side of Fred Gertner to see the method of cutting up the model, which Dorothy had made of plasticine and dental resin, or watching George Jennings make the moulds. Mr. Jennings, who always worked in a battered old bowler hat, was a superb mould maker and a great deal of the successful withdrawal of the small, delicate parts of the figures from the moulds depended on his skill. Once, however, he had to make a crafty substitution of one of the heads of Doris Lindner's group of two lambs when he lost one. No one noticed that the group emerged from the moulds with the same head on both lambs.

Miss Doughty, with her keen grasp of artistic problems, learned a great deal in a very short time and was soon able to cut up her own models and bring the numbered pieces to the factory. Bob Bradley, who was brought into casting and fitting up the birds after the first two, remembers that she used to stay at the factory until two groups had been built up to her satisfaction and one of these approved models would be called the 'Standard' and used by the craftsmen as the touchstone for assembling all the models in the series so that each one would be as close to the artist's conception as possible. The assemblers would incise their particular mark under the base of the model, Bob Bradley using his initials RB, a practice he continued even after he became foreman of the department.

Dorothy was always prepared to learn from the craftsmen but was more prepared to insist that the painters reproduced the exact colours she wanted. George Evans was the first to paint the birds, although subsequently Harry Davis did a number.

The Bluebirds on Apple Blossom, the third pair in the series, marked a great step forward, with the flowers produced by hand flower making. Antonio Vassalo taught a group of girls to do this intricate work, which was a slow and difficult task in the early days. The making of these early groups of foliage was a lengthy process, with the clay being pressed onto real leaves to provide the shape. This, of course, became impractical in winter so leaf and petal moulds were made in plaster of Paris, into which the clay was pressed. The flower makers used to make their own clay on a Monday morning, rather like a glorified pastry making session, they used to call it, mixing the clay powder with gum arabic that had been melted down on the stove previously—a very sticky business!

Naturalism was Dorothy Doughty's aim and the birds required more from the flower makers than the decorated trays. New techniques were required and Mary Leigh worked closely with Dorothy to develop them; finally, in 1938 becoming responsible for the flowering of all the Doughty models. Miss Leigh was a fine flower maker and a great character. She only had one leg, having had the other cut off by a train when she was younger. One day, Len Morris, the mould maker, made a plaster cast from her remaining leg and Mr. Dyson Perrins paid for a cast leg to be made from this, which she used to wear. She was highly imaginative, used to have at least three birthdays a year and claimed that one of her ancestors was the pirate, Captain Henry Morgan. She used to keep her turps in a bottle that she said had belonged to the famous pirate, although the other girls were sure that it was an ordinary pop bottle. Miss Leigh's influence was very strongly felt and the subsequent forewomen of the flower makers, Mrs. O'Brien and Mrs. Hudman, were to build on the well-laid foundations.

Dorothy was a great source of inspiration to the workers in the factory and as each subsequent bird subject seemed to pose more and more problems her answer to any pessimists who claimed that the problem was impossible was 'we can do it!'

The next pair of birds to be produced were Virginian Cardinals on Orange Blossom, modelled from a tame pair in Dorothy's studio. The red colour on the cock was extremely hard to reproduce and required many trials by Harry Davis before the combination of colours that would fire in different stages, producing this splendid effect, could be found. The leaves and flowers of this model are very beautiful and the delicate hand-made stamens anticipate a number of the even finer later subjects.

For the next subject Alex Dickins suggested an inexpensive figure suitable for Christmas presents, a single model without flowers—a single Indigo Bunting on a Plum Twig. Dorothy fought against this, claiming that no one would want a bird model without flowers, and was allowed to put three small leaves on it and that was all. So the model was made from her own tame bird but it was very dull; no one wanted it in fact and it was a complete failure, only about six or seven being made. The single Bunting, without doubt, ranks as one of the rarest and most desirable of anything made at Worcester. Dorothy was later to be allowed to make a fully flowered pair of Indigo Buntings.

The last two pairs of birds to be produced before the beginning of the war, Chickadees and Baltimore Orioles, were a great contrast. The Chickadees, charmingly twisting and turning around twigs of larch, have a simple branch support above a round plinth but the Baltimore Orioles on colourful tulip trees, have rectangular bases that are partially hidden by the leaves of the tree, suggesting the greater degree of planning of the base for the provision of wooden plinths that were to come later.

In 1938, with war clouds looming, the Company installed a small laboratory at the top of the mill and this was used for experiments concerning bodies and glazes chiefly for fireproof porcelain. Most of these had been obtained from Europe and the growing troubles on the Continent led the Company to the realisation that the source of supply might be cut off. Thus Worcester was well placed to help the country's war effort with the supply of raw materials and special laboratory equipment previously obtained from Germany. The laboratory was equipped with grinding cylinders for making small trials, laboratory crushers, special stirrers and simple physical apparatus for determining the mechanical strength of ceramic ware and its thermal shock. To this laboratory in 1938 came Paul Rado, who had had a special training in hard-paste porcelain in Czechoslovakia and is now the Company's chief chemist.

The testing time of the war years was ahead.

Chapter V

The 1940s and 50s

The war imposed stringent restrictions upon china manufactories in this country, the chief being that production of rich ornamental and decorated ware virtually came to an end.

Worcester was allowed to carry on production of a certain quantity of fine wares, especially the Doughty Birds, for the United States market, as it was vitally necessary for the country to earn dollars in order to pay for lease lend. Many of the younger craftsmen and artists had joined the forces, many others were working in factories producing war equipment and this shortage of skilled staff put a great strain upon those remaining. Undecorated white ware was still produced, of course, for the home market and the forces, although only to a very limited extent. Those who lived in England during the war years will vividly remember the red-letter days when word spread around the community that the china shop had received a consignment. As a boy myself in those days I can recall joining a queue at dawn to wait hours for the shop to open, with instructions to buy something. 'But what?' I asked, 'Oh anything they have,' was the reply, and my cup was full when I returned proudly carrying a Staffordshire sugar bowl.

About one-third of the Worcester factory was taken over by the Ministry of Aircraft Production as a shadow factory. Mr. Tom Lunn, now the Company's chief development engineer, remembers coming to the factory on 23rd May 1941 on which day production of insulators for use in aircraft radar and radio equipment began. These insulators were being made by the Steatite and Porcelain Products Ltd., firm of Stourport, in Worcestershire, but so greatly were they needed that Worcester was also called upon.

Shortly after this, early in 1942 the Welwyn Electrical Laboratories Ltd., of Welwyn Garden City in Hertfordshire, started production of resistors for wireless equipment in another part of the factory. The tubes were obtained from Steatite at Stourport and they were wound, glazed and fired in Worcester in a special kiln, building of which was begun in 1940. These departments remained separate, the Art Director, Mr. Simmonds, taking control of the Steatite insulators and Dr. Aronovsky taking over the Welwyn resistors until

Mr. R. Cyples took charge. A large number of Worcester workers moved over to these departments and at one time over two hundred were engaged on this work, a very large proportion of them being women. Two twelve-hour shifts were worked every day for the first year, but this was found to be too hard for the younger girls and it was changed to two eight-hour shifts per day.

The factory was made a high security area and was guarded through the night by Home Guard sentries. Many of the factory workers took their turn at such duties as fire watching, but Worcester suffered relatively little damage from enemy air action during the war, no bombs landing within a mile of the Porcelain Works.

The fire watching teams, under the eagle eye of Percy Burgess, had their moments of excitement when they had to put out minor fires around the factory or cover up gaps in blackout curtaining so that enemy aircraft could not see the lights. The nightly reports would make a book in their own right, the comments of those on duty often being expressed in very strong terms; for instance:

> 'How many times has it got to be reported about the Bucket at the top of the Fireproof Casters steps. It runs out so needs replacing. Bucket at top of girl china casters steps empty and turned upside down (has been for some days now)';

or an altercation between Harry Davis and Percy Burgess:

> 'The iron door on landing will not lock. H.D.' 'This door will lock. P.B.'

When there was no air raid on, the long night hours were made easier by darts or billiards, although the report books have their moments of anxiety:

> 3 fire buckets in shot room all used for other purposes and now empty. Only two billiard cues usable, as usual;

to be followed by:

> Wholesale Warehouse black-out not sufficient, light shows through sides of curtains. Only one cue again. Can anything be done?

In 1943 Dr. W. G. Wearmouth, an eminent physicist, joined the Company to take control of a completed laboratory, having separate physical and chemical laboratories and ceramic and engineering departments. Here special experiments on bodies and glazes were carried out and new equipment for the development of pilot plants for the factory was made. Here, experiments on the making of alumina sparking plugs were started. Tom Lunn had produced the first successful half dozen examples by late 1944 and the showroom (outside of which were taken the group photographs shown in this book) was turned into a special factory, producing thirty thousand sparking plugs a week.

Thus Worcester served the war effort but the end of the war was in sight. Percy Burgess, the engraver, noted the signs in his notebook:

> Fireguard duties finished on September 12th 1944, the protective net was removed from factory windows two days later and black-out finished on September 17th.

Shortly after this date, at Christmas 1944, Mr. C. W. Dyson Perrins' two sons, Mr. G. A. and Col. C. F. Dyson Perrins, joined the Board of Directors and Dr. Wearmouth was appointed to the Board on 18th June 1945.

Some interesting small figures were introduced during the war years, very few of them doing very well. Doris Lindner continued her series of small dogs, produced a charming number of 'Zoo Babies' (groups of playful animals), and made a fine model of the horse 'Bogskar', the winner of the 1940 Grand National, shape 3330. The latter was a complete flop and probably only two were made. Miss Lindner explained the failure by saying that winners of annual horse races often lose their popularity by the following year. Gwendoline Parnell continued the series of 'London Cries' and made some beautiful Chinoiserie Figures which were followed up by Miss Pinder-Davis, who also made a group of 'Watteau' figures. Eva Soper produced a new range of small birds and an interesting group of seven models dealing with children in wartime Britain—3346/7, 3351/2, 3369/70 and 3382 (Plate 179). These latter did not do very well, possibly they were too poignant. They certainly are very effective—the painful terror of 'The Rescue' and 'Take Cover', the sadness of 'The Letter' giving news of the death of a loved one, the relief and pride of the children looking up at the 'Spitfire' and the humour of 'Salvage' with the children taking their rags and paper to the collecting centre and even the dog bringing his favourite bone to help the war effort.

The Doughty Birds continued—birds that had already gone into production were steadily being made until the total number of the limited edition had been completed. A number of new models were produced during the war years and also the models of four English bird groups were made (3392/6) but were not brought into production.

The Bob White Quails were yet another failure. Alex Dickins suggested another inexpensive pair of birds, without flowers, that would be bought by sportsmen and the quails were favourite game birds. Dorothy did not like the idea of no flowers and 'for life and beauty' she added a pair of tiny mottled babies to the hen. Because sportsmen did not shoot quail when there were chicks, during the close season, and they did not want these appealing babies staring them in the eye, few people would buy them and the edition was closed at twenty-two pairs. Originally a pair cost 275 dollars, but they are now so sought after by those who wish to have a complete collection of the birds that a typical recent auction sale price in the United States was 37,000 dollars. The Quails proved very difficult to colour—the feathers having such subtle mottling, and it is hard to realise that they were so ill considered originally, as now they appear so attractive, but that is being wise after the event. Dickins wanted the feathers to be even more naturalistically depicted than they were but Dorothy was then heavily engaged in war work and could not find the time to make the change.

The Crab Apple Sprays were designed to go with the Bluebirds as a group and were first modelled with White Admiral butterflies but Dorothy realised that they would not have emerged from the chrysalis stage before the crab apple had finished blooming. So she put on instead the Holly Blue and the Orange Tip. The Mocking Birds were modelled and the first white trials produced around the time of Dunkirk and Dorothy pointed out that the sprays of peach blossom, which she had gathered from a tree by the stable wall of her house, had somehow formed themselves into Churchill's patriotic V sign. The Apple Blossom and Bees were made to go as table decoration with the Bluebirds and were issued in 1941. In the same year the pair of Indigo Buntings on Blackberries were issued and the cock is one of the most extraordinary coloured birds of the whole series with feathers that give the impression of being fluffy and wet.

Through these years Dorothy had worked hard on war work, being involved in the experimental side of aircraft production and also driving an ambulance. She fell ill in January 1943 and in the Autumn of that year the family moved to Falmouth, to a cliff-top house with a garden studio whose walls were lined with bird cages. The Birds lost their founder in 1945 when Alex Dickins died but his widow continued to take a great interest in the series and Dorothy went on working, producing models.

The war had ended and the Company decided to carry out some very necessary and extensive rebuilding. Many of Chamberlains original buildings, including the Chamberlain Tea Room block, were pulled down and a new porcelain block was built, production starting in February 1947.

Slowly things began to get back to normal. The employees who had served in the forces began to trickle back and helped the Company to recover from the effects of the war. A promising group of youngsters joined Robert Bradley as rich ornamental casters and were responsible for producing the fine limited edition figures. One of these—William Allen—was to take over as foreman of the department when Bob Bradley retired in 1968. Some fine flower makers continued the steadily growing improvement in that department, under successive foreladies—Mary Leigh, Mrs. O'Brien and Mrs. Hudman.

The men's painters department began to build up again and among the more important painters of the late 1940s and 50s were:

Harry Ayrton, fruit
Harry Davis, foreman
Gerald Delaney, fruit
John Freeman, fruit
Peter Love, fruit
William Powell, birds
Horace Price, fruit

Daisy Rea, flowers
William Roberts, fruit
Raymond Rushton, landscapes, gardens
Richard Sebright, fruit
Harry Stinton, cattle
James Stinton, game birds
Edward Townsend, foreman from 1954

A great number of young painters joined as apprentices from the late 1940s. Although there was no longer an articled apprenticeship system, the youngsters would be put under one or more of the seniors for tuition and also were sent to the Art School for one whole day a week, learning design, general drawing and art. At first they used to have lessons in pottery making but these lessons were not popular with the school as there seemed to be more throwing of the clay about the room than on the wheel. The youngsters were certainly a lively lot, no doubt living up to the traditions of the past. Some of their pranks would have made their predecessors envious—such as the occasions when they tied all the chairs up to the ceiling, or made large paper aeroplanes with tails dipped in paraffin which, when lit and thrown, made a fiery sight. Fruit put out for the still life classes lasted no time at all, the apprentices taking turns to have bites out of the apples and pears or thieve the grapes while the instructor's back was turned.

By this time the senior painters were losing the previous reserve over passing on their secrets and the youngsters received great help, which enabled them to attain a high standard in a reasonable time. Horace Price, for instance, would show them how he could transform any minute specks on a piece into birds in the sky or another part of the scene, so that the piece would be perfect. The boys served an apprenticeship of approximately seven years, being paid on a rising flat rate basis, until they were accounted proficient enough to go on piece rate.

In 1948 a fine service was produced for the Maharajah of Baroda. A green and acid gold border was designed and a number of possible centres were sent to the Maharajah, who chose a beautiful depiction of a pig sticking scene. The same year saw the purchase by the Company of 30, Curzon Street, a fine Georgian house in London's West End which was built in 1771. This building is now the headquarters of the Royal Worcester group, the ground floor is let to the Worcester Royal Porcelain Company as their London showrooms and a number of special exhibitions have been put on there.

The year 1948 was also memorable for the issuing of the first limited edition equestrian model by Doris Lindner, the magnificent statue of Princess Elizabeth on Tommy, the police horse. This statuette was made at the request of Queen Elizabeth, now the Queen Mother, to commemorate the taking of her first Trooping the Colour by the Princess. The Princess sat for Doris Lindner at Buckingham Palace and after the sitting the King asked to compare the model against the Princess wearing the uniform of Colonel in

Chief of the Grenadier Guards and he expressed himself delighted in every respect. The Royal model also sat for Harry Davis so that the colour standard would be accurate and the statuette, issued in a limited edition of a hundred, is very true to life and although the horse is standing still and quiet the modelling of the muscles gives the animal plenty of movement. The statuette is now the most sought after of Worcester's equestrian models and one had the honour of being sold at the auction rooms of Sotheby in London for £1,800, a collectable piece in its own time.

The statuette was used as the linking item in a fine black and white film made in 1950 and shown on the major cinema circuits. Entitled 'The Doctor Ordered Clay', it presented a brief history of the Company, showed Warmstry House, Dr. Wall's factory, as it was then standing and followed the processes involved in producing the statuette. First was shown Doris Lindner putting the finishing touches to the plasticine model in her Chelsea studio, then, on the factory, Fred Gertner beginning the cutting up, his sharp knife cutting surely through the head of the horse at the correct angle to allow the moulded pieces to fit perfectly. Then was seen the making of the moulds, followed by the casting and fitting up of the statuette by Robert Bradley and its subsequent firing and shrinkage in size. The painting of the statuette by Harry Davis is followed by the stages of making and decorating useful wares and vases, including scenes of Tim Ayrton painting fruit and Ivor Williams gilding a vase.

In 1950 the great biscuit kilns that had served the factory for so long were finally superseded by gas-fired tunnel kilns, which not only were more efficient and cleaner in use but produced a finer quality ware. About this time a considerable amount of pattern W1414 was being produced which had a ground-laid border with a double gold line. The production of this pattern was stopped when it was realised that some of the plates were being painted on by amateur painters and, worse, were being faked by painting a Worcester-type subject in the centre and signing it with a collectable signature. I have only recently seen a Highland Cattle subject of very poor quality signed 'I. Stinton', purporting, of course, to be by John Stinton.

The following year was the bicentenary of the founding of the Worcester Porcelain Company in June 1751 and the special occasion was marked by the opening of the Dyson Perrins Museum by Princess Elizabeth on 8th June 1951. The great collection of early Worcester porcelain built up with loving care by Mr. C. W. Dyson Perrins, plus the original Company museum collection, was bequeathed to a Trust that was established to administer it. Among the Trustees were the Mayor and Town Clerk for the time being of the City of Worcester.

The museum that was opened by Princess Elizabeth was the old Company showroom, and in this building the Princess was shown the magnificent collection of Worcester porcelain, earthenware and china which, with the addition of the many items donated by the Company, such as the complete series of the American Doughty Birds, ranks as the finest and most comprehensive collection of Worcester in the world. Princess Elizabeth was also shown around the factory, making a special request to meet Harry Davis, who had painted the colour trial of the equestrian statuette.

The bicentenary was also marked by a major exhibition of Worcester porcelain of the Dr. Wall period at the Curzon Street showrooms, arranged by the English Ceramic Circle, which ran for five months. The exhibition did not include any blue and white wares and only a few pieces of onglaze transfer printing, so it was not really representative of the production in the early years. However, the display of the finest of the coloured wares from such great collections as the Rous Lench, Rissik Marshall and Dyson Perrins Collections, plus pieces from the Royal Collection, made the exhibition one to be long remembered.

For the wedding of Princess Elizabeth in 1947 the Company produced a number of important presentation services. Tea services in the Dr. Wall and Flight styles were presented by the Company and by the citizens of the City of Worcester. A magnificent dessert service was presented by the Brigade of Guards, the service having the crests of the different Guards Regiments in the centre surrounded by a beautifully controlled maroon ground-laid border and fine gilding. This service is still in regular use in Buckingham Palace.

The Coronation of Queen Elizabeth in 1953 was the occasion for the making of the special presentation vase surrounded by the ten fabulous Queen's Beasts, made by the six members of the Fine China Association—Copeland, Derby, Doulton, Minton, Wedgwood and Worcester. This great vase, $25\frac{1}{2}$ inches high, $11\frac{1}{2}$ inches in width and weighing 29 lbs., was designed by John Wadsworth, Minton's Art Director, who had held a similar post at Worcester from 1915 to 1929, but all the firms had a hand in its making. Worcester was responsible for the making of two of the ten Beasts, which fitted into niches on each face of the ten-sided vase. Skilled artists went from each factory to co-operate in the decorative work, which was all done at the Minton factory, and Worcester's representative was William Ashley, the gilder. Also made were eleven copies which were presented by the Duchess of Gloucester to the seven Commonwealth countries and the four Mother countries of the United Kingdom.

Worcester was producing some magnificent pieces itself at that time. Dorothy Doughty was continuing to bring out a number of new bird models, which included the immensely difficult Magnolia Warblers, the largest of the bird subjects. Dorothy had absorbed so many of the skills of the Worcester craftsmen through watching them intently and asking such pertinent questions when she used to come to the factory that she was now able to 'cut up' her own models. These she made in plasticine mixed with dental resin (acrylic resin) to prevent distortion and she would bring the cut-up pieces to Worcester, remaining at the factory until the first two cast figures had been assembled to her satisfaction by Robert Bradley. The Magnolia Warblers were too big to be practical, the huge pair requiring over 80 moulds weighing $4\frac{1}{2}$ hundredweight. No matter with what care they were fitted up and fired every one was splitting and breaking as it cooled. It was decided to have one final go at making them and if that failed the subject would be scrapped. Bob

Bradley was given permission to make any alterations he felt necessary and, realising that the trouble was caused by the hot air imprisoned in the hollow interior splitting the china as it burst out, he cut 'windows' at certain positions in the base of the giant Magnolia leaves which eased the cooling problems.

A pair of figures which caused nearly as many problems were numbers 3473/4, a pair of Balinese and Siamese dancers, modelled by Miss Pinder-Davis. These are probably the richest and most sumptuously decorated figures made by Worcester (Plate 183) and the fact that, although the limited edition is only twenty-five pairs, the edition is not yet completed after twenty years points to the difficulty of making these pieces.

Most of the figures made at this period, however, were small ones. Days of the Week modelled by Freda Doughty, animal subjects by Doris Lindner, Chinese subjects, proverbs and sayings by Pinder-Davis. Many candle extinguishers—resurrected from the nineteenth century—were produced and the list of them current in 1955 are Japanese, Dr. Fox, Mandarin, Witch, Diffidence, Confidence, Hush, Granny Snow, Mr. and Mrs. Cordle, Owl, Cook, Monk and Nun; only Monk and Nun are still produced. Granny Snow was said to have been modelled on an old character who lived in Severn Street, near the factory. One failure among these small figures were the pair of Red Riding Hood and Wolf shapes 3510 and 3511, which were said to be so realistic that they frightened the children for whom they were designed.

In 1953 Ronald Van Ruyckevelt was appointed to the Company's design staff particularly to give closer day by day supervision to the production of the Doughty Birds. He worked with her at Falmouth and was able to coordinate her wishes with the work at the factory. From this time the production of the Birds went ahead faster and more models could be introduced. Van Ruyckevelt was to produce a great number of important models of fish, flowers and birds for Worcester as staff modeller.

On 30th September 1954, the Worcester Royal Porcelain Company became a Public Company with Mr. C. W. Dyson Perrins as its Honorary President, although he was to die the following year. As well as manufacturing, the new public company acted as a holding company for the growing number of outside firms in the field of electronics and industrial ceramics that were now in the group such as Palissy Pottery Limited, a Stoke-on-Trent earthenware factory purchased in 1958.

The growing complications of the size and spread of activities of the group led Worcester to set up a holding company in 1958, named Royal Worcester Limited. This new Company of which Mr. J. F. Gimson was also Chairman, was able to control all the ceramic and electronic activities of the group, leaving the Worcester Royal Porcelain Company to concentrate on its own products. The productions of the Company had been popularly known as 'Royal Worcester' for a long time and still continue to be so known in popular usage.

The 1950s marked the introduction of a number of fine limited editions: horses and bulls modelled by Doris Lindner, fish and flowers by Ronald

III. Superbly decorated ewer and basin, painted with 'Limoges Enamels' on cobalt ground by Thomas Bott in 1868, gilding by Josiah Davis. The scenes depict the Norman Conquest from designs by Daniel Maclise and are 'The marriage of Harold and Aldyth' on the ewer and on the basin 'William in the hunting field informed that Harold has taken the crown of England'; 'Harold, whilst wounded at York, is informed that William has landed' and 'The death of Harold'. Height of ewer $11\frac{1}{2}$ inches, mark number 1 with 68 under the circle and signed 'T Bott 1868' under each piece. Shown at 1871 Exhibition.

IV. Group of finely decorated small pieces of the 1860's, in the glazed Parian 'ivory porcelain' body. Top row, dolphin and shell, shape 6/92 decorated with Raphaelesque colours, mark 1 with '66' under the circle; the bucket with lion heads, shape 6/32, painted with birds by Hopewell; spill of Kerr & Binns shape painted with butterflies and grass on a celadon ground; bottom row, 'New three claw spill', shape 10/50 and 'Japanese form', shape 505, painted with feathers probably by Rea and a pair of hand vases, shape 6/35 painted with heathers.

Van Ruyckevelt and Edwardian and Victorian human figure subjects by Ruth Van Ruyckevelt. But the ornamental wares which made the most impact on the decade were the Doughty Birds.

The supply of birds indigenous to the United States available for study in England was very limited and Miss Doughty was having to go to extreme lengths to find new ones. So the Company decided to send her to America to model a new series.

In 1953 she went on the first visit to the States on the Eastern seaboard and she spent nearly three months in New York, Virginia, the Carolinas, Florida, Georgia and Tennessee. She met Dr. Cushman Murphy of the American Museum of Natural History and learned how to make sketch models of flowers in crêpe paper, wire, wax and paint, so that her quick sketches of the birds as she saw them in the life could be transported safely. The models that arrived at the factory on her return showed incredible freedom of movement, great naturalness and artistic balance of birds and flowers. Such studies as the Myrtle Warblers, Blue-Grey Gnatcatchers, Bewick's Wrens, Scarlet Tanagers, Oven Birds, Parula Warblers, Phoebes, Yellow-throats, Downy Woodpeckers and Hooded Warblers date from this visit. A pair of the beautiful Parula Warblers were given to President Eisenhower by the Queen when she visited the United States in 1957 and Dorothy was greatly honoured at this Royal Seal of approval given to her models. She enjoyed this trip to the States very much, seeing for the first time in their natural surroundings the birds that she had loved for so long.

It was not only the birds, of course, that took her attention. In the case of many of the subjects it was the flowers that came first and she would then decide on a suitable bird to place on them. It is illuminating to give her own account of one of these subjects—Yellow-throats and Water Hyacinth—as quoted in the Doughty Bird Book:

> Running gradually south to Okeechobee we found masses of Water Hyacinth in every river, lake and pond. I paddled in, hoping not to meet a Water Moccasin, and gathered some of these exciting flowers. There was a slight breeze blowing, which tore the fragile petals to ribbons as I carried them the few yards to the car, and I had to go back for more and transport them in a hastily constructed tent. Back in the hotel I worked feverishly, and Connie (Connie Dickins) helped me, nobly cutting out hundreds of petals which I made up into flowers. Alexander Sprunt, the ornithologist, happened to be in this hotel and I saw him for the first time one evening with one of his Nature Ramble classes of adults sitting in a semi-circle around him while he read out to them a list of the birds which they had seen together on that day's trip, and each one marked them in his own notebook with keenest delight and enthusiasm.
> 'So we saw a Night Heron.'
> Everyone wrote that down.
> 'And then those Egrets, do you remember?'
> Everyone wrote that down too.

'And then that Red Tailed Hawk.'

One lady held up her hand.

'Yes?'

'Please,' she said, 'I nearly saw him. Can I count that?'

'Certainly not,' said Sprunt severely and passed onto the next item. He deputed one of his game wardens to drive us in a jeep for a whole day over the endless flat Everglades, looking for birds. Towards evening we came once more onto a sandy road and there in the middle of it was a turtle with a long pointed tail.

'That is a Soft-shelled Turtle', he said. 'They come up from that swamp on the right and cross the road to lay their eggs in those sand-dunes on the other side. When they are gone the vultures, who have been watching, dig up the eggs and eat them'.

I begged him to stop, that I might get out and examine this strange creature more closely and also rescue her from any car that might run over her. She was about ten or eleven inches across, quite round, and black, with a nose like an elephant's trunk. I picked her up by the edge of her shell and she struggled wildly and strongly. I carried her to the side of the road nearest to the slope of about fifty feet that led to her swamp and put her down there.

Instantly she was off, not crawling as a turtle should, but at a breakneck gallop, leaping and bouncing about eight feet at a time, for all the world like some jumping frying-pan at speed, and in a few seconds was gone. We still worked at the Water Hyacinth and I tried to put a Least Bittern with it, but had to give that up. He was too big. I consulted Sprunt as to what small bird might correctly be shown with these plants. He promised to think and later on in the evening he came racing up the stairs.

'Yellow-throats', he said. 'They frequent the sides of ponds and streams.' So Yellow-throats it was, and I am grateful to him.

This trip made a profound impression upon Miss Doughty and it was decided to send her to the States again in 1956. This time she went to Texas, New Mexico and Arizona, where in the arid deserts she was to come across some of the most dramatic subjects in the whole series. The terrifying desert landscapes should have daunted a well brought-up elderly English lady but it must be remembered that she was the daughter of the author of 'Arabia Deserta'. When she returned to Worcester she held an audience of workers from the factory spellbound for several hours while she gave a virtuoso lecture on her trip describing how she went down the Colorado on donkey back to find the Canyon and Cactus Wrens, descended into the terrible Sunset Crater to depict the Lark Sparrow on the lava-ash, and crossed the Arizona deserts at night where she was captivated by the little Elf Owl living in the great Saquaro trees. Her lecture was a tour-de-force, unforgettable by those fortunate enough to attend it, those she called the 'bird workers', especially memorable for her extraordinary ability to whistle the songs of the birds.

An innovation was the modelling of two wall models, the Scissor-tailed

Flycatchers and the extinct Carolina Paroquets, which she had to produce from Museum skins. Several models could be issued in an alternative white edition—the Lazuli Buntings and Scissor-tailed Flycatchers. A few of these editions still remain unfinished at the time of writing and this applies especially to some of the series of English Birds, the models of which Dorothy had finished before her death. Some birds of the English series surpass their American cousins in their difficulties—the tiny Chiff Chaff perched half way up a huge spray of Hogweed or Cow Parsley, the beautiful English Redstarts on Gorse that require some 1,200 separate handmade pieces to build up into the completed pair. Many of these figures require up to thirty different enamel colours fired in a number of kiln firings to produce the correct effects.

There is no doubt that Dorothy Doughty made a great personal impression upon the staff when she made her infrequent visits to the factory. She would be very firm about what she wanted and highly critical of anything of which she disapproved, but she could be full of praise when it was merited. She brought out an idea of the award of points to the painters for the painting of various parts of the birds and foliage and would always give a report upon each one at the end of her visit. A personal message to the Flower Making Department, that preceded detailed instructions on the making of the flowers, shows her own attitude to her work and makes clear the fantastic idolatry that she generated:

> The models of the Doughty bird series are all portraits of living birds and flowers. It is not enough that they should be beautiful pieces of china. They must, equally, be true to nature in every detail as far as we can possibly make them.
>
> 'We' is an important word there. A picture or even a statue can be the work of a single artist's hand, but a model in china must, by its very nature, be entrusted through its various stages to many hands in many departments, so a model in china is not the work of a single artist but of a team.
>
> In this series, the flower makers are very important members of the team, because every single thing they make and put on the model is vital to it. The tiniest stamen, or even a little bit of stem, if it were wrongly formed, would make that part untrue to nature and the whole model would be wrong, and nothing that could be done in any other department afterwards could put it right again.
>
> The originals in this series have all been modelled from life, and those of the latest models were made among the woods and mountains of America direct from the wild birds and flowers growing there. I have made them as true as I possibly can—please help me to keep them true.
>
> There is another thing I think we should remember about these models. They cost so much to make that by the time they are sold in the big shops in America they are very expensive indeed, and also very difficult to get.
>
> Naturally, when people buy such valuable things they take a lot of care

of them so that they shall last a long time, and not get easily broken like cups and saucers. And when the time comes that any particular bird reaches the end of its limited edition and there are no more to be bought anywhere, those which are already owned by various people begin to increase in value and are then often sold second-hand for more than they originally cost in the shops. That is what the Americans call 'scarcity value'. As time goes on, the models get rarer and rarer, until they finally end up as Collectors' pieces—which are taken *such* care of that they will last a very long time indeed, perhaps even hundreds of years.

You wouldn't like, any more than I should, that your work, treasured like that, should be anything but your best work—and here I should like to tell you how much your flowers are admired in America today. So many people said to me when I was over there, 'How beautifully the flowers are made', and I always felt very proud on your behalf.

Dorothy's humbleness of mind was in direct contrast to her positive character and in her introduction to the Doughty Bird Book she said 'I find it difficult to write about my own work, embarrassing in fact, because in my heart I am bitterly aware that it is never as good as it ought to be; never as good as I had hoped; never what each portrait promised to be in its easy early stages'.

One of her last statements about her work was very moving:

My work with the birds has been a joyful thing. In this tortured world one of the happiest ways of spending a life is to work closely with nature.

Although the miraculous perfection of birds and flowers, and indeed of all wild things, is beyond the power of man to portray in any medium, he or she who strives towards it, learns to see ever more deeply, to glimpse something of the Infinite, and to feel a privileged and very humble person.

In 1957 Professor Robert W. Baker, Professor of Ceramics at the Royal College of Art, came to Worcester as Art Director. Two of his former leading students, Peter Ewence and Neal French, followed him to join a Design Staff that was to play an increasingly important part in the history of the Company in the 1960s.

Chapter VI

The 1960s and into the 70s

As the 1960s dawned, the directors of The Worcester Royal Porcelain Company, headed by Mr. J. F. Gimson as Chairman and Mr. J. D. Milne as Managing Director, were Mr. G. Adams, Professor R. W. Baker, Mr. A. Dutton, Mr. W. J. C. Kendall and Mr. E. H. A. Wheen as Secretary.

Important additions to the Board in the next eleven years were Mr. A. F. Street in 1961, who became Chairman on the retirement of Mr. Gimson in 1967; Mr. A. T. Wright in 1964 who became Works Director and resigned in 1970 and Mr. W. B. Dunn who became Managing Director in 1967, resigning on 31st December 1970, being replaced by Mr. R. Steven on 2nd January 1971.

Mr. Gimson remained as a valued consultant for many years, giving the Company the benefit of his vast knowledge of the ceramic industry. The appointments to the Board of Dr. J. N. Aldington, Mr. L. D. Chandler, Mr. J. B. C. Clifford, Commander S. W. Collier, Mr. G. N. L. Dalzell-Payne and Mr. R. W. Zrike during the period brought in a blend of skill in ceramics and business.

The Company was at last earning the sort of profits that the products justified and Royal.Worcester wares were being keenly bought throughout the world.

The decade opened with the Company establishing a factory in Jamaica. A lot of ground work had been laid for this, the aim being to manufacture ware made from local clays by islanders. Many colourful Jamaican style patterns were produced, some being contributed by Noel Coward, the actor and playwright, who was a resident of the island. The mark used was the words 'Island Worcester' inside a scroll of palm fronds. The factory, founded in 1961, was eventually taken over by the Jamaican Government.

One of the most important events of the decade was the purchase by the Trustees of the Dyson Perrins Museum of the Victorian St. Peter's School building. This fine school, in which so many of the factory employees had been educated, was opened as the new Museum by Viscount Cobham, the Lord Lieutenant of Worcestershire, on 12th May 1967. In these noble

surroundings this incomparable collection, so strong in Victorian and twentieth-century Worcester, can now be seen to its best advantage and attracts
over 100,000 visitors a year. The purchasing, restoration and fitting out of the
Museum was due to the benevolence of the late Mrs. Freda Perrins, the widow
of Mr. C. W. Dyson Perrins, who generously gave the Trust over £100,000
to supplement the existing fund. The name of Dyson Perrins is perpetuated
in the title of the Museum, but the collection is kept continually refreshed by
generous gifts of recent work by The Worcester Royal Porcelain Company
and also of different periods from many others, such as the Friends of the
Dyson Perrins Museum. In fact, there can be no doubt that the Museum
contains the finest collection of Worcester porcelain and china in the whole
world and is the perfect place for studying the development of the Company's
history and work.

A venture which was deserving of better support by the public was the use
of a number of Scottie Wilson designs. Scottie's work first came to the
attention of the Company in the early 1960s. He was born in Glasgow but
went to live in Canada where he started painting, being inspired by the theme
of Red Indian totem poles which are frequently to be seen in a stylised form
in his work, although swans, flowers and trees are also very common. The
Company provided sections and segments of plates on which the artist
painted his black patterns. These patterns, as shown typically in Plate 212,
were put on earthenwares made at Palissy Pottery and were never very
successful, possibly being too highly priced for the market at which they were
aimed. They were liked by many artistic people, especially by Lord Snowdon
when he visited the factory in 1966. Scottie Wilson, now aged eighty, is still
drawing and painting.

The death of Dorothy Doughty in 1962 led the Company to ask Ronald
Van Ruyckevelt to produce a new series of models of birds for the American
market, as the subject was now so popular in that country. Van Ruyckevelt
went to America to model a number of splendid editions of gamebirds some
of which are already in production. This gamebird series shows the birds in
naturalistic sizes with the emphasis primarily on the birds themselves, the
foliage being of secondary importance, although this was still as accurately
produced as for the Doughty subjects. What made the series a step forward
was an incredible sense of movement in the birds, the Mallard for example,
caught apparently in the act of taking off and it is quite a while before the
viewer can see how the support of the bird above the water is done. It almost
makes one feel that before very long a model will be produced by the Company with a bird or fish or horse actually in the air, supported by nothing at all.
Other superb creations in the gamebird series have been the Ring-Necked
Pheasants, the cock with its fantastic life-sized and naturalistically coloured
tail feathers (Colour Plate XVII). Also by Van Ruyckevelt are a fine series of
flower subjects, tropical groups such as Bougainvillaea and Passion Flower
naturalistically painted. A fine series of Edwardian and Victorian female
figurines, started by Ruth and now continued by Ronald Van Ruyckevelt,
includes such beautiful creations as The Tea Party with three ladies and a girl

taking tea at a table set with a miniature service, or the more recent Charlotte and Jane, depicting a lady and a girl watching a game of tennis. These groups, and the singles and pairs in the series, have all the qualities of nineteenth-century Dresden and attract a great following of collectors, as do the Nursing Sister series, the models taken from actual Sisters at the London Teaching Hospitals.

It was in the 1960s that the models of Doris Lindner reached a height to which no other ceramic equestrian studies had approached. Like all the other Worcester modellers she went to great pains to make her original model an accurate representation of the subject. Whether she was preparing an equestrian group of a famous person on a particular horse, such as Prince Philip on his polo pony, or Marion Coakes on Stroller, the great show jumper, or else preparing a model of a particular breed of horse or bull, she would go to any length to get the character and movement correct. Her magnificent study of Arkle, the Duchess of Westminster's famous steeplechaser, brought out that indefinable something that made the animal the best loved horse in racing. It is possible to feel his majestic, lively presence as, with ears pricked, he shared the whole crowd's evident enjoyment in his flawless jumping (Plate 195). When modelling a horse or bull study she would seek out a particular best of breed and study the creature in all its moods for many days, doing drawings, taking photographs and making her plasticine model. When the model of the Jersey Bull was completed the owners were horrified to find that she had shown the animal swishing its tail. 'He never does that', they exclaimed, 'he has been taught to stand perfectly still for the judges'. But Doris Lindner was able to show them photographs in which he *was* swishing his tail and this moment of truth is preserved in the model.

The custom is for the Company to present number one in the edition to the owner or rider of the particular animal. The first of the edition is, naturally, a more valuable model than the later numbers although, as has been explained, great care is taken to ensure that each model is as perfect as possible a re-creation of the original Standard, any pieces that fall short of this being ruthlessly destroyed. The working plaster-of-Paris moulds are constantly being replaced at the slightest sign of wear and it is true to say that number 500 should be as perfect a replica of the original as number 1. Although many of the earlier series of limited editions were not numbered under the bases the most recent series are and they are sold with certificates certifying their number in the edition.

One of the most recent series is of great Generals on horseback, modelled by Bernard Winskill, beginning with Napoleon and Wellington. Napoleon was the first ceramic model that Bernard Winskill had produced and the illustration of this splendid study (Plate 211) shows that yet another fine and sensitive modeller can be added to the long line running back to James Hadley.

Many of these modellers have been free lance, providing the Company with one or more models per year, but it should be realised that there is a fine modelling and design department at the factory. Here, under the advice of

Professor R. W. Baker, who is now an Art Consultant to the Company, are produced the new models, new vases and ornaments and the special designs to be put on them.

Whilst limited editions are the 'jam' of the Company's production, the 'bread and butter' comes from the superbly designed tea, dinner and oven-to-table wares, the present design team for which is headed by Peter Ewence, Neal French and Kathleen Hills.

Worcester's recent designs range from a few based on traditional patterns from Worcester's past, to the most modern in the industry. It is not always easy to persuade the public that a Company with Worcester's great traditions cannot just produce shapes and patterns from the past but should take a forward looking approach or otherwise art would stagnate.

The most dramatic advance in the production of useful wares has been in the field of hard porcelain. This fine body, fired to a very high temperature of over 1400 degrees centigrade, looks so fresh and clean, has such attractive patterns and will stand up to flame and cooking in a domestic oven; it is not surprising that it has had a great success in Britain. What is possibly surprising is its tremendous success in Europe and the Far East, areas where hard porcelain has been traditionally made for a long time.

Demand for the porcelain increased enormously through the 1960s and led to the necessity of a separate factory to produce the ware. The last photograph in this book shows the fine new single storied factory, built between the River Severn and the canal basin in the Diglis area. The factory went into production in the Summer of 1970 and is planned so that the production flows from the one end, where the raw materials enter, to the other, where the finished porcelain is dispatched. Provision is made for quadrupling the production of porcelain but although much of the laboriously heavy handwork has been done away with by the use of the most modern machinery, most of the decorating is still done by hand and the final results are as fine as anything in the past.

An interesting venture has been in the making of hard porcelain ornamental ware, the first such to be made in this country since the eighteenth century. The brilliant modeller Arnold Machin has made a number of fine models, from the first dramatic set of Four Seasons, a limited edition of fifty sets bought in its entirety by Thomas Goode & Co. of London, to the beautiful Night and Day shown in Plate 209. There is an extraordinary timeless quality of the hard glaze, requiring no enamel decoration to provide a dramatic effect.

The making of porcelain figurines posed many new problems but they were all successfully overcome. The figurines are now made and decorated by a small team and the most recent pieces are delightful figures in an eighteenth-century style modelled by Neal French, intended for table centre decoration.

With the enormous increase in production and the necessity to control it accurately, a computer department was established in 1967 under the control of Mr. A. Wardner. This department was the successor of a punched card system begun in 1964, and progressively more complicated machines were used leading to the present I.B.M. System 360, Model 20/5 Disk Computer. This machine produces all order sheets and packing notes, order analyses and customer invoices, sales ledger and statements, control of quantities going through the kilns and quality and loss control, wages up to gross, annual stock valuation and market analysis. The first computer to be used on a large scale in the ceramic industry in this country, it has allowed Management to operate with accurate and up-to-date information and there is no doubt that it has played an important part in the great improvement in the profitability of the Company. Some other local companies are helped by being allowed time on the machine.

In 1970 a new film was made by the Company, this time in colour. Entitled 'The Partridge Tureen' it linked a love story set in London and the Worcestershire countryside with scenes on the factory, cleverly cutting from one to the other. With music but no dialogue, it was intended for international showing and presented a much more modern image than the first film made twenty years earlier. The new film, made available for hire to clubs and organisations, was as much a 'soft sell' production as the earlier one had been a 'hard sell', and reflected the 'swinging' London scene of the late 1960s.

A number of commemorative pieces were produced in the decade: printed jugs, mugs and trays for the Shakespeare quater-centenary in 1964; a limited edition mug for Prince Charles' Investiture in 1969; a limited edition bowl for the 450th Anniversary of the Mayflower in 1969, printed from a fine engraving showing the ship in the centre of the bowl and around the outside a list of the names of the original passengers with their coats of arms; and the most recent, a limited number of plates decorated with Caernarvon Castle, made in 1970 for Royal Worcester Industrial Ceramics, number one of the edition going to Prince Charles. Most of the cricket tourists who come to play in England have a plate produced with their autographs printed in gold.

The great tradition of making services for special orders has continued to the present day, with orders such as that from the Sultan and Government of Brunei, numbering some 4,925 pieces.

In these days of growing mass production and the consequent lowering of artistic quality and craftsmanship it is comforting to see that Worcester still sets great store on continuing the training of its young artists and craftsmen into whose hands will pass the flame of tradition. A new method of training is about to go into force in that all apprentices in the skilled potting and painting departments as well as receiving their normal training in their own department will attend a special training school under artist Mrs. Lorraine Howe and the training officer Mr. R. Seward. This school, which will also run refresher courses for more senior artists and craftsmen, aims at teaching appreciation of a wide range of arts and skills; to give a fuller idea of the importance of the pupil's work relative to the finished products, to develop a sense of competence and pride of work and to develop a greater range of expertise and ability so that a youngster does not get pushed into the first department he thinks of, but will eventually work where his best skill and happiness lies.

The present painting departments are basically divided up into the men's and the women's departments under the direct administration of the decorating manager. In these departments is done the painting of figurines and the freehand painting on pieces ranging in size from the great 1286 and 1428 shapes, through coffee and tea services, down to the diminutive thimbles delightfully painted with birds, flowers, or fruit and each bearing the signature of the artist. Such thimbles have been a great tradition of Worcester, running back into the early nineteenth century, although these early ones are seldom marked. The present ones are, naturally, marked and although, since the late 1960s, year-mark codes are no longer used, they still remain pretty pieces and are popular as wedding presents. Some thimbles are decorated with litho prints, but these will not be signed. If a girl had a name that was too long to go on a thimble it was a general custom to shorten it, for example Miss Twinberrow would sign 'Twin'. A fruit painted tea or coffee service can be a composite of the work of a number of different painters, or the work of one.

Another department is the Decorators, where moulded patterns such as the Blind Earl are decorated and patterns requiring building up with raised enamel spots are done.

The days are long past when the painters would get sixpence for a plate centre, and now a commendable wage can be earned in conditions of work that are much more pleasant than in earlier days. When Daisy Rea first came to the factory the paintresses worked by the light of naked gas jets, a very dangerous method of lighting when they were using turpentine and fat oil as mediums for their colours. In an even earlier day the light would be provided by tallow candles stuck in the neck of old bottles—two of these having only just been discovered in an old factory cupboard in a room being redecorated. Now the painters work in bright and attractive rooms, with plenty of light, and although artificial strip lighting is provided it is seldom in use, the painters preferring to work by natural light as long as possible, even on a dark winter afternoon with just a glimmer of daylight remaining.

If one's image of a ceramic factory is based on ideas of dirt and grime, of great big bottle ovens belching out smoke and fumes, one would get a great surprise on seeing the new porcelain factory. Clean and light, with delightful surroundings, bounded by the River Severn on one side and the canal basin on another looking like a little Venice with boats of all sorts, it is one of the most up-to-date factories in the country. The old factory is being modernised in sections but it is still managing to retain its outward appearance of character.

Nowadays the quantities of gold and colour used have reached enormous proportions. Over £100,000 worth of gold and platinum is used each year by the gilders, and the painters and decorators have 6,680 different colours available, all the gold and colour being under the control of David Palmer. The pattern room, under William Corfield, keeps the huge range of different patterns in order, a task now made many times more complicated than in the past because of the necessity of setting out the patterns for all the different shapes. The whole of china production is under the control of John Lance, the China Works Director, and as well as the decorating departments, he controls the making of china with the help of Mr. Glanville Hooper, china making manager and Mr. Robert Clarke, decorating manager. A large number of separate departments come under this group, such as the ornamental making department under William Allen, with Alan Sheppard's flower makers, George Morris's mould makers and the decorating departments including the printers under Stan Woodyatt, the lithographers under Mrs. Dorothy Knee, the gilders under Ivor Williams and the burnishers under Miss Dorothy Purser.

The porcelain production is under the control of Alan Philpott, the Porcelain Works Director, the making stages being under Reg Cyples and the decorating under Harold Burdon.

Relationships between management and staff have always been good. Throughout the 110 years dealt with by this book there has not been one major strike, a sure testimonial both to the loyalty of the staff and to their pride in their work. The number employed at the Worcester Royal Porcelain Company factory has now risen to over 1,200 and at the beginning of the year 1972 it was true to say that the Company had not only survived 220 years but had come 'through difficulties to honours', as R. W. Binns foresaw, and a discerning examination of the photographs of the most modern pieces in this book, will, I am sure, suggest that the glory of the latter house is greater than the former.

Chapter VII

Worcester painters, gilders, modellers and the pattern numbers

An enormous number of artists and craftsmen have worked for Royal Worcester since 1862 and the greater majority are noted in the details that follow. The list is divided into three separate parts, the painters, followed by the gilders and then the modellers. A subsequent section lists the patterns attributed to known artists.

The list of painters is as complete as I have been able to make it, but may not include some who were only at the factory for a short while.

A very important point to bear in mind is that up to about the year 1900 it was not usual for a painter to sign a piece. A few painters seem to have been the exception to this rule, and signatures are sometimes to be seen on important pieces. Sometimes the painters used initials or monograms, for instance Edward Raby junior generally using an ER monogram mark on the front of the vases, but again these were exceptions.

The list of special subjects of the painters, that follows, should help to ascribe a painting to a particular artist, especially if the year of manufacture of the piece is carefully considered to make sure that he was at the factory in that particular year.

Many marks appear under the base of some pieces; as well as the factory trade mark, a registered number may be found; nearly always a shape number is to be found (see Appendix I) or a written pattern number on useful wares (see the last part of this chapter); workmen's marks are often to be found in bewildering quantity: incised or impressed marks for the maker, written symbols for the groundlayer, printer, painter or gilder, and guidance is given on these in the sections that follow.

Some complications are to be found in ascribing some workmen's marks, especially numbers, which tend to get passed onto a new workman when the previous one leaves. Printers' marks are especially difficult and the only certain ones that it has been possible to pin down are K for Alf Harris, P for Percy Osborne, W for Walter Scrivens and G for George Harris—these usually being in the same colour in which the print is done.

The space devoted to the life of a particular painter does not necessarily reflect the importance of that artist, as it has not been possible to find out much about some of the earlier painters. The work of some is referred to more fully in the respective chapters of the book.

It is felt certain that an understanding of the character and life of the craftsman or artist who made a particular work of art will add greatly to one's enjoyment.

Subjects of Royal Worcester Painters

Apple blossom, Bevan,

Australian flowers, R. and W. H. Austin, L. Flexman, Johnson, Taylor

Birds, R. and W. H. Austin, Baldwyn, Hill, Hopewell, Locke, Osborne Powell, Wm. and Walter Sedgley, W. Stinton, Jas. Stinton, Townsend

Birds of Paradise, W. H. Austin, Sedgley

Birds' nests, R. H. Austin, Baldwyn, Bradley

Birkett Foster style, J. Bradley snr., Perling, Salter, J. Williams

Blackberries, K. Blake, W. Hale, M. Miller

Butterflies, Bradley, Copson, Hopewell, C. Johnson, R. Rea, Sherriff, Mrs. Stevens

Cattle, Davis, Perling, Townsend, Scyner, H. Stinton, John Stinton

Chrysanthemums, Raby

Cooper Subjects, Perling

Corot style, H. Davis, G. Evans

Cottages, Bray, R. Rushton

Exotic Birds, Freeman, G. Johnson

Feathers, R. Rea, J. E. Sherriff

Fish, W. H. Austin, Bradley, Davis, Eaton, Holloway, G. Johnson, Salter, Scyner

Flamingoes, E. Johnson, G. Johnson, W. Powell

Flowers, Bates, Miss Everitt, Phillips, Raby, D. Rea, Ricketts, Roberts, Shuck, Stanley

Flowers—early Worcester style, Phillips, Stanley

Fruit, R. H. Austin, W. H. Austin, Ayrton, Bee, Bowkett, Budd, Chivers, Copson, Creed, Delaney, English, L. Flexman, Freeman, Hale, Harper, Hawkins, Higgins, C. Johnson, D. Jones, Leaman, R. Lewis, Lockyer, Love, Maybury, Mosley, Price, Ricketts, F. Roberts, W. Roberts, Schwarz, Scyner, Sebright, Shuck, Telford, Townsend

Game centres, J. Bradley, James Stinton

Hadley style flowers, May Blake, Chidley, Farley, Hood, M. Hunt, W. Powell, D. Rea, Sedgley, Sharples, Spilsbury, Twinberrow

Heathers and heaths, Shaw, Taylor

Ivy, Gwillam

Japan gold sprays, Callowhill Bros., Copson

Landscapes, Davis, R. Gyngell, R. Lewis, R. Rushton, Salter, I. Williams

Landseer subjects, J. Bradley, Perling

Mediterranean scenes, G. M. Evans, Sedgley

Moonlight scenes, Baldwyn, Sedgley
Orchids, Roberts, Shuck, Stephan
Peacocks, Harbron, Jarman, Martin, White, Bray
Pheasants, Jas. Stinton, H. Stinton
Plant centres, Hundley, Webster
Rosa Bonheur subjects, Perling
Roses, Bevan, Chair, Cole, Flexman, Freeman, Hawkins, Hundley, Sedgley
Seabirds and Seascapes, Sedgley
Seaweeds, Bradley
Sheep, Allen, Barker, Davis
Ships, Rushton
Still life, J. J. Ayrton, Bagnall, Hawkins, Hundley, Stanley
Swans flying, Baldwyn, George Johnson
Thistles, Hundley
Tiger Lilies, Chamberlain
Wild flowers, Hundley, Marsh, Miss D. Rea, Taylor, M. Blake

Royal Worcester Painters and Artists

ABDUL, see Platt.

ADAMS, Harry William. b. 1868, d. 1947. Educated at a private school, worked for eight years at Worcester Royal Porcelain Company in the 1880s and signed E. P. Evans' autograph book in 1887. Studied in Paris 1895–6, made several visits to Switzerland and painted landscapes, a speciality being snow scenes. Taught life drawing at Worcester Technical College and was a member of Royal Society of British Artists and many other societies. One of his paintings of a snow scene is in the Tate Gallery.

AITKEN, Mrs. R. (See Van Lachterop)

ALLEN, James. b. 1923, started 1937 under Wm. Powell painting birds, and Harry Davis painting sheep, left factory in 1955 and returned in 1971. Brother of William Allen, foreman of men's ornamental casting department.

ARNOLD, Miss Annette, b. 1951, started 1966, painting rich ornamental, marking 'O'.

ARTHORNE, H. Came during Second World War, here for a few years painting 'cut oranges', signed 'H. Art'.

AUSTIN, John. Signed E. P. Evans' autograph book in 1887.

AUSTIN, Reginald Harry. b. 1890, d. 1955. In his young days had medals for drawing, at Worcester specialised in birds, flowers, fruits and general subjects, including Australian flowers and plants, and flowers and birds on blue scale pieces. Left the factory in 1930 and did freelance designing with his brother, eventually joining Paragon China in the Potteries as resident designer where he painted design ordered by Queen Elizabeth the Queen

Mother for the birth of Princess Margaret Rose (a design of lovebirds, marguerites and roses). Did not like the Potteries and returned to Worcester to work free lance.

AUSTIN, Walter Harold. b. 1891, d. 1971. Like his brother, R. H., he was a brilliant draughtsman and won several medals in national competitions for plant drawing in black and white; he won the King's Prize for examination held in drawing the 'life of two plants from seed to death' out of 13,000 competitors and chose a watch of which he was very proud. At the factory, specialised in fish, flowers and fruit and also, like his brother, did a great quantity of freelance water colours, a particular favourite being magnificent delphiniums with an unusual quality of blue, 'first painted in white and then in pure blue directly over the white'. Painted on Sabrina ware. Spent a whole year studying delphiniums before he ventured to paint them. Left factory in 1930 in the depression and did part-time painting on furniture for the firm of Rackstraw's in Worcester; his flowers on bedroom furniture were said to be so realistic that butterflies would fly through the bedroom window and land on them; these pieces are signed. He worked off and on at this until about 1948 when demand for this sort of furniture ceased. One day a group of carpenters were standing around admiring him painting; one said 'how does he paint those flowers without any to copy from', to be answered by another 'don't be daft, he makes the b . . . .'s up'. The price was a matter of negotiation— about 7s. 6d. for a bureau fall or a front of a drawer or £1 for a wardrobe. When asked for a price he would stand back, suck his cigarette and say 'you know, there's a lot of work in that' and eventually a price would be agreed. He would not work in September, when he went to Scotland or Ireland for the fishing— angling being his favourite recreation, although also very fond of tennis.

AYRTON, Harry (Tim). b. 1905. Started at the factory in January 1920 and retired in 1970, although continues to paint part-time. Was put under Hawkins for the first seven years, doing numerous subjects. From the end of his apprenticeship he painted fruit until about 1930 when he was put onto filling in the castle subjects for about two years. He continued with fruit for two years and then went onto painting fish and horse models and also doing fruit. In 1942 he went into the glost kiln working on the Welwyn resistors returning to the painting department in 1946. In his younger days he did a lot of cycling, especially with the other members of the 'Terrible Seven'—Bee, Townsend, Bagnall, Twilton, Mosley and Stanley. Also very fond of gardening. Feels that differences in fruit painting styles have now been ironed out and the painting is more uniform; everyone had his own style at one time. See Plate 191.

AYRTON, James John. b. about 1897, d. 1918. Brother of above. Came to factory about 1913 and put under Mr. Hawkins and did a number of apprentice pieces, mainly still life, signed. Went into the forces in 1915, served in

France, came home on leave at the Armistice, returned to France and was killed by a horse kicking him in the chest.

BACH. See Greatbach.

BADHAM, Arthur. b. 1935. Started at the factory in 1951 painting models and free-hand subjects. Enjoys all sports.

BAGNALL, William (Bill). Very promising painter who left factory in 1930s because of lack of money. One of the 'Terrible Seven' apprenticed in 1918, he left to take a fish and chip shop in Guildford. His fruit painting was very fine and he also did still life subjects. Worked for Crompton Potteries and died of cancer.

BAKER. Flower painter of Kerr & Binns period, running a few years into the Worcester Royal Porcelain Company period.

BAKER. Noted as a flower painter but nothing known. Around first years of twentieth century.

BAKER, Miss Anne. Paintress, also worked in Design Department, later went to Canada.

BALDWYN, Charles Henry Clifford. b. 1859, d. 1943. Started at the factory in 1880 and left in 1904 although a note in Mr. E. P. Evans' hand states that he left in 1909. Father was a piano tuner. Charley was a great specialist in the painting of birds, particularly swans and smaller birds which he painted from the life, a special favourite being moonlight scenes. Also did a number of water colours and exhibited at the Royal Academy, Plate 124. See separate section (page 251) for excerpts from his father's diary. Frequently seen personal mark is 'BY'. After he left the factory he did freelance water colour painting, employing an agent—Weave—and a lot of his work was sold in the North of England.

BALL, William Henry. b. about 1842. Apprenticed 3rd February 1857.

BAND, W. Painting ferns and flies in early 1880s.

BANKS, Gerald. Apprentice in the 1950s.

BARKER, Ernest. b. 1890, d. 1956 aged 67. Put under Harry Davis and specialised in sheep subjects in Davis style, flowers and blue tits on pussy willow. Generally on very small pieces and on plaques intended for mounting in silver and also did old style flowers in the centre of service and dessert plates. He retired from the factory in 1956 but for a number of years before that did not paint but was otherwise employed. See Plate 107.

65. Royal Worcester and Grainger Pilgrim flasks. Above, from left, 6/290, 16 embossed flying storks, bronzed and gilt, b. blue landscape; Grainger, pâte-sur-pâte flowers on green ground; shape 6/202, imperial red ground, raised and chased gold sprays; Grainger, b. blue ground, classical figures in gold and silver cut up red. Below, shape 504, pencilled ivory and modelled gold; 6/210, embossed Chinese potting subjects, coloured; Grainger, ivory, dry dull pink ground, pearl spots edged up with raised gold; and raised gold Persian pattern filled in with salmon pink, blue and gold.

66. Beautiful pierced vase and cover of Persian design, shape 603, decorated in Japanesque style, ivory pencilled and gilt, Japanese storks in gold, panels by S. Ranford, vase modelled by James Hadley, height $9\frac{1}{4}$ inches, 1880. See page 8.

67. Three different styles. Left, Persian shape and decoration, 783, 18 inches; centre, German Renaissance style, 1409, tones of old ivory, 18 inches; right, faience in style of faïence D'Oiron, imitation jewels inserted by E. Béjot, dated 1866.

68. Beautiful moulded and pierced vase in Persian style, with cream ivory glaze, shape 980, 17½ inches.

69. Moulded and pierced fluted vase in Persian style decorated in old ivory, shape 988, 15 inches, year 1892.

70. Indian slipper shoe, shape 1180, giving the appearance of being a piece of carved ivory but actually Parian decorated with old ivory, $6\frac{1}{2}$ inches long, 2 inches high. See page 9.

71. Fine vase, lacking cover, shape 1199, in Eastern style, decorated with raised gold on a blush pink colour and blue handles, height with cover 22 inches.

72. Vase and cover, shape 804, Persian style, pencilled ivory ground with painted poppies and corn, the pierced neck and handles stained ivory and gold, 23 inches, date 1892.

73. Spiral vase and cover in Eastern style, shape 883, dragon feet and handles, pencilled ivory ground, bronze and gold birds and sprays in panels alternating with pierced bronze, 23 inches.

74. One of a pair of Potters vases, ivory porcelain, each side with deeply sunk panels with figures in alto relievo in the style of the Italian Renaissance illustrative of sixteenth-century Italian potters. The scenes on this vase are 'The Modeller' and 'The Potter' with heads at the shoulder of Maestro Georgio and Luca della Robbia. On the other vase are 'The Painter' and 'The Furnace' with heads of Michaelangelo and Raphael. The embossments tinted by the Callowhill brothers. Only 2 pairs of these vases were produced, one in gold and bronzes being sold to an American at the Paris Exhibition of 1878. See page 14.

75. Beautiful mounted shell in style of Italian Renaissance, shape 1051, old ivory and bronze, painted sprays and scrolls in green by James Crook, $14\frac{1}{2}$ inches high, 13 inches length, date 1885. See page 9.

76. Exquisite mounted shell and angel handle in style of Italian Renaissance, shape 785, $13\frac{1}{2}$ inches, elaborate piercing and gold beading, beautifully painted with a classical scene on a very translucently thin body by the Callowhills.

77. Candlestick in Italian Renaissance style, shape 1506, pencilled ivory, bronze and tinted red and gilt, 15 inches, date 1892.

78. An old photograph showing 3 superb pieces: a centre-piece, shape 1354, in style of Italian fifteenth century, in ivory porcelain decorated with tints of red and green combined with old ivory, richly gilt, surmounted with 'The Sower', height 32 inches, modelled by Hadley and decorated by Josiah Davis; pair of candlesticks, shape 409, similar decorations, 22 inches.
See page 9.

79. A fine rustic table-centre fern stand, '10 years after', shape 1167, decorated in stained ivory and gilding. The embossed name 'HADLEY' may be seen to the right of the left-hand tree stump. Although James Hadley made the model he did not, of course, make the actual piece, length $18\frac{1}{2}$ inches, date 1886, The pairs of figures could also be made separately as 1234 shape. See page 5.

80. Two-figure comport, modelled by James Hadley.

81. Countries of the world, modelled by James Hadley. Above, from left to right, shape numbers 839, 837 and 840. Below, 836, 851, 1874, 835, 1875, 914 and 913. Note that all these have the same shaped base. They could be sold white glazed, or with tinted faces (as 851, 835 and 914 are shown) up to full naturalistic colours, as shown on 836, heights between 6 inches to 7 inches.

82. Magnificent and rare fully fitted pair of oil lamps, shapes 1239 and 1240 (figures as 114), decorated with stained ivory and gilding, height to base of metal fittings, 20 inches.

83. Range of candle extinguishers. Above, from left to right, shapes, Mr. and Mrs. Caudle, 7/71 and 72; Owl, 7/73; Abbess and Praying Monk, 7/70 and 7/67. Centre, Witch, 2543; Town Girl, 6/380; Toddie (one of Helen's Babies), 6/856. Below, Hush, 2844; Diffidence, 7/58; Toby and Punch, 6/889; Coleridge and Orton from Tichborne Trial, and Monsieur Reynard, 7/62.

84. Another group of extinguishers, differently coloured. Above, right, is The Cook, 7/74. Centre, left to right, Japanese, Nun; Mandarin, 2568; Witch; Granny Snow. Below, Budge (Helen's babies) middle, Monk. *Messrs. Godden of Worthing Ltd.*

85. Group of candle extinguishers; participants in the Tichborne Trial. Arthur Orton lifts off his butcher's block on which is impressed the letters 'AO'; Coleridge, the attorney, is made to fit over Orton, extinguishing his claim to the Tichborne fortune. Decorated in black enamel, height of Coleridge 3¾ inches. See page 12.

86.   Group of dogs. Above, from left, 267, 374 and 444. Below, 387, length 15 inches.

87. 'The health of the King', one of a pair, shape 1383, decorated in stained ivory, decorated coat and gilt, 14 inches, year 1898.

88. Set of 4 busts. Above, right, Maestro Georgio, 906. Below, left to right, Raphael, 905; Michaelangelo, 904; Luca della Robbia, 907. Above, left, 'The Modeller', 2067; Maestro Georgio is decorated in stained ivory and gilt, the others in old ivory.

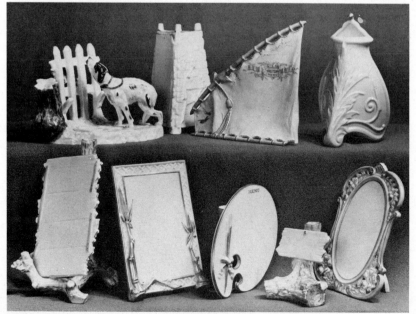

89. Group of menu cards and a hungry dog menu holder. Above, left to right, shapes 1013, 1916, G803, 1917. Below, 1636, 1283, 2342, 1637 and 2341, mostly stained ivory decorated; the menu would be written on in grease pencil, so that it could be wiped off.

90. Cup and saucer from the service pattern W836, painted large and small sprays and flies by Edward Powell. Gilders mark T R underneath base for George Roberts, mid 1880s.

91. Imposing jardinière stand and jardinière, shape 1925, decorated in stained ivory with painted thistles, probably by Hundley, height 49 inches. The cost of this in 1897 was 14 guineas.

92. An old photograph showing the cupid ınkstand on ebony plinth, shape 1623, presented to Benjamin Williams Leader with the Freedom of the City of Worcester, in ivory porcelain richly gilt with chased and burnished gold, inkstand 9 inches high and 16 inches long. See page 3.

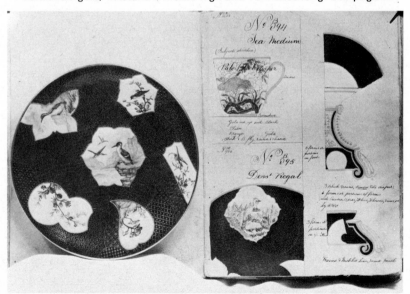

93. Example of a page of one of the Company's pattern books showing patterns B894 and B895. On the left is shown a dessert plate of pattern B895, noted in the book as blue black ground, reserving 6 forms or portions of forms with painted birds, flies, flowers, views, etc., by O H C (Octar H. Copson). The gold decoration and oddly shaped forms are typical of the Japanesque period. The drawings on the right show how the comports were to be decorated, and pattern B894 above is an example of the typical gold stork decoration in which the Callowhill brothers specialised.

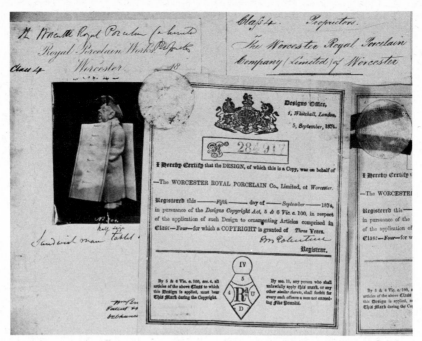

94.   Example of design registration particulars, registering one of the
Men menus, shape 440, on 5th September 1874, giving the diamond
shape mark that would subsequently appear on the shape. It should
be clearly understood that a diamond mark is not a factory trade mark,
nor does it show the date on which the object was made, which would
be after the date of registration. The photograph is interesting in showing how a card menu was added to the 'sandwich man tablet'.

95.   Set of 6 'Men menu holders', shape 440. *From the collection of
Mr. M. Traub.* These are not particularly rare, but the set of Politician
menu holders, shape 512, shown on the photograph in the front, are
exceedingly rare. Left to right, Disraeli, Cairns, Mornington, Bright,
Gladstone and Lowe. See page 12.

96. Umbrella stand in a design of bamboo, in earthenware with green and brown glazes, height 29 inches.

97. Umbrella stand, shape 561, unglazed and undecorated, height 27 inches.

98. Vase, shape 636, pink coloured clay body decorated with pâte-sur-pâte (underglaze slip) flowers, gilt handles, 9 inches high, year mark R for 1880. Bill Pointon, the figure maker, told Mr. Gimson that he had decorated this vase. See page xxiv.

99. Photograph of the inauguration meeting of the Porcelain Works Cycling Club, taken in front of the showroom on 2nd April 1887. Mr. E. P. Evans is in the front in the centre with the big black beard, a few places to his left may be seen R. W. Binns himself, with the great white beard and bowler hat. See page 32.

100. The Aesthetic Teapot, shape 870; a skit on Oscar Wilde and the Aesthetic Movement, marked under the base 'Fearful consequences through the laws of Natural Selection and Evolution of living up to one's teapot'. Male on one side, female on the other, brilliantly coloured in enamels in 'greenery, yallery' colours, mark 1 and code for 1882, 6 inches high.

BARKER, William. b. about 1841. Apprenticed in late 1850s (?), died 1895. Lived at Richmond Villa, Portland Street. May also have been employed as a gilder.

BATES, David, (senior). b. 1843, d. 1921. At the factory from about 1855 to 1880. Bates had his early training at the factory, claiming that this was the only way he could obtain such skills, and did floral subjects of great quality, such as on the 'Beauties at the Court of King Charles' subjects and on Pattern number 8575. Left the factory to devote himself to landscape painting on canvas and is now regarded as one of the country's leading painters of the late nineteenth century. His son David Noel Bates also became a well known canvas painter and changed his name to David Bates Noel to avoid confusion. See Plate 46.

BEE, William (Bill). Fruit painter, starting at the factory about 1918 as an apprentice and was one of the 'Terrible Seven'. Left the factory in the 1930s in the depression.

BÉJOT, Eduard. At factory from about 1870 to 1880, at first decorating pierced vases in his Paris Studio then came to Worcester, finally returning to Paris where he had pieces sent to him. Did fine gilding and designs on chased gold, never repeating his subjects. A pair of Indian style vases decorated at Worcester by Béjot cost £600 and were presented to Queen Victoria by some ladies of Worcestershire. Died in Paris in 1885, aged 49.

BELL, Mrs. Elizabeth. Painter of Moss Rose Pattern, mother of Maude.

BELL, Miss Maude (later Mrs. Mountford). Came to factory about 1904–5. Was foremistress for a few years and left in 1931. Her mother was also a paintress.

BELLMAN, Mrs. Paintress under Daisy Rea in the 1920s and 1930s.

BETTISON, Keval. b. 1948, came 1971.

BEVAN, William Charles. Painter of rosebuds and apple blossom in 1880s.

BEVINGTON, Walter. An apprentice in the 1850s continued into the 1870s.

BILLS, Mrs. Anthea. b. 1949, started 1970, free-hand painting and marks 'AB'.

BINNS, Albert. Son of Mr. R. W. Binns, died 1882 aged 20. At the factory for two years doing rare experimental work, especially sgraffito work on large earthenware plaques, such as dog subjects. Died following a fall from a damson tree while gathering fruit, death being from peritonitis for it seems that in eating some of the fruit he swallowed a stone. See Plate 59.

H

BLAKE, Charles. Signed E. P. Evans' autograph book in 1887, left 1894.

BLAKE, Miss Kitty, 1905–53, specialist in blackberry subjects and flowers painted in Autumnal tints in the Hadley style. A very vivacious personality, always seemed to have bright red lips and a cigarette hanging from them. During odd minutes she used to paint water colour posters advertising future events on the factory, peopling the paintings with factory characters disguised in various ways. See Plate 148. The blackberry and buttercup and clover patterns were her own design.

BLAKE, Miss May. Hadley-style rose painter, not related to Kitty. b. 1885, taught by Frank Hadley, roses, sweet peas, violets. Mark no. 2.

BLAKEMORE, Tony. b. 1944, started as a caster in 1969 and moved to men's painters in 1970.

BLOODWORTH, Miss May. Came 1905 and retired 1967. Trained by Mrs. Handley and finally worked in Progress Department. Sister of Mrs. Pearson. Her mark was the number 22.

BOOTH, Walter Robert. At factory about 1875–90. A neat flower painter. Later became one of the pioneers of the film industry. Pattern book notes pattern B198 as painted by him.

BOTT, Thomas. b. 1829, d. 1870. A great enameller, inventor of the Limoges Enamel style. He was born near Kidderminster and his first training was at Richardson's glass works at Wordsley, near Stourbridge, where he went in 1846, some of his painted glass being exhibited at the 1851 Exhibition. He used to amuse the landlady where he lived by drawing cupids which she enjoyed, often asking him to draw some more 'little devils'. Did portrait painting in oils and the Richardsons found him so talented that they thought he would be better employed at Worcester where he went in 1853. He was employed on the Shakespeare service and the following year developed his Limoges enamels. Studies for some of these were loaned by Sir Alfred Lechmere and others. Gilding on his vases was generally chased and not burnished and he also did many plaques. A relation noted in a diary that he decided to work on his own account selling direct to customers but this caused difficulties with the Company and Mr. Binns is said to have told him that he was 'killing the goose that laid the golden eggs'. His work fetched great prices at the time and the pressure of work is said to have accelerated his death. See Colour Plate III and Plate 47.

BOTT, Thomas John. b. 1854, d. 1932. Son of the above, employed at Worcester from about 1870 to 1885 or 1886 doing Limoges enamels in the style of his father. In 1886 would appear to have painted free lance at the home of C. H. C. Baldwyn and later went to Brown-Westhead, Moore in 1889 and afterwards to Coalport to become Art Director, remaining with them until his death. See also page 28 and Plate 47.

BOULLEMIER, Lucien. b. 1876, d. 1949. Figure painter, better known on Minton pieces, but at Worcester for a short period painting cupids and other subjects. Did the portraits on the Imperial Vase, Colour Plate X.

BOWEN, Christopher. Apprentice in 1950s, painting fruit, left to go to Hornsey College of Art.

BOWKETT, David (name pronounced as in French—'bouquet',. At factory from about 1950 to 1960 painting fruit at first, then Doughty Birds. Went to Cornwall and took a public house subsequently doing freelance painting of country houses etc. on 'blanks', which he still produces.

BOYLE, Shaun. b. 1955, came 1971.

BRADLEY, Edith. Sister of Gladys came about 1908 and here about nineteen years.

BRADLEY, Gladys. Flower painter from about 1911 to 1943—signed generally M. Brady as the paintresses were often not allowed to sign their real names especially when these were rather long.

BRADLEY, James (senior). b. about 1810, employed about 1852 to 1860s. Kerr & Binns painter of Landseer subjects (Stags in torrent etc.) and some pieces in Birkett Foster style; also birds and crests.

BRADLEY, James (junior). b. about 1848. Painter of dogs and various subjects, also circles of birds in Japanese style, signed E. P. Evans' autograph book in 1887.

BRAY, Frederick. Before First World War; did vases with cottage scenes with shaded black effects at top and bottom produced by spraying. Killed in action in Palestine in 1916.

BRECKNELL, Joseph. b. 1827. Designer and decorator for Chamberlain and Kerr & Binns, carried on into eariy years of Worcester Royal Porcelain Company. As well as being a painter he was also a fine gilder.

BROOK, Mary (married name Nicholls). Excellent painter under Mrs. Pearson & Miss Rea, left in 1950s.

BRUTON, William. Died during First World War while training in England.

BUCKINGHAM, John. At factory from the 1880s but was primarily a teacher of art at Worcester School of Art. An atheist and a stern disciplinarian. If there was a book he wanted he would go without food to obtain it.

BUCKLE, David. b. 1946. Started at factory 1962, doing models and free-hand painting. Hobbies—nature study and vintage motor cars.

BUDD, Richard. Came as an apprentice about 1927–8 and left after about four years, before his time was up. Afterwards taught china painting and did a considerable amount of freelance painting on 'blanks' specialising in game-birds and fish.

BULLOCK, Carolyn (later Mrs. Hammond). At factory for two years from 1968, before leaving to get married.

BURGESS, Leonard. A nephew of the Callowhills, he was a fine decorator, especially doing raised gold paste work which he introduced in the late 1870s. His brother Frank was also at Worcester but left and went to America. His son, Percy, became Foreman engraver, retiring in 1970, and Percy's son, David, continues in the fine family tradition at the factory to this day. He perfected a method of acid printing and raised paste printing, and with friends made a quantity of his own china and earthenware.

BURNS, Christopher. b. 1953. Started as a caster in 1969, moving into men's painters in 1970, fruit and general.

BURTON, Miss Susan. b. 1946, started 1970, marks 'SB'.

CALLOWHILL, James. b. about 1839, employed about 1855 to 1880s. Very fine all-round decorator specialising in figure subjects, heads and chased gilding, particularly doing storks and grasses in gold. Also did some free-lance work with his brother. A note in an old book says that in 1882, with his brother T. S. he left the works and went to America. Mark ℐℭ (J C conjoined). See also page 93.

CALLOWHILL, Thomas Scott. b. about 1841, employed about 1855 to 1880s. Brother of the above, also a fine all-round decorator, doing similar work. Did the heads on the Dudley déjeuner service. Mark was ℭ (T S C conjoined). The Worcester Trades Directory of 1885 lists both Thomas Scott and James as 'Artists' then living in Worcester. See also page 93.

CALLOWHILL. Four Callowhills won prizes at the Worcester School of Art in 1885, as noted in the local newspaper: Clarence, James C., Ralph and Sidney, but it is not known that any of these worked at the factory.

CHAIR, Henry (Harry). d. 1920. Painted at Worcester for forty-two years, specialising in roses; contemporary of George Owen, whose pierced ware he decorated with festoons of flowers. Was a small plump man and was once heard to remark to a visitor—'Ah! Every three strokes I put on this plate—two for me and one for the gaffer!' Lived at Hawthorne Cottage, Bath Road.

CHAMBERLAIN, Henry. Came to factory in 1889, apprenticed 1891. Painted tiger lilies and other subjects but left to go to Australia about 1907, foreman of Hadley factory painters, also did freelance painting.

CHIDLEY, Arthur. Well-painted Hadley-style flowers, under Walter Sedgley. Left factory to become a newspaper illustrator and worked on the Crippen trial doing sketches of the case as cameras were not allowed in Court.

CHIVERS, Frederick H. Fruit painter of late nineteenth century up to early 1900s, later went to Coalport, but returned about 1930 for a few years. Achieved his peculiar broken up mossy backgrounds by stabbing it with a chewed-up match stick. Died in 1965, aged eighty-four.

CHURCHMAN, James. b. about 1842. Apprentice in late 1850s and painted on into 1870s. Pattern books note B182 as 'flowers natural by J. Churchman'.

CLARKE, James. b. 1839, at factory 1850s–60s.

COLE, George H. d. 1912. Fine painter of roses and other flowers. Used to paint flowers with only one firing involved. Often painted on blanks with scenes of Malvern, these will be unmarked. See also page 113.

COLE, Mildred. Apprenticed about 1914.

COOK, John. Apprentice in 1950s painting fruit, left to go to Hornsey College of Art.

COOPER, Derek. b. 1942. Started at factory 1963 painting models. Hobbies sailing and riding. Left in 1968 to go to Canada.

COOPER, Donald. Apprentice in late 1940s.

COPPIN, Tony. b. 1954, came 1971.

COPSON, Octar H. At factory from about 1875. Mainly fruit but also flowers. Some oil landscapes known, dated 1879.

CORBETT, Miss Gladys. An apprentice with Mrs. Pearson, was very talented but left factory about 1914 because of insufficient money.

COSFORD, Ezra G. B. Came to factory 1890 and apprenticed same year.

COX, Brian. Apprentice in 1950s painting fruit and the small dog models.

CREED, Nigel. b. 1947. Started in factory 1965. All-round painting. Hobbies swimming and motor cycling and does water colour landscapes for his own enjoyment.

CREESE, Charlie. b. 1911. Came to factory 1925 to Pattern Room for a year and then to painters under Hawkins and then Harry Davis. Painted the Rural Scenes and Cathedrals and signed C. Creese. Also painted the early

Lindner horse groups. Left painters about 1938 to go into groundlayers to help his uncle, continuing after his uncle died. After service in the army he returned to groundlayers, where he still is. His Uncle Charles got him the job at the factory; Uncle Charlie's sister's son was Horace Price, the painter, and when Horace heard about it he is reputed to have said 'for Christ's sake don't let Charles start down in that dump'.

CRESSWELL, Keith. b. 1935. Apprentice 1952-5, fruit and flowers on vases, and still life. Now paints free lance on canvas.

CROOK, James. From about 1885, doing gilt decorative motifs, died 1895.

CRUMP, Elsie. Paintress from about 1900, left between the two world wars.

CRUMP, J. Painter of landscapes, birds' and dogs' heads in mid-nineteenth century.

DANGERFIELD, Miss Emily (later Mrs. Walker). 1919-29. Came aged fourteen to help with the start of the Recreation Club and then began to paint Hadley-style flowers under Kitty Blake, then under Daisy Rea doing figurines and general painting. Nicknamed 'Safety-meadow' by the girls and then 'Puck' as she looked like the girl playing 'Puck' at the Worcester Theatre Royal.

DARE, Stephen. Fruit painter 1972-74.

DAVIS, George. Signed E. P. Evans' autograph book in 1887.

DAVIS, Harry, b. 1885, d. 1970. At factory 1898-1969. Foreman painter 1928-54. His grandfather was Josiah the fine gilder and his father Alfred was a china presser. Harry came to the factory on his thirteenth birthday in 1898 as a talented young painter taught drawing by Josiah, but his first job was to be set to wash down the Museum steps—'that will teach you to handle a brush', he was told. After twelve months he was formally apprenticed as a painter, and this was to be the last actual indenture of an apprentice on the form dating back to the eighteenth century (see page 35). He was fortunate in being apprenticed to Ted Salter, a true and sensitive young artist. They had a common interest in fishing—both in catching and painting fish and in 1900 Harry won a fishing club prize for a roach caught in the River Teme and a South Kensington national book prize for a water-colour study of that same fish. The shock of Ted Salter's inexplicable suicide remained with Harry until his last days and in an attempt to ease the blow the Management remitted their share of Harry's earnings, a welcome concession, for the lad was quickly able to hold his own with his more senior colleagues. Landscape painting had always attracted him and he did a great number in the classical style of Claude and the melting colourings of Corot. Every one was an original, for he avoided easy repetition. 'Harry', one of the travellers said to him, 'if you're ever stuck for an idea, just put your name on a plate—I can sell it'. But he was never stuck for an idea and the neat signature 'H. Davis' grew steadily in repute. He made a great speciality of sheep in pastoral or Scottish mountain settings, woodland and garden scenes, rural cottages and town subjects, an extraordinarily wide range. He married in 1910, joined the army in 1916, keeping his artistic hand in by the drawing of diagrams for instruction purposes and painting a backcloth for a regimental show. After the war he took on the demanding task of painting the double service for Ranjitsinji. In 1928 William Hawkins, the foreman, retired and Harry was appointed in his place. Much of his time was now claimed by the calls of administration and training. As a means of aiding training he etched a series of subjects including Cathedrals and Castles providing a printed outline which under supervision could be completed by less experienced hands; some of these are still done to this day. Other etchings which followed were of game birds, fish and coaching scenes and as most of the painters would not sign their own name to the colouring in of these subjects, so Harry himself used the fictitious name of H. SIVAD (Davis back to front). During the Second World War Harry worked on the painting of a number of the Doughty Birds and other special pieces. After the war he did the colour standard for the study of Princess Elizabeth on Tommy, the Princess sitting for him at Buckingham Palace. In 1952 his services to the industry were rewarded by the presentation of the B.E.M. and although he relinquished the position of foreman in 1954 he continued to paint in his studio at the factory until a few months before his death in 1970 working especially on the production of a magnificent series of plaques decorated with Corot-type scenes. To celebrate Harry's seventy years of working at the factory, in 1968, the Company arranged a special holiday for him and his wife in Scotland, which would have been his first visit to the Highland scenes that he painted so well, but his wife's illness and death upset this plan. He remained to the end a man of unfailing courtesy, for ever amazed that anyone should be interested in him or his work, an honest and conscientious craftsman of great integrity. Examples of Harry Davis's work are shown in Colour Plates XII and XIII.

DAVIS, J. Signature on some flower-painted pieces in the Hadley style dated 1900.

DAVIS, Josiah. b. 1839, d. 1913. Grandfather of Harry Davis, at factory from about 1855, fine decorator, specialising in plant decoration and gilding. See Plate 47.

DAVIS, William A. Signed E. P. Evans' autograph book in 1887.

DEAKINS (or Deakin), Charlie H. d. 1923. Worked at Worcester in nineteenth century, signed E. P. Evans' book in 1887, but left to do freelance painting, his work often being found signed on Coalport plates. Did elaborate raised and chased gold pattern of peacocks on branches and gilding over raised paste. Returned to the factory about 1911. Did not have a nose and wore a black patch over the space, the disfigurement said to have been caused by 'smelling a flower'.

DELANEY, Gerald. b. 1933. Came to factory in 1948 and left 1954, returned in 1971. Fruit painting under Ted Townsend, never on full production but signed most of his pieces, left 1973.

EATON, Miss Mary. b. 1873, d. 1961. Hadley painter. Trained at Taunton School of Art then in London. Worked at Worcester but early this century went to Jamaica and then in 1914 went to New York working at New York Botanical Gardens for twenty years as official botanical artist. Made a major study of American flora and painted a series of over seven hundred illustrations of wild plants. Awarded by Royal Horticultural Society their silver gilt Grenfell Medal in 1922 and gold Grenfell Medal in 1950. Returned to England in 1947, having retained her British nationality and received a personal letter from Lord Halifax thanking her for her services on behalf of Britain and its cause during Second World War. See Plate 148.

ENGLISH, Paul. b. 1955. Joined painting department in 1971, painting fruit subjects, left 1974.

ERDMAN, Miss Christine. b. 1950. Started 1965 painting rich ornamental, marking 'E'.

EVANS, George M. b. 1899, d. 1958. Landscape painter, first Worcester painter to do Corot-style. Later did colouring in of Sedgley's Mediterranean outline scenes—these generally signed 'H. George'. During the slump left to go to Doultons but returned to Worcester to be one of the first Doughty Bird painters. No one else was allowed to touch the birds and he would paint them and place them in the kiln himself.

EVANS, Miss Gertrude (Gertie). Paintress of high quality, transferred to Pattern Room during First World War to help with records. Left to get married.

EVANS, Stewart. b. 1950, came 1971.

EVERETT, Miss Hilda. From 1920s to early 1930s painter of flowers of all kinds, only female apprentice to William Hawkins.

EVERETT, T. Painter of flowers, late nineteenth century, mark used T E; his eyesight deteriorated and he became an insurance agent.

FARLEY, Miss Gladys. Hadley rose and flower painter at factory from about 1906 to early 1920s, great friend of Kitty Blake, married Rev. Edward King-dom and moved to Christ Church, Tottenham Court Road, London. Had four children—the ladies in the factory were sure that they intended to produce the twelve Apostles. (Method of Hadley painting style was that the colour background was put on roughly, then badgered with a large badger brush, breathed on and then the lights picked out.)

FARMER, Mrs. Doreen. b. 1941, started 1956, paints rich ornamental wares, marking 'DF'.

FILDES, Miss Ellen Margaret (Madge). Came about 1910–11 as an apprentice, trained in Hadley rose painting. A live wire, she was a leading light in Worcester Royal Porcelain Company Recreation Club concerts with Daisy Rea. Left about 1923–4 to become a nurse, went to Margate as a sister tutor. Her grandfather, Samuel Hill, had worked at the factory.

FLEXMAN, John. b. 1895, d. 1958. Rose painter from 1910–22, painting in a studio of his own. Served in the Royal Artillery in the First World War and was wounded in action. Left in 1922 to do freelance china painting, then returned to the factory in about 1925 for a year, painting his own designs. He left again to illustrate his wife's books of children's stories.

FLEXMAN, Louis (Lou). b. 1897, d. 1934. Fruit painter from 1911. When Roberts died, Lou took over the painting of the Tudor pattern (two apples, raspberries and leaves); when Lou went the pattern was carried on by Lockyer, only one person at a time being allowed to do it. Lou was wounded in the leg during the First World War while serving with the Royal Artillery and walked with a limp. Left factory in 1920s to paint water-colour landscapes and did a great deal of etching. He was killed in a road accident.

FOWLER, Leslie. Apprentice late 1940s.

FREEMAN, John H. b. 1911. One of the foremost present fruit painters. A native of Worcester, joined the Company in 1925 specialising in the painting of fruit, floral groups and individual roses. Hobby gardening.

FULLER, John. b. 1940. Came to factory 1955, under Horace Price, painting rose centres on plates, fish subjects and many thimbles. Moved to Doughty Bird production with W. Nicholls.

GATES, Christopher. Apprentice in early 1960s, painted horse models; killed on a motor cycle.

GEORGE, H. See George M. Evans.

GODFREY, Ron. Late 1930s flower painter, did not return after war.

GOODWIN, F. Painter in 1880s and 90s doing very fine fruit.

GOODWIN, J. Apprentice before Second World War, went into Territorials and did not return to the factory. Was a professional footballer for Worcester

City, then transferred to Birmingham City and then Bradford, finally becoming a coach.

GRAVES, P. Painter of sprays in early 1880s. (This might also be Percy Groves.)

GREATBACH, Charles A. Painter of flowers last quarter nineteenth century. Went to Locke's and then did coach painting in Birmingham. On Locke pieces sometimes signed 'C Bach'.

GREEN, Miss Doris. Paintress under Mrs. Pearson in late 1930s, only here two years, straight from school.

GREEN, Mrs. Emma. Painted roses in the 1910s, used mark number 8.

GRIFFITHS, Mrs. Freda. b. 1931. Forewoman of lady paintresses and figure paintresses. Started at factory in 1946, painting flower subjects, figurines and rich ornamental. Left 1971.

GRIFFITHS, Miss Lybbe. General paintress, was in 'The Sunday School Team', a team of women fire watchers during Second World War.

GROVES, Mrs. Alice. Flower paintress, late nineteenth century, her daughter Elizabeth (later Mrs. Gegg) later worked as Mr. Binns' assistant until 1893.

GROVES, P. See Graves.

GUMMERY, Henry. Landscape painter, turn of century.

GUNSTER, Lionel. Apprentice in late 1940s to early 1950s.

GWILLAM. Apprentice in 1850s, did thimbles painted with roses, toy mugs with groups of flowers.

GYNGELL, Albert. d. Jan. 1894. (Apparently pronounced with a hard G.) Landscape painter but as an apprentice in the 1850s did 'grass and flies', roses and corn sprigs. A number of oil and water-colours known. Lived in Waverley Terrace, Bath Road.

HALE, William. d. circa 1928–30. Came to factory in 1874, put under John Hopewell. Painter of fruit, flowers and birds, also had a considerable experience in decorating ornamental goods in the Cloisonné style. He was the last of the 'decorators'—those able to do all the decorative arts—painting, gilding, ground laying etc. Did a small amount of the 'Fern & Heath' pattern on stained ivory, comprising old English flowers, white and pink backed up with fern. Factory was on short time when he was taken ill and died. He was quite a character, used to hit the bottle hard all the weekend and really only surfaced by Tuesday, when he had to start working hard again to earn enough money for the next weekend; by Saturday he was spruced up and ready to go.

HALFORD, Amos. Began as a painter, transferred to ground laying about 1924–9.

HANDLEY, A. Painter of figure subjects on vases dated 1869.

HANDLEY, Mrs. Susan. Painter of Hadley roses and foremistress. Told by Frank Hadley in 1907 that she was not wanted any more, went home, had a stroke and died—aged sixty-nine. Was at the factory in 1887, came from Coalport, mother of the Stevens girls.

HANLEY, A. Painter of a cupid on a Claw spill vase in the 1880s.

HARBRON, William (Nicky). Came at age of fourteen in about 1908. Went to First World War and did not return to the factory. Hadley-style painter, painting roses and peacocks.

HARPER. Came from Potteries during First World War, painted fruit and signed 'Harper'. Only here a short while.

HARRIS, Mrs. Wyn. b. 1933, used Mark Z, left in 1956, returning in 1967, now uses Mark 7.

HARRISON, M. E. Around 1903 did paintings of mother and child scenes and 'Il Moschettier'.

HARTSHORN, James. Victorian period painter of landscapes.

HARVEY, Mrs. Florence. b. 1923, at factory 1937 to 1963, returned to factory in 1967. Mark F, up to 1963 and FH after 1967.

HAWKER, E. Painter of flowers in late nineteenth century, Mark EH.

HAWKER, Malcolm. Apprentice in 1950s.

HAWKINS, William A. d. 1930. At factory 1874–1928. For many years foreman of the men's painters department. His own particular line of painting was portrait and figure subjects and still life. A particular speciality was Meissonnier's 'Cavalier', Gainsborough's 'Blue Boy' and Reynold's 'Mrs. Carnac'. Many still life subjects were put on the centres of service plates or on vases. A great deal of time was devoted to the supervision of the painting department, not always an easy task with such as the 'Terrible Seven' apprentices to deal with. In his youth he was a keen athlete and an ardent long distance cyclist and a leading member of the works cycling club. In his leisure hours he executed many beautiful figure and portrait subjects in miniature on ivory and other mediums. On his retirement he was presented with a beautiful bowl, which he had painted himself, a clock and a presentation book in which all the leading men painters had painted an example of their work. His last years were spent watching cricket and it is noteworthy to remark that everyone who knew him spoke of him as a fine gentleman and a kindly foreman. He was only once known to lose his temper badly and that was during an Armistice Day two minute silence; the hooter blew to signify the beginning of the silence and all the painters were sitting quietly when in came John Osborne with a great clatter. Mr. Hawkins threw him outside, returned to the silence and when it was over went to the Pattern Room and had a row with Osborne. His work was initialled 'WAH' before the use of full signatures became common in about 1900.

HAYWARD, Mrs. Beryl. b. 1932, started 1947, marks 'BH'.

HENCHER, John. Apprentice in late 1940s–50s. Flowers and general, left to become an actor and subsequently was ordained in the Church of England.

HENDRY, James. Landscape painter coming to the factory when he was seventeen in the 1920s. Left the painting department because of insufficient wages and became a ware carrier. Did not return to the painting department after service in the Second World War. Was Scottish and loved cycling in the Scottish Highlands and purply Highland landscapes are known from his brush. He had many interests, being a keen member of the Cyclists' Touring Club, the 'Rough Stuff' Fellowship and the Paddle Steamer Preservation Society.

HENRY, H. b. 1917, started 1973, fruit painter (real name Hryncewicz).

HIGGINS, Frank. b. 1940. Started at factory 1957 doing figures, painted fruit etc. Apprenticed to Harry Davis. Hobbies handicrafts and sport, left 1972.

HILL, Albert. b. 1841. Apprenticed at factory 25th October 1859, tinting figures and doing turquoise and gold decoration. Later did free-hand painting of a very neat style, often birds, and did a lot of outside free lance work, including some for Locke's factory. Had his own private china painting classes for ladies and had his own muffle kiln in his garden. Exhibited at Howell & James exhibitions and won a prize of a silver locket in 1882 for china painting, which is now owned by Madge Fildes, his grand-daughter, who was a Hadley painter. Left in the 1890s, and did some work for Hancock's colour works in Diglis, Worcester.

HOLFORD, Amos. Apprentice 1920s–30s, cottage scenes.

HOLLOWAY, Melvyn. b. 1940. Started at factory 1955, doing models and free-hand, especially fish; apprenticed to Harry Davis. Hobby motor racing, left factory in 1971.

HOOD, Ambrose. Hadley-style flower painter in the early twentieth century. Left during First World War and did not return to the factory.

HOPEWELL, John. b. 1835, d. 1894. At factory from about 1855 to 1890. Noted in boy painters' book in the late 1850s as doing grasses, hawthorn, pansy wreath, holly and mistletoe but later went onto naturalistic bird subjects, of which he became a master. Pattern books note numbers 9170, 9357 and 9664 and many others as painted by him. See Colour Plate IV.

HOUGHTON, George. Pattern books note pattern B 160 as 'View in centre by G. Houghton'; also painted figure subjects in 1880s.

HUGHES, Alan. Apprenticed to Harry Stinton and did some Highland Cattle in the master's style, at factory from about 1956 to 1960. Left to work for a solicitor.

HUGHES, Carol. b. 1948, started 1964, general subjects. Mark H.

HUNDLEY, George. Second half of nineteenth century; noted in boy painters' book in 1854 as doing slight plants, later did flower painting and raised enamels of birds and plants. Said to be a very sanctimonious man.

HUNDLEY, W. Henry. Brother of George, a very rapid painter of flowers. He would come in the morning at four a.m. and by the next day have a full service finished, with two firings. Lived in Comer Gardens, Worcester and had a small market garden, selling his vegetables in the market. Used to paint postcards with flower subjects and sell them in the local public houses at 2d. each. Did raised enamel work of a heavy type by adding dry white into the enamel, making it stiffer. Marked HH.

HUNDLEY. There were a great number of other Hundleys at the factory in the late nineteenth century (seven in 1887 signed E. P. Evans' autograph book) and it is very difficult to sort out which is which, or what work they did.

HUNT, Kevin. b. 1955. Joined 1971 painting limited edition subjects.

HUNT, Miss Mildred (Millie). Came about 1906 and painted between the two world wars. Specialised in flowers in the Hadley style, became Mrs. Johns on marriage.

HUNTLEY, Stanley. Apprentice in 1950s, had hopes of becoming an actor.

HUSSELL, John. Apprentice in 1950s, painting birds.

IGOE, Mary. b. 1956, started 1971, thimbles, bird plates. Mark MI

IVOR. See WILLIAMS, Ivor.

JAMES, H. Painting sprays of berries in 1879.

JARMAN, William (Bill). At Hadley's factory and then with Worcester Royal Porcelain Company specialising in peacocks, these often produced with a brown print then a wash of colour put on with gum and water, dried, then washed over again in oils. Painted roses in Hadley style. Went to the war in 1914 and afterwards became a masseur.

JEFF, Miss Barbara. b. 1944, started 1959, castles, cathedrals etc. Marks 'J'.

JENNINGS, Miss Mary. Grand-daughter of Mr. Jennings, mould-maker; very clever painter under Miss Rea, mainly doing figures in the late 1920s but not here very long.

JOHNS, Mrs. M. See Mildred Hunt.

JOHNSON, C. Painted geese and hens in farmyard subjects around 1900.

JOHNSON, E. Pattern B 611, dessert, described as '3 sprays of leaves and berries, Autumnal tints on enamels by E. Johnson'.

JOHNSON, George B. From 1880s, d. 1938. A clever bird painter, specialising in game subjects and he also painted many of the 'exotic' birds in the reproductions of eighteenth-century scale blue and exotic birds. Did storks and flamingoes in appropriate settings of lake and river scenery. Also reproduced Chamberlain style landscapes in low tones. Master in his own field, always studied from nature direct and employed most of his spare time in doing oils and water colours. A very tall man, with a beard. Had retired by 1933. See Plate 148.

JOHNSON, Malcolm. b. 1944, came to factory in 1967 painting fruit etc. Hobby stage design. Left 1971.

JONES, Derek. b. 1930, started at the factory 1944, models and free-hand subjects. Hobbies sport and cartoon drawing.

JONES, Ernest. Boy apprentice in 1888.

JONES, Yvonne. Paintress early 1960s, signing thimbles etc. 'Y. Jones'.

JOYNER, Simon. b. 1956, started 1973, limited editions.

KAUL, I. A German girl who came to Worcester at start of Second World War and painted flowers on plates, found to be too expensive for general sale and she did not stay long. One signed plate seen (dated 1940) has a blue scale border in scrolls, cut by flowers and a central spray of flowers.

KIMBERLEE, Ian. b. 1942, started 1974, cathedral and castle plates.

KING, Peter. Apprentice in 1950s.

KNOTT, Doreen (later Mrs. Martin). Factory painter until her marriage in 1962 and continued to do outside work. Painted thimbles and figurines.

LAFFORD, Stuart. b. 1953, started 1972, limited editions.

LANDER, Jenny and Mabel. Sisters employed at the Hadley factory painting sweet peas, roses and violets, they moved to the Royal Worcester Company in the 1910s.

LANE, Albert (Bert).

LAWRENCE, Miss Jean. b. 1951, started 1970, free-hand painting and thimbles, marks 'JL'.

LAWTON, Stephen. Kerr & Binns decorator, possibly into Worcester Royal Porcelain Company period doing enamel and gilt decorations.

LAYLAND, Mrs. Louisa. Employed from late nineteenth century until 1920s, did most of the scale blue ground on the unglazed ware, including that for the miniature vases for Queen Mary's dolls' house.

LEAMAN, Brian. b. 1936, started 1969, fruit painter and has a great interest in flower painting.

LEWIS, Arthur C. (Ocker). Hadley factory painter of storks in landscapes and irises who moved over to Worcester Royal Porcelain Company but left in depression and became an insurance agent. Died in Kidderminster aged about fifty-four in the 1930s.

LEWIS, Ernest. Apprenticed painter in 1888.

LEWIS, J. A Locke factory painter of birds, such as small robins.

LEWIS, James Henry Liseron (signed J. H. Lewis). At Coalport before coming to Worcester. A fine decorator—painter, gilder, raised gilding etc. Produced book of 'Designs and Adaptations' in 1896—pencil drawings. Left factory to do freelance water-colour painting, producing two large or four small canvases a week (for 12s. 6d. each, providing all materials himself) on a mass production basis, many for a local weekly art lottery. These were landscapes mainly, and many are now in the USA. His son, Percy, became a fine gilder for Worcester, retiring in 1969.

LEWIS, Richard (Ricky), b. 1941. Was a professional soccer player joining the factory in 1961, accepted as apprentice of Harry Davis and his landscape painting is very like that of his master. Also fruit and models. Hobbies football and squash. Left 1970.

LEY. See Miss Lily Whiteley.

LEYLAND, Mrs. Paintress under Daisy Rea, specialised in a 'maize' ground colour (flesh), mended Royal Lily pattern.

LLEWELLYN. Came during First World War for a few years, painting roses.

LLOYD, Frederick. Decorating with bronzes and colours on lotus candlesticks etc. Late nineteenth century.

LOCKE, Edward. b. 1829, d. 1909. Floral compositions, later started his own factory. Apprenticed to Grainger's, 1845. Probable mark ⅊. See page 23.

LOCKE. A large family of Edward Locke included Frank, Beatrice and Kate who were painters, but seldom signed.

LOCKYER, Thomas Greville (Tom). d. 1935. At factory from just before 1914 until his death. Specialist fruit painter. In forces during war and was wounded in the leg leaving it permanently stiff and he walked with a limp, producing a war pension for him. His fruit painting style was very like that of Frank Roberts, doing dessert fruits with mossy backgrounds. When Lou Flexman left he took over the 'Tudor Pattern'. His spare time was occupied by making water-colour studies from nature and he also did woodwork, at which he was an expert; also liked classical music.

LONG, William. Apprenticed under Harry Davis in the late 1920s. Was killed in the Grenadier Guards during the last war.

LOVE, Peter. Painted fruit. Came before 1950, left about 1956 but returned for a year or so. Died following an operation.

LYN, C. See Maslyn.

LYNES, Harry. Apprentice in 1950s, painting fruit.

MARGETTS, Mrs. Pauline. b. 1951, started 1967, paints rich ornamental and thimbles, marks '6', or signs P. Sheph.

MARIE, L. See M. Milward (pseudonym).

MARSH, W. Doing patterns B 684 and B 737—wild flowers. (Might be Herbert Marsh, noted in E. P. Evans' autograph book as dying in 1888.)

MARTIN, Harry. Came before First World War. Specialised in rose painting in the later Hadley style and peacocks. Not here very long.

MASLYN, Carola. Paintress early 1960s, signing thimbles etc. 'C. Lyn'.

MASSEY, Douglas. Apprentice in 1950s—fruit and general.

MAYBURY, Leighton. b. 1929. Came to factory during Second World War as an apprentice. Fruit painter, left and returned again. Left and returned yet

101. Pieces modelled by Hadley in the Kate Greenaway style. Left, shape 944; centre, boy and girl hats pierced as sugar sifters, 800; right, one of pair, shape 826, in front cat in barrel pepper, 930, all tinted and gilt. Shapes 800 were later reproduced as shapes 2725/6.

102. Four figures. Above, left, Bringaree Indian, shape 1243, pencilled ivory and shot silk; right, Yeoman of the Guard, 1362, 7¼ inches. Below, Indian metal beater, 1207, stained ivory and decorated (beater missing); gold brocade maker, 1203, stained ivory and gilding; the other Indian craftsmen in the series are 1204, 1222 and 1226.

103. Hadley modelled children. Above, top, left, shape 888, right, 901, both in Kate Greenaway style. Below, left, group of Goldsmith's schoolboys 'Smile', shape 1263 in unglazed biscuit china; right, boy skater from Russian table decoration, shape 1595, stained ivory, base broken, date 1892. Modelled by Hadley. See page 25.

104. The fantastic Chicago Exhibition vase, $52\frac{1}{2}$ inches high, ivory porcelain, embossments and handles coloured and gilt, body ornamented with modelled gold and bronze scrolls, cupids, etc., shaded with green, festoons of flowers of the four Seasons painted by Raby, 4 figures on plinth and one on cover coloured in old ivory. One only made in 1892–3. *Photograph taken in the Dyson Perrins Museum.* See page 26.

105. Two pieces made in the Chicago Exhibition year. Dessert plate, shape 1120, pencilled and stained ivory, green and richly gilt, Chicago Exhibition 1893, special mark, and smelling bottle (with metal screw top) embossed bird and 'Chicago 1893', shape 1649. See page 26.

106.   Jugs and small vases. Above, left to right, shapes
1373, 1438 and 1507. Below, 1948, 2083 (lacking cover)
and 1639.

107.   Cups of different shapes. Above, left, moustache
cup of tankard shape (has moustache protector inside), on
celadon ground, pattern 8820; right, coffee, pattern Z793,
painted blue tits by Ernest Barker. Below, left, 'trembleuse'
deep shape saucer, scaled blue ground, raised gold, mark
for 1874; centre, heart-shaped mark for 1895; right,
Empress tea cup, shape 1471, painted daisies and roses,
pattern W4018, mark P E for gilder Alfred Price.

108. George Grainger in the doorway of his shop at 19, The Foregate, Worcester, now the premises of W. H. Smith & Son. This was the retail shop and showroom of the firm, the factory being at St. Martin's Gate. The windows are full of pierced and painted vases, some glass is to be seen in the ground-floor left-hand window and some large female figures in the middle first-floor windows. See page 18.

109. Beautiful Grainger green and white Parian and celadon clay vase with modelled and applied swans and rushes, 11 inches high, not marked, c. 1870.

110. Three pieces with hand-modelled and applied flowers. Left, Grainger plate, Parian, decorated old ivory, rose in dry colours and gilt; right, Royal Worcester regal plate, pencilled ivory, raised blackberry spray by Raby, coloured by J. Callowhill; below, Grainger dish, unglazed Parian, undecorated flowers applied over a blue slip.

111. Grainger teacup and saucer, richly pierced, decorated with dry colours and richly gilt. The making of a double pierced vessel, like the cup, involves two separate cups, the larger one pierced, the smaller one placed inside and a separate rim put on over the two.

112. The 3 main Stintons at Grainger's factory. Above, left, shape G493, painted by James; right, G955, stained ivory, painted game birds by James. Below, pierced vase, G963, turquoise blue and gilt painted by James; centre, dessert plate, b. blue ground, white enamel and raised gold spots, painted scene by John senior in 1860s: right, shape G1020 (lacking cover) painted by John junior. See page 18.

113.   Group of Grainger workmen during an outing, about 1895: the tall one at the rear is George Cole, second from the left in the back row is James Stinton, fourth from the left is John Stinton junior (in front of Cole); in front row, second from the left is John Stinton senior with white beard, on his left is John Osborne, on the far right is Brown, kilnman, in front with violin is Fred Norris, printer.

114.   Group from the Hadley factory during an outing to Malvern, about 1900. James Hadley is standing at the left in the front, Frank Hadley is seated on his right, Howard Hadley is seated next but one, with white boater, and Lou Hadley is standing farthest right at the rear. Some of the workmen, such as the one between Frank and Howard, may be seen on the Royal Worcester Cycling Club photograph.

115. Attractive early Hadley 'Art Pottery' terra-cotta plaques, intended for framing; the plaques incised with verse as follows. Above, from left, 'Oh what a plague is love, I cannot bear it'; 'But woe to tell here she stumbled and fell'; 'T'other day as she passed me, she looked t'other way and would not spy me'. Below, 'Dear Willy would a wooing go'; 'Where are you going to my pretty maid?'. c. 1895–6. See page 22.

116. Early Hadley factory wares of 1896–1900. Left to right, pair of candlesticks, faience body, coloured clays and gilt, shape 141/3; opaque faience body, thinly glazed, stylised design, shape F103/1; candlestick, 9½ inches, faience body, clay mounts, green monochrome decoration, shape F117A/6, mark 14; square vase, red and blue lotus design, shape F116, mark 13, *without* 'Hadley's Worcester England'.

117. Later Hadley factory wares, all with Mark 15, and 1902–5 date except for jardinière. Above, left, shape 148A/50, gold bands and painted peacocks by Jarman; right, fine jardinière, shape 2498, pattern mark 145–74; painted storks in yellowish landscape by Walter Powell in 1912, height 10 inches. Below, left to right ewer shape 242B/77–54, painted stocks in yellowish landscape by Walter Powell; oval boat shape 254A/69–54, painted pheasants in landscape; shape 247B/50–62, painted pheasants in landscape by Jarman. *The large jardinière from the collection of Mr. R. Checketts.*

118. Hadley factory figures. Above, left, Kreuger and Chamberlain, coloured bronzes; right, Uncle Sam and John Bull shaking hands across the Atlantic Ocean, shot silk decoration. Below, pair of Italian Musicians decorated in bronzes and ivory, shape 143/54. See page 20.

119. A rare photograph of the Hadley factory in Diglis Road; Roland Blake standing in the doorway. See page 19. *Photograph loaned by his daughter.*

120. Studio photograph of James Hadley, kindly loaned by a descendant, inscribed on back 'For Frank, 1881' (i.e. Frank Hadley). *Taken by Bennett of Worcester.*

121. One of the photographs shown at the High Court action brought against the firm of Locke & Company. A group of Locke pieces are shown in a local shop window, on the bottom shelf and stacked up on the centre display stand, decorated with typical birds and flowers on a blush ivory ground in imitation of Royal Worcester. See page 23.

122. Group of Royal Worcester painters in 1899 or 1900. Left to right, standing, Frank Roberts, Baldwyn, George Johnson, Sebright, C. Greatbach, Hawkins, Hale and Ricketts; seated in front, left to right, E. Sadler, Robert Rea and Salter; the 2 apprentices in the front are Harry Davis, left, and Richardson.

123. Fine large vase, shape 1957, solid underglaze blue cover, neck, handles and foot, underglaze painted landscape painted by Edward Salter, raised and tinted gold exotic bird on branch by Tom Morton senior, 18½ inches high, mark for 1899.

Note: from Plate 123 onwards all pieces shown are Royal Worcester.

124. Photograph of the beautiful water-colour painting of 'Teazles' by Charles Baldwyn in 1884, exhibited at the Royal Academy exhibition of 1887. See diary of Henry Baldwyn, Appendix III. *The property of Mr. Rodney Baldwyn.*

125. Large vase and cover, shape 2007, painted in early Art Nouveau style in 1899, height 23½ inches. *From the collection of Mr. R. Checketts.*

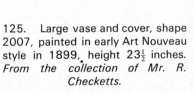

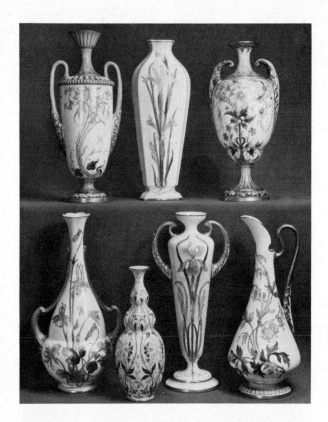

126. Vases in Art Nouveau style. Above, left to right, shapes 2129, 2177, 2031. Below, 2164, 2167, 2150, 2146. All from the year 1901 and most marked 'Leadless glaze'. See page 42.

127. Busts of Queen Victoria, shape 1230, 25 inches, King Edward VII and Queen Alexandra, on pedestals, in unglazed Parian.

128. Fine statuette of 'The Violinist', shape 1487, decorated in stained ivory and traced gilt, height 9¾ inches, mark for 1898.

129. Well-modelled pug dog, mark for 1900, naturalistic in size and with a matt glaze, marked under the paw, shape 355. Another version was made of a pug squatting.

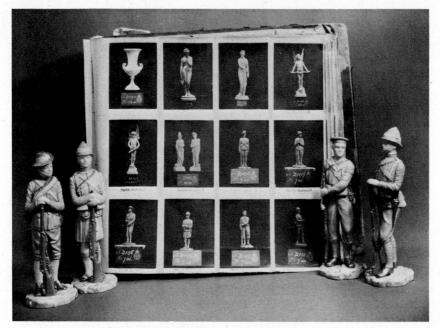

130. Four of the set of 6 Boer War Soldiers, coloured dry browns and bronze, about 7½ inches, shown with a page of the photographic shape book to show the remaining 2 figures and the other shapes between 2100 and 2111. *From the collection of Mrs. M. MacGeoch.*

131. A range of the beautiful Sabrina ware pieces. Above, left to right, 161, 2174, 1376, 1897. Below, straight spill, 867, 2175, 1215, 2266, 2240. See page 34.

132. Figures of musicians. Above, left to right, 465, 2071, 1803. Below, 1803 and 465.

133. Afternoon tea-set of fluted shape, made in 1882, decoration in the Persian style with painted mulberry spray diaper, richly modelled bands and borders in bronze, round tray $14\frac{1}{2}$ inches.

again, remaining for some five years. Left finally in the 1950s doing free lance work painting on 'blanks' for a local antique dealer doing an incredible range of subjects: fruit, landscapes, gamebirds, regimental uniforms, miniature services, signing the work LEIGHTON (at the Worcester factory he signed L. MAYBURY) but these pieces do not carry the word WORCESTER.

MCHARG, Mona. Flower paintress of small pieces.

MILLER, Miss Michelin (Micky). Apprenticed to Kitty Blake and painted blackberries in her style. Left to get married in the late 1950s.

MILWARD, Miss Marie. Painted flowers, signed MM, left 1971.

MOLD, Miss Margaret (married name Hughes). Came in 1951, left 1959, worked in Mrs. Pearson's department painting flowers and general.

MOLLOY, Miss Pauline. b. 1951, started 1966, marks 'Q'.

MONA. See McHarg (pseudonym).

MOODY, Miss Gillian. b. 1944, started 1964 painting rich ornamental, marking 'M'.

MOORE, Laura. Apprentice in about 1914.

MORRIS. In boy painters' books of 1850s, painting roses, pansies and forget-me-nots.

MORETON, Violet. Apprenticed 1918, left 1920.

MORTON, John C. Signed E. P. Evans' autograph book in 1887.

MORTON, Thomas (senior). Did raised gold and exotic sprays from 1880s until about 1906, he also modelled birds and sprays.

MORTON, Miss Violet. Came about 1918 under Daisy Rea, left in the 1920s to get married. Daughter of Tubby Morton, the gilder.

MOSLEY, George. Came as an apprentice about 1919, one of the 'Terrible Seven'. Fruit mainly and also birds (bullfinches, robins, etc.). Left about 1939 to go into Territorials, did not return to the factory, d. 1973, used mark GM monogram on small mugs.

NASH, Albert Edward. Apprenticed as a painter 1887.

NEWMAN, Robert. Apprentice in 1854 books doing French-style flora groups.

NEWMAN, (? George). Brother of above, a flower painter.

NICHOLLS, William. b. 1933, started at factory 1950 under Harry Davis in painting department for ten years doing fruit, bird subjects, Corot landscapes and later Doughty Birds; since 1960 in charge of quality control of rich ornamental wares, left 1972.

NOAKE, Walter. Apprentice painter, coming to factory in 1886, being put down as an apprentice in 1888.

NORTON, Miss Paula. b. 1949, started 1966, marks 'P'.

NORWOOD, Allan. Apprentice late 1940s to early 50s. Painted a lot of thimbles, went to Heatherley Fine Bone China who started up in Worcester for a short while in the early 1960s.

OSBOURNE, John H. At factory for over seventy-one years, finally working in the pattern department, keeping the 50,000 or more patterns in order. A strict disciplinarian, he would walk to and from work from his home in Stonehall Common (some seven miles from Worcester) every day on a meal of a piece of dry bread, bringing his own candle to work with him. Had a fine head of wavy auburn hair and never went bald. Taught in Sunday Schools for many years; late nineteenth to twentieth century, b. 1859, d. 1947, was in charge of decorating at Graingers.

OWEN, Mrs. Judy. b. 1946, started at factory 1962, marking '4'.

PALMERE, Charles. About 1867–80. Figure subjects of fine quality, also Tenniers style figures.

PARKER, F. Apprentice fruit painter turn of nineteenth century.

PAYNE. Came about 1918 with the Flexmans but left to become a poultry farmer, it is believed.

PEARSON, Mrs. I. b. 1900. Came to factory in 1915 eventually becoming forelady of lady decorators' department. Did raised enamelling and Egyptian style patterns from 1924. In 1927 the girl painters' department was divided in two, Mrs. Pearson being in charge of one part and Daisy Rea of the other. A large number of the girls left in the 1930s because of lack of work.

PEPLOW, David. b. 1941 in India, came to factory in 1961 and had a wide all-round training in many departments: ground laying, gilding, decorating, aerographing, repairing and finally in the men's painters.

PEPPIN. Second half of nineteenth century, painting cupids in clouds and Watteau scenes.

PERLING, Robert F. From about 1855 to 1885. Landscape subjects, especially Landseer & Cooper subjects. See Plates 50 and 52.

PERRY, Miss Diane, b. 1947. Started at factory in 1962, painted general patterns, mark figure '2' at first, now signs D. Perry. Enjoys athletics and horse riding.

PHILLIPS, Ernest John. From 1890, d. 1932. Fine flower painter, specialising in the neat and highly finished groups in the early Worcester style, done especially on plate centres. He had a brilliant sense of colour and accuracy of touch. A keen horticulturist and his spare time was taken up with the care and culture of flowers from which he made water-colour studies for use in his work.

PIGGOT, John. Apprentice in 1950s, painting flowers and fruit.

PLATT, Peter (Sam). b. 1935. Started at factory 1951, models and free-hand painting. Hobby gardening. Nicknamed 'Sam' as there were four Peters in the Department at the time and it was causing confusion, also called 'Abdul' as he went very brown in the sun. Some of his fellow apprentices would take his signature off thimbles and replace it with his nicknames as a joke, and some of these fired signatures will be in existence.

PO-HING. Probable name of a Cantonese painter who painted at the Royal Worcester factory about 1870, work in the Cantonese style. See Colour Plate V.

POINTON, William (Bill). Came as an apprentice in the 1870s. Known as a figure maker and modeller but did some vases decorated with coloured clay flowers.

POOLE, Raymond. b. 1935. Started at factory 1950, painting models. First apprentice to start on bird models, being put on the Humming Birds at a time when their decorating was not going well. In the RAF 1953–5. Hobbies cactus growing and photography. Left, 1971.

PORTER, James. Painter of various subjects, turn of century.

POWELL, Edward. In the 1880s painting fern and butterfly subjects, died 1st July 1895. See Plate 90.

POWELL, Michael. b. 1945, started 1966, limited editions.

POWELL, Walter. Hadley artist from about 1900 moving over to Royal Worcester Company for a short time. Specialised in the painting of storks, was still painting in 1912.

POWELL, William. b. 1878, at factory from 1900 to 1950. Fine specialist painter of British bird subjects and flowers. He spent most of his spare time in the country and devoted many years to the study of birds, painting them with great accuracy. He was a hunchback and a dwarf, but the most cheerful of men that one could meet. The Company put him to paint in the gilding room so that visitors (who were not allowed to go through the men's painting department) could see a painter at work and his cheerful personality greatly impressed the visitors, many of whom, returning to the factory in recent years, ask about the little hunchback who was perched upon his specially high stool doing his beautiful birds, always willing to stop and talk. His contented approach to his work is typified by one remark he made to a visitor who asked him why he did not ask for more than 6d. per plate for his paintings, to be met with the answer, 'I am well contented'. A box camera would always be with him when he went for a walk in the country so that he could photograph the birds for future study. In his last years he got very slow and Ted Townsend clearly remembers the first sight he had of the men's painting department on returning from the Second World War and seeing Powell surrounded by huge piles of plates requiring bird paintings to complete an order for Canada. Ted was put onto the job of helping to complete the order, even though the pattern book of this pattern to this day notes 'Birds by Powell'.

PREECE, Miss Linda (married name Wilson). b. 1947, came 1963, at first signed L. Preece, now signs L. Wilson (married Paul Wilson, gilder). Enjoys archaeology.

PRICE, Horace H. b. 1898. At factory from 1912. d. 1965. Painted fruit of all kinds, also Hadley and Worcester-style flowers. In First World War and lost the second finger on his right hand through shrapnel. Stayed in the men's painters right through Second World War and took over as foreman of the apprentices in 1945. Keen fisherman and would often go fishing with many of the other anglers in the factory; also fond of motor cycling and gardening. In his last few years worked shorter hours, stopping work about four or four-thirty p.m., being taken home in a Company car.

PULLEIN, James. Painter of neat flowers, such as a plate with ivy leaves in 1875.

RABY, Edward (senior). Flower modeller, produced in the 1860s and 1870s a number of large plaques with modelled and applied flowers, son of Sam Raby, Bristol flower modeller.

RABY, Edward I. From about 1870 to 1896. Floral artist, later at Doultons. Probably drew flower sprays which were engraved for printing and colouring, although he probably did not do the engraving. Such engravings would have continued years after they were originated. Used a monogram mark ℛ. Was an uncle of Harry Davis and son of the above Edward Raby. A keen Salvationist, he directed the Worcester Salvation Army Songsters and became a deacon in the Congregational Church.

RABY. There were four Rabys signing E. P. Evans' autograph book in 1887 —Harry O., E. J. (Edward jnr.), Frederick and Samuel (see modellers).

RADFORD, Samuel. Decorator and foreman in Victorian period.

RAINER, Miss Janet. Paintress. Commenced in 1964, painter of flowers, figure subjects and birds.

RANFORD, Harry. Son of Sam Ranford, gilder in the last part of the nineteenth century. Harry went to USA and founded a colour business there after painting flowers at Worcester Royal Porcelain Company.

RANFORD, Samuel, (Sam). b. about 1840, employed from about 1855 to 1890. Mainly known as a superb gilder (gilding and jewelling of the Dudley déjeuner service) but also did fine raised gold decoration of Japanese storks and painted branches of fruiting cherries. See Plate 28.

RATCLIFFE, Edward. b. 1929, apprentice in late 1940s to early 1950s.

REA, Miss Daisy. b. 1894, started at factory September 1909. Painter of flowers in either Hadley-style or groups of English flowers, in early days especially on stained ivory. Was nicknamed 'Scissors' because she was so thin that if she stood with arms on hips she looked like a pair of scissors. Began under Mr. Sedgley in the Hadley painting department painting Hadley roses then moved over to Royal Worcester painters. Later did figure painting, her mark number being '33'. Became forewoman of paintresses and worked with Freda Doughty at Sissinghurst to show her how to do the china colours on her first figures of Mischief, Tommy, Michael and Joan. She was paid 7s. 6d. per week for training the apprentices and had to make up the rest by doing piece work. Retired as forelady (position taken on by Mrs. Griffiths) but continued painting or, in Mrs. Griffiths' absence, looking after the girls. One of the great characters of the factory, still painting her beautiful floral subjects on tea-sets, see also pages 46–47.

REA, Miss Grace. Paintress, sister of Daisy Rea, came to the factory in 1929. Started off in the Litho department and started painting by having lessons from Daisy in the evening. Did figures, especially the 'Longies' of Ethelwyn Baker. (The Victorian Musicians so-called because of their long legs—sometimes called 'legs eleven') and the limited edition of King George the Fifth and Queen Mary.

REA, Robert T. No relation of the above. Worcester Royal Porcelain Company painter of butterflies, feathers, etc. in the 1870s and 80s, signed E. P. Evans' autograph book in 1887.

RICHARDSON, H. From 1891 painting flowers into early twentieth century.

RICKETTS, William. From 1880s to about 1933. Painter of flowers and especially fruit, his speciality being vases and ornaments with painted fruit in artistic groupings. His style of painting differed from most in that he produced a precision of outline. Used two different oils in the enamel medium which fought against each other which gave the broken-up appearance of background, typical of his work. Painted water colours in his spare time and exhibited at the Royal Academy. Chief recreation was music. Was over seventy when he retired and did not live long after that. He was a very reserved man. Lived at 20 Dineley Cottages, Bank Street, Barbourne, died just before the Second World War.

RIGBY, Mrs. Pat. Commenced in 1951. Paints the Vatican figures and rich ornamental, marking '9'.

ROBERTS, Frank. From about 1880. d. 1920. Very fine fruit painter, also did flowers and could trace and raise gold. The present apprentices are given Roberts' work as practice work in their training. Roberts kept very much to himself. See Colour Plate XIV.

ROBERTS, George. Pair of ewers seen painted with blossom, bees, butterflies and birds, signed underneath 'Painted by Geo. Roberts 1917'—no one knows anything about him and he may have been an apprentice for a short time. There was a George Roberts who signed E. P. Evans' autograph book in 1887.

ROBERTS, Miss Nina. b. 1952, started 1967, marks 'B'.

ROBERTS, William. b. 1915. Started at factory in 1930 and still employed on fruit painting. Hobbies—photography and gardening.

ROBINSON, Miss Susan (later Mrs. Chambers). At factory for a few years in the 1960s and did oil painting, mainly portraits, in her spare time. Left on marriage.

ROSE, Miss Annie. Came about 1912 and was at factory about ten to twelve years. Worked mainly on useful wares, especially on stained ivory.

ROSS, Miss Joan. Paintress, started in factory in 1965, later went into Design Department.

ROUND, Fiona. b. 1956, started 1973, thimbles, bird plates. Mark FR.

RUSHTON, Frank R. Late nineteenth century.

RUSHTON, Josiah. b. 1836. Employed from about 1852 to 1871. Fine painter of figure subjects. Painted series of 'Beauties at the Court of King Charles', did many reproductions of famous paintings by Gainsborough and a number of plaques. Also did canvas portraits and submitted one to Royal Academy in 1880 giving his address as 15 Foregate Street, Worcester. Mark: sometimes used J R monogram and dots: *JR*. See Plates 55 and 56.

RUSHTON, Raymond. b. 1886, d. 1956. Fine landscape painter, specialising in pictures of old-fashioned manor house gardens, old cottages and gardens in bright colours and also castle subjects in monochrome. Did a series of gardens at Royal Palaces. A prize winner at the National School of Arts in his earlier years and remained a painstaking worker, putting a wealth of detail into his painting. Fond of fishing in his spare time and was an accomplished pianist, playing at the Fountain Inn (opposite the factory) in the evening for beer money. Did a considerable amount of the colouring in work of the Castles and Cathedrals scenes, designed in outline by Harry Davis. Also did seascapes. Did a lot of work for calendar and Christmas card firms. In his last years became crippled with arthritis, his hands and joints became very swollen and he had difficulty in holding a brush, his legs became deformed and he had great difficulty in turning his head. Did not sleep at all well and often dozed off at work, retired in 1953 (see Frontispiece).

SADLER, Thomas E. Flower painter, late nineteenth century, signed E. P. Evans' autograph book in 1887.

SADLER, W. J. Painter at Royal Worcester, then Hadleys, then Pountneys.

SALTER, Edward (Ted). From about 1886 to 1902. Fine painter of landscapes and fish subjects. Harry Davis was apprenticed to him and, as Salter was a very keen angler, he would often take Harry on a fishing trip, setting him to draw and paint the fish he caught. (see Frontispiece)

SALTER, Edwin. Signed E. P. Evans' autograph book in 1887. Died 1902 and is possibly the same person as Edward Salter, above.

'SAM'. See Peter Platt.

SANDAY, Arthur. Apprenticed as a painter in 1888.

SANDAY, William Thomas Croft. b. about 1846. Decorator, did some experimental trials of metal plating on china. Apprenticed 26th October 1859.

SANDAY, William. Apprenticed as a painter 1886.

SCHWARZ, Bernard. b. 1947, came 1962, painted mainly cottage subjects, a little fruit and Doughty Birds. Left to work for Van Ruyckevelt in 1968 and returned in 1971.

SCYNER, David. b. 1949, painter of cattle, fruit, fish and flower subjects.

SEBRIGHT, Richard (Dick). b. 1870, d. 1951. Fruit painter at Worcester for about fifty-six years to the late 1940s. Probably the finest fruit painter even among the many fine exponents in his day and must rank as one of the finest fruit painters of any period. He was also a master of many branches of flower painting and exhibited several water-colours of flower studies at the Royal Academy. He painted direct from nature and spent a lot of his spare time in making careful water-colour studies from ripe fruits for later use at the factory. He was too painstaking a painter to make any money at the job and even after the Second World War he was only earning about 45s. per week. Each piece was given great care and deep thought and in the 1930s, when the painters were getting 6d. per plate centre, he refused to simplify his painting in an attempt to paint more quickly and so earn a decent wage. His own colleagues regarded him as the finest fruit painter ever and he was a very religious man—'all he thought of was religion and fruit'—and he never married, living with his sister all his life. He became very ill, from religious mania it was said, during the last six months he was painting at the factory. He would be working away and suddenly start shouting that he could see angels all around him in the painting room and would get very angry with any girls singing on the factory complaining that they should not be singing hymns, when in reality they would be singing popular songs (see Frontispiece).

SEDGLEY, Thomas. b. 1880, d. 1950. Started as a painter, then worked in the pattern room with John Osbourne, at factory for fifty years. Taught at Worcester Art School and also in the Methodist Sunday School. In his spare time did excellent illuminated addresses.

SEDGLEY, Mrs. E. Widow of above. Paintress, still at the factory (1971). In her early days her pseudonym was 'Willis', when the ladies were not allowed to use their own names. b. 1909, started at factory 1924, used number 29.

SEDGLEY, Walter. From 1889 to 1929. Painter of roses and other flowers, golden pheasants, also general subjects and especially Italian garden scenes. Was apprenticed in 1891. His colleagues regarded him as the finest of the Hadley rose style painters and he taught many of the later painters of the style. No relation to Thomas Sedgley. Died in the early 1930s from T.B. of the spine. Pseudonymous signature on printed and coloured pieces 'Seeley'.

SEELEY, see Walter Sedgley.

SERRA, Miss Filippa. b. 1951, started 1966, cathedral and castle plates etc.

SHEPH, P. See Margetts (her maiden name was Shephard).

SHARPLES, Miss N. Few years painting Hadley-style roses in the late 1940s and early 1950s.

SHAW, George. See under Gilders; brother of Thomas Shaw.

SHAW, Thomas. b. 1855, d. about 1919, apprenticed 1868. Noted in pattern books as painting pattern B 138 (small group of flowers and background small spray) and B 188 (heath and fern centre). Left c. 1890 to manage a pub.

SHERIDAN, Miss Jennifer. b. 1952, started 1968, marks '2'.

SHERRIFF, James E. (senior). b. about 1825, Kerr & Binns floral artist.

SHERRIFF, James E. (junior). Son of above. Royal Worcester painter of butterflies, grasses etc. Pattren 8880 is noted as being by J. Sherriff (one large fly, three small ones, gold grass and fern sprigs, green grass in background). Some of his work kept as copying subjects for apprentices. Died October 1885.

SHERWOOD, Mrs. Angela. b. 1949, started 1966, painting rich ornamental wares marking 'AF'.

SHUCK, Albert J. b. 1880, d. 1961. Painter of fruit, orchids and other flowers. A very quiet and reserved man who would only become animated when talking about his favourite subject—painting.

SKERRETT, James. b. 1954, started 1969, limited editions.

SIEVERS, Gustav. Figure subject painter, late nineteenth century, doing Tenniers subjects.

SIVAD, H. See Harry Davis.

SMART, C. b. 1947. Started at factory 1962, painting fruit and models. Hobby coin collecting.

SMITH, Christopher. Left factory 1970.

SMITH, John. b. 1934. Started at factory 1950 painting fruit and models. Hobby gardening, left factory 1971.

SMITH, Mrs. Loraine. b. 1942, started at the factory 1957, marking 'LS'.

SMITH, Walter. Signed E. P. Evans' autograph book in 1887.

SOUTHALL, Jack. See under gilders. His signature seen on a jardinière painted with peacocks in the style of Jarman and white storks on Sabrina ware.

SPARKES, Miss Dorothy. b. 1935, started 1951, cathedral and castle plates etc.

SPARKS, George. b. 1804, d. 1874. Outside decorator in Worcester 1836–1854. See G. Godden's *Victorian Porcelain* (Herbert Jenkins, London, 1961).

SPILSBURY, Miss Ethel. Came before First World War, trained in the Hadley style, painted flowers, particularly violets. Worked with Kitty Blake, interested in social work and left to join the army, it is thought.

SPRAGUE, George. Signed E. P. Evans' autograph book in 1887.

STAIT, Mrs. Edith. Paintress, was over seventy when she left in about 1965.

STANLEY, Jack. b. 1905. At factory 1919–1933. Started at age fourteen and put under Ernest Phillips for flowers and William Hawkins for figure subjects and still life. One of the foremost painters of his time, portraits such as Meissonnier's, 'La Bixe', Hals', 'Laughing Cavalier', and Mrs. Siddons and coaching scenes. He etched a number of copper plates with the Mrs. Siddons and Meissonnier subjects, in faint outline for colouring in. One of the members of the 'Terrible Seven' and was getting a good deal of work and as much overtime as he wanted in the early years of the depression, married and within a few weeks the supply of work dropped leaving him in a very difficult financial position. Went onto painting the early Doris Lindner dog figures, getting only 3d. per figure, involving two firings. Finally left the factory in 1933 to work for the gas board. When he left the factory he was presented with a large spill vase painted with cattle by Harry Stinton. In his apprenticeship days he was awarded the prize for the best painting of an item from the City Museum—bearded tits—also did a bit of modelling, taught to him by Gertner, in particular a model of a mouse, that was fired in china, but found too difficult to do in the days when knowledge of supporting figures was not very great; d. 1972.

STEADMAN, Mrs. Christine (née Lloyd). Here from 1965 to 1966, painted some thimbles.

STEPHAN, E. Late nineteenth-century painter of flowers, especially orchids. Probably came from Germany. Daughter painted at Coalport. Two Stephans signed E. P. Evans' autograph book in 1887—John and George, the latter noted as 'left' in 1896.

STEPHENS, Mrs. Fay. Started at the factory in 1949, painting mainly figurines marking them 'Y' at first and later 'F S'. Has also produced some landscape painted plates signed 'Fay Yarnold'.

STEVENS, Ada. Paintress apprenticed in 1887, daughter of Mrs. Susan Handley.

STEVENS, Annie. Sister of above, painted free-hand floral sprays, from 1880s.

STEVENS, Laura. Sister of above, did enamelling from 1880s, left early 1930s.

STEPHENSON, Thomas. b. about 1847. Decorating in bronzes and colours on elaborate pieces at end of nineteenth century, signed E. P. Evans' autograph book in 1887.

STINTON, Arthur. b. 1878, d. 30th December 1970. Eldest son of John Stinton junior. Was first articled to Grainger's factory, after the amalgamation of 1889, by Mr. E. P. Evans, and remembered Mr. Evans well—'if his top hat was on the back of his head when he arrived in the morning he was known to be in a good mood'. Not one of the best of the painting Stintons, he did some flower painting and some colouring in and went to Locke's factory. Did not remember how he came to leave but went to a Brierley Hill glass firm as a decorator.

STINTON, Harry. b. 1882, d. 1968. Second child of John Stinton junior and nephew of James. Started at factory 1896. Distinguished himself at National Art School, taking several medals in open competition at South Kensington. Studied for many years under his father and did the same Highland Cattle scenes, although his palette of colours was different, using more purples. It is said that his father kept all the large vases for himself leaving Harry to do the smaller and lower-paid pieces in his early days. John and Harry painted so many Highland Cattle scenes that their colleagues claimed that they grew to look like the cattle. They were both heavily built and had shaggy eyebrows which helped to give this impression and they kept themselves very much to themselves. Harry had a club foot from birth and had a lot of illness in his young days, spending a lot of time in hospital. His hobbies were fishing and chess and he did a lot of fishing with his great friend Harry Davis. Painted an English cattle water-colour scene which he gave to Harry Davis as a wedding present. In the years 1908–12 or so produced a large number of extremely fine water-colours, of subjects ranging from his china subject of cattle, to game-birds—the subject of Uncle James—landscapes—the speciality of his father, and sheep—the speciality of Harry Davis. It is becoming increasingly clear, the more of his water-colours that are seen, that he must be regarded highly among the English water-colour painters of this century. Retired from the factory 1963. See Colour Plate XI.

STINTON, James. b. 1870, d. 1961. Youngest son of John Stinton senior, specialised in the painting of gamebirds, especially pheasants on the ground or flying, and grouse. Painted first at Grainger's and then at Royal Worcester factory working on ornamental pieces and also on plate centres and coffee and tea services. Did a great deal of water-colour painting of gamebird subjects. Retired in 1951. See Colour Plate XI.

STINTON, John (Senior). b. 1829, employed about 1846–95. Grainger painter specialising in landscapes with figures. In the wages books of 1846–51 he first appears earning only a few shillings a week. Had five sons, three of whom became painters—John, Walter and James.

STINTON, John (Junior). b. 1854, d. 1956 in his 102nd year. Eldest son of John Stinton senior. John Stinton and Harry Davis undoubtedly rank as the finest Worcester landscape painters of the twentieth century and must rank among the finest landscape painters on china of all time. Began at Grainger's in 1889, moving over to Royal Worcester Works. Specialised in ordinary cattle subjects and then in Highland Cattle in landscapes from 1903, but also did English cattle and old castles and landscapes for plate centres. (Chepstow,

Kenilworth and Ludlow being his favourites.) A genial old man, he was an inveterate smoker, never painting without his pipe going all the while. All the Stintons used oil of cloves as a medium for their colours—it kept the colours open, stopping them from drying too quickly—and there was always a strong smell of cloves in their room. John, Harry and James always used to arrive together in the morning, proceeding to the painting room in that order and their fellow workers would refer to them as the Holy Trinity. In his spare time John was a horticulturist and also did a number of water colours. Retired in 1938. See Colour Plate XI.

STINTON, Kate. Daughter of John Stinton junior, and paintress at Royal Worcester factory.

STINTON, Walter. Son of John Stinton senior—fourth of five sons, about two years older than James. Painted first at Grainger's and then went to Locke's. Did landscape painting, including some New Zealand scenes. Left Locke's factory to work for a Droitwich firm making hydraulic windmills. Had three children and painted cards for them every Christmas for them to give to their grandparents. Very fond of dancing but got rheumatic fever from, it is said, sleeping in a damp bed. Died 1950.

It may be helpful to give a short family tree of the main Stinton family painters:

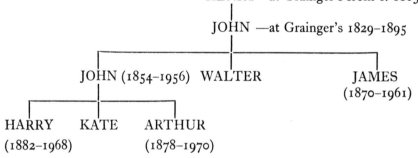

STOKES, Ernest William. Signed E. P. Evans' autograph book in 1887.

STUBBS, Arthur. Apprentice in late 1940s doing most styles.

SUTTON, Frederick N. Painted figure subjects and heads on plate centres in 1880s, signed E. P. Evans' autograph book in 1887.

TALBOT, Percival. Apprenticed in 1890.

TAMPLIN, Paul. b. 1937, started 1974, cathedral and castle plates.

TANDY, Michael. b. 1942. Started at factory 1966 painting models, left 1970.

TANDY, John. b. 1945, started 1960, limited editions.

TANSELL, John. Apprentice in 1950s.

TARENDALE, Miss Jane. b. 1953, started 1968, marks 'I'.

TAUNT, Miss Gertie. At factory from 1910s, painting Hadley-style flowers. Left to go to Lea & Perrins and then worked for a milliner painting straw hats.

TAYLOR, William. b. about 1828. Floral painter from about 1845, was still doing flower subjects in 1870. Shown on photograph with Thomas Bott and Josiah Davis in late 1860s, Plate 47, and was obviously regarded highly. The pattern books are full of patterns noted as being painted by him—e.g. 8337 (tea service) crossed wild flowers, grass and fern covering surface and 8893 described as 'Australian Centre by Taylor', i.e. Australian flowers.

TEAGUE, Mrs. Mary Anne. Forewoman paintress before Daisy Rea and after Mrs. Handley, employed until 1920s.

TELFORD, Alan. b. 1947. Fruit and flower subjects. Left factory 1971.

THORNTON, Miss Mary. Apprenticed paintress in the 1890s.

TISDALE, Caroline (Carry). Paintress from about 1900 to 1920s, specialised in raised white enamel dotted flowers.

THOMPSON, Anthony. b. 1947. Started at factory 1963, models and free-hand painting. Hobbies photography, hiking and swimming, left 1971.

TOWNLEY. See Edward Townsend.

TOWNSEND, Edward (Ted). b. 1904. Started at the factory in 1918, was assistant foreman painter under Harry Davis in 1939, went into the forces in 1942, returned to factory in 1947. Became foreman of the men painters when Davis retired from this position in 1954. He always managed this arduous task with great understanding, kindness and yet great firmness, and this position which took up so much time with the training of the younger painters and the painting of the first colour standards of the limited edition models, allowed him little time to paint his fine free hand subjects. However, in 1971, he retired from this position but still continues to paint. His speciality is fruit and sheep but he can tackle most subjects, such as birds, cattle and fish. In the 1920s and 30s used the pseudonym 'Townley' if tinting in the cheaper outline prints.

TWILTON, Charlie. d. about 1967–8. Started at the factory 1918 or 1919—one of the 'Terrible Seven', aged about sixteen. His colleagues described him as a good painter but rather slow and not able to earn enough money. Left in the depression to do car spraying at Saunders Garage in Worcester.

TWINBERROW, Miss. Painter of Hadley roses in the early 1930s—called 'Twin' by everyone. Came when middle-aged and did not stay long. Being one of the few Hadley-style painters at that time she worked on her own and did not mix much with the other style paintresses.

UNDERHILL, Mrs. Virginia. b. 1952, started 1968, marks '8'.

UPTON, Nicholas. b. 1950, came 1971.

VAN LACHTEROP, Shirley. Here for about ten years in late 1940s, used 'V' mark.

VASS, Julia. b. 1954, started 1971, thimbles, bird plates. Mark JV.

VICKERS, Miss Judy. b. 1946, started at factory 1965, painting rich ornamental, marking 'V'.

VILES, Alfred E. B. Signed E. P. Evans' autograph book in 1887.

WALDRON, Francis. Painting group centres in the 1880s, signed E. P. Evans' autograph book in 1887 and left about 1890; born 1862, died 1939.

WALDRON, Mrs. Rosemary. b. 1951, started 1967, paints rich ornamental thimbles, marks 'R'.

WALDRON, Susan, b. 1955, started 1971, thimbles, bird plates, mark SW.

WALE, John Porter. b. 1860 in Worcester, studied at Worcester School of Art and was employed at the Royal Worcester factory from about 1876 to 1878 as a floral and landscape painter. Later went to Derby.

WALL, H. Locke factory painter of gamebirds, c. 1900.

WALLCRAFT, A. Painted the outline printed cottage subjects about 1958, not here long.

WALLEY, William. Signed E. P. Evans' autograph book in 1887.

WARD, Stephen. Came 1973, fruit painting, left 1974.

WATKINS, A. W. (Jack). Apprenticed to Walter Sedgley and only at the factory a short while. Left to join Worcestershire Regiment in 1914 and went on after the war to an exciting life as an air pilot in Africa. Died 1971.

WEAVER, James. b. about 1839. In the boy painters' book of 1854 being paid for grass and flies and cornflowers. At factory from about 1853 to 1870 dying in the 1890s. Had a son who worked at Copelands. Pattern 8725 (dessert) is described as 'neat centre of grass and flies by Weaver'.

WELLS, Luke (senior). About 1852–65. Painter of dogs and other subjects.

WELLS, Luke (junior). Painter of dogs, Watteau subjects etc., c. 1860s and 1870s.

WEBSTER, Thomas. In boy painters' book of 1854 being paid for hawthorn and slight plants. For the Royal Worcester Company he painted plant centres on dessert patterns 8810, 8869, 8881 and 8929.

WESTWOOD, Derek. Apprentice in the 1950s, some fruit and flowers, was drowned in the river Teme while on leave from the RAF.

WHATMORE, David. b. 1949, started 1972, game bird centres.

WHITE, Charles. b. 1885. Started at Hadley's in 1900 painting peacocks and roses, left in 1910 to go to Doulton's for two years.

WHITFORD, Christopher. b. 1952, started 1971, limited editions.

WHITELEY, E. Painter of flower subjects.

WHITELEY, Miss Edith. Here for a few years, left during First World War.

WHITELEY, Mrs. Lillian. Came and left before First World War, mother of Lily and Edith.

WHITELEY, Miss Lily. Paintress under Daisy Rea, pseudonym being 'Ley'. Employed from 1910s to 1940s, her number was 30.

WHITFORD, Christopher. b. 1952, came 1971.

WIGGETT, Anthony V. Apprentice painter after Second World War, left to go into Fire Service.

WILD, Nigel. Apprentice in the 1950s.

WILLIAMS, Frederick. Signed autograph book of E. P. Evans in 1887.

WILLIAMS, Henry. Painting wreaths in 1880s, signed E. P. Evans' autograph book in 1887.

WILLIAMS, Ivor. b. 1927 (not the gilder of the same name), landscape painter, taught by Harry Davis, not at Worcester long, did some Corot subjects in late 1940s leaving in 1948. Sometimes signed 'Ivor'.

WILLIAMS, Joseph. b. about 1805. Little is known about his early career but employed from at least 1850s. Animal subjects, scenes, rustic figures in style of Birkett Foster, copies of famous paintings such as Turner's 'Fighting Temeraire', painted in the 1860s and 1870s. See Plate 51.

WILLIAMS, Walter. Painted fish in mid-1880s.

WILLIS. See Mrs. E. Sedgley.

WILLOUGHBY, Walter. Apprenticed 27th October 1859, awarded medals for science and art 1857–8. Aged twenty-seven at death, dying from T.B. There was also a James Willoughby at the factory.

WILSON, Derek. b. 1930. Apprentice in 1950s, painting flowers and Doughty Birds.

WITHEY, Miss Angela. b. 1953, started 1968, mark '3'.

WOOD, George, signed E. P. Evans' autograph book in 1887.

WOODWARD, Alan. b. 1949, started 1974, cathedral and castle plates.

YARNOLD, Fay. See Mrs. Fay Stephens.

YOUNG, Anthony. b. 1956, started 1972, limited editions.

YOUNG, Jack. Apprentice before First World War, about 1910, painting Hadley-style flowers and birds on small pieces such as two-and three-handled miniature loving cups, signed 'J. Young'.

Royal Worcester Gilders and their marks

Gilders' marks were generally put on in red, sometimes in black, only very occasionally in gold on special pieces, or by Tom Morton. Initials generally indicate fully trained gilders, other marks generally indicate apprentices. Girl gilders first came to Royal Worcester in 1905 from Hadley's. Marks such as dots are placed in different positions on the base, or in relation to the trade mark, to show whose mark it is. The mark was generally placed thus so that any pieces found to be badly gilded could be traced to the workman, it was not done for calculating piece rate pay, as this was done by checking the quantity on the spot. Gilders seemed to delight in giving each other nicknames, often of an outrageous sort, which would be unthinkable in the painting department; these nicknames are given in brackets, or in the details.

MARK

ALLEN, George. From late nineteenth to early twentieth centuries.

ALLIES, Mrs. Daisy (nee Attwood). Came from the Hadley factory in early 1900s, employed to c. 1943, died in 1960s.

APPLETON, Mrs. Margaret (née James). b. 1921, came in 1936, left in 1939 to go into the NAAFI, returned in 1951 and became charge hand.

L
A on
ornamental ware
or by the stamp

ASHLEY, William H. (Biffo). b. 1913, came in 1928 under Tom Morton and did raised colour and general gilding. In

First mark
÷

V. 6 plates painted by early painters; top row left, basket pierced, oval panel painted with Elizabeth Bagot, Countess of Falmouth and Dorset, after Sir Peter Lely, by Josiah Rushton, flowers painted by David Bates; right, painted cupids in clouds by Thomas Bott; second row, left, Queen Victoria service shape but not pierced, birds in panels on gold ground and turquoise borders, bird in centre by John Hopewell; right, pierced, turquoise and gold border painted in centre with 'Morning on the Sea Coast' after F. R. Lee, R.A., by R. F. Perling; bottom row, left, Vitreous Ware plate·painted with a Cantonese subject by Po-Hing; right, pierced and gilt borders with oval panels painted with feathers and flies probably by J. E. Sherriff and in centre with White Tailed Eagle by Luke Wells. All plates with mark 4 impressed except the last which is unmarked and all are china except where noted.

VI. Magnificent pair of Negro and Negress with water pots, shapes 1126 and 7, modelled by James Hadley, the moulded signature 'Hadley' appearing on the side of the columns on which the pots rest. Decorated in the subtlest forms of stained and shaded ivories with gilding, impressed and printed shape and factory marks (Mark 5) code letter Z for 1888. Height of male 18 inches and of female 17 inches. The qualities of this pair are typical of the many fine figures made in this style.

1952 he did the Worcester work on the Queen's Beasts and also worked on the various presentation services to the Queen—the Guards and the Company services. Was foreman of the printers' department from 1955 to 1960 but 'hated the bloody job, was pushed into it and progressed backwards'. A keen fisherman and cyclist.

On later work and ornamental
Wᴙ

BEECHEY, James. b. 1878, d. 1961. Came from Grainger's, later did aerographing.

JB

BEVAN, William Charles. Late nineteenth century.

BOMFORD, Oliver. Late nineteenth century.

BRECKNELL, Joseph. Gilder and painter, see page 85.

BRIGHT, Henry Charles. From 1880s, left about 1937 and died about 1942; his father was a master tailor and Bright's work was characterised by being neat and firm. Was nicknamed 'The Colonel' because he was a member of the Volunteers, a mounted regiment; once on parade, the horses all being taken from milk floats, someone from the crowd shouted out 'Milko'—his horse immediately stopped and refused to move. Was also called 'Cocker' and used to take parties around the factory; had whiskers and a pointed beard.

BT

BROWN, Albert. Late nineteenth to early twentieth century, was nicknamed 'Yokohama', for no known reason.

BROWN, Edward. Twentieth century.

BURGESS, Leonard. See under painters.

CHAIR, William. Late nineteenth to early twentieth century.

? CW

CARPENTER, Miss Katharine, came 1939.

· to the right of 'China'

CHARTERS, Peter. b. 1937, came 1952.

· · above trade mark, also
I —

COLLINS, David. b. 1947, came 1962, nicknamed 'Nobby'.

◯ or ·

K

MARK

CREESE, Charles. Was hump-backed and nicknamed 'Crinky', started as a gilder but later was a ground layer —died about 1942; uncle of Charlie Greese, the present ground layer.

CC

DAVIES, Frederick Henry. Late nineteenth century.

? HD

DAVIS, 'Dummy'. Was deaf and dumb, early twentieth century.

DAVIS, Josiah. See under painters.

DAVIS, Will. Worked under Mr. Thorpe, c. 1910s–1930s.

DEAKINS, Charley. See under painters.

℞
(i.e. C and D conjoined)

DUDLEY, Tom Owen. Late nineteenth to early twentieth century.

EVANS, Ernest. Under Percy Lewis, c. 1910s–1930s.

EVANS, William. b. 1870, d. 1964, at factory from 1880s, retired 1949. Had a large white moustache, burnt at one side from continual smoking.

WE

FIRKINS, John. b. 1937, came in 1952 under Ivor Williams.

·· to the left of the star.

FOULES, Lawson. From about 1951–4, nicknamed 'Chico'.

FUGGER. Was deaf and dumb and had a habit of jumping over chairs. Employed in the first quarter of the twentieth century.

GLOVER, Alfred. Nicknamed 'Grovy'. Employed from 1910s to 1930s.

AG

HALE, William. Raised and chased gold in 1880s. See under painters.

WH

HAND, George. Late nineteenth to early twentieth century, had mutton chop whiskers.

GH

HAYNES, Thomas. From late 1880s to about 1905, went to Australia.

TH

MARK

HANCOCKS, Dennis (nicknamed 'Pegnose'). b. 1931, came 1947, under Ivor Williams.   DH or D

HAYES, Harold, late nineteenth century.

HOOPER, Alfred, nicknamed 'Snuffy' as he was always taking snuff; died about 1938.

HUDSON, Edward. b. 1931, started at factory in 1946, played in the works' football team.

HUNDLEY, Ernest. Late nineteenth to early twentieth century, nicknamed 'Culley'.

HUNDLEY, George. Late nineteenth to early twentieth century.

HUNDLEY, Henry. Late nineteenth to early twentieth century.

HUNDLEY, Walter. Late nineteenth to early twentieth century.

ICKE, Miss Christine. b. 1951, came 1967.   · in right-hand corner of base

JACKSON, Edwin. Nicknamed 'Natty'. Employed in first quarter of twentieth century.   J

JONES, Brian. b. 1950, came 1966.   J

LAWTON, Stephan. From the Kerr & Binns period possibly into post 1862 Royal Worcester period.

LEA, Henry George. Late nineteenth century.

LEWIS, Harry. Brother of Percy, always wore a bowler hat, was very small and nicknamed 'Splooch', also conducted visitors around the factory, retired in 1960.   HL

LEWIS, James H. L. Father of Harry and Percy, see under painters.

LEWIS, Percy. b. 1887, d. 1971. Came to Hadley's Factory in 1901 and moved to Royal Worcester in 1905, finally   PL retiring in 1969 through failing eyesight. Always worked in a cap. A fine singer in his youth and had the chance of becoming a professional. Could forecast everything that happened, after it had happened. A very tough character, at the age of eighty he came into the gilders room, jumped onto a beam about six feet six inches high (Percy was only five feet tall) swung right over the beam and jumped down again. A young gilder who tried to do the same thing failed.

LIPSCOMBE, Fred. Nicknamed the 'Professor' or 'Lippy' was at factory from late 1880s until he was aged eighty-one. Took parties round the factory.   L

LLOYD, Frederick W. Always wore a top hat and frock coat to work and was very well read; from late nineteenth to early twentieth century, nicknamed 'Tacker'.

MATTHEWS, Albert. Early twentieth century.   BM

MATTHEWS, Thomas. Late nineteenth century.

MAYGLOTHLING, Miss Ethel. b. 1899, at factory about fifty years, retiring about 1963.

MORTON, Tom, senior. From 1880s, left about 1906 and went to the Potteries. The name was sometimes spelt MORETON.   TM

MORTON, Tom, nicknamed 'Tubby'. Was in the Boer   TM
War and the First World War and died about 1936, aged about fifty-eight, son of above; the last gilder to specialise in modelled raised colour and gold work.

NEWTH, Charlie. Turn of the century.   N

PEARCE, Miss Winifred E. b. 1913. Came about 1927   · under the trade
under Mrs. Allies, was forewoman 1947–9. Went to Wedg-   mark.
wood for a year, returning to Worcester. Specialised in colour edges and banding, she and Mrs. Appleton were the only women able to do this.

PERKINS, Arthur, nicknamed 'Perky'. From 1880s to early twentieth century.

MARK

PHIPPS, William. b. 1885, d. 1960, did raised paste work and aerographing, was in First World War and captured in 1918. Came from Hadley's and was a fine musician, able to play most instruments but concentrated on the French Horn, playing in the Worcester Municipal Band. Foreman gilder 1938–45, retired in 1950.

WP
or . · .

POWELL, Miss Betty. At factory for several periods between 1939 and 1965.

· by 'Royal'

PRICE, Albert. Late nineteenth to early twentieth century.

PRICE, Alfred, nicknamed 'Nocker', employed from 1880s to mid-1930s, eventually became caretaker of the Museum.

PE

RADCLIFFE, Tom. b. 1942, came 1958 under Ivor Williams and became a ground layer in 1963.

T

RANFORD, Samuel. b. about 1840, one of the finest gilders of the late nineteenth century. See under painters. Marks S and R conjoined.

$

ROBERTS, George Topham. Went to Hadley's as foreman from Royal Worcester in late nineteenth century.

TR

ROGERS, Alfred. b. 1837, employed in second half of nineteenth century, to first quarter of twentieth century, died 1927, aged 80.

AR

ROGERS, Charles. Came before Second World War and was killed in the RAF. Was goalkeeper for Worcester City.

ROWBERRY, Mrs. Grace. b. 1895, came in 1911 under Frank Hadley, later a paintress.

· · ·

RUSSELL, Ken. b. 1934, came 1950 under Ivor Williams, doing both useful and ornamental ware; very keen motor cycle rider. One of the leading younger gilders.

K on ordinary ware or KR or K Russell on very special pieces.

SANDAY, W. T. C. See under painters.

X·

SHAW, George. Raised gold and bronzes at the end of the nineteenth century, brother of painter T. Shaw; their father and mother were both at the factory.

MARK

SHEPPARD, Henry William, nicknamed 'Dummy'. b. 1870, d. 1950. Was deaf and dumb and a diabetic. Had to have insulin injections at the factory twice a day and was a very timid man.

S
(probably HS in the nineteenth century)

SMITH, Dick. Came 1965 doing raised colour work, left 1967.

R

SOUTHALL, Jack. Came from Kinver near Kidderminster. Employed late nineteenth to first quarter of twentieth century.

X

SOUTHALL, Wallace. Died very young from consumption; not related to Jack or William. Employed late nineteenth century.

IX

SOUTHALL, William. Brother of Jack, died of consumption. Employed late nineteenth to first quarter of twentieth century.

WS

TAYLOR, Henry. b. about 1827, d. 1888.

TEAGUE, Henry. Late nineteenth to early twentieth century, worked on the Chicago vase, was mainly a printer.

THOMAS, Brenda (later Mrs. Eastment). Now in South Africa.

· by 'made'.

TURNER, Robert. b. 1914, started in 1928 as lodge boy, was encouraged to become a gilder by Mr. Wadsworth, now works in acid shop.

÷

TYLER, Edwin. b. about 1828, employed from c. 1850.

WAINWRIGHT, Mary (later Mrs. Swierczynsky). b. 1925, came 1940 under Mrs. Allies, left and returned again after marriage.

· · close to the stamp

WILD, Nigel. b. 1937, came 1952, nicknamed 'Squiggy'.

· · to the right of the stamp, or N

WILLIAMS, Ivor J. b. 1922, came 1936 under Percy Lewis for seven years doing general gilding and red colour work. Lost the middle finger of his right hand and a toe. During

IJW

the war was charge hand at the Stourport Steatite Works. Returned to the factory in 1945 as foreman gilder, over all the other older and more senior men, who accepted this because of his superb gilding technique. Designed and gilded the Churchill Urn and many other magnificent pieces, such as the special services for Princess Elizabeth at her wedding and Coronation, the original designs for the gold printed 'Hyde Park' pattern and the dish for Sir Leonard Woolley (now in the Ashmolean Museum at Oxford). One of the foremost gilders of the present day.

WILLOUGHBY, James. b. about 1844, employed c. 1860 onwards.

WILSON, Paul, nicknamed 'Mad Eric'. b. 1943, came in 1960 'as a last resort' under Percy Lewis, enjoys motor racing, old Biblical manuscripts and history.   PW

WITHERS, Art. Late nineteenth to early twentieth century.   IO

Modellers

ACHESON, Anne. C.B.E., A.R.B.S. Free lance. She was Irish and did a number of Irish subjects—Lough Neagh Mary etc. in the 1930s.

AUMONIER, Eric. Free lance in the 1930s doing rather strange stylised animals.

AZORI, A. Paris modeller of the 1950s whose more usual medium was terracotta.

BAKER, Miss Ethelwyn. Free lance, modeller of the 'Longies', in the 1930s. The back of her figures generally marked with a cross in a circle mark, a symbol she liked to have put on them by the painter.

BARGAS. Free lance modeller in the 1930s.

BETZEMAN. Free lance modeller in the 1930s.

BLAKE, Geraldine. Free lance in the 1930s doing equestrian models.

BRAY, Miss Jessamine. Free lance modeller in the 1930s.

BROCK, Sir Thomas, R.A. 1847–1922. Born in Worcester, educated at School of Design in Pierpoint Street, Worcester, and was apprenticed at the factory. He went to London in 1866 as a pupil of John Foley, R.A., and when the latter died in 1874 Brock completed the outstanding main commissions of O'Connell in Dublin, Lord Canning in Calcutta and Lord Gough in Dublin. His later most important work was the Queen Victoria Memorial outside Buckingham Palace and he also produced fine monuments in many major buildings, such as that of Lord Leighton in St. Paul's, the Longfellow bust and Gladstone statue in Westminster Abbey, the Raikes Memorial on the Thames Embankment and the South African War Memorial in Worcester. In 1913 Worcester made him an Honorary Freeman of the City. His paternal grandfather was a designer at Grainger's.

CANE, Miss Margaret. Free lance in the early 1930s.

CHAROL, Madame D. French lady, free lance. Came to the factory a number of times in the 1930s and is remembered for the quantity of vaseline she put on her eyebrows.

CLEMINCIN. French free lance, worked in the early 1920s.

CROFTS, Miss Stella. b. 1898, d. 1964. From an early age was lame and crippled by T.B. in the bones but was able to go to the Central School of Arts and Crafts in London and made a particular study of animals and their movements from the life at the London Zoo. She then went to the Royal College of Art as a student of sculpture and pottery. Exhibited at the Summer Exhibitions of the Royal Academy (nine groups between 1925 and 1962) and apart from her Royal Worcester models she made and finished all her groups herself, having her own kiln, her father acting as business manager and potter's labourer until he became too old. Her signed work is exhibited in many public Museums.

DOUGHTY, Miss Dorothy. One of the greatest ceramic modellers of this century. She was born at San Remo in Italy, in 1892, her father being Charles Doughty, traveller and poet, whose major work *Arabia Deserta*, was the inspiration of Lawrence of Arabia. As a girl she studied at the Eastbourne School of Art and became a keen naturalist and ornithologist. Details of her modelling of the birds are given earlier in this book and she also produced a magnificent series of Alpine flowers, modelled in china by her own hands, some examples of which can be seen in the Dyson Perrins Museum, to which collection they were given by Freda Doughty. There can be few modellers whose work can have had such an immense importance as Dorothy's to a ceramic firm of long standing. She died in 1962 on 6th October. For further details see Chapters 4 and 5 and Plate 166.

DOUGHTY, Miss Freda. Sister of Dorothy. Produced the models of a large number of charming children subjects made by Worcester from 1931. Many of these were modelled from real children. She moved in 1943 from Sissinghurst in Kent to Falmouth with her sister. All her models were made in plasticine. For further details see Chapter 4 and Plate 166. Died Jan. 1972.

ELLIS, A. R. and Elsie K. Husband and wife, freelance modellers who worked in the 1940s.

EVANS, Eric. Employed at the factory with F. Gertner, came from the Potteries.

EVANS, Ernest. Works modeller, son of George.

EVANS, George. About 1870–1910. Modelled the smallest version of 'Bather Surprised' and Imperial Vase and a large bamboo bird cage with monkey on top, 1878.

EVANS, Sydney. Son of George.

EWENCE, Peter. b. 1934 in Wiltshire, where the chalk trout streams and beech woods fostered a love of natural beauty, and a practical joy in painting was encouraged by his grandfather and father, artists both. From an early age he was interested in the ceramic remains of early cultures and he studied at the Salisbury School of Art. From there he went to the Royal College of Art, graduating in 1959 and being awarded a silver medal for work in the copper-plate printing process. He became a staff designer for the Royal Worcester Company, working closely with Dorothy Doughty, supervising the interpretation of her work at the factory and developing many new series of garden and wild flowers. As designer he has been deeply associated with the development of new tableware and oven-to-tableware in both china and porcelain for which he has made several market surveys of the United States. Coping with a large garden in the quiet beauty of the Malvern Hills still leaves time for his study of ancient ceramics, and he has produced a great number of papers and drawings on the subject.

FOY, Miss Peggy. Free lance, worked for the Worcester Company in the 1950s.

FRENCH, Neal. b. 1933, studied first at Mid-Essex Technical College and School of Art where he won the Sidney Taylor Silver Medal as the outstanding student of the year. Developed a special talent for sculpture and modelling under Huxley-Jones. In 1953 entered the Ceramic School of the Royal College of Art where he studied under Prof. R. W. Baker and graduated with the Diploma Des. R.C.A. First Class in 1958 and the silver medal for ceramic modelling. He was granted a travelling scholarship which enabled him to spend some time in Italy studying the work of great Italian sculptors. He joined the design staff of Royal Worcester under Prof. Baker and succeeded F. M. Gertner in completing the series of statuettes of members of the Papal Household in uniform. Has since modelled tableware shapes and a series of

small table ornament figures for porcelain. In his spare time produces terra-
cotta models of children's heads and collects early teapots.

GARBE. Produced the models for the King Edward VII and George V and
Queen Mary Coronation plaques.

GERTNER, Frederick Martin. 1886–1960. Worcester born, worked in his
father's firm as a wood carver. Attended evening classes at the Victoria
Institute in Worcester, winning a bronze medal for sculpture and a scholarship to the Royal College of Art, School of Sculpture. Taught at Llanelli as
Assistant Art Master about 1913. Came to Royal Worcester in 1915 as works
modeller, responsible for most of the shapes until he died in 1960, while still
employed. Modelled all the historical series and the first two of the Papal
Guards. Trained his son Paul. See Plate 162.

GERTNER, Paul. Son of above, b. 1930 in Worcester, joined factory as trainee
modeller in April 1950 and took responsibility of modelling department in
1960 on his father's death.

GREAVES, Miss Rachel. b. 1908, Sheffield College of Art from 1924 to 1932,
subsequently doing freelance modelling until 1950 when she joined the staff
of Birkdale Preparatory School until her retirement in 1970. Her free lance
models for Worcester were not proceeded with.

GUERO. Free lance, worked in the 1930s.

HADLEY, James, 1837–1903. Lived at 1, Beechwood Villas, Battenhall,
Worcester. The most important Worcester modeller of the nineteenth
century. He left the direct employment of the Company in 1875 but continued
to supply designs and models on a free lance basis. In 1896 he set up his own
factory, see pages 19–22, but this concern was amalgamated with the Royal
Worcester Company in 1905.

JONES, E. J. Modeller of many class 1 and 2 busts and figures, see page 159,
worked in the Kerr & Binns period.

KIRK, W. Boyton, 1824–1900. Modelled Shakespeare service and many early
Parian figures. Son of a Dublin sculptor.

LEIGH, Miss Mary. Flower modeller and designer of the 1930–50 period,
who had worked under Antonio Vassalo. She had a wooden leg.

LINDNER, Miss Doris. Born at Llanyre, Radnorshire. Studied sculpture at
St. Martin's School of Art, in London, the British Academy in Rome and at
Calderon's Animal School in London. First models done for Worcester in
1931 were a group of dogs, typified by 'Bill', number 2931, a dog that belonged

to a friend, Col. Fortescue, but the first number in the recorded list is 2865 —'Cora'. Many of the early subjects were not ones she liked doing, but were financially necessary; now she is able to do subjects that give her great pleasure. A very exacting modeller, achieving great accuracy and incredible movement. Will spend a great deal of time in studying the subject and has had many exciting experiences while doing so. Her Circus Horses were modelled at Bertram Mills' circus, which she followed round while they were on a tenting tour. At one performance she went to her accustomed seat just before the start, realised she had left her tools outside and hurried out to get them, to be met by a line of stallions rushing towards her. Remembering that if a lion charges you are recommended to stand your ground and stare him out she did just that and all the stallions veered away from her. While modelling the Santa Gertrudis bull a photographer turned up who wished to take a photograph of her with the bull free. They took off his bridle and the animal went wild, charging everyone in the corral. Doris just rescued her precious plasticine model and then returned to see the fun of the photographer being chased by the bull. The animal was finally roped and tied up by a marvellous eighty-year-old Mexican. Her first work on a model is done by thinking—quite blankly looking at a wall, where the idea will appear; a simple armature is then made and work begins in plasticine. She prefers working in plasticine for models intended for bronze, which require much rougher treatment. She makes models for casting in bronze, and also does abstract stone carving; all the work is done in her home in a beautiful Cotswold village. Her most recent major commission is a half life-size bronze of Arkle to stand on Cheltenham racecourse. See Plate 193.

LOVEGROVE, David. Works modeller, b. 1933 in North Staffordshire but not from a Potteries family; studied at Newcastle-under-Lyme School of Art and Stoke-on-Trent College of Art and after National Service worked for Doulton's and other Staffordshire factories, until coming to Worcester in 1963.

MACHIN, Arnold. b. in North Staffordshire, taught at Burslem in the 1940s, at the Royal College of Art in the 1950s and became a master at the Royal Academy in the 1960s. Has two terra-cottas in the Tate Gallery and is a fine modeller in bas-relief, one of these of the Queen being used as the design of a British postage stamp and he also designed the Australian coinage and Britain's new decimal coinage. Has always had a great feeling for ceramic sculpture and his models for Worcester's new porcelain have a masterly handling of drapery, foliage and form which could be thought of as Baroque or Rococo except that it has much greater freedom.

MITCHELL-SMITH. Free lance, twentieth century.

MORRIS, Len. b. 1915, joined Company in 1930 as mouldmaker's labourer under Bill Blake. Became a mouldmaker himself and has also produced a number of models.

PARNELL, Miss Gwendoline (accent on first syllable of name). Related to the Parnells of Ireland. Her grandmother was one of the ladies-in-waiting to Queen Victoria. Her sister, Edith Farmiloe, was an illustrator of children's books. Had studio in Chelsea producing pottery figures from about 1916 to 1935 and subsequently worked for the Royal Worcester Company. Was always very well-dressed, rather in the Victorian style, and carried a parasol. She was known as 'The Duchess'. She liked the painter to put 'GMP' (her initials) under the base of the figures.

PINDER-DAVIS, Miss. Free lance modeller of the 1940s and 1950s mainly known for her Chinoiserie figures, including Balinese and Siamese dancers. See Plates 183 and 186.

POINTON, William. b. about 1860. Staff modeller, produced 2645/6 and other shapes.

PROTAT, Hughes. A leading sculptor of the early Victorian period, modelling master at the Stoke and Hanley Schools of Art and worked for Minton's up to about 1858. He also worked for Wedgwood's and in the early 1870s went to London. Would appear to have produced some free lance models for Worcester.

REEVES, David. Staff designer and modeller from about 1953 to 1965, originally trained as a painter. Left Worcester to go to Kilkenny Design Workshop Ltd. in Ireland and has recently been appointed Head of Ceramics at the Central School of Art and Design, London.

RUYCKEVELT, Ronald van. b. 1928. Full time student at Wimbledon for three years and at the Royal College of Art for three years, in the school of ceramics. Passed out with an associateship and was awarded the Diploma Des. R.C.A. after one year of industrial practice. Began to work as a designer for Royal Worcester in August 1953, and in the following year won the British Pottery Manufacturer's Federation Travelling Scholarship. He was closely associated with the production of the Doughty Birds and his first modelling for the Company was his own series of small American Birds. Later he began his famous series of Tropical Fish and Flowers for which he visited Florida to gain first-hand information. On a subsequent visit to America he made extensive studies for his series of game fish. In 1965 he made yet another trip to America to do preliminary work on an entirely new series of gamebirds which promise to be among the most outstanding models in existence. In order to study the fish in greater detail he would catch one and rush it back to his hotel, putting it into his bath while he made drawings at great speed. The hotel was most helpful and put a refrigerator at his disposal so that he could keep his fish fresh, although there was not much room left after a large dolphin had been squeezed in. He also has his own business in Malvern where he manufactures ormolu and china flower subjects, which are distributed by Royal Worcester. See Plate 205.

RUYCKEVELT, Ruth van. Wife of above, born 1931 at Raynes Park in Surrey. Studied for six years at Wimbledon School of Art and there met her husband, Ronald. They married in 1953 and moved to Worcester. In 1958 she was commissioned to produce the first of the Victorian figurine series. She was for several years on the staff of the Malvern College of Art and is now on the staff of Malvern Girls' College. Has a great knowledge of costume.

SOPER, Miss Eva L. Daughter of George Soper, Fellow of the Royal Society of Painter Etchers and Engravers, who was the founder of a wild life sanctuary continued by Eva and a sister. She had plenty of opportunity to study birds which were very tame, never caged, fed from the hand and frequently came into the studio. Her introduction to the Worcester Company in the 1930s was through Mr. Alex Dickins who was handling her original models of birds completed in her studio, where she had installed an electric kiln.

STABLER, Mrs. Phoebe. d. 1955. A talented artist and designer, carried out works for the Worcester Company in the 1930s; wife of Harold Stabler, a partner in the Poole Pottery firm (Carter Stabler & Adams) and a designer, potter and silversmith. Examples of her work are in the Victoria and Albert Museum. Also worked in bronze.

STEVENS, Miss. Free lance, worked in the 1950s.

TOFT, Charles. b. 1831, d. 1909. Modelled parian busts for Worcester in the Kerr & Binns period. Studied at the Stoke-on-Trent School of Design and according to family tradition joined Minton's at the age of fifteen, i.e. in 1845. This date is probably too early and may refer to his employment at Worcester. Left Worcester sometime in 1854 for Bristol; in the late 1860s he was an instructor at the Birmingham School of Art and employed by Elkington's, a firm famed for their silver and plated wares. He seems to have begun at Minton's about 1872. Skilful modeller of Parian busts but is best known for his intricate and painstaking copies of the early French inlaid 'Henri Deux' earthenware. He afterwards joined Wedgwood as chief modeller and in 1889 established a small pottery at Stoke. His son, Albert (1862–1949) was employed at Wedgwood.

VASSALO, Antonio. Maker and designer of flowers in the 1930s and trained the girls who made the flowers for the early Doughty Birds. Specialised in 'flowering' cigarette boxes and trays. Was a chain smoker, always seeming to be surrounded by cigarette smoke. Left in the 1930s. See Plate 178 and page 53.

WILLIAMS, Miss Sybil. Free lance in 1930s.

WINSKILL, Bernard. During his schooldays this current Worcester modeller developed a deep love of horses and his main interest was in painting and modelling and his first jobs were in the world of hunting, horse shows and breeding stables. He attended St. Martin's School of Art and then Kennington School of Art where he concentrated on sculpture. Became a designer and modeller and also bred horses. Has recently modelled a fine series of Generals on horseback for Worcester. See Plate 211.

The following section relates to the various pattern numbers and in particular the patterns that have the names of individual artists listed against them in the factory records.

The pattern number series continued the system started by Chamberlain which had started at 1 and run up to 5,000 by 1852; continued by Kerr & Binns from 5,000 into the 7,000s and had reached 7247 on 10th July 1862. This series continued to 9699 which was reached in August 1876 and then changed to a B prefix—usually written on the pieces with B over the number. This continued to B 1081, reached in May 1883 and the next series had a W prefix which ran up to W 9999 in 1913 being replaced by a C prefix. This ended at 3390 in 1928 and continued with a Z prefix series, which is still current.

There are some important points to make about pattern numbers. They generally applied to useful wares—that is tea, dinner and dessert wares, but could occasionally be used on some more ornamental pieces. The number would be written onto the base of the piece by either the printer, painter or gilder but not every piece of a service would necessarily have its pattern number and it is not unknown for a mistake to be made, for example a wrong number being written onto a pattern. The date of introduction of a pattern number is only indicative of its first use and some patterns could continue in use for many years, or drop out of use and come back again later. So the only certain indication of the year of manufacture is the code mark. The main use of pattern numbers is to enable purchasers to quote the pattern number in order to be able to obtain replacements and they are recorded in a pattern book which gives either a section of the plate or a complete drawing out of the pattern, generally done by the pattern room manager, although some of the painters would occasionally paint their own patterns into the pattern book in water colours. A good example of what a page of a pattern book looks like is shown in Plate 93. Just because the following list of pattern numbers does not include a certain number it should not be assumed that it is not a painted one, as not all patterns had their painter entered. One reason was that everyone at the time knew that Mr. X always painted any pattern that was of, say, hippopotamus and there would be no need to indicate this. Fruit was another complication in that so many trained painters of fruit existed that the work could be put out to any of them and a service could be painted by quite a few different hands. This is quite clearly seen with signatures on the pieces, but is not so easily appreciated on pieces made before signatures became common.

As will be seen, the pattern books frequently indicate the name of the painter who is to do the pattern, but a very strong warning must be given. If the painter who was appointed to do the pattern was away ill, or had left the factory or had died when an order for that pattern was received it is obvious that another painter would be appointed to paint the order. So it is necessary to check the year of painting of the piece from the code mark to see if the painter was still at the factory at the time. Up to about the year 1900 painters, in general, were not allowed to sign their work at the Worcester Royal Porcelain Works and unless the style of painting or subject indicates clearly who the painter is, it is safer to rely on the ascription in the pattern books. Where only initials are given, or the ascription is not very clear, I have made a positive ascription in brackets when certain. In the case of the Stintons, if the pattern refers to gamebirds it is obviously James Stinton who is referred to, but where the subject is cattle the reference to Stinton could be to either John junior, or Harry. It is also often difficult to know which Austin is referred to unless the books state R. Austin—i.e. R. H. Austin or H. Austin —i.e. W. H. Austin, who was generally known as Harold. All references to Sherriff are, of course, to the younger Sherriff. Where two painters' names are coupled it should be understood that each did their own particular subject; as, for example, pattern 9170, 'birds and flower centre, by G. Hundley and J. Hopewell', this must be understood as Hundley painting the flowers and Hopewell the birds. One strange feature in the pattern books is the omission of any ascriptions to the Callowhills. Admittedly their work was mainly on ornamental pieces but it was probably a case of everyone recognising their work and style and there being no point in indicating the name. The illustration of pattern B 895 (Plate 93) also shows B 894 which has no painter ascribed to it, although it could well have been one of the Callowhills, who are known to have specialised in such favourite subjects as raised gold storks

PATTERN NUMBER	TYPE OF SERVICE AND/OR DATE OF INTRODUCTION	PATTERN	PAINTER
7247	10th July 1862		
7728	5th July 1866		
8075	14th April 1869		
8337	Tea	Wild flowers, grass and fern	W. Taylor
8487	Dessert	Wild flowers, grass and fern	W. Taylor
8514	Dessert	Wild flowers and grass	W. Taylor
8515	Dessert	Panels and centre of wild flowers	W. Taylor

PATTERN NUMBER	TYPE OF SERVICE AND/OR DATE OF INTRODUCTION	PATTERN	PAINTER
8575	Dessert	Circular group of flowers	D. Bates
8606	Dessert (basket edge)	Large bending fern centre	W. Taylor
8725	Dessert	Neat centre of grass and flies	Weaver
8793	Dessert	Wild flowers and flies	Taylor
8804	Dessert	Large fern and heath and gold fly	Taylor
8808	21st January 1870		
8810	Dessert	Cross plant centre	Webster
8828	Toilet set	Lily of the valley sprigs	W. Bevan
8867	23rd February 1871		
8869	Dessert	Plant in centre	Webster
8870	Dessert	Side plant and small sprigs	Bates
8880	Dessert	Large and 3 small flies, gold grass	J. Sherriff
8881	Dessert	Plant centre	Webster
8909	Dessert	Bird, grass, fern and flies	Bradley
8929	Dessert	Vibernum	Webster
9005	Tea	Large butterflies, flowers and grass	J. Bradley
9024	Dessert	Wild flowers, heathers and heath	W. Taylor
9038	Dessert	Birds, flies and flowers	Bradley
9040	Dessert	Spray and 5 scattered flies	W. Taylor
9041	Tea	Large and 3 small groups wild flowers	W. Taylor
9065	Tea (tankard) (14th February 1871)	Now by	Mr. Sherriff
9066	Tea	Flies and flowers	W. Taylor
9067	Dessert	Large cross fern	Webster
9164	Dessert	Birds	Bradley
9170	Dessert	Birds and flower centre	G. Hundley and J. Hopewell
9171	Dessert	Spray of apple blossom	Taylor
9306	Dessert	Plant centre	G. Hundley
9307	Dessert	Plant centre	G. Hundley
9357	Dessert	Wild flowers one side, bird on enamel other side	G. Hundley and J. Hopewell
9409	Dessert	Plant centre	G. Hundley
9422	Dessert	Grass and flies and insects, gold ferns cut up red	J. E. Sherriff
9456	Dessert	Full centre	G. Hundley
9458	Dessert	Spray of wild flowers	Cop (?Copson)
9459	Dessert	Plant centre	G. Hundley
9470	Dessert (basket)	Flowers on one side	Copson
9473	Tea	Spray of roses, 2 sprays forget-me-nots	W. Bevan
9478	Dessert	Veined flowers	W. Bevan

VII. Above. Pair of vases, shape 1969, thickly applied ground painted with '11' green, painted by C. H. C. Baldwyn with continuous scenes, including Patty's Farm, Cropthorne, near Evesham ; height 15½ inches.

VIII. Below. A page from the presentation book to Mr. E. P. Evans with a panel of typical Baldwyn bird subjects and on the left sketches of birds from the life by Baldwyn.

IX. Left. Fine Hadley factory vase and cover, shape and pattern number $\frac{272}{93\cdot62}$ painted in typical late Hadley flower style, mark number 15, height $21\frac{1}{2}$ inches; the blue clay mounts contrast effectively with the gold and set off the splendid paintings of chrysanthemums.

X. Right. The Imperial Vase, shape 2219, designed by F. Thorpe, modelled by George Evans and painted by Lucien Boullemier with portraits of King Edward the Seventh and Queen Alexandra in their Coronation robes; a panel on the reverse contains the Royal Arms, richly emblazoned, the whole vase decorated in underglaze scale blue and finely gilded; height 27 inches, made in 1902 when the original cost was £130 (see Chapter 3).

PATTERN NUMBER	TYPE OF SERVICE AND/OR DATE OF INTRODUCTION	PATTERN	PAINTER
9490	Dessert	Flowers painted on enamel	Copson
9492	Tea	Festoons of ivy	Gwillam
9613	Tea bamboo	Painted flies	J.E.S. (Sherriff)
9632	Dessert Vienna	Spray Japanese flowers, gold fern and fly	J. E. Sherriff
9634	Dessert	Large spray roses and one fly	E.S.
9636	Dessert	Half circle of flowers, thistle and heath	G. Hundley
9664	Tea	Bird on enamel and gold sprays	J. Hopewell
9684	Dessert	Bird on spray in underglaze colours	J. Bradley
9685	August 1876	This series terminated at number 9699	
B29	Dessert	Circle sprays of flowers, grass and fly	J. Sherriff
B138	Dessert	Small group flowers background small spray	T. Shaw
B160	Dessert	View in centre	G. Houghton
B168	Dessert	Sprays in Japan style	J. Churchman
B170	Dessert	Plant centre	G. Hundley
B171	Dessert	Plant centre	G. Hundley
B182	Tea	Gold flowers cut up, flowers natural	J. Churchman
B186	Dessert	Large orchid spray	E. Stephan
B188	Dessert	Heath and fern centre	T. Shaw
B189	Dessert	Plant centre	G. Hundley
B198	Dessert	Pricked by	R. Booth
B203	Tea	Scattered flowers and heaths	T. Shaw
B207	Dessert	Full Mazarin view	J. Bradley
B262	Dessert	Full orchid centre	J. Stephan
B285	Tea	2 panels on cup, 3 on saucer	R. Booth
B319	Dessert	Centres painted	T. Shaw
B258	October 1880		
B379	Tea	Petals	R. Booth
B383	Dessert	Gold panel as B402 Japan sprays	J. Churchman
B384	Tea	Japan style sprays b. blue, cut up gold	J. Churchman
B409	Dessert	Bird's nest on the ground and spray of flowers	E. Stephan
B480	Dessert	Flowers cut up red	J. Churchman
B489	Tea	Large spray with two birds and 2 small sprays	J. Hopewell
B503	Dessert	Grass and spray and gold fly	J. E. Sherriff

PATTERN NUMBER	TYPE OF SERVICE AND/OR DATE OF INTRODUCTION	PATTERN	PAINTER
B505	Dessert	Bird and spray in panel	O. H. Copson
B506	Dessert	Fish and seaweed	J. Bradley
B513	Tea	Spray with gold grass	G. Hundley
B521	Dessert	Spray of flowers and gold grass cut up red	T. Shaw
B523	Dessert	Nicely painted plant one side and butterfly	Johnson
B533	Dessert	Gold and colour spray and butterfly	J. E. Sherriff
B543	Dessert	Plant centre	G. Hundley
B544	Dessert	Plant centre	G. Hundley
B550	Dessert	Grass in centre, gold grass at back	Mr. Hundley
B556	Dessert	Large fly in enamel, gold fern cut up red	J. E. Sherriff
B560	Dessert	2 birds and painted spray	Mr. Hopewell
B563	Dessert	Sprays of flowers on side, bird on other in b. blue	O. H. Copson
B571	Dessert	Bird and spray	J. Bradley
B575	Tea	Small birds	Mr. Hopewell
B583	Dessert	Large spray one side, gold grass at back	G. Hundley
B588	Dessert	Flowers in centre on raised enamel	G. Hundley
B591	November 1886		
B599	Dessert	Plant centre	G. Hundley
B611	Dessert	3 sprays leaves and berries, autumnal tints	E. Johnson
B613	Dessert	Violets (or any other flower) on one side and spray of heath on other	G. Hundley
B623	Dessert	6 Butterflies and insects scattered on ivory ground	J. E. Sherriff
B638	Dessert	2 small sprays and 5 scattered flies	J. Bradley
B641	Tea	Plant one side, spray on other, painted to nature	O. H. Copson
B664	Dessert	Japan style birds and sprays	O. H. Copson
B684	Dessert	Wild flower plant up to edge of plate	W. Marsh
B688	Dessert	Group roses or other flowers	G. Hundley
B690	Dessert	Flowers coloured proper and 2 Japan birds	O. H. Copson
B694	Tea	3 sprays and small birds	J. Hopewell
B706	Dessert	Painted large fish and seaweed	J. Bradley
B718	Tea	Faint grass and fern, berries and 3 flies	R. T. Rea
B720	Tea	Japan sprays	J. Churchman

PATTERN NUMBER	TYPE OF SERVICE AND/OR DATE OF INTRODUCTION	PATTERN	PAINTER
B722	Dessert	Fruit	O. H. Copson
B728	Tea	Flowers, berries and 2 butterflies	R. T. Rea
B737	Dessert	Wild flower up to edge	Mr. W. Marsh
B739	Dessert	Spray and butterflies	O. H. Copson
B742	Tea	Sprigs and butterflies	Mrs. Stevens
B743	Dessert	Japan spray and 2 birds on spray	O. H. Copson
B744	Dessert	Plant centre	G. Hundley
B748	Ice plate 6 in.	Japan spray on one side	O. H. Copson
B769	Tea	Gold grass cut up red faintly painted grass at back, 6 scattered flies on cup	R. T. Rea
B770	Tea	Sprays in brown, touches of white enamel	G. Hundley
B808	Dessert	Semicircular spray with bird and 2 flies	Mr. Hopewell
B813	Dessert	2 birds, fly and flowers on enamel	O. H. Copson
B826	Dessert	Plant centre of flies	Johnson
B827	Dessert	Plant centre	G. Hundley
B832	Dessert	Plant centre	W. Marsh
B838	Dessert	Bird and spray one side, 2 sprigs and butterfly	J. Hopewell
B841	Dessert	Large spray and fly in dark Worcester blue	O. H. Copson
B850	Dessert	Wild flowers up to edge	W. Marsh
B851	Dessert	Large Japan spray	O. H. Copson
B857	Dessert	Large plant painted proper and gold grass at back	G. Hundley
B876	Dessert	New plant centre	W. Marsh
B878	Tea and Dessert	Plant centre	G. Hundley
B880	Dessert	Plant centre	G. Hundley
B883	Dessert	3 sprays of leaves and berries	E. Johnson
B890	Dessert	Group wild flowers and bird on raised enamel	Hundley and Hopewell
B892	Dessert	Large painted spray	O. H. Copson
B893	Dessert	Large spray and 1 small spray	Johnson
B895	Dessert	Birds, flies, flowers, views, etc.	O.H.C. (Copson)
B897	Dessert	Large spray, black fruit, etc.	O. H. Copson
B900	Dessert	Japan spray in centre	O. H. Copson
B902	Dessert	Plant centre	W. Marsh
B910	Dessert	Painted wreath, gold grass, butterfly centre	G. Hundley

PATTERN NUMBER	TYPE OF SERVICE AND/OR DATE OF INTRODUCTION	PATTERN	PAINTER
B911	Tea	Bird and spray one side, spray other	J. Hopewell
B913	Dessert	Wistaria, lilies, ferns, passion flowers, roses and orchids in different centres	G. Hundley
B914	Dessert	Landscape and flying birds	O. H. Copson
B915	Dessert	Plant starting from border	W. Marsh
B916	Dessert	Large spray in underglaze colours, cut up with gold	O. H. Copson
B920	Dessert	Bird and spray centre	J. Hopewell
B923	Dessert	Full game centre	J. Bradley
B926	Dessert	Faintly-painted flying storks	O. H. Copson
B928	Dessert	Plant centre	G. Hundley
B931	Dessert	Large painted side spray	F. Roberts
B932	Tea	Full painted game and bird subjects	J. Bradley
B958	Dessert	Large spray painted proper, 2 flies and leaves	J. E. Sherriff
B963	Dessert	Bird and spray centre	J. Hopewell
B966	Dessert	Faintly painted landscape in hard kiln colours, 2 small birds in distance and 2 large birds	O. H. Copson
B967	Dessert	Plant centre	G. Hundley
B973	Dessert	Large bird's nest and 1 bird	J. Bradley
B983	Dessert	Fish and seaweed	J. Bradley
B985	Dessert	Flies and flowers proper	J. E. Sherriff
B986	Dessert	Japan spray, 2 birds	O. H. Copson
B991	Dessert	Full spray, fruit on enamel painted proper	W. Hawkins
B994	Dessert	Painted exact as B998	F. Roberts
B995	Dessert	Autumnal tints and flies	O. H. Copson
B997	Dessert	Large spray and sprigs of blossoms and leaves	G. Hundley
B998	Dessert	Cluster on one side, painted fly, gold acorns	F. Roberts
B1001	Dessert	Fish and seaweed	Jas. Bradley
B1006	Dessert	Spray in two golds, traced, flowers, flies and insects	J. E. Sherriff
B1009	Dessert	Yellow gold spray cut up, flowers and flies proper	J. E. Sherriff
B1010	Dessert	Flies, gold grass cut up red	G. Hundley
B1011	Dessert	Japan fruit spray raised and chased fruit	O. H. Copson
B1014	Dessert	Wreath of clustered flowers and 1 other	G. Hundley
B1015	Dessert	Wild flowers and ferns one side, 2 flies and foreign birds	J. Hopewell

PATTERN NUMBER	TYPE OF SERVICE AND/OR DATE OF INTRODUCTION	PATTERN	PAINTER
B1016	Dessert	Plant centre, gold grass cut up red	G. Hundley
B1019	Tea	1 large side spray	O. H. Copson
B1020	Dessert	Heath and fern centre	G. Hundley
B1022	Dessert	Large bird's nest, a little gold wheat, small birds	Mr. Baldwyn
B1023	Dessert	Large Japan spray raised and coloured flies	O. H. Copson
B1030	Tea	Fern and butterfly	E. Powell
B1031	Dessert	Wild flower springing from side	Johnson
B1040	Dessert	Yellow goldfish cut up red, seaweed edge	J. Bradley
B1041	Tea	Sprays, raised and chased flies	H. Chair
B1043	Tea	Birds and sprays	J. Hopewell
B1048	Tea	Bird, spray and flies	O. H. Copson
B1050	Dessert	1 double gold feather in green and yellow-gold and 6 scattered feathers	R. T. Rea
B1052	Tea	Leaves, birds, flowers and flies	O. H. Copson
B1056	Dessert	Fruit centre	G. Hundley
B1058	November 1881	Group centre	G. Hundley
B1060	Dessert	Large b. blue spray, cut up gold, flies and flowers in underglaze colours and traced gold	R. T. Rea
B1065	Dessert	1 b. blue leaf, cut up gold, faint heath and ferns	F. Roberts
B1067	Dessert	Plant centre	G. Hundley
B1070	Tea	Spray of flowers, heath etc.	T. Shaw
B1074	Dessert	Yellow goldfish cut up red, green goldfish cut up black, large spray of seaweed proper	J. Bradley
B1076	Tea	Gold sprays cut up red, flowers and 2 flies	J. E. Sherriff
B1077	Tea	Large autumn spray and small spray	C. Johnson
B1079	Dessert	Plant centre	G. Hundley
W1	May 1883	(last B number is 1081)	
W3	Dessert	Japan spray	W. Hawkins
W4	Dessert	Plant centre	G. Hundley
W5	Dessert	Wreath round plate	G. Hundley
W6	Dessert	Bird and spray centre	J. Hopewell
W10	Dessert	Plant centre	G. Hundley
W11	Dessert	Plant centre	G. Hundley
W13	Dessert	Flies and spray at back	J. E. Sherriff
W14	Dessert	Japan bird and spray starting from border	Bott and Baldwyn

PATTERN NUMBER	TYPE OF SERVICE AND/OR DATE OF INTRODUCTION	PATTERN	PAINTER
W15	Dessert	Group centre	G. Hundley
W23	Dessert	Large spray of fruit	Ranford
W24	Dessert	Parrot on spray and sprays	Johnson and Salter
W25	Dessert	Botanical plant from Curtis' Work, name of plant at back of each plate	C. Johnson
W26	Dessert	Large fruit spray and 2 flies	J. E. Sherriff
W27	Dessert	Sprays, grasses, flies in underglaze colours	E. Powell
W29	Tea	2 sprays and 3 flies	J. E. Salter
W32	Tea	Large and small spray	H. Chair
W35	Dessert	Bird and spray centre	J. Hopewell
W37	Dessert	Wild flower plant	Ranford
W39	Tea	Spray of gold cut up and spray of flowers	E. Powell
W69	Dessert	Bird and spray centre	J. Hopewell
W70	Dessert	Plant with heath at back	F. Roberts
W71	Dessert	Plant centre	G. Hundley
W74	Dessert	Japan style sprays	H. Chair
W82	Dessert	Japan sprays	H. Chair
W84	Dessert and Tea	Cluster of flowers and 1 butterfly	G. Hundley
W86	Dessert	Spray and 1 butterfly	J. E. Sherriff
W87	Dessert and Tea	Spray and 2 or 3 butterflies, no painting on tea ware	J. E. Sherriff
W93	Dessert	Worcester bird and spray	Bott and Baldwyn
W96	Dessert	Gold leaves and 2 or 3 flies	J. E. Sherriff
W101	Tea	Sprays cut up and flowers	H. Chair
W102	Tea	Sprays, raised and chased Japan style	H. Chair
W103	Tea	Berries, flowers and 2 flies	R . . . (?Rea)
W108	Dessert	Full centre	G. Hundley
W139	Dessert	Full painted centre subjects after Landseer	J. Bradley
W157	Dessert	Large spray and birds nest, 4 or 5 birds flying, sky red	Bott and Baldwyn
W158	Dessert	Large spray and 4 flies	R. T. Rea
W160	Tea	Leaves and faintly painted heath at back	W. Hawkins
W169	Dessert	Fish part in and part out of water and water plant	E. Salter
W170	Dessert	Large painted spray across printed pattern	G. Hundley
W171	Dessert	Large spray one side and fly the other	W. Ricketts
W176	Dessert	Heath and fern centre	G. Hundley

PATTERN NUMBER	TYPE OF SERVICE AND/OR DATE OF INTRODUCTION	PATTERN	PAINTER
W184	Dessert	Plant centre	G. Hundley
W192	Tea	Japan sprays, stems cut up gold, flowers proper	J. Churchman
W198	Dessert	Game subjects one side	G. Johnson
W202	Dessert	Game subjects one side	G. Johnson
W203	Dessert	Spray of fruit across plate	H. Ranford
W205	Dessert	Large spray of flowers	H. Ranford
W208	Dessert	Plant cluster	C. Johnson
W215	Dessert	Plant centre	G. Hundley
W217	Dessert	Spray of gold, large and small fly proper	J. E. Sherriff
W228	Dessert	Worcester bird spray, 1 bird etc. in each panel and in centre	Baldwyn and Bott
W234	Tea	One large spray and flies	R. R. . . (?Rea)
W239	Messrs. Kittel's order September 1881		
W243	Dessert	Card in centre with view, with spray, celadon ground	J. Bradley
W245	Dessert	Bird and spray centre	J. Hopewell
W253	Dessert	As W243 but on pink ground	J. Bradley
W262	Dessert	Spray of fruit	H. Ranford
W265	Dessert	Spray of fruit, card off centre with view	H. Ranford
W267	Dessert	Large bird and spray, with a view in off-centre circle	G. Johnson
W272	Dessert	Faint seaweed, off-centre card with fish in water	E. Salter
W273	Dessert	Water, seaweed, shells and fish	E. Salter
W274	Dessert	Pale pink ground, off-centre card with landscape, with birds and spray in enamel colour in imitation of oil painting	T. J. Bott
W280	Tea	Leaves, berries, heath and butterfly	F. Roberts
W289	Tea	3 sprays of flowers	T. Shaw
W291	Dessert	Basket pierced gold and colour sprays and fly	H. Ranford
W293	Dessert	Bird and spray panels and centre	T. J. Bott
W294	Dessert and Table	Plant centre to dessert wares	G. Hundley
W295	Dessert	3 panels of Autumn leaves, centre fruit spray	H. Ranford
W296	Table china and Dessert	Plant centre to dessert	G. Hundley

PATTERN NUMBER	TYPE OF SERVICE AND/OR DATE OF INTRODUCTION	PATTERN	PAINTER
W298	Dessert	Bent spray on side	T. Shaw
W302	Tea Tankard	Japan sprays	H. Chair
W304	Tea Tankard	Sprays and grass	T. Shaw
W305	Tea Tankard	Sprays and flies	J. E. Sherriff
W320	Tea	1 large and 2 small African flies	J. E. Sherriff
W322	Dessert	Full centre, subjects after Landseer	J. Bradley
W343	Table china and Dessert	Group centre to dessert	G. Hundley
W346	Dessert	Plant centre	G. Hundley
W347	Tea Tankard and Dessert	Group centre to dessert	F. Waldron
W353	Dessert	Plant centre	G. Hundley
W372	Dessert	Wreath running round plate	E. Raby
W374	Tea	3 sprays of heath	F. Waldron
W388	Dessert	Full centre, beautifu leaves, begonia etc.	F. Roberts
W393	Dessert	Large cluster of leaves and berries, fly and heath	F. Roberts
W395	Dessert	Large spray	W. Hawkins
W397	Dessert	Bird and spray	J. Hopewell
W401	Dessert	Bird and spray	J. Hopewell
W453	Dessert	Spray in white and gold	J. Bradley
W455	Coffee Tankard	Painted birds and sky	Bott
W466	Tea Tankard	Painted spray and fly in each panel	H. Ranford
W470	Tea	Sprays and berries	R. T. Rea
W479	Dessert	Painted spray at back of circle by 5 inch circle subject etched in brown after Birkett Foster	E. Salter
W480	Dessert	Spray at back of scroll on celadon ground	H. Ranford
		scroll with painted head	F. Sutton
W484	Dessert	Plant centre	C. Johnson
W485	Dessert	4-inch white centre faintly etched landscape, spray and sprig at side	Ricketts
W487	Dessert	4 or 5 birds and sprays etched	C. Baldwyn
W489	Dessert	4-inch circle one side of plate marine subject etched in brown, 4 fishes and seaweed all over	E. Salter
W493	Dessert	Small fern plant, 2 small flies in centre	W. Band
W494	Dessert canvas embossed	Canvas tinted and large spray of fruit	W. Hawkins

PATTERN NUMBER	TYPE OF SERVICE AND/OR DATE OF INTRODUCTION	PATTERN	PAINTER
W496	Dessert seconds	Fern and 2 small flies	W. Band
W497	Dessert canvas	1 large fish, seaweed at back	E. Salter
W499	Dessert	Landscape after Birkett Foster etched in proper colours	C. Baldwyn
W500	Dessert	Blossom spray across centre	E. Raby
W503	Dessert	Sprays crossing	G. Hundley
W505	Tea fluted	Worcester birds etc. fly in saucer	T. J. Bott
W522	Dessert	Gold sprays cut up, 10 small birds painted	E. Salter
W523	Dessert	Landscape, several small birds, gold grass	E. Salter
W527	Dessert	Green bronze leaves, 2 butterflies	E. Powell
W531	Tea	Sprays, green bronze and traced gold	H. Chair
W537	Dessert	3 coloured flies	J. E. Sherriff
W545	Dessert	Etched wreath and 17 small birds around border, centre with moon and cloud scene, black spray and bat	C. Baldwyn
W548	Dessert	Slight bird and spray centre, one fire	J. Hopewell
W551	Dessert	Group centre	G. Hundley
W559	Dessert Parian	Spray of gold, 3 flies and flowers	J. E. Sherriff
W561	Dessert	Plant or spray centre	G. Hundley
W562	Dessert	Bird and spray centre, one fire	J. Hopewell
W566	Tea	Sprays of flowers and heath	T. Shaw
W567	Dessert	Japan plant in centre	H. Ranford
W568	Table china and Dessert	Plant centre to dessert	G. Hundley
W570	Dessert	Large bent spray	T. Shaw
W578	Dessert	Group centre	G. Hundley
W584	Dessert	Bird and spray centre, one fire	J. Hopewell
W601	Dessert	Painted water all over, open shell with seaweed in hard kiln colours, seaweed in the shell one side, printed gold net on other side	T. J. Bott
W603	Dessert	Japan spray and bird in ground on one side	T. J. Bott
W605	Dessert	Fruit centre	H. Ranford

PATTERN NUMBER	TYPE OF SERVICE AND/OR DATE OF INTRODUCTION	PATTERN	PAINTER
W617	Table china	Gamebird on spray	G. Johnson
W623	Dessert	Painted bird and spray	E. Salter
W628	Table china and Dessert	Australian centre	G. Hundley
W630	Dessert	Bird and spray, Autumn leaves and berries	T. J. Bott
W643	Dessert	Cluster of flowers, grass and sprigs	T. Shaw
W659	Tea Tankard	Birds, bronze leaves	T. J. Bott
W660	Dessert	Large bent spray	T. Shaw
W662	Dessert	Large bird and spray	T. J. Bott
W664	Dessert	Large spray, green and brown bronze	H. Chair
W665	Dessert	Full heath and fern centre	G. Hundley
W667	Dessert	Plant centre	H. Ranford
W668	Dessert	Bent spray of heath	T. Shaw
W669	Dessert	Full plant centre	H. Ranford
W670	Dessert	Gamebird and spray	G. Johnson
W671	Dessert	Bird and spray, gold and bronze grass	J. Hopewell
W672	Dessert	Water, 1 large and 2 small fish and seaweed	E. Salter
W673	Dessert	Large plant and flowers	W. Hawkins
W675	Dessert and Tea	Flowers and leaves	G. Hundley
W677	Dessert	Heath and fern centre	G. Hundley
W678	Dessert	Heath plant	T. Shaw
W681	Dessert	Spray one side plate	T. Shaw
W682	Dessert	Australian centre	G. Hundley
W687	Dessert	1 large and several small birds flying	G. Johnson
W693	Dessert and Tea lobed	Stone ground, Japanese centre, moon in white, large and small birds	C. Baldwyn
W699	Dessert	Full heath and fern centre	G. Hundley
W708	Table Crown and Dessert and Tea Tankard	Flies and flowers	E. Powell
W709	Dessert	2 flies and flowers	R. T. Rea
W710	Tea	Sprays	H. Chair
W713	Tea, Apple Blossom handle	Apple blossom and leaves	W. Bevan
W714	Tea, Rosebud handle	Rosebud and leaves	W. Bevan
W726	Dessert	Full spray centre	H. Ranford
W728	Dessert	Heath plant	G. Hundley
W732	Tea Tankard	Sprays of heath	T. Shaw
W735	Dessert	Sprays	T. Shaw
W736	Dessert	Spray and 2 flies	R. T. Rea
W749	Dessert	Plant centre	G. Hundley
W750	Dessert	Plant centre	G. Hundley

PATTERN NUMBER	TYPE OF SERVICE AND/OR DATE OF INTRODUCTION	PATTERN	PAINTER
W756	Dessert	Leaves, 3 flies in bronze gold and colour	R. T. Rea
W757	Dessert	Pencilled ivory, fruit and flowers	W. Hawkins
W758	Dessert	Large spray of flowers in centre	H. Ranford
W759	Dessert	Gold grass, flowers and 2 flies	R. T. Rea
W763	Dessert	Flowers and 1 large fly	J. E. Sherriff
W764	Dessert and Tea	Bird and spray centre	T. J. Bott
W780	Tea	Large spray in sombre colours	W. Hawkins
W790	Dessert	Water, seaweed, small fish	E. Salter
W800	Tea Blackberry embossed	Tinted flowers	W. Hawkins
W802	Tea Blackberry embossed	Coloured spray	W. Hawkins
W804	Tea Blackberry embossed	Coloured spray	W. Hawkins
W822	Dessert	Water, open shell and seaweed	T. J. Bott
W823	Dessert	Game hunting scenes	G. Johnson
W835	Dessert	1 large spray	H. Chair
W836	Dessert	Large and small spray, 2 butterflies and fly	E. Powell
W856	Tea	Large spray	T. Shaw
W866	Dessert and Tea	Sprays	H. Chair
W880	Dessert	Semicircular spray	T. Shaw
W881	Dessert	Heath and fern centre	G. Hundley
W910	Dessert	Large spray of chrysanthemums	H. Ranford
W919	Dessert	Landscape and game centre as W202	G. Johnson
W920	Dessert	Plant centre	G. Hundley
W925	Table china	Game and landscape in centre	G. Johnson
W928	Tea	Fancy birds in 4 panels	T. J. Bott
W932	Dessert and coffee	9 sprays form the word 'Atalanta', seascape in centre	J. Bradley
W935	Dessert	Several birds, landscape and sky	G. Johnson
W943	Dessert	Figure in centre painted in rose pompadour	F. Sutton
W944	Dessert	Landscape and a number of small gamebirds	G. Johnson
W947	Dessert	Bird and spray centre, one fire	J. Hopewell
W948	Dessert	Heath (Plant) centre	G. Hundley
W950	Dessert	Cluster of flowers (French style)	H. Ranford

PATTERN NUMBER	TYPE OF SERVICE AND/OR DATE OF INTRODUCTION	PATTERN	PAINTER
W951	Dessert	Large chrysanthemum spray	H. Ranford
W952	Dessert	1 spray	T. Shaw
W955	Dessert	Painted fish and seaweed in centre	E. Salter
W956	Dessert and Tea	Turquoise birds	E. Salter
W957	Dessert and Tea	Small birds in turquoise	E. Salter
W959	Dessert	2 large birds in metals and gold flowers	T. J. Bott
W967	Dessert	Spray and berries	W. Hawkins
W983	Tea	7 small turquoise birds, raised and chased grass	E. Salter
W984	Dessert	Modelled enamelled spray	W. Hawkins
W996	Dessert	Spray and 3 flies	E. Powell
W998	Dessert	Full landscape with female and swan	A. Handley
W1008	Coffee	Gold and colour sprays and painted flies	J. E. Sherriff
W1012	Dessert	Plant centre	G. Hundley
W1018	Dessert	Bird and spray centre	J. Hopewell
W1023	Dessert	Large spray stencilled	G. Hundley
W1035	Dessert	Spray in dry colours cut up gold, 1 bird in metals	T. J. Bott
W1044	Dessert	1 double, 3 single shells, fish and seaweed	E. Salter
W1045	Dessert	Landscape and a number of small gamebirds	G. Johnson
W1079	Dessert	Heath and fern centre	G. Hundley
W1080	Dessert	Heath and fern centre	G. Hundley
W1081	Dessert	One fire bird centre	J. Hopewell
W1092	Dessert	2 large birds in metals and flowers	T. J. Bott
W1099	Dessert	Bronze and gold sprays, flowers proper	W. Hawkins
W1105	Dessert	Spray cut up gold, 2 birds in metal	T. J. Bott
W1122	Tea croquet	2 sprays on cup, 3 on saucer	W. Band
W1124	Dessert	1 large and 2 small sprays	T. Shaw
W1132	Dessert	Plant centre	W. Ricketts
W1136	Dessert	Raised and chased flowers and 2 flies	T. Shaw
W1139	Dessert	Large Cinerarre spray, or other spray if ordered	W. Hawkins
W1146	Coffee	Landscape and gamebirds	G. Johnson
W1153	Tea	Spray and bird and 2 flies painted in purple	J. Hopewell
W1171	Dessert	2 large fishes and seaweed slated out and painted	E. Salter
W1173	Dessert and Tea	Spray or cluster one side, spray opposite	W. Hundley

PATTERN NUMBER	TYPE OF SERVICE AND/OR DATE OF INTRODUCTION	PATTERN	PAINTER
W1180	Dessert and Tea	1 large fish and water in dessert, no painting on tea	E. Salter
W1184	Dessert	2 birds, 4 flies and wreath, birds and landscape centre	T. J. Bott
W1187	Dessert	Large spray, raised and chased flowers	H. Chair
W1199	Tea Tankard	1 large and 1 small spray	P. Graves
W1202	Tea	1 large and 1 small spray Japan style	H. Chair
W1206	Dessert	Spray of raised and chased natural grasses	E. Powell
W1207	Dessert and Tea	Bent spray raised and chased grass	E. Powell
W1208	Dessert	Sprays of raised and chased natural grasses	E. Powell
W1223	Dessert	Plant across centre from Miss B.'s drawing	W. Hundley
W1241	Dessert	Plant centre	T. Shaw
W1244	Tea Tankard and Dessert	Bird and sprays (+3 flies on dessert)	J. Hopewell
W1250	Tea	Large and small spray and 1 bird in turquoise cut up blue	J. Hopewell
W1253	Dessert (seconds)	Slight centre	F. Waldron
W1263	Dessert	Cluster of flowers	G. Hundley
W1268	Dessert	Raised and chased gold grass, 3 coloured flies	E. Powell
W1269	Dessert	Celadon ground, bent spray, leaves gold, flowers proper	G. Hundley
W1276	Dessert	Gamebird, and landscape in centre	G. Johnson
W1277	Dessert and Tea	Large and small pink spray	H. Chair
W1281	Dessert	Large spray, green bronze leaves	H. Chair
W1285	Dessert	2 large and 2 small fish in metals, seaweed and water	E. Salter
W1292	Dessert	Cluster of roses or other flowers	E. Raby
W1293	Dessert	Chrysanthemum printed in brown, painted in hard kiln colours	W. Hawkins
W1295	Dessert	Chrysanthemum printed in brown, painted in hard kiln colours	W. Hawkins
W1298	Tea	Large plant spray	W. Hundley
W1300	Tea	Green and yellow gold-fish cut up, seaweed and water	E. Salter
W1301	Tea	Cluster and spray	F. Waldron
W1314	Dessert	Full heath centre	G. Hundley
W1317	Tea Tankard	Spray, faint heath and ivy	T. Shaw

PATTERN NUMBER	TYPE OF SERVICE AND/OR DATE OF INTRODUCTION	PATTERN	PAINTER
W1330	Dessert	Small gamebirds, landscape and sky	G. Johnson
W1334	Dessert	Bent cluster of roses or other flowers	E. J. Raby
W1347	Dessert	2 birds in metals cut up colour	T. J. Bott
W1357	Dessert	Slight bird and spray centre	J. Hopewell
W1363	Dessert	Plant centre	G. Hundley
W1364	Dessert	Spray, shining flowers, bird in metals cut up colours	T. J. Bott
W1366	Tea	Large and small spray	T. Shaw
W1371	Dessert	Bent spray, flowers proper	R. T. Rea
W1372	Dessert	2 birds and spray	J. Hopewell
W1373	Dessert	5 b. blue panels with flies, groups and bird painted old Worcester style	T. J. Bott
W1381	Dessert	Flowers and sprays	W. Hawkins
W1382	Dessert	Small game, several birds, landscape and sky	G. Johnson
W1388	Dessert	Fish and weed in various metals and a little water	E. Salter
W1392	Dessert	2 gamebirds and landscape	G. Johnson
W1424	Table china and Dessert	Roses on ivory ground	W. Hawkins
W1428	Table Gadroon—1884 China	Dresden flower style	H. Chair
W1431	Tea	Spray	H. Chair
W1444	Dessert	Ivory ground, spiral spray	W. Booth
W1449	Dessert	Celadon ground, raised and chased flowers and fly	T. Shaw
W1462	Dessert	Large spray fruit, leaves gold	W. Hawkins
W1472	Dessert	4 or 5 fish in metals, cut up colours, weed and water	E. Salter
W1503	Dessert	Faint landscape, 2 large and 2 small birds in metals	T. J. Bott
W1504	Dessert	Seascape centre painted	J. Bradley
W1505	Dessert	Spray in green and yellow and gold	E. Powell
W1506	Dessert	Gold ferns, 3 metallic flies cut up black	E. Powell
W1509	Dessert	Full centre mohair ferns, 3 flies in metals	E. Powell
W1517	Dessert	Leaves and flowers, autumnal tints	W. Ricketts
W1523	Coffee	Ivory ground, large and small spray and 3 flies	R. T. Rea
W1533	Dessert seconds	Spray one side, sprig the other	G. Hundley

PATTERN NUMBER	TYPE OF SERVICE AND/OR DATE OF INTRODUCTION	PATTERN	PAINTER
W1563	Dessert	Gold spray, painted bird	Osbourne
W1564	Dessert	Spray in pink and bird painting in a card	Osbourne
W1565	Dessert	White panel, birds in metals, spray in dry colours	T. J. Bott
W1566	Dessert	White panel, sea views and landscape, 12 or 13 birds on surrounding diaper ground	J. Bradley
W1588	Tea	1 spray in cup	W. Hawkins
W1608	Dessert	Painted fish and seaweed and water	E. Salter
W1609	Dessert	12 subjects printed in brown, fish and seaweed, filled in	F. Williams
W1610	Dessert	Large spray flowers proper, pale gold spray	H. Chair
W1623	Tea Tankard	Large and small spray in turquoise, bird and fly in purple	J. Hopewell
W1629	Dessert	Large bent spray, gold leaves cut up red	G. Hundley
W1645	Dessert	Spray with bird and nest	Osbourne
W1649	Dessert	Sprays autumnal tints	W. Hawkins
W1652	Dessert	Bent group of chrysanthemums	E. Raby
W1654	Dessert	Metal spray 2 birds and flowers	E. Salter
W1655	Dessert	Spray of leaves, autumnal tints	W. Hawkins
W1657	Dessert	Large spray flowers, modelled yellow gold leaves	G. Hundley
W1663	Dessert	Large spray from edge	J. Lewis
W1664	Dessert	Painted fruit	E. Raby
W1668	Dessert	Spray of roses	W. Hawkins
W1670	Dessert	Fruit spray printed in carmine by Litho process (1st noting)	Coloured by the Boys
W1681	Tea	Spray on enamel, flowers proper	G. Hundley
W1691	Dessert	Bird nest centre	E. Raby
W1692	Dessert	Spray of roses in centre	E. Raby
W1695	Tea	Embossed geranium leaves and heath coloured proper	W. Hawkins
W1723	Table Crown	Bird centre	J. Hopewell
W1729	Dessert seconds	Spray or cluster	W. Hundley
W1730	Dessert	Slight bird centre, one fire	J. Hopewell
W1733	Dessert	Fish and water centre	E. Salter
W1734	Dessert	2 birds and spray	J. Hopewell

PATTERN NUMBER	TYPE OF SERVICE AND/OR DATE OF INTRODUCTION	PATTERN	PAINTER
W1738	Dessert	Chrysanthemum centre	E. Raby
W1764	Tea	Pansies, carnations and wistaria in varied colours	F. Waldron
W1755	Tea Butterfly handle	Ferns varied and fly	J. Hopewell
W1770	Dessert	Fish and water, bronze seaweed	W. Williams
W1774	Dessert	Fish, seaweed and a little water	E. Salter
W1778	Dessert	Diaper ground, 1 large 2 small birds, gold clouds	C. Baldwyn
W1780	Tea	Spray of roses, metallic leaves	W. Hawkins
W1797	Dessert	Painted chrysanthemum	E. Raby
W1801	Dessert	Autumnal spray	W. Hawkins
W1808	Coffee Tankard	Large and small spray chrysanthemum	E. Raby
W1812	Coffee	Spray cut up gold and 2 birds in metals	T. J. Bott
W1852	Table china	Large and small spray, all white, gold leaves	H. Chair
W1867	Dessert	Spray on straw ground	E. Raby
W1868	Dessert	Spray on ivory ground	H. Williams
W1871	Table china	Spray on ivory rim	E. Raby
W1884	Coffee	Spray	W. Bevan
W1900	Dessert seconds	Cheap bird and spray in centre	J. Hopewell
W1902	Dessert	Rifle Regiment Crest, spray in centre	W. Hawkins
W1905	Dessert	Orchids on straw ground	E. Raby
W1923	Dessert	Slight bird and spray	J. Hopewell
W1950	Dessert	Painted kitten in centre	J. Bradley
W1952	Dessert	One fire bird centre	J. Hopewell
W1953	Dessert	Spray and 2 birds, renascent style [*sic*]	T. J. Bott
W1956	Dessert and Tea	Side group	G. Hundley
W1958	Dessert	Cluster of flowers	G. Hundley
W1966	Table china	Large spray flowers on enamel	W. Ricketts
W1973	Dessert	Cluster of flowers, autumnal leaves	G. Hundley
W1988	Coffee	Moonlight subjects in dry colours, 2 small birds	E. Salter
W1989	Dessert	2 birds painted in dry colours	T. J. Bott
W1992	Dessert	Slight bird and spray centre	J. Hopewell
W1994	Tea Tankard	Large Japan spray	H. Chair
W1995	Tea Medium	2 Japan sprays	H. Chair
W2009	Tea Tankard	Mohair fern, 3 Mayflies	R. T. Rea

134.   An old photograph showing 11 typical shapes painted by John Stinton in the early years of this century. See page 109.

135.   Three fine vases painted by Harry Davis with scenes in the style of Claude. The pair of vases, shape 2340, have rich blue ground; the centre vase, shape 2354, has green ground. See page 88.

136. Vases painted by Harry Davis, showing his great range of styles. Above, left, pair of vases, shape 2452 (lacking covers), Claude type subject with turquoise ground, date 1920; right, 2151, red and gold mounts, painted in 1903. Below, left, pair of vases, shape H313, typical Highland Sheep subjects in 1921, gilding by Henry Bright; right, shape 1410, stained ivory mounts, English style landscape.

137.   Vases painted by Harry Davis in the French style of Corot and a
pair painted with Polar Bear subjects on an ice-cold matt blue ground
lay. Above, left to right, shapes 2098, 2128 (both turquoise ground
painted in 1900); pair of ewers, 2115, blue ground, painted in 1903.
Below, pair of vases, 1764 (lack covers) in 1903, and 2194 blue
ground, year 1901. See page 88.

138. Finely-pierced vases by George Owen, all signed. Shown at right is a photograph showing George reticulating the large vase shown above. The vessels below, left, are painted with flowers. See page 31.

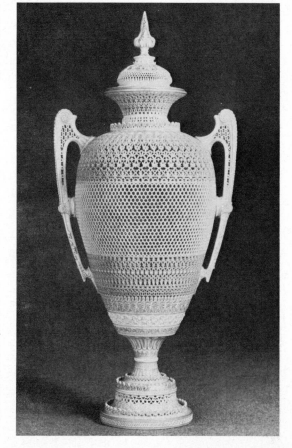

139. Fantastic pierced vase by George Owen (signed G. Owen in the paste under the foot), shape 1481, richly perforated with some 5350 holes, decorated pencilled ivory and pale turquoise with rich filigree gilding, made in 1892 and exhibited at the Chicago World Fair in 1893, height 7 inches. This is probably one of the most difficult ceramic items ever made. See page 31.

140. Old photograph of a fine vase, shape 2354, painted still life by William Hawkins in finely chased gold panel with raised gold design, height 15 inches. See page 47.

141. Old photograph of group of vases decorated with gold conventional designs of the period 1914–18, on powder blue and maroon grounds. Above, left to right, shapes 2576, 2671 and 2472. Centre, 2572, 628, 2476, 2670. Below, 2573. Heights from $5\frac{3}{4}$ inches to $9\frac{1}{2}$ inches. See page 41.

142. Five figures of the 1920s and 30s, the outside ones being in crownware, left 2481, right CW151. Centre, left to right, 3030, 2693 and 2689. The crownware is in blue and gold. See page 48.

143. Group of rare pieces of the 1920s and 30s. Above, left to right, 2612, 3204, 2623. Below, 3127, 2605, 2983.

144. A range of figures. Above, left to right, 2908, 2907 (the latter in biscuit has been inaccurately coloured) and 3620. Below, 2645, 2646 (khaki colours) and 2917 (height $6\frac{1}{4}$ inches in crownware). These figures are often found just in the white.

145. Vase and cover, shape CW292, printed and painted under-glaze, lustred and glazed over-glaze, made in 1924 in crownware, 11 inches high. Crownware mark. See page 48.

146. Worcester coffee set of Mocha shape, in fitted box with Birmingham-made silver gilt spoons; painted Highland Cattle subjects by Harry Stinton. *Collection of Mrs. D. Howell.* See page 40.

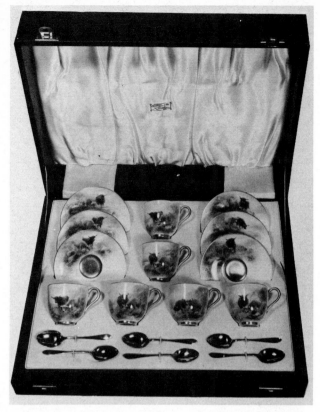

147. Fine water colour by Harry Stinton, showing his superb drawing technique and highly developed sense of perspective. One peculiar feature of the Highland Cattle painted by John and Harry Stinton is that the beasts' feet are never shown but are always hidden in the water or grass. *Private collection.* See page 47.

148. Six Worcester painters. Above, left to right, by Miss M. Eaton on Hadley F106B/78–53; spill, shape G923, painted blackberries by Miss K. Blake; cabinet cup, painted fruit by F. Parker, shape 2115; vase painted by E. Barker. Below, left, plate painted by R. H. Austin; right, plate by George Johnson in 1901.

149. Photograph of the Men Painters department, plus a few paintresses, taken in 1928. Left to right: back row, in doorway T. Lockyer, A. Shuck, H. Price, R. Austin, W. Bee, J. Stanley, H. Ayrton; second row, C. Creese, H. Everett, Wm. Powell, E. Sharples, W. Long, J. Freeman, A. Halford, E. Barker, R. Rushton, G. Mosley, W. Bagnall, E. Townsend, H. Davis, W. H. Austin, H. Stinton, James Stinton, E. Spilsbury, J. Hendry, W. Sedgley; front row, seated, Kitty Blake, R. Sebright, E. Phillips, W. Ricketts, W. Hawkins, G. Johnson, John Stinton, W. Hale, Millie Hunt.

150. Two toby jugs and covers. Left, 2856, yellow, black, red and gold, date mark for 1931, 6½ inches; right, 2850, red, black, and green, date mark for 1929, 7 inches. *Private collection.*

151. Models by Gwendoline Parnell of the early 1930s. Above, left to right, 3111, 'The Masque'; 3154, 'The Drummer'; 3108, Amaryllis. Below 3138, 'The Planter's Daughter', height 7¼ inches.

152. Models by Gwendoline Parnell of the early 1930s. A pair of limited edition statuettes of King George V and Queen Mary, shapes 3089–90, height 9 inches. Left, 'Good luck to your fishing' or 'Cupid Kneeling', shape 3095, 5¼ inches; centre, 'Spring', 3342, painted by Miss M. Fildes, and loaned by her. See page 54.

153. Two models by Geraldine Blake of the early 1930s. Left, 'Banbury Cross', 3165, 8 inches; right, 'The Highwayman', 3166.

154. Pair of Bluebeard and Fatima, shapes 2903 and 2904, 10¼ inches and 10 inches, modelled by Sybil Williams and Jessamine Bray, bold enamel colours. See page 52.

155. Beautiful and fairly rare group of Giraffes, shape 2895, modelled by Stella Crofts, decorator's mark, GE for George Evans, made in 1931, Height 8 inches. See page 52.

156. Three curiously beautiful and rare figures of the early 1930s. Left to right, 'Pierrot', one of pair of bookends modelled by Doris Lindner, shape 2867, height $8\frac{1}{2}$ inches; 'Lute Player', of the 'Longie' figures, shape 2899 (the others in the series being 2898, 2901 and 2902), modelled by Ethelwyn Baker; Horse by Eric Aumonier, shape 2877. See page 52.

157. An old photograph showing shape 2899 set up as a lamp, early 1930s. These lamps were specially designed using Worcester figures, by Charles Selz of New Cavendish Street, London. See page 52.

158. Group of commemorative pieces. Above, left to right, limited edition porcelain mug for the Investiture of the Prince of Wales in 1969; plaque for Edward VII's Coronation; crown top pot pourri, shape 2516, b. blue ground, painted with Windsor Castle by R. Rushton in 1911, height 6 inches. Below, mask jug transfer printed in Dr. Wall period style for Coronation of Queen Elizabeth in 1953; plaque for Coronation of King George VI modelled by R. Garbe; beaker, shape 1205, for Golden Jubilee of Queen Victoria in 1887 and plaque for Coronation of George V in 1911.

159. Commemorative plates. Above, left to right, Beauchamp Mayoral plate of 1896; Shakespeare Quater-centenary; West Indies Cricket Tourists of 1962. Below, Emmanuel Thomas, Mayoral plate of 1911; Walter Holland, Mayoral plate of 1887; Baden Powell Relief of Mafeking in 1900; Dr. Wall and scenes of Worcester in 1909. The Mayoral and Dr. Wall commemorative plates are very common ones. The Emmanuel Thomas plates were made in a total of 8,350, supplied at a cost of £22-16-8d per 1,000. See page 75.

160. A duplicate of the fantastic pair of miniature hexagonal vases and covers made for Queen Mary's doll's house, with hand-painted underglaze blue scales and 'fabulous' birds in the Dr. Wall style by George Johnson, beautifully gilded and yet only $1\frac{3}{10}$ inches, high, shown against the point of an ordinary size pencil. See page 50.

161. Reproduction of old Worcester shapes and patterns. Above, left to right, pattern W5752, b. blue border, flowers and landscapes in turquoise panel; pattern W5321, green borders, painted flowers, gilder's mark PE; 'dry blue' flowers and gilding; shape 2126 in Flight Barr & Barr Style, b. blue ground, pearls and gold snake handles, painted fabulous birds; plate in Dr. Wall style, scale blue ground and painted fabulous birds. See page 50.

162. Frederick Gertner modelling one of the Papal Guard series, the Trooper of the Papal Swiss Guard, a limited edition subject, height 15 inches, shape 3580. See page 40.

163. One of the historical uniform series modelled by Frederick Gertner, Officer of the 29th Foot, the Worcestershire Regiment c. 1812 period, height 12 inches, first made in 1954 and still in production, shape 3535.

PATTERN NUMBER	TYPE OF SERVICE AND/OR DATE OF INTRODUCTION	PATTERN	PAINTER
W2017	Tea Medium	Straw ground, 2 birds painted and flowers, leaves in metals cut up colours	T. J. Bott
W2021	Dessert	Landscape, swans, water etc. on lower part of centre	E. Salter
W2046	Dessert	Spray and moss, autumnal tints	G. Hundley
W2056	Dessert	Side group, autumnal colours	G. Hundley
W2063	Tea	Roses	T. Shaw
W2064	Dessert	Figure head centre	F. Sutton
W2078	Dessert	Large spray one side	W. Ricketts
W2096	Dessert	Fish, seaweed and water	E. Salter
W2106	Dessert seconds	Slight bird and spray centre	J. Hopewell
W2108	Tea	Red sun, teazles and birds	J. Bradley
W2113	Dessert	Ruff and sun, spray other side	C. Baldwyn
W2114	Dessert	Gamebird and faint landscape from drawings by Thorpe	G. Johnson
W2116	Coffee Tankard	New owl decoration	T. J. Bott
W2124	Dessert	Shells, fish, seaweed and water	E. Salter
W2135	Dessert	Shells, fish, seaweed and water	E. Salter
W2137	Dessert seconds	Printed in carmine, filled in regular colours	W. Hawkins
W2142	Tea	Flower sprays	W. Hawkins
W2157	Dessert	Semicircular spray	F. Waldron
W2160	Tea	Frog and mice in dry colours cut up gold	G. Johnson
W2161	Tea	Frog and flies in dry colours cut up gold	G. Johnson
W2181	Tea	3 fruit and flower panels in saucer	E. Raby
		Wreaths on saucer	H. Williams
		Cupid and clouds in panel on cup	F. Sutton
W2186	Tea	Mohair ferns, neutra at back	W. Ricketts
W2194	Tea	Owls and moonlight scene, 1 bird on other side	G. Johnson
W2197	Dessert	Bird and spray centre and gold grass	J. Hopewell
W2203	*Tea—Mortlocks Old Worcester shape. Order for Standish 1886*		
		2 groups and sprig, wreath in cup	W. Waldron
W2210	Tea	Geranium leaves, green and brown bronze leaves	W. Hawkins
W2244	Dessert	One fire bird centre	J. Hopewell

M

PATTERN NUMBER	TYPE OF SERVICE AND/OR DATE OF INTRODUCTION	PATTERN	PAINTER
W2247	Coffee	Wreath of roses	Waldron
W2258	Tea Tankard	2 sprays	W. Ricketts
W2269	Dessert	Shell fish and water	E. Salter
W2281	Dessert	Frog playing violin and leaves	G. Johnson
W2331	Dessert	Floral centre varied	E. Raby
W2356	Dessert	2 birds and spray	J. Bradley
W2364	Dessert	Bent spray round centre	R. T. Rea
W2365	Dessert	Fish water and seaweed	F. Williams
W2394	Dessert	Dry colour spray	J. Lewis
W2460	Dessert	Chrysanthemum spray in brown filled in	W. Hawkins
W2461	Dessert	2 sprays of leaves	W. Hawkins
W2464	Dessert	Fish centre	E. Salter
W2465	Dessert	1 large 1 small fish, seaweed and water	E. Salter
W2467	Dessert	Rich fish centre in metals etc.	E. Salter
W2468	Dessert	Fish, weed and water	E. Salter
W2469	Dessert	Marine subject	E. Salter
W2470	Dessert	Fish, seaweed and water	E. Salter
W2471	Dessert	Fish centre	E. Salter
W2520	Tea Duke	Maroon ground, wheat, barley, oats etc. in gold and bronze	W. Hawkins
W2541	Tea Medium	3 sprays of flowers, 3 sprays of grasses	G. Hundley
W2571	Dessert	Group, autumnal tints	W. Ricketts
W2579	Dessert	Mohair fern dry colours, cut up raised gold	J. Lewis
W2591	Dessert	Spray dry colours, cut up raised gold	J. Lewis
W2635	Tea Ho	Varied sprays, cut up raised gold	J. Lewis
W2639	Dessert and Tea	Raised and chased mohair fern and mayflies	R. T. Rea
W2648	*1887*		
W2652	Coffee	Bronze leaves, modelled sprays in old metals	W. Buckingham
W2653	Coffee	Sprays in underglaze colours	W. Hawkins
W2655	Coffee	2 sprays in underglaze colours	W. Hawkins
W2656	Coffee	2 sprays in underglaze colours	W. Hawkins
W2678	Coffee	Roses	H. Chair
W2695	Table china	Canton spray, filled in flat wash of red	W. Hawkins
W2739	Dessert	Heath and fern centre	G. Hundley
W2749	Dessert	Spray and landscape in dry blue	F. Waldron

PATTERN NUMBER	TYPE OF SERVICE AND/OR DATE OF INTRODUCTION	PATTERN	PAINTER
W2758	Tea Randolph	Sprays	H. Chair
W2778	Dessert	Sombre spray in panels, raised gold	Hale
W2792	Dessert	Mohair fern in gold, 2 flies in metal	R. T. Rea
W2836	Dessert	Flower panels and centre	E. Raby
W2917	Tea Tankard	Cluster of flowers and sprig	G. Hundley
W2920	Coffee	Flowers in underglaze colours, cut up	W. Hawkins
W2929	Dessert	Bent spray	G. Hundley
W2993	Dessert	Australian spray	G. Hundley
W3001	Dessert	Gamebird hard kiln colours and bronze spray	G. Johnson
W3007	*Table China Order for Messrs. Phillips 11th June 1888*		
W3030	Dessert seconds	Bird and spray	J. Hopewell
W3169	Dessert	Varied plants	W. Ricketts
W3294	Dessert and Tea Tankard	Printed chrysanthemum sprays filled in and shaded	H. Chair
W3306	Tea Old Worcester low flute	Purple sprays old Worcester style	W. Hawkins
W3313	Dessert	Lamp black printed tinted sombre colours fish	E. Salter
W3316	Dessert	Group and sprigs Dresden style	W. Hawkins
W3360	Dessert Shell	Parian body, cloissoné spray and raised gold	Hale
W3369	Tea Old Worcester flute	Sprays of fruit old Worcester style	W. Hawkins
W3752	Dessert	Spray, spider and web	F. Roberts
W3972	*Service done for Williams, Rochdale—1893*		
W4084	Dessert	Birds-spray and moonlight side of centre	CB (Baldwyn)
W4085	Dessert	Landscape in centre	Baldwyn
W4109	Dessert (Basket pierced) and coffee	Birds and flowers	C. Baldwyn
W4116	Dessert	Bird centre	CB (Baldwyn)
W4162	*Table China 25th October 1893*		
W4213	Dessert	Sprays cut up gold	ER (?Raby)
W4214	Dessert	Spray centre	ER (?Raby)
W4278	Dessert	Fish and landscape	ES (Salter)
W4289	Tea Tankard	Sprays in panel	ER (?Raby)
W4358	Dessert	Group of fruit and flowers	WH (Hawkins)
W4359	Dessert	Wreath	WmB (?Bevan or Briton)
W4760	*Table Vitreous and Tea Crested service for Gurkha Reg. 30th October 1894*		
W4908	Dessert	Prismatic and gilt mounts, birds	CHB (Baldwyn)
W5432	*Coffee Set done for Osler with crest 21st March 1898*		
W5540	Dessert	Bird and spray centre	GJ (?Johnson)

PATTERN NUMBER	TYPE OF SERVICE AND/OR DATE OF INTRODUCTION	PATTERN	PAINTER
W5602	Dessert	Orchids in centre	FR (Roberts)
W6235	Dessert	Cluster of flowers	T. Shaw
W6429	*Set done for Goode & Co. 2nd September 1902*		
W6490	*9th September 1902*		
W6765	*New chromosprays 1903*		
W6893	Dessert	Ruins in panels and centre	J. Stinton
W6977	Dessert	Group of flowers side of centre	RS (?Sebright)
W7087	Dessert	Ruins and landscape centre	H. Davis
W7099	*Set done for show rooms April 1904*		
W7123	Dessert	Hard kiln colours fruit	F. Roberts
W7226	*July 1904*		
W7356	Tea	Pheasant	J. Stinton (i.e. James)
W7711	Dessert	Fruit centre	F. H. Chivers
W7799	Dessert	Marine view	H. Davis
W7804	Dessert	Flowers	W. Hale
W7814	Dessert and Tea	Flowers and background, painted fly	RS (?Sebright & RR Rushton)
W7890	Dessert	Fruit centre	F. H. Chivers
W7896	Dessert	Fruit centre	F. H. Chivers
W7948	Dessert	Painted fruit centre hard kiln colours	FP (?F. Parker)
W8154	*21st October 1907*		
W8256	Dessert	Full painted cattle centre	J. Stinton (John)
W8276	Dessert	Gamebirds and landscape	G. Johnson
W8377	Dessert	Gamebirds and sky and woodland	Jas. Stinton
W8437	Dessert	Game centre	Jas. Stinton
W8474	Tea	Dog rose and sprig off side	GC (?Cole)
W8500	*April 1909*		
W8540	Dessert	Fruit centre	RS (?Sebright)
W8542	Dessert	Group of flowers in panels and centre	E. Phillips
W8544	Dessert	Full plant and background	EP (?Phillips)
W8557	Dessert	Flower sprays	GC (?Cole)
W8558	Dessert	Fruit and background	RS (?Sebright)
W8572	Ring Ash Tray	Landscape	R. Rushton
W8574	Dessert	Gamebirds and landscapes	J. Stinton
W8598	Dessert	Full centre, game and landscape (also cattle)	J. Stinton
W8670	*October 1909*		
W8676	Dessert	Roses	F. Roberts
W8686	Tea	Crimson Rambler	FR (Roberts)
W8698	Tea	Flowers	FR (Roberts)
W8709	Dessert	Castles	JS (John Stinton)
W8711	Dessert	Cattle	J. Stinton
W8740	Dessert	Spray, old Worcester style	E. Phillips

PATTERN NUMBER	TYPE OF SERVICE AND/OR DATE OF INTRODUCTION	PATTERN	PAINTER
W8762	*14th March 1910*		
W8778	Dessert	Bent spray old Worcester style	E. Phillips
W8793	Dessert	View	R. Rushton
W8860	Dessert	Full fruit centre	R. Sebright
W8972	*August 1910*		
W9052	Table china	Landscape	R. Rushton
W9134	Dessert	Painted fruit	G. H. Cole
W9157	Table china	Rose spray	F. Roberts
W9190	*December 1910*		
W9191	Dessert	Fruit centre	G. Cole
W9254	Table china and Tea	Roses	G. Cole
W9277	Dessert	Stratford views printed in grey, painted by	R. Rushton
W9296	Dessert	Roses and background	F. Roberts
W9303	Dessert	Gamebirds and landscape	JS (Stinton)
W9306	*24th July 1911*		
W9315	Dessert	Game and woodland	J. Stinton (James)
W9331	Mocha	Flowers	G. Cole
W9345	Dessert and Table	Fruit	A. Shuck
W9385	Tea	Roses	H. Austin
W9395	Dessert	Cattle	H. Stinton
W9401	Dessert	Exotic birds	G. Johnson
W9408	Table	Rose groups	G. Cole
W9414	*July 1911*		
W9427	Table	Gamebirds	J. Stinton (Jas.)
W9428	Table	Gamebirds	J. Stinton (Jas.)
W9429	Table	Fish centre	H. Davis
W9437	Mocha	Pigeons	G. Johnson
W9438	Mocha	Swans, bird at back	G. Johnson
W9443	Table	Fish centre	H. Davis
W9444	Dessert	Fish centre and panel	H. Davis
W9445	Table	Game centre	J. Stinton (Jas.)
W9447	Dessert	Flowers	E. Phillips
W9448	Dessert	Game centre	G. Johnson
W9459	Table	3 flower sprays	C. Phillips
W9463	Dessert	Bent spray printed in brown coloured	H. Austin
W9467	Service plate	4 panels of Shakespeare views	R. Rushton
W9479	*October 1911*		
W9494	Dessert	Full cattle centre	J. Stinton (John)
W9495	Dessert	Shakespearean views	R. Rushton
W9511	Dessert	Fruit centre	R. Sebright
W9512	Plate 8 in.	Game centre	Jas. Stinton
W9513	Plate 8 in.	Game centre	J. Stinton
W9515	Plate 8 in.	Fish centre	H. Davis
W9516	Plate 8 in.	Fish centre	H. Davis

PATTERN NUMBER	TYPE OF SERVICE AND/OR DATE OF INTRODUCTION	PATTERN	PAINTER
W9517	Plate 8 in.	Fish centre	H. Davis
W9527	Dessert	Birds nests, all different	F. Roberts
W9531	Dessert	Cattle centre	H. Stinton
W9534	Mocha	Fruit, gold centre	F. Roberts
W9535	Mocha	Fruit, gold centre	F. Roberts
W9536	Mocha	Venetian views	R. Rushton
W9539	Mocha	Raised filigree daisies	L. Burgess
W9542	Tea	Flowers on stained ivory	W. Powell
W9551	Dessert	Fruit and background	H. Martin
W9555	Dessert	Cattle centre	H. Stinton
W9556	Dessert	Fruit centre	R. Sebright
W9557	Dessert	Dresden flower centre	E. Phillips
W9559	Dessert	Landscape	F. Roberts
W9567	Dessert	Moss Rose and background	F. Roberts
W9570	Dessert	Game subject side of plate	J S (Jas. Stinton)
W9571	Dessert	Bird centre	E. Barker
W9572	Plate 8 in.	Duck in centre	J. Stinton (Jas.)
W9573	Dessert	Sundial and birds in centre	E. Barker
W9575	Dessert	Gamebirds and landscape	Jas. Stinton
W9576	Plate 8 in.	Full fish centre	H. Davis
W9577	Dessert	Birds and background	E. Barker
W9578	Dessert	Castle centre	R. Rushton
W9580	Plate 8 in.	Game centre	J. Stinton (Jas.)
W9584	Dessert	Bird and spray and background	E. Barker
W9589	Dessert	Litho spray and fly coloured	W. Ricketts
W9592	Dessert	Litho spray and fly coloured	W. Ricketts
W9594	Dessert	Roses in panels by Phillips landscape centre	R. Rushton
W9598	Dessert	Chamberlain landscape and castle	G. Johnson
W9627	Tea	Birds and landscape in fabulous old Worcester style	G. Johnson
W9628	Tea	Landscapes in panels	R. Rushton
W9630	Tea	Festoons of roses	E. Phillips
W9633	Tea	Landscape	R. Rushton
W9636	Dessert	Fruit centre	R. Sebright
W9639	Dessert	Flamingoes centre	W. Powell
W9645	Dessert	Cattle centre	J. Stinton (John)
W9651	Table	Flower centre and panels	E. Phillips
W9661	Dessert	Landscape centre	R. Rushton
W9664	Dessert	Flamingoes in landscape	W. Powell
W9665	Dessert	Chamberlain landscapes	G. Johnson
W9666	Dessert	Birds in centre	E. Barker

PATTERN NUMBER	TYPE OF SERVICE AND/OR DATE OF INTRODUCTION	PATTERN	PAINTER
W9667	Dessert	Birds in centre	E. Barker
W9668	Dessert	Flower groups old Worcester style	E. Phillips
W9669	Dessert	Venetian grounds	R. Rushton
W9672	Tea	Pigeons	G. Johnson
W9676	Mocha	Violets	W. Hale
W9677	Dessert	Birds and foliage	W. Powell
W9678	Dessert	Flamingoes	W. Powell
W9701	*2nd December 1912*		
W9719	Dessert	Full gamebird centre	W. Powell
W9720	Dessert	Fish centre	H. Austin
W9721	Dessert	Landscape	H. Davis
W9724	Dessert	Bird centre	E. Barker
W9736	Service plate	Flamingo centre	W. Powell
W9749	Table	Landscapes in panels	F. Bray
W9752	Dessert	Cattle centre	Jas. Stinton
W9760	Dessert	Heath flowers	A. Shuck
W9761	Dessert	Waratah flowers	A. Shuck
W9762	Dessert	Flowers	A. Shuck
W9797	Dessert	Fruit in panels	A. Shuck
W9798	Dessert	Fruit in panels	A. Shuck
W9805	Tea	Roses and moss background	H. Martin
W9806	Tea	Roses and moss background	H. Martin
W9821	Table	Shakespearean views new Litho print touched up by hand	R. Rushton
W9831	Service plate	Shakespearean views new Litho print touched up by hand	R. Rushton
W9832	Table	Shakespearean views new Litho print touched up by hand	R. Rushton
W9833	Service plate	Shakespearean views new Litho print touched up by hand	R. Rushton
W9834	Table	Shakespearean views new Litho print touched up by hand	R. Rushton
W9835	Service plate	Shakespearean views new Litho print touched up by hand	R. Rushton
W9855	Nile shape	Flowers	E. Phillips
W9856	Plate 8½ in.	Fruit centre	R. Sebright
W9857	Plate 8½ in.	Fruit centre	R. Sebright
W9872	Dessert	Fruit centre	R. Sebright
W9891	Dessert	Group of flowers with a view	W. Ricketts
W9892	Dessert	View, old style	R. Rushton
W9893	Dessert	Flamingo centre	W. Powell

PATTERN NUMBER	TYPE OF SERVICE AND/OR DATE OF INTRODUCTION	PATTERN	PAINTER
W9896	Table	Tudor cottage	L. Burgess
W9903	Dessert	Bird and spray and sprig other side	W. Hale
W9906	Service plate	1. Claude landscape	H. Davis
		2. Still life subject	W. A. Hawkins
		3. Fruit	R. Sebright
W9912	Dessert	Wreath of wild rose	R. Austin
W9914	Dessert	Birds, spray of fir, background	E. Barker
W9915	Dessert	Flower centre	E. Phillips
W9916	Dessert	Spray across plate	W. Hale
W9918	Mocha	Figure and Italian garden	W. Sedgley
W9919	Mocha	Figure and Italian garden	W. Sedgley
W9930	Dessert	Fruit centre	R. Sebright
W9935	Dessert	Old style fruit centre	R. Sebright
W9936	Dessert	Blackberry spray	W. Hale
W9948	Service plate	Festoons of roses	E. Phillips
W9953	Dessert	View of old style centre	R. Rushton
W9957	Dessert	Roses in centre	A. Shuck
W9958	Dessert	Fruit and moss background	L. Flexman
W9967	Table	Raised gold border by hand	A. Glover
		Castle series centre touched up	R. Rushton
W9978	Table	Fruit centre	R. Sebright
C4	Dessert	Printed spray touched up	J. W. Sedgley
C5	Table	Stratford views	R. Rushton
		Litho touched up	
C8	Dessert	Old Worcester fruit centre	E. Phillips
C9	Dessert	Fish centre	H. Davis
C10	Dessert	Game in centre	J. Stinton (Jas)
C13	*24th June 1913*		
C14	Plate 8 in.	Peacocks and peacock feathers colour and gold work	W. Powell
C17	Mocha	Yacht subjects	R. Rushton
C19	Tea	Flower group old Worcester style	E. Phillips
C22	Dessert	Claude landscape	F. Roberts
C23	Tea	Fruit band round cup and saucer	F. Roberts
C37	Tea	Flowers	E. Phillips
C38	Tea	Fruit old Worcester style	E. Phillips
C39	Dessert	Flowers	E. Phillips
C49	Dessert	Full sheep centre	E. Barker
C55	Dessert and Tea	Full fruit and background	F. Roberts
C57	Tea	Wild rose	R. Austin

Note: From this date it was general for painters to sign and therefore I have not continued the list beyond here.

PATTERN Z160 *Cottages in Worcestershire and Warwickshire.*

Harvington, Ripple, Wick, Mary Arden's House, Elmley Castle, Welford on Avon Little Comberton, Offenham, Cropthorne, Tewkesbury, Anne Hathaway's Cottage Fladbury.

PATTERN Z161 *English Cathedrals.*

Durham, Canterbury, Gloucester, Worcester, Hereford, Ely, Lichfield, Norwich, St. Pauls, Salisbury, York, Wells.

PATTERN Z162 *Castles.*

Windsor, Ostermouth, Warwick, Kenilworth, Raglan, Chepstow, Kilchurn, Pembroke, Barnard, Alnwick, Bothwell, Arundel.

Appendices

List of Shapes and their Numbers from 1862

An * before the shape number means that the shape is a common one, † means very common. A ‡ means that the shape is rare, § extremely rare. Class 1 and Class 2 figures might be called relatively rare, at least, except where noted. Against a number of the shapes from the 1920s are given the names of the modellers. These shape numbers are generally found under the bases, impressed, incised, printed or written. They should not be confused with registered numbers, generally prefixed with R N or some such abbreviation, or pattern numbers on useful wares. Some of the words are spelt in a rather odd way in the records, and where this would cause confusion the spelling has been corrected.

Class 1—Busts

1	Queen Victoria
2	Prince Albert (Modelled by E. J. Jones)
3	Prince Albert (Modelled by E. J. Jones)
4	⎰Lord Palmerston
5	⎱Lord Brougham
6	Sir Walter Scott (Modelled by C. Toft)
7	James Watt
8	Professor Wilson
9	⎰Prince of Wales
10	⎱Princess of Wales
11	Richard Cobden
12	Washington
13	Lincoln
14	Lincoln
15	⎰Charity
16	⎱Hope
17	⎱Faith
18	Charity, half-veiled
19	The Bride, veiled
20	Clytie
21	Sabrina
22	Shakespeare Size 1
23	Shakespeare Size 2
24	Shakespeare Size 3
25	Thomas Moore
26	William Dargan
27	Mozart

28   Beethoven
29   Handel
30   ⎰Ajax
31   ⎱Apollo
32   ⎰Peace
33   ⎱War
34   Clytie—large size
35   Young Augustus
36   General Grant
37   ⎰Summer
38   ⎱Winter
39   Washington 2nd size
40   Bacchante Bust
      Also
      Bishop of Gloucester
      Flora
      Peabody
      ⎰Spring
      ⎱Autumn
      Derby
      Millar
      Titania
      Robert Burns
      General Sir Henry Havelock
      Mr. & Mrs. R. W. Binns
      Locke

Class 2—Statuettes over 8 inches in height

1   Evangeline, reclining
2   Evangeline, as a nun
3   Evangeline and Benedict (her father)
4   Ariadne on rock (modelled by Kirk)
5   Hesione
6   ⎰Charles I
7   ⎱Cromwell
8   Lord Elcho
9   ⎰King Lear
10   ⎱Hotspur
11   The Fop
12   ⎰Comedy
13   ⎱Tragedy
14   Hermione
15   Lady Macbeth
16   Psyche
17   Little Dorrit
18   Boy and Butterfly
19   ⎧Earth
20   ⎪Air
21   ⎪Fire
22   ⎩Water
23   Dr. Hahnemann
24   Polyhymnia
25   Euterpe

26	⌠Isambard Brunel
27	⌡Stephenson
28	⌠Night
29	⌡Morning
30	Volunteer Rifleman
31	⌠Ceres
32	⌡Pomona
33	⌠Spring
34	⌡Autumn
*35	⌠Morning Dew
*36	⌡Evening Dew
37	Christ and Mary
38	Guardian Angel
39	Wounded Soldier
40	⌠Henda and Hafed
41	⟨Romeo and Juliet
42	⌡Faust and Margaret
43	Raphael's Boy on Dolphin
44	Uncle Tom and Eva
45	Britannia
46	Paul and Virginia
47	⌠Peace Blessing the Arts
48	⌡Plenty Bestowing her Gifts
49	⌠Boys and Nest
50	⌡Companion Group
51	⌠Cupid Stealing a Kiss
52	⌡Companion Group
53	⌠Before the Wind
54	⌡Against the Wind
55	Young Hercules and Serpent
56	Sappho
†57	⌠Joy
†58	⌡Sorrow
59	Nymph startled by a viper
60	Cupid, for suspending
61	⌠Music
62	⌡Poetry
63	Shepherd Boy and Dog
64	⌠Paris
65	⌡Venus
66	⌠L'Allegro
67	⌡Il Penseroso
68	Flora
69	⌠Listening Figure
70	⌡Companion
71	Sabrina
72	⌠Ariadne reclining
73	⌡Bacchus reclining
74	⌠Diana
75	⌡Venus
76	Fame

Groups from Midsummer Night's Dream

77	Quince and Flute
78	Bottom and Snout

79   Wall and Bottom
80   Thisbe and Moonshine
81   Egeus and Hermia
82   Theseus and Hippolyta
83   Lysander and Hermia
84   Demetrius and Helena
85   Oberon and Titania
86   Titania and Boy
87   Puck pulling a flower
88   Titania and Bottom
89   A set of Season figures (small)
90   Summer, a floating figure
91   Canova's Venus ⎫ Pair
92   Canova's Venus ⎭
93   Winter ⎫ floating figures, pair
94   Summer ⎭
95   Bacchante
96   Goat
97   ⎰Venus
98   ⎱Iris
99   Fisherwoman
100 Hunter
101 ⎰Skipping Girl
102 ⎱Boy and Ball
103 ⎰Paul
104 ⎱Virginia
106–8 Dancing Bacchante
109 Peace
110 Peace, without wings
‡111 Entomologists
‡112 Entomologists
115 Theodora
†116 ⎰Liberty
†117 ⎱Captivity
118 Skipping male figure with brass rope
121 Dresden flower boy and girl
123 Japanese lady and gentleman
125 New large Grecian Water Carriers (4 sizes)

Class 3—Candlesticks, tapers etc.

1   Renaissance candlestick
2   Dresden candlestick
3   Candelabrum for the Prince service
4   Terminal candlestick—Music and Poetry
5   Female caryatids
6   Male and Female, style of Louis XV (Charles Toft)
7   Boys with branch and companion
8   Fawn terminal candlestick
9   Egyptian candlestick
10   Corinthian candlestick
11   Dolphin candlestick
†12 Tri-dolphin candlestick
13   Boy with torch and companion

XI. Group of vases painted by John, James and Harry Stinton. Top row, from left, shape H179 painted by Harry in 1929, shape 2491 by Harry in 1929 ; pair of Grainger pierced vases painted by James ; bottom row, left, shape 2336, painted by John in 1914, gilding by Henry Bright, height 14 inches ; right, shape H179 painted by John in 1924. (Notice the much more purply effects by Harry).

XII. Worcester china plaque superbly painted with a landscape by Harry Davis. The imaginative use of colour, inspired by French painting, the fine drawing and incredible skill in perspective show why the work of this painter is now so appreciated. Size $5\frac{1}{5}$ x $6\frac{4}{5}$ inches.

14 Embossed candlestick
15 Pillar
16 Griffin taper
17 Foot taper
18 Boy and Drum taper
19 Persian taper
20 Fluted flat candlestick
21 Fluted flat candlestick and shells
22 Small taper, classic ornament
23 Ring-handled taper and extinguisher
24 Boy taper with shell on shoulder
25 Florence taper
26 Duck taper
27 Science plaque, with alto-relievo for 4 lights
28 Truth
29 Pompeian candlestick
30 Louis XVI candlestick
31 Medieval candlestick
32 Grotesque candlestick
33 Plain candlestick on 8 claws
34 Mermaid candlestick
35 Boy and sheet
36 Plume Taper
37 New draped candlestick
39 Grecian candelabrum
40 Japanese juggler candlestick
41 Corinthian candlestick with double branch
42 Two figure candelabrum
43 Set of 3 Japanese candlesticks
44 Figure candelabrum
45 Boy and dolphin candlestick
46 Medieval figure candelabrum

Class 4—Centres, Baskets and Dessert Ornaments

1 Dresden centre
2 Watteau pierced pillar centre
3 Kremer centre
4 Centre with figures of Faith, Hope and Charity
5 Centre with 3 nymphs
6 Dolphin and triple shell centre
7 Sabrina centre
8 Centre for Prince dessert—candelabrum and basket
9 Large basket for Prince dessert, cross-handled with boys
10 Small basket for Prince dessert, cross-handled with boys
11 Sweetmeat vase for Prince dessert, 3 boy supporters
12 Wine cooler for Prince dessert, with boys
13 Female cream ewer for Prince dessert, small size
14 Small sugar basket for Prince dessert
15 Plain basket compotier for Prince dessert, 3 sizes
16 Salt for Prince dessert
17 Salt for Prince dessert
18 Salt for Prince dessert
19 Boy on snail comport

N

20 Boy on frog comport
21 Boy on dolphin comport
22 Boy on mussel shell comport
23 4 standing boy seasons comports fitted with baskets
24 4 sitting boy seasons comports fitted with baskets
25 4 groups of boys standing, illustrative of the seasons
26 4 groups of boys standing, fitted with comports
27 4 groups of boys standing, fitted with comports
28 Falcon figure comports
29 Dolphin and triple shell comport
30 2 shells and cupid without dolphin
31 Shell, storks and baskets
32 Dolphin and single shell
33 Greek head supporting a shell
34 Witley tazza
35 Ram's head comport
36 Cornucopiae
37 Pattern flower bowl with boys and shield
38 Oval flower bowl with heads and scroll
39 Raglan comport
40 Tri-griffin centre
41 Swan and tazza
42 Medieval jug and goblet
43 Renaissance jug and goblet
44 Blackberry jug and goblet
45 Plain jug and goblet
46 4 comports with boys, in Louis XVI style
47 Centre with 3 boys and masks
48 Caryatid figure of Sabrina
49 Embossed ice bowl and stand
50 Bath centre piece, fruit on foot
51 Puck salt
52 Salt
53 Conch-shell salt
54 Oyster shell on triton
55 Dolphin salt
56 Tripod salt
57 Bucket salt
58 Menu Tablet
59 Menu Tablet, smaller
60 Flora flower bowl on fountain
61 The Queen's centre
62 The Queen's grape basket
63 The Queen's wine cooler
64 The Queen's bon bon
65 The Queen's biscuit stand
66 The Queen's compotier
67 The Queen's compotier (small)
68 Bath sweetmeat
69 Male and female salt
71 2 figure comport
72 2 figure comport
75 Shell and grotto centre
77 Double shell comport
78 Single shell comport

79	Boy and shell comport
83	Shell dessert plate
86	Top shell of 4/84 on 3 shell feet
87	Shell
88	Swan and shell
90	Caryatid sweet with basket on foot
91	Sitting seasons figures fitted with 4/82 shell top
*92	Mermaid and shell
*93	Shell and lizard on coral
*94	Shell on coral
95	Shell on coral, number 4/13
100	Grape wagon on wheels

Class 5—Brackets, plaques, pedestals

1	The Asheley bracket
2	The season bracket (four)
3	The consol bracket
4	The scroll bracket 3 sizes
5	Bracket decorated with boys and foliage
6	Angel head bracket
7	Oblong plaque—nereids (after Clodion)
8	Oblong plaque—tritons (after Clodion)
9	Square plaque male and female fawn
10	Round plaque female fawn
11	Round plaque male fawn
12	Pedestal with ram's head and festoons
13	Truncated column
14	Small pedestal for busts
15	Small fluted pedestal
16	Small square pedestal
17	Pedestal for Raphael vases
18	Pedestal for Sabrina vases
19	Pilaster
20	Pedestal as lampstand
21	New bracket
22	Basket bracket
23	Angel head bracket
24	Wheat and bow pocket
25	Barrel bracket
26	Bow bracket
27	Large bow bracket
28	Bamboo and ivy pocket
29	New scroll bracket
30	Japanese lion head bracket
31	Angel head bracket
32	Scroll bracket
33	3 angel head bracket
34	4 seasons set of brackets

Class 6—see after Class 10

Class 6 for use as the main series which continues to this day.

Class 7—Small figures, match boxes and extinguishers

1	⎰Small Dresden figure standing
2	⎱Small Dresden figure standing
3	⎰Small Dresden figure sitting
4	⎱Companion
5	⎰Infant Bacchus
6	⎱Companion
7	Girl in shell
8	⎰Infant St. John
9	⎱Infant Christ
10	⎰Boy and faggots
11	⎱Companion
12	Broken pitcher
‡13	Charbonnier (a coalman)
‡14	Monkey cobbler
‡15	Monkey cobbler, smaller
16	Cupid captive
17	⎰Boy on dog
18	⎱Companion
19	Shell and coral
‡20	The young sculptor match-box
21	Shakespeare studying (after Roubillac)
‡22	Snipe fishing
‡23	The monkey host
24	Cock and rat
25	Dogs and rat
26	Shell with griffin
27	Fox and rushes
28	Dog and pheasant
29	Fox and goose
‡30	Bear and pole match-box
‡31	Shakespeare's house
‡32	Monkey sprinkler
‡33	Greyhounds chained
34	Large shell and coral
‡35	Bear and drum
36	China cigar tray
37	Mastiff recumbent
‡38	Jocko jug
‡39	Don Catsquali
40	Cone-shell
41	Oyster shell on triton
42	Cigar tray
43	Water can sprinkler
44	Ring tray
45	Ring tray, square
46	Ring tray, oblong
47	Ring tray, tripod on stand
48	Ring tray, trident and shell
49	Altar pastille
50	Small jewel box and stand
51	Medici cigar tray
52	Leaf Jewel tray
53	Mice and egg vase

54   Nautilus and coral
55   Twig-handled reticule basket

Designs à la Grandville (56–62)

‡56   Extinguisher—The Philosopher
‡57   Extinguisher—The Lawyer
58   Extinguisher—Diffidence ⎫
59   Extinguisher—Confidence ⎬ Jenny Lind
‡60   Extinguisher—Greyhound
‡61   Extinguisher—Giraffe
62   Extinguisher—Fox
‡63   Match-box—the orphan bird
‡64   Match-box—old granny
‡65   Match-box—'let us out'
‡66   Match-box—the noisy nest
67   Extinguisher—Monk
68   Extinguisher—Nun
69   Extinguisher—Friar
70   Extinguisher—Abbess
71   Extinguisher—Mr. Caudle
72   Extinguisher—Mrs. Caudle
73   Extinguisher—Owl's head
74   Extinguisher—The Cook
75   Extinguisher—Night
76   Extinguisher—Morning
77   Extinguisher—The torch
78   The Toby taper
‡79   The Zouave
‡80   The schoolmaster
‡81   Egg and mice
‡82   Canaryensis bottle
83   Rose
84   Violet
85   Cupid
86   Fly
87   Key border
88   Flat
89   Flat bottle with heads
90   Match-box—oake pattern
‡91   Match-box—Gothic
‡92   Match-box—puss in trousers
‡93   Match-box—owl
‡94   Match-box—sick mouse
‡95   Match-box—tomato
‡96   Match-box—embossed (small)
‡97   Match-box—oval
‡98   Match-box—dog's head
100   Sachet box
102   Scent bottle
103   Scent bottle
104   Scent bottle
106   Match-box and stand
107   Italian renaissance cigar tray
108   New shell
‡110   Rhinoceros

Class 8—Flower pots etc.

1	Flower pot with embossed ferns
2	Flower pot with embossed ferns (smaller)
3	Flower pot with lion's head and festoon
4	Flower pot with lion's head and festoon (smaller)
5	Flower pot with fluted column
6	Flower pot with basket pattern
7	Flower pot with basket pattern (smaller)
8	Flower pot with rustic pattern
9	Flower pot with leafage
10	Flower pot plain
11	Flower pot with handles
12	Flower pot embossed ivy and hop wreaths
15	Lotus flower pot
16	Lotus flower pot
17	Lotus flower pot

Class 9—Butter tubs, honey pots etc.

1	Butter tub with cow top
2	Butter tub with Vandyke heads
3	Butter tub with primrose wreath
4	Butter tub with strawberry wreath
5	Butter tub with ferns
6	Butter tub with clover and nettles
7	Butter tub with fluted pattern
8	Bee hive honey pot
9	French hive honey pot
10	Fluted honey pot
11	Ivy honey pot
12	Partridge game pot
13	Muffinier, plain
14	Muffinier, fluted
15	Muffinier, with heads and festoons
16	Bread plate, Gothic pattern
17	Bread plate, plain centre
18	Knife to match
19	Embossed bread tray
20	Custard cup and cover

Class 10—Inkstands, caskets, spill pots etc.

‡1	King John's Tomb, as an ink
‡2	King John's Tomb, as a casket
‡3	The Ariosto ink
‡4	Owl ink with reliefs
‡5	Owl ink plain body
‡6	Pompeian ink, double spout
‡7	Grotesque ink
‡8	Helmet ink
‡9	Donkey and panniers as an ink

‡10   Goat head ink
11   Shell ink
12   Casket
13   Casket with goat's head
14   Casket (new)
15   Small font on pedestal
16   Small font on low
‡17   Warrior inkstand
18   Monkey casket or tobacco box
19   Holly spillpot
20   Acorn spillpot (large)
21   Acorn spillpot (small)
22   Corinthian spillpot
23   Terminal spillpot
24   Gothic spillpot
25   Gothic spillpot (small)
26   Wheat spillpot
27   Wheat spillpot (small)
28   Reed spillpot
29   Indian corn spillpot
30   Beaker (large)
31   Beaker (small)
32   Square spillpot
33   Union Corn spillpot
34   Gothic spillpot, pierced
35   Gothic spillpot, smaller
36   Lotus spillpot
37   Scroll spillpot, on 3 legs
38   Bamboo spillpot
39   Vernon spillpot
40   Barrel spillpot
41   Dresden embossed card tray, pierced
42   Griffin patera
43   Draped spill
44   Old 3 claw spill
45   Peach ink
46   Nut taper
47   Plum box
48   Vine stand
49   Bird and nest ink
50   New 3 claw spill
51   Pedestal spill
52   Jar spill
53   Flange spill (2 sizes)
56   Chinese spill
58   Seaweed spill
59   Walnut box
62   Crocus spill, large
63   Crocus spill, small
64   Small jar spill raised figures of spring and autumn
65   Figured inkpot
66   New spill with 3 heads for feet
67   Spill

Class 6—General Class

1	Medici vase, no foot
2	Renaissance vase
3	Renaissance vase
4	Bohemian vase, pierced (with glass lining)
5	Bohemian vase, pierced
6	Bohemian vase, smaller
7	Grecian vase, 3 female figures, and cover
8	Swan and bullrushes vase
9	Swan vase, plain
10	Dolphin vase
11	Embossed cruche
12	Kremer vase
13	Kremer ewer and tray
14	Warwick vase
15	Rose water ewer and dish
16	Renaissance tazza on pedesta
17	Bullrush beaker
18	Bullrush beaker, smaller
19	Satyr head vase, fluted and cover
20	Small tri-rhyton
21	Large tri-rhyton
22	Snake rhyton
23	Horse rhyton
24	Bull rhyton
25	Sphinx rhyton
26	Swan rhyton
27	Tri-griffin amphora
28	Small griffin amphora
29	Altar violet
30	Tri-bucket for violets
31	Twin bucket
32	Twin bucket with heads
33	Triple amphora and stand
34	Audley flower stand
35	Hand vase
36	Hand and trumpet vase
37	⎰Roman flower girl and pierced basket
38	⎱Neapolitan boy companion
39	Blackberry vase on pedestal and cover
40	Oak vase and cover
41	Griffin and shell
42	⎰Boy and sheaf
43	⎱Boy and sheaf, companion
44	⎰Boy and amphora
45	⎱Boy and amphora, companion
46	⎰Water carrier, male, 2 water pots
47	⎱Water carrier, female
48	Boy with globe
49	Triple Carthage violet
50	Single Carthage violet
51	Triple Athens violet
52	Pierced card tray with horn
53	Triple bottle, antique

54	Sette amphora (7)
55	Single violet amphora
56	Egg-shaped violet
57	Egg-shaped violet with Grecian Ornament
58	Embossed strawberry leaf violet and cover
59	Low Chinese violet
60	Flower goblet Athenium ornament
61	Persian flower-holder
62	Persian flower smaller on plinth
63	Small tazza with snake heads
64	Low basket violet with cover
65	Basket violet with panel on 3 legs and cover
66	Square rustic violet
67	Pierced flower basket
68	Cross-handled basket and cover
†69	Shell basket—still made
70	Large tazza with snake handles
71	Ely tazza on pedestal
72	Swan amphora
73	Chatsworth bottle
74	Fontaine beaker
75	Elizabethan beaker
76	Paris vase
77	Medallion beaker
78	Louis XVI vase
79	Bickerton flower vase
80	Wyatt vase
81	Gille vase
82	Chalice vase
83	Mermaid violet
84	Fan flower holder
85	Dove vase
86	Athens tube
87	Athens cup and stand
88	Roman cup and stand
89	Violet, raised flowers, pierced top
90	Dagmar horn
91	Large swan and nautilus
†92	Dolphin shell violet
93	Plain vase violet
94	Triple shell
95	Trident, triple shell and dolphin
96	Triple shell without dolphin
97	Sette amphora
98	Flowered vase, 4 tubes
99	Flowered vase, 3 tubes
100	Parakeet basket
*101	Large conc shell—still made
102	Triple dolphin and globe
*103	St. Aubyn vase
104	Triple basket
105	Feather vase
106	Dolphin shell and bullrush violet
107	Renaissance spill, or arabesque violet
108	Tri-dolphin and deep shell

109	Draped neck vase
110	Plain goblet, or Louis XIV cup
111	Tri-dolphin flower vase, Grecian top
112	Ribband vase
113	Ram's head spill vase
114	Palissey vase
115	Raphael vase
116	Prague vase
117	Beaker vase
118	Lion head vase
119	Single basket
120	Group of 4 baskets
121	Griffin shells without griffin
122	Beaded bottle
123	Embossed pilgrim bottle
124	Plain pilgrim bottle, satyr heads
125	Vase, lion heads
126	Flora bust
127	Cupid violet
128	Triple griffin and trumpet vase
129	Ring-handled vase
130	Alexandra vase
131	Dolphin-handled vase
132	French snake-handled vase
133	Rope handle vase
134	Worcester bouquet holder
135	Jewelled cup
136	Plain tazza
137	Tall snake-handled tazza
138	Renaissance spill, Arabesque goblet, altered
139	Sedge nest
140	Dragon bottle
141	Cupid-handled jardinière
142	Jardinière without handle
143	Tri-dolphin shell
144	Butterfly vase
145	Butterfly tazza
146	Butterfly horn
147	Jewelled violet
148	Shell horn
149	Snake and ivy bottle
150	Vase
152	Small shell
155	Lion head spill
158	Pierced foot vase, also without pierced foot
159	Pierced foot vase, also without pierced foot
160	Pierced foot vase, also without pierced foot
*161	Plain cylinder, pierced foot (2 sizes still made for fruit)
162	Spill
163	Dudley pilgrim vase
164	Elephant handle vase, with or without pierced foot
165	Lizard vase
166	Reed bottle, gourd shape
167	3 legged bowl
168	Triple cupid flower vase (as Goode's)

169	Vase
170	Lizard bottle
171	Dudley pilgrim bottle, embossed
172	Pierced flower stand and horn
173	Egyptian vase
174	Fish bowl
175	Square medallion vase
176	Butterfly vase, no figure
177	Boy, butterfly and snail vase
178	Circular bottle
179	Spill
180	Nymph trough, 3 parts
181	Amphora trough, 3 parts
182	Chinese vase
183	Lion and basket
184	Springing lion
185	Antelope
186	Boy and boat
187	Japanese flower-holder
188	Japanese flower-holder
189	Square vase
190	Square vase, tall
191	Hexagon vase
192	Square vase
193	Shell
194	Tortoise
195	Cauldron
196	Elephant and panniers
197	Sedge vase
198	Swan and horn
199	Oblong jardinière
200	Pierced tray
201	Plain beaker
202	Pilgrim vases 1, 2, 3 and 4
203	Chinese, spill pierced
204	Japanese vase
205	Globular dragon flower bowl
206	Dragon jardinière
207	Triple Japanese bottle
208	Elephant
209	Camel
210	Pilgrim vases, potters scenes embossed (2)
211	Honeysuckle spill vase
212	Stork spill
213	Spittoon flower bowl
214	Boy and jar
215	Little piper
216	Potters vases as 6/189
217	Monkey spill
218	Triple dolphin and flat shell
219	Cushion violet
220	Squirrel in stump
221	Japanese vase
222	New pilgrim birds
223	Pottery vase

224	Stork vase
225	Lozenge vase
226	Double draped vase
227	Bird and rush
228	Oblong rustic violet
229	Boy and barrel
230	Vase on pedestal
231	Cruche
232	Rope handle basket
233	Beetle violet
234	Tall spill
235	Lizard violet
236	Square diaper jardinière

1872

237	Oval basket, 3 sizes
238	Stork vase with tortoise base
239	Japanese dog number 1
240	Egg basket, 6 holes and cups
241	Egg basket, 4 holes and cups
242	Rustic trough, straight
243	Rustic trough, crescent
244	Trellis trough, straight
245	Trellis trough, crescent
246	Trellis trough, small
247	Water can
248	Large conc shell
250	Napkin basket
251	Large pilgrim figures
252	New pilgrim heads
253	Japanese déjeuner set
254	Japanese kettle
255	Heart shape vase
256	Head-handled jug
257	Tortoise box
258	Tusk spill, frogs
259	Spill, pierced foot
260	Dragon-handled jug
261	Bullrush pot
262	Boat on rock
263	Embossed lamp vase
264	Plain lamp vase
265	Rustic season comport
266	Bird cylinder
267	Pug, sitting
268	Pug, standing
269	Japanese dog number 2, with ball
270	Bamboo and wicker flower pot
271	Dragon gondola
272	Monkey vase
273	Wicker and lotus flower pot
274	Japanese gondola
275	Primrose spill
276	Japanese dog number 3

277	Tall basket with ivy
279	Oval kettle
280	Plain basket
281	Square top elephant-handled vase
282	Medallion basket
283	Silkworm vase
284	Square pierced violet
285	Frog and snake
286	Pierced teapot
287	Cane basket
288	Suspending shell bowl
289	Wicker and ivy vase
290	Duck pilgrim vase
291	Dolphin jug
292	Bamboo cheese stand
293	Japanese figure, also a hexagon stand
294	Lotus leaf and frog
295	Hawk
296	Dove
297	Japanese cylinder
298	Pierced Japanese vase
299	Stork card tray, pierced
300	Japanese grotesque figures
301	Elephant head foot jardinière, pierced and cover
302	Pierced cylinder
303	Pierced jardinière
304	Jug

1873

305	Cane flower pot
306	Wheat and poppy bowl with snake handles
307	Wheat and poppy bowl without handles
308	Hexagon vase and stand
309	Lobed vase
310	Lotus bowl
311	Lotus tray with flowers
312	Vase raised leafage and flowers, pair
313	Mice and egg, pair
314	Fern stand
315	Large jardinière
316	Japanese box pierced cover
317	Round Japanese pierced box and cover
*318	Tailor bird bracket, pair
319	Pomegranate vase
320	Tall vase
321	Japanese triple amphora
322	Tall embossed vase
323	Chess player vase
324	Sedge nest bracket, pair
325	Pierced spill
326	Pierced jardinière
327	Landscape moulded vase
‡328	Kitten
329	Pierced spill

330	Stork vase
331	Square Japanese pierced vase
332	Kylin candlestick
333	Embossed jardinière
334	Boy and frog
335	Triple cupid centre
336	Japanese tray
337	Flower pot
338	Bamboo basket
339	Lotus sugar box
*340	Frog and lizard cup and saucer
341	Boy and boat with plinth
342	Japanese pilgrim flask with flies
343	Japanese pilgrim flask with birds
344	Fluted lamp vase
345	Ring-handled vase and cover
346	Bacchus flower vase, 3 figures
347	Boy and faggot
348	Dolphin salt
†349	Mermaid salt
350	Tripod
351	Japanese salt, round
352	Renaissance salt
353	Shell and coral
‡354	Woodcutter and musician
‡355	Pug standing, life size
356	Mermaid taper
357	Wicker vase
358	Bird salt
359	Lotus cream
360	Fruit box and cover
361	Wicker salt
362	Leaf
363	Small vase
364	Globe flower holder
365	Bird salt
366	Bracket, bird and nest / Bracket, fly / Bracket, plain
367	Double cylinder teapot
368	Jardinière
369	Fruit teapot
370	Ribbon teapot
371	Fluted spill
372	Pilgrim, flowers
373	Bird ink
374	Skye terrier

1874

375	Bouquet holder
376	Owl
377	Parrot
378	Cock and hen group and single
379	Stork comport

380	2 Girls of period—town and country
381	Money bag (old)
382	Rustic cruet
383	Russian flower bowl
384	Round egg basket with 6 holes
385	Vienna comport and figure
386	Vienna comport and cup
387	King Charles' dog
388	Square embossed jardinière
389	Flower bowl
390	Fruit violet
391	Fruit violet
392	Hand menu holder
393	Japanese sitting musician
394	Bracket
‡395	Grotto centre
396	Pagoda vase
397	Ring-handled vase
398	Bowl
399	Square Japanese vase
400	Square Japanese jardinière
401	Egg shape vase
402	Round bowl
403	Jardinière
404	Oblong jardinière
405	Bowl
406	Cupid and double basket
407	Boy comport
408	Round fluted basket (2)
409	Candelabra
410	King Charles' dog
411	Cockatoo
‡412	Fisherman and hunter figures (17 in.)
413	Toilet box
414	Florist figures, boy and girl
415	Amphora, single, groups of 4, 7 and 10
‡416	Hanging dove (2)
‡417	Japanese frame, frogs
418	Tankard, elephant handle
419	Narrow neck jug, elephant handle
420	Pilgrim vase with storks
421	Square jardinière
423	Stork jardinière
424	Gourd
‡425	Persian vase (large size)⎫ modelled with 'Feramorz introduced as a
‡426	Persian vase (small size)⎭ poet' and 'Ganed the slave of love'
427	Cut top vase
428	Slipper number 2
†429	Oval basket raised floral (Dr. Wall type)
430	Oval basket raised floral (Dr. Wall type)
431	New boy and amphora
432	Stump spill
433	Stump spill
434	Stump jug
435	Oblong mignonette jardinière

436	Ribbon gourd
‡437	Shoe number 4
‡438	Shoe number 3
‡439	Shoe number 1
*440	Men menu holders (6)
441	Lotus violet
442	Bracket
443	Spitz dog
444	St. Bernard dog
445	Bowl
446	Square Italian jardinière
‡447	Italian mirror frame
448	Ribbon menu
449	Florist figure and trough
450	Pierced floral holder
451	Bamboo menu
452	Bamboo flower pot
453	Dolphin comports
454	Square wicker basket
455	Bath sweet
456	Triple cupid centre
457	Dragon menu
458	Italian vase
459	Violet
460	Tassel violet
461	Boy and shield shell trough
462	Double kneeling cupid comport
463	Bird and basket
464	Pierced casket
465	Musicians
466	Dancing cupids
467	Stork
468	Scroll bracket

1875

469	Falcon
470	Basket, raised flowers
471	Swan
472	D.V. Basket
473	Elephant
474	Italian cup and stand
475	Oval jewel
476	Cupid comport
477	Pierced basket, overhead handle and figure
478	Pierced basket, side handles
479	Pompeian flower holder
480	Essex basket
481	Griffin and shell
482	Tall, square candlestick
483	Horse and panniers
484	Small Grecian figure
485	Lesbia
†486	Bather surprised—3 sizes
487	Roman female (28 in.)

XIII. Beautiful Royal Worcester coffee set painted with London scenes by Harry Davis in 1926. The perfect effects of the foggy atmosphere and the colour of the buildings make it hard to realise that the original raw enamel colours undergo a considerable change during firing.

XIV. Five vases of differing ground colours ; top left, shape 2059,
turquoise ground, panel painted with fruit and flowers by Hawkins
in 1901, marked 'Leadless Glaze', gilded by Wallace Southall ;
centre, shape 1742, Royal Blue ground, panel painted with fruit and
flowers by Hawkins in 1900 ; right, shape 2156, Calabash ground
(slightly lighter than Barr's Orange) painted with orchids by Frank
Roberts in 1904 ; bottom row, left, shape 2059, Matt Blue ground-
lay, painted with flying swans and gold rushes by C. H. C. Baldwyn
in 1901 ; right, shape 2130, maroon ground, panel of fruit painted
by Hawkins in 1901.

488   Tall square candlestick, pierced nozzle
489   Wicker basket
490   Stump vase plain and another with squirrel
491   Renaissance bracket
492   Toilet box and cover
493   Rustic basket
494   Italian vase and cover
495   Grecian flower bowl, 3 female figures
496   Elephant
497   Clock vase
498   Jug stands, 4 sizes
499   Frog violet with 1 or 2 frogs
500   Italian spill
501   Pierced jardinière
502   Round vase pierced
503   Wicker vase
504   Double plain bottle
505   Japanese form, tall and two small forms
506   Bitch pug
507   Italian bucket
508   Triple basket and rope
509   Jardinière
510   Snake-handled basket
511   Money bag violet
§512 New menu holders—6 different statesmen
513   Owl
514   Low basket (4)
515   Japanese menu holders 1 male and 2 females
516   Brush basket
517   Wicker basket ink
‡518 Group of cats
519   Snake-handled vase
520   Sèvres-shape vase
521   Boat money box
522   Swell money box (2 figures by money box)
523   Wicker basket
524   Mermaid and nautilus shell
525   Nautilus on pedestal
526   Gourd vase
527   Square bamboo flower pot
528   New claw spill, raised flowers
529   Gate
530   Winter figures, pair
531   Head spill, raised flowers
532   Swan and cupid or swan without cupid

1876

533   Ewer and stand
*534 Dancing Bacchante pair
535   Cupid, shell top
*536 Humming bird bracket
‡537 Japanese juggler with 3 pots
538   Lotus
539   Corner bracket

o

540	Dove and basket
541	Boys on dolphin, pair
542	Pilgrim bottle
‡543	Japanese juggler candlestick
544	Violet
545	Jardinière
546	Pierced basket
547	Watteau figures, male and female, pair
548	Hexagon vases
549	Flower holder
550	Dachshund
551	Dürer
552	Reubens
553	Bottle
554	Tub, set, tray and teapot
555	Melon teapot, box and cream
556	Double fish
557	Jardinière
558	Triple dolphin and deep shell
559	Triple dolphin and deep shell
560	Dante
‡561	Stork and umbrella stand
562	Pilgrim flask
563	Japanese candlestick
564	Square jardinière with tubes
565	Leaf
566	Brighton basket
567	Elephant-handled vase and cover (2 sizes)
568	Vase
569	Cabbage leaf jugs (as Dr. Wall)
570	Jardinière
571	Boy and girl with cat and dog, pair
572	Monkey and tortoise
573	Jardinière
574	Bottle
‡575	Italian centre ($22\frac{1}{2}$ in. width)
576	Vase and cover (18 in.)
577	Jam pot and cover
578	Double cupid comport, standing
579	Double cupid comport, sitting
580	Indian vase
581	Pottery figure, female decorating vase
582	Lobed Indian vase
583	Long neck Indian vase
584	Fan dish
585	Square violet with tubes
586	Owl candelabra
587	Love bird bracket
588	Bamboo and dragon flower pot
589	Lotus
590	Triangular jug
591	Bamboo flower holder
592	Medieval men with baskets (4)

1877

593	Swan and stump
†594	Eastern Water carriers (2 sizes)
595	Photo frame
†596	Kneeling water carrier, male (see 637)
597	Fox
598	Perforated teaware
599	Perforated goblet, vases, jug and stoppered bottles
600	Candlestick
601	Lotus
‡602	Grotesque figures, pair (as Mansion House dwarfs)
603	Pierced vase and cover
604	Pierced vase with tubes
605	Bottle, raised storks
606	Pierced vase
607	Group of 6 bottles
608	Love bird flower holder
‡609	Athlete figure
610	⌠Cockatoo and frame
611	⌡Magpie and frame
612	Japanese bamboo vase
613	Pierced vase
614	Tub set, 4 cups and saucers
*615	Diamond tea set
*616	Diamond déjeuner set
617	Kettledrum set and 3 cups and saucers
*618	Tub tea set
619	Violet
620	Triple jam pot
621	Square vase with panel
622	Boy and drum boxes, pair
623	Basket
624	Hexagon and diamond dessert plates, pierced
625	Square and round dessert plates, pierced
626	Elephant on pedestal
627	Vase with pipes
628	Vase
629	Shell on dolphin
630	Bottle
631	Bamboo flower holder
632	Stump
633	Wheel violet
634	Elephant-handled vase
635	Clock
636	Vase
†637	Kneeling water carrier, female to 596
638	Tub cruet
639	Vase, tall Japanese form
640	Vase, low Japanese form
641	Tea caddy
642	Love bird stand
643	Violet
644	Napkin basket
645	Triple amphora

*646 Tub kettle (2)
647 Rope bucket for Cockatoo frame
648 Bamboo basket

1878

649 Flower holder
650 Horn (3)
‡651 Double horn for suspending
652 Vase
653 Vase
654 Violet, pierced foot
655 Vase (3)
656 Teapot
657 Square teapot
658 Vase with raised hops
659 Bramble basket
660 Easel photo stand
‡661 Figure, newspaper boy date calendar
662 Boy bracket, 2 boys or 1 boy or no boys
663 Seau
664 Lion head jardinière
665 French figures
666 Square leaf violet
667 Swiss figures, male and female
668 Persian candlestick
669 Persian vase
670 Jardinière
671 Lotus comport
672 Leaf (3)
673 Persian vase
674 Persian vase
675 Persian vase
676 Persian vase
677 Persian vase
678 Square teapot with flowers, no stand
679 Leaf cup and saucer
680 Vase
681 Low kettle
682 New violet
683 Bracket pierced or not pierced
684 Bracket with 2 boys
685 Vase, embossed rope
686 Triple vase (2)
687 Lotus taper
688 Lotus candelabra
689 Flower holder, three tubes
690 Candlestick
691 Vase
692 Vase

1879

693 Bamboo egg basket
694 Lobed vase and stopper

695   Violet
696   Double fan flower holder
697   Kettle (2)
698   Triple shell
699   Groups of tubes—15, 7 or 6
700   Embossed slipper
701   Owl and bamboo flower-holder
702   Jug
703   Pierced vase
704   Bird menu
705   Piano candlestick
706   Group of bottles
707   Pierced vase and cover
708   Bird and lotus
709   Water lily
710   Menu and flower-tube
711   Frog and rush-handled jardinière
712   Spill on 3 pedestal feet
713   {Triple tube on stand (2) / Single tube on stand (2)}
714   Vase, 7 necks and pierced
715   {Watteau centre with figures / Watteau comport with figures}
716   Pierced bottle
717   Pierced vase
718   Scroll flower holder plain or with tortoise
719   Bag bracket
720   Vase with elephant handles
721   {Persian pierced goblet / Persian half-pierced goblet}
722   Vase, plain with trumpet neck
723   Vase, rope handle and pierced at edge
724   Folio flower holder
725   Persian cruche (2)
726   Figure candlestick
727   Persian goblet
‡728   Artillery centre
729   Menu stand
730   Hexagon vase and cover
731   Bag and boat
732   Card and drum violet
733   Persian vase embossed
734   Boy and pillar
735   Water bottle and stopper
736   Large pierced vase and cover
737   Shell bracket
738   Pierced goblet
739   Persian ewer
740   Double spouted kettle (2)
741   Flower holder
742   Plain vase
743   Pierced vase with or without foot and cover
744   Pierced vase
745   Bag violet
746   Tall goblet

747	Pierced vase or half-pierced vase and cover
748	Pierced teapot
749	Pierced ink
750	Shell and coral flower holder
751	Tall bottle and stopper
752	Tortoise and amphora
753	Wicker basket (2)
754	Single amphora (2)
755	Plain form (2)
756	Lotus and poppy vase
‡757	Lord Derby and Lord Salisbury group
‡758	Statesmen pair of figures and baskets
759	Pierced vase and cover
*760	Orchid bracket

1880

761	Square vase pierced corners
762	Rustic menu
763	Pierced shoe
764	Japanese menu
765	Lotus flower holder, 3 flowers
766	Candle extinguishers—Helen's babies
767	Bowl with pierced cover
768	Bowl with pierced cover
769	Oval basket
770	Vase
771	Square pierced vase
772	Orchid vase
773	Double Queen Anne boy and girl comport number 1
774	Double Queen Anne boy and girl comport number 2
775	Single Queen Anne boy and girl comport number 1
776	Single Queen Anne boy and girl comport number 2
777	Single Queen Anne boy and girl comport number 3
778	Single Queen Anne boy and girl comport number 4
779	Persian cruche (and a miniature)
†780	The Martin jug (6 sizes)
781	Toy kettle
782	Dragon ewer
783	Persian ewer (3 and a miniature)
784	Persian vase (3 and a miniature)
785	Renaissance shell with angel handle
786	Elizabeth and Raleigh pair of figures
787	Queen Anne candelabra, boy and girl, 3 nozzles
788	Shell spout jug
789	{ Ewer with embossed swan Italian Florentine style { Ewer without swan and a miniature
790	Fowl
791	Pierced caddy
792	Bottle
793	Duck and amphora
794	Town and country girls, pair candle extinguishers
795	Vase and cover
796	Juggler candlesticks, pair

797	{Group of water lilies / Group with flowers
798	Candlestick without foot
799	Small Watteau comports, pair
*800	Sugar sifter figures, boy and girl
801	Star shape (?)
802	Stork and lotus taper
803	Pierced candelabrum (25 in.)
804	Vase and cover, pierced handles (22 in.)
805	Group of 19 tubes
806	Round Japanese form vase?
807	Violet
808	Vase (2)
809	Vase and stopper
810	Violet
811	Caryatid candelabrum
812	Vase
813	Fountain group, boy and girl with water pot
814	Embossed spill
815	Vase
816	Pierced ewer
817	Pierced candlestick
818	Group of angular tubes
819	Bamboo teapot, box, cream, jug
820	Fluted tea set
821	Bamboo flower pot (3)
822	Cabbage leaf
823	New embossed jug
824	Double egg basket

1881

825	Hide and seek group (boy and girl each side of tree trunks)
826	Boy and basket on shoulder—pair
827	Boy and basket at foot—pair
‡828	County courtship group
829	Pierced vase and stopper
830	Vase
831	Lotus candlestick
832	Oval lotus comport
833	Round lotus comport
834	Pierced caddy
*835	Irishman
*836	Yankee
*837	Chinese
*838	Hindoo
*839	Italian
*840	Negro
841	Ewer (loose spout)
842	Persian ewer and stopper
843	Persian ewer, long neck and stopper (15 in.)
844	Pierced vase 4 bird foot
845	Pilgrim vase flat side
846	Ewer
847	Bamboo bracket or spill (2)

848	Pierced vase
849	Clematis vase, also a plain form
850	Vase (3 sizes and a miniature)
*851	John Bull
852	Stork and bamboo flower-holder (18 in.)
853	Lotus leaf
854	Vase, tall neck (2 sizes and a miniature)
855	Sugar and cream with pierced handles
856	Howard's extinguishers
857	Vase (4 sizes)
858	Bamboo basket (2 sizes)
859	Vase and cover
860	Plain jar
861	Violet
862	Jardinière with 3 figures
863	Double violet
864	Tall pierced vase and cover (22 in.)
865	Embossed tea set
866	Plain violet (4 shapes)
867	Plain violet, shapes 5 and 6
868	Conche ash tray
869	Acorn pepper and salt
870	Aesthetic teapot
871	Vase and cover
872	Lotus flower pot
873	Tall lotus candelabrum (3 or 5 lights)
874	Spiral vase ('fairy' lamp base)
875	Vase
876	Persian ewer and cover
877	Persian ewer and cover with panels
878	Frog and shell ash tray
‡879	Lotus and tortoise violet
880	Boy and girl with baskets, pair

*

1882

881	Pierced ewer
882	Oil and vinegar cruet
883	Spiral vase, dragon foot and cover
884	Wicker pot pourri
‡885	Vase with 4 dragons (24 in.), Chinese style
886	Wicker vase and cover (18 in.)
887	Pheasant vases (pair)
*888	Boy and girl figures on chair (Kate Greenaway style)
889	Punch and Toby extinguishers (pair)
890	Square coffee pot
891	Coffee pot (16 in.)
892	Coffee pot (15 in.)
893	Figures, boy and girl with baskets
894	Large pierced vase and cover
895	Lobed Persian vase and cover (22 in.)
*896	Group, boy and girl pulling basket
*897	Group, boy and girl holding basket
898	Dragon candlestick
‡899	High-heeled shoe

900	Bamboo toast rack
*901	Boy astride chair and girl holding knee (pair similar to 888)
902	Double shell bracket
903	Coastguardsman (18 in.)
904	Bust of Michaelangelo
905	Bust of Raphael
906	Bust of Maestro Georgio
907	Bust of Lucca della Robbia
908	Napkin vase, draped at neck—2 sizes
909	Plain vase
910	Flat with lily candlestick
911	Bamboo-handled vase
912	Lotus cruet
*913	Scotchman (Scotsman)
*914	Russian
‡915	Large Monk
916	Globe violet
917	Wicker flower-holder, 3 low and 1 tall pots
918	Vase and cover
919	Shell ice dish and plate
920	Bamboo spill
921	Bamboo panel sugar and cream
922	Vase and cover, pierced panels
923	Vase and cover, pierced panels
924	Bamboo pierced spill
925	Wicker and ivy spill
926	Spill, embossed panels
927	Wicker basket, strap handles
*928	Tortoise on mussel shell
929	Globe and wicker violet
930	Dog and cat pepper, owl and owl in stump
931	Vase and cover as 841 ewer, no spout
932	Vase and cover as 923 but plain
933	Tusk bracket, pierced
*934	Chocolate jug, mask spout (2 sizes) and cover
935	Vase and cover and a miniature
936	Double early English comport, girl standing, boy sitting
937	Double early English comport, boy standing, girl sitting
938	Double early English comport, single boy, or candlestick
939	Double early English comport, single girl, or candlestick
940	Embossed butter dish and cover, as 865

1883

941	Persian vase, pierced panels and cover
942	Vase pierced handles 3 sizes and a miniature
943	Vase 2 sizes and a miniature—early Persian style
944	Boy and girl figures
945	Wicker and ivy vase pierced at top or unpierced
946	Bamboo salad bowl (2 sizes) and a plate
947	Vase, 3 elephant feet, embossed panels
948	Vine leaf plate (Mr. Starrs)
*949	Pair Cairo Water Carriers (21 in.)
950	Horn candelabrum and bracket
951	Pierced vase on pedestal and cover (26½ in.)

952	Vase, pierced at handles
953	Jug, scale body and scroll handle
954	Lotus lamp and reservoir (linings extra)
955	Lotus lamp and reservoir, low shape
956	Pair embossed spills
957	Frog and lotus flower pot (2 sizes)
958	Leaf and lotus flower pot (3 sizes)
959	Grotesque flower-holder (shape of a dog)
960	Queen Anne rustic boy comport
961	Queen Anne sleeping girl comport
962	Rustic boy and basket on back
963	Rustic girl holding basket
964	Rustic girl and 3 branch candelabrum
965	Rustic boy and 3 branch candelabrum
966	Rustic boy and girl comport
967	Rustic boy and girl comport
968	Low lotus candelabrum, 3 lights
969	Lamp, embossed fish
†970	Tusk jug, 5 sizes
971	Grotesque jug
972	Square coffee pot pierced
973	Pierced ewer, as 891
974	Embossed ewer
975	Hexagon vase and cover
976	Dragon vase
977	Pair of trays, quail and young
978	Embossed teapot and coffee pot, as 865
‡979	Queen's vase and cover in Indian style
980	Pierced vase and cover
981	Panelled vase
*982	Vase (5 sizes including miniature and toy)
*983	Lotus and tortoise tray
984	Pierced spill, 3 sunk panels
985	Pierced bottle, as 854 (small)
986	Dragon-handled ewer/cruche
987	Flower-holder, elephant feet
988	Vase and cover, spiral pierced (2 sizes)
989	Raised flower holder on 4 feet
990	Renaissance ewer
*991	Violets—6 different forms
992	{Low basket twisted handle pierced (4 sizes) {Low basket twisted handle not pierced (4 sizes)
993	Oval embossed basket (2 sizes)
994	Double shell flower-holder, coral handle
995	{Shell and coral menu {Shell and coral menu, shell in front
996	Shell
997	Triple shell, coral handle
‡998	London Cries figure—Ye watchman
‡999	London Cries figure—Ye ratte killer
‡1000	London Cries figure—Ye prison basket
‡1001	London Cries figure—Ye brush man
‡1002	London Cries figure—Ye water man
‡1003	London Cries figure—Ye marking stones man

1884

1004	{ Leaf salad bowl, pierced edge { Leaf salad bowl, small size, not pierced
1005	Wicker and ivy spill, as 925
1006	Bamboo spill, pierced as 924
1007	{ Ice pail with handle { Ice pail, no handle
1008	Dog and cat menu
1009	Double shell, dragon handle
1010	Pierced vase and cover (22 in.)
1011	Mask spouted ewer
1012	{ Basket, oval, pierced (3 sizes) { Basket, oval, not pierced (3 sizes)
1013	Hungry dog menu
1014	Ewer with 4 panels
1015	Dragon ewer embossed, or plain
*1016	Lady and gentleman of George III's reign, pair
1017	Oval bowl, 4 elephant head feet (2 sizes)
1018	Round bowl, 4 elephant head feet (2 sizes)
1019	Square bowl, 4 elephant head feet (2 sizes)
1020	Candlestick, 3 elephant head feet
1021	2 handled vase (3 sizes including miniature)
1022	Vase and cover
1023	Tennis cup and saucer
1024	Vase (2 sizes)
1025	Vase and stopper
1026	Cruche, dragon handle
*1027	Pair figures—'100 years ago'
1028	Embossed scale jug (Starr)
1029	Double gourd vase and dragon
1030	Vase, flared top
1031	Vase and stopper
1032	Pair musicians—girl with tambourine, boy with banjo
1033	Owl lamp and plain lamp
1034	Vase and cover
1035	Gourd dragon jug
1036	Frog and toadstool ringstand
1037	Wicker vase
1038	Embossed caddy and cover
1039	Plain globular caddy and cover
1040	Ewer and a plain form
1041	Ewer (2 sizes)
1042	Ewer
‡1043	Owl candlestick
1044	Ewer
1045	Gourd basket
1046	Figure group, boy and girl with pitchers
†1047	Claret jug (4 sizes)
1048	Flat dragon-handled ewer (2 and a miniature)
1049	Bamboo sticks, groups of 3 and 7 tubes (4 sizes, $2\frac{1}{2}$–$5\frac{7}{8}$ in.)
†1050	Spiral candlestick (2 sizes)
1051	Figure-handled centre on pedestal
1052	Pair figures
1053	Vase, conc shaped

1054   Double tier basket
1055   Renaissance horn
1056   Horn candlestick
1057   Primrose flower holder
1058   Violet flower holder
1059   Conventional primrose
1060   Vase (2 sizes)
1061   Lobed vase and stopper (2 sizes)
1062   Boy bracket
1063   Girl bracket
1064   Vase and cover (2 sizes)
1065   Cruche and a miniature
1066   Bamboo spill and tube
1067   Teapot

1885

1069   Menu and salt holder
1070   Pair dancing figures (Hogarth-style)
1071   Vase and cover
1072   Boy comport (Hogarth-style)
1073   Girl comport (Hogarth-style)
1074   Honeycomb vase (2 sizes)
1075   Vase
1076   Vase (2 sizes)
1077   Vase (2 sizes)
1078   Square vase with dragon
1079   Vase (3 sizes)
1080   Basket (3 sizes)
1081   Dragon vase
1082   Vase
1083   Lotus, tortoise and frog tray
1084   Pair Egyptian female musicians (2 sizes)
1085   Orchid bracket
1086   Vase and cover on human pedestal
1087   Centre dish on pedestal
1088   Lotus candlestick
1089   Vase (5 sizes)
1090   Bamboo-handled ewer
1091   Vase
1092   Watteau-style figure candelabra, male
1093   Watteau-style figure candelabra, female
†1094   Jug (6 sizes)
1095   Bamboo chamber candlestick
1096   Figure candelabra (castanet), 2 lights
1097   Figure candelabra (banjo)
1098   Figure candelabra (castanet), 1 light
1099   Figure candelabra (banjo)
1101   Round watering pot, 1 or 2 handles
1102   Goat table centre with boy and girl (10 × 13 in.)
1103   Pair boy and girl sugar dusters
1104   Square pierced cup and saucer
1105   Oval watering pot, 1 or 2 handles
1106   Pair of figures, artist and model
1107   Wicker embossed vase

1108   Vase, 4 pierced handles
1109   Vase (3 sizes)
1110   Lotus salad bowl
1111   Melon jug
1112   Pot pourri vase and cover with or without snakes
1113   Pierced ewer and stopper
1114   Double figure candelabra, 3 lights, a boy killing snake
1115   Double figure candelabra, 3 lights, girl with bird's nest
†1116   Tusk ice jug—7 sizes and a goblet
1117   Vase
1118   Vase and cover, 2 yoked heads
1119   Tortoise and salt
1120   Pierced dessert plate and stand
1121   Lotus candelabrum, 5 lights
1122   Wicker plate
1123   Ewer
1124   Boy candelabrum, 2 lights
1125   Girl candelabrum, 2 lights
‡1126   Negro and water pot
‡1127   Negress and water pot
1128   Toy teapot
1129   Pair figures—sailor boy and girl
1130   Grotesque stork ewer
1131   Renaissance ink
*1132   Claret jug (3 sizes)
1133   Vase and cover, pierced handles (2 sizes)
1134   Vase and cover
1135   Spiral vase and cover, pierced
1136   Ewer (3 sizes)
1137   Violet, tall pierced handle
1138   Violet, plain handle
1139   Low violet, pierced handle
1140   Pair monkey candlesticks

1886

1141   Pair boy and girl candlesticks
1142   Vase and cover (2 sizes)
1143   Lobed ewer (2 sizes)
1144   Chelsea-style ewer and a miniature
1145   Shell flower-holder
1146   Tall lamps, heads at foot
1147   Lamp
1148   Ewer
1149   Bottle and plain bottle
1150   Fairy lamp vase
1151   Lotus flower-holder, 3 buds
1152   Boy comport (as 960)
1153   Girl comport (as 961)
1154   Double figure comport (as 966)
1155   Scarf bracket
1156   Lamp with claw foot and heads
1157   Lamp, plain foot and heads
1158   Bottle (B and D) and plain
1159   Ewer

1160	Jug
1161	Ewer
1162	Ewer
1163	Bottle
1164	Bottle
1165	Vase—942 with 1048 handle
1166	Ewer—1028 with 782 handle
‡1167	Table centre—4 figures '10 years' (20 × 11 in.)
1168	Vase and cover perforated neck (2 sizes)
1169	Vase and cover perforated neck (2 sizes)
1170	Oyster plate
1171	Pair monkey and lotus
1172	Pair lamps boy and girl on each
1173	Pair jardinières boy and girl on each
1174	Double figure comport
1175	Pair of boy and girl candlesticks
*1176	Vase dragon handles (5 sizes including miniature and toy)
1177	Boy comport
1178	Girl comport
1179	Ewer Italian style
1180	Indian slipper shoe
1181	Vase and cover (18 in.)
1182	Vase
1183	Shell teapot, sugar box, cream and 2 sizes open sugar
1184	Vase
*1185	Bamboo jug (9 sizes)
‡1186	Indian craftsman, figure of Bakshiran, the old potter, aged 104
1187	Ewer pierced panel neck and cover
1188	Frog and bullrush spill
1189	Pair sleeping boy and girl comports
1190	Mouse and wicker candlestick
1191	Persian ewer
1192	Vase, pierced handle and a small size on foot
1193	Vase pierced handles
1194	Vase and pierced cover
1195	Vase embossed foot and pierced neck
1196	Bamboo déjeuner set—Tray, teapot, open sugar, cup and saucer, cream and plate
1197	Shell dish on coral foot
1198	Fluted mustard, pepper and salt
1199	Vase and cover (2 sizes)
1200	Vase Persian style 19″
‡1201	Renaissance clock case
*1202	Pair French fisher boy and girl and miniature
1203⎱	Indian craftsman figure of Shaban, the gold brocade maker
1204⎰	Indian craftsman figure of Karan Singh, the trinket maker
1205	Jubilee jug and goblet
*1206	Pair miniature Eastern water carriers
1207	Indian craftsman figure of Haji Mijak, the coppersmith
*1208	Melon dish (2 sizes)

1887

1209	Cucumber dish (2 sizes)
1210	Embossed figure scent bottle

1211	Plain figure scent bottle
1212	Wicker fairy lamp
1213	Round wicker lamp, embossed
1214	Vase and cover (3 sizes)
1215	Drumstick vase
1216	Vase, low neck, as 784 (2 sizes)
1217	Oval shell salad bowl
1218	Ewer
1219	Somers shell coffee cup and saucer
1220	Bamboo shell coffee cup and saucer
1221	Coventry fluted déjeuner service
1222	Indian craftsman figure of Munnasall, the clay figure maker (also see 1226)
1223	Flower-holder
1224	Flower-holder
1225	Chocolate jug, as 1047 (2 sizes)
1226	Indian craftsman figure of Nazir Hassan, the ivory miniature painter
1227	Ewer
1228	Shell strawberry bowl and plate
1229	Jug (5 sizes)
1230	Bust of Queen Victoria (25 in.)
1231	Pair round fern comports, single figure
1232	Pair round fern comports, single figure, small
1233	Fern centre, double figure
1234	Pair fern centre double figure triangular basket
1235	Pair oval fern comports, single boy and girl
1236	Spiral candlestick
1237	Pair monkey and lotus tapers
1238	Severn basket (3 sizes)
1239	Figure lamp as 1114—bird's nest
1240	Figure lamp as 1114—snake
1241	Triple wicker fairy lamp
1242	⎧Boy and girl fern pots, as 938 ⎩Boy and girl fern pots, as 1141
*1243	Pair of Bringaree Indians, male and female (2 sizes)
1244	⎧Lion handle chamber candlestick ⎩Chamber candlestick, no handle
1245	Mouse taper
1246	Fringe orchid bracket
‡1247	Boy comport 'Australia'
‡1248	Girl comport 'Africa'
1249	Pair round fern comports, single figure and rails, boy and girl as 1231
†1250	Miniature Cairo water carriers
1251	Leaf chamber candlestick
1252	Oval fluted sugar and cream on foot
1253	Sugar box and cream ewer
1254	Bamboo celery basket (3 sizes)
1255	Goat head jug (3 sizes)
1256	Mortuary vase and cover (3 sizes)
1257	Globe vase (4 sizes)
1258	Lion head jug (5 sizes)
1259	Pierced ewer honeycomb neck
1260	Ewer not pierced and a miniature
1261	Vase tall neck (20 in.)
‡1262	Goldsmith's schoolboys 'Frown'

‡1263 Goldsmith's schoolboys 'Smile'
1264 Vase and cover
1265 Renaissance ewer (3 sizes)
1266 Large vase and cover, figure handles
1267 {Loving cup
{Loving cup with 3 tusk handles
1268 Plain shape vase (9 sizes)
1269 Fairy lamp, 3 shells and coral feet
1270 Fairy lamp, 3 shells and coral feet
1271 Fairy lamp, plain shape with 3 small flower tubes
1272 Fairy lamp, plain shape with 3 small flower tubes
1273 Fairy lamp, with indented edge
1274 Scalloped shell (3 sizes and a double)
1275 Wicker candy box and cover (2 sizes and a plain form)
1276 Vase and cover embossed head handle (2 sizes)

1888

1277 Fairy lamp
1278 Fairy lamp
1279 Vase pierced handles (2 sizes)
1280 Griffin candlestick
1281 Rose jar and cover
1282 Fluted cracker jar and cover
1283 Bamboo menu
1284 Basket (4 sizes)
1285 Vase and cover (2 sizes)
*1286 Rose jar and cover (3 sizes) small and medium still made for fruit painting
1287 Double leaf (2 sizes)
1288 Cabbage leaf
1289 Folio menu
1290 Figure candelabra, 3 lights
1291 Figure candelabra, 3 lights
1292 Mower candelabrum, boy (and figure only)
1293 Mower candelabrum, companion girl (and figure only)
1294 Candy box and cover (2 sizes)
1295 Centre
1296 Greek ewer, pierced handle
1297 Cylinder ewer
1298 Apple caddy
1299 Ink and sugar
1300 Wicker candy box (2 sizes)
1301 Ink
‡1302 Boy and stile, boy and gate, crescent trough, straight trough, rabbits
1303 Lamp with double cupid pedestal
1304 Plain piano candlestick
1305 Dessert dish
1306 George IV spiral sugar sifter
1307 Vase and cover and another with head handle
1308 Cache pot
*1309 Ewer (3 sizes)
1310 Embossed jardinière (2 sizes)
1311 Embossed vase and cover (2 sizes)
1312 Stuart rose jar and cover
*1313 Melon rose jar and cover

164.   Historical series modelled by Frederick Gertner. Above, left to right, Charles I and II, Sir Walter Raleigh, Edward VI. Below, Anne Boleyn, Henry VIII, Mary Queen of Scots and Queen Elizabeth. These figures, first made in 1916, are still in production.

165.   Models by Freda Doughty. Above, left to right, Sister, 3149; Fortune Teller, or Mother Machree, 2924; Babes in the Wood, 3302; Joan, 2915; Spain, 3070; Mischief, 2914; Holland, 3074; and Tommy, 2913. See page 52.

166. A snapshot of Dorothy Doughty (seated) and her sister Freda Doughty in their garden at Falmouth.

167. Two of the most popular of the Freda Doughty models. Left, Grandmother's Dress, 3081, and Boy with Parakeet, 3087, $6\frac{1}{2}$ inches and $7\frac{7}{8}$ inches. These can be made in a number of different colours and are still in production. See page 53.

DAYS OF THE WEEK FIGURES

168. The series of Days of the Week figurines, modelled by Freda Doughty; the shape numbers may be seen under the figures, 7 boys and 7 girls, which have undergone a few changes since they were first introduced, and they are still produced. See page 52.

MONTHS OF THE YEAR FIGURES

169. The series of Months of the Year, modelled by Freda Doughty; they run from January, above left, to December, below right, and their shape numbers may be seen under the figurines, which are still in production. See page 52.

170. The first pair of Doughty Birds, the American Redstarts on Hemlock, shapes 3112 and 3113, modelled by Dorothy Doughty in 1935, height $7\frac{3}{4}$ inches. The cock, on the right, has black and orange tail feathers, the hen has bluish-grey crest, olive green back and tail feathers and brilliant yellow markings. The plain, stepped, circular white base is typical of the early Doughty Birds, this pair being limited to 66. See page 55.

171. Magnificent pair of American Doughty Birds, Phoebes on Flame Vine, shapes 3548 and 3549. Such models reflect the climax of Dorothy Doughty's modelling of the American series in the 1950s, fine proportion and balance, hand flower making of superb quality and naturalistically painted. The hen bird, with creamy white breast and pale green tinted grey feathers, has insects in her beak ready for the chick, who perches beneath a spray of flame vine of gorgeous orange and white colour, limited edition of 500 pairs, height $9\frac{3}{4}$ inches. See page 67.

172. Superb pair of English Redstarts on Gorse, modelled by Dorothy Doughty and first produced in 1968. The specially designed bases and plinths, the proportions and balance and the flower making which comprise some 1,200 separate hand-made pieces which build into the complete assembly, add up to what is probably the finest ceremic bird creations ever made. The bright yellow and green gorse reflect the orange reds of the cock Redstart as he is captured in the act of landing on the gorse, height of cock 11 inches with plinth. See page 69.

173. Some fairly rare animal figures of the 1930s watched over by the exceedingly rare Pigeon, coloured naturalistically, height 7 inches, length 8 inches (no mark). Wilfred the Rabbit, 2842, precedes in date the small Doris Lindner dog subjects. *The pigeon is in the collection of Miss G. C. Hoskins.*

174. A great range of the small dog, fox and kitten studies, modelled by Doris Lindner and made in the 1930s. *From the collection of Mrs. Heirs.* See page 52.

175. Fine large dog subject modelled by Doris Lindner, one of a pair of Afghan and Borzoi, 3425 and 3426 of 1947, height 9 inches, length 16 inches.

176. Hog hunting subject, modelled in 1936 by Doris Lindner, and still produced, length $9\frac{1}{2}$ inches, height $8\frac{1}{2}$ inches.

177. Photograph of Robert Bradley, foreman caster, assembling a Dorothy Doughty model of a Mocking Bird on Peach Blossom. The tail, which is clearly seen to be hollow as are all the cast pieces, is being stuck up to the body with liquid slip, then the bird and the numerous other pieces will be slowly and carefully built up on the branch of blossom. On the bench by the window may be seen a fully assembled pair of Mocking Birds, and also some examples of Freda Doughty's model 'Sister', all in raw, unfired, bone china. See page 56.

178. Photograph of Antonio Vassalo making the little flowers which were put on boxes and trays in the early 1930s. It was watching Antonio making the little flowers by hand, petal by petal, out of the solid clay, that gave Dorothy Doughty the inspiration of having the flowers on her bird models made by hand. See page 56.

179. Figures of the late 1930s and 40s. 'Salvage', 3370; right, 'Take Cover', 3351, show the humour and terror to be found in equal quantities in wartime England (the other shapes in the series of 7 are 3346, 3347, 3352, 3369 and 3382, modelled by Eva Soper; The Wolf (3511) modelled by Miss Stevens, height 8 inches. *'Salvage' owned by Miss Rea, 'Take Cover' by Mrs. Harvey.* See page 61.

180.   The visit of Princess Elizabeth to open the original Dyson Perrins Museum in 1951, to commemorate the bi-centenary of the founding of the Worcester Porcelain Company. Princess Elizabeth is being shown part of the Victorian Collection by Mr. Dyson Perrins, on the Princess' right is Mr. Joseph Gimson, the Managing Director, to his left is Mrs. Freda Perrins and on her left the Mayor of Worcester of that year, Alderman Norton. *Photograph by Berrows Newspapers.* See page 64.

181.   Part of the magnificent dessert and coffee services made for presentation to Princess Elizabeth by the Guards Regiments, on her marriage; gadrooned edge, maroon ground and gilding, with the crests of the Guards Regiments in the centre. See page 65.

182. A duplicate of the superb urn in which the Freedom of the City of Worcester was presented to Sir Winston Churchill in 1950. The urn has a beautiful painting of Worcester Cathedral by Harry Davis and fine hand gilding by Ivor Williams. The original is now on exhibition at Chartwell.

183. The wonderful pair of Siamese and Balinese Dancers modelled by Miss Pinder-Davis, shapes 3474 and 3473. A limited edition series of 25 pairs, started in 1951 and not yet completed, height 21 inches and 17 inches, beautifully painted and gilded. See page 66.

184. Chinoiserie subjects by Miss Pinder-Davis; the large pair, left, shape 3447, and right, 3446. Above, left, frame shapes 3494; right, 3502. Below, left, 3499; centre, 3500; right, 3492. These are in the white. but could be coloured and are not very common. See page 66.

185. Set of 4 Chinoiserie figures, from the left L'Oiseau, La Miroir, La Fleur and Le Panier, modelled by Azori, all in biscuit. The shape numbers of these beautiful figures are shown by their drum bases.

186. Papal Guard series modelled by Neal French and Frederick Gertner in limited editions. Left to right, shapes 3594, 3589, 3580, 3595, height 15 inches.

187. Set of 6 beautiful children subjects modelled by Neal French. Left to right, 3748, 3755, 3756, 3757, 3754, 3747. These subjects, made in 1962, did not sell and did not go into production, although a very few coloured and white examples are in existence.

188. Some old Worcester shapes that are in current production, in the white, their shape numbers by the side. Above, left to right, 2536, 1947, G971. Centre, 429, 69, 6/92, 4/94. Below, 3567, 3566, 2351 and 349.

189. Lamp and candlestick forms still in production. Left to right, 3284, 3544, 3762, 1969, 1050, 3283, 1957.

2363 H314 1691 1428 1572

H162 H175 H169 2713 2710 2826 2701

2048 H261 H279 H277 H291 H278 1286

ORNAMENTAL WARE. PATTERN-PAINTED FRUIT

190. Vases, pot pourris and covers in current production, painted with fruit subjects. Pot pourris generally have an inner dust cover and an outer cover. The H prefix numbers are shapes that originated at James Hadley's own factory. These shape numbers should be found under the base of the finished piece. See page 41.

191. Rose jar, or pot pourri, and cover, shape 2048, first made in 1899 and still a popular shape for fruit painting. This typically modern style of completely freehand-painted fruit with mossy backgrounds, every subject different, is painted by Harry Ayrton. See page xxiii.

192. Three of the popular cottage, castle and cathedral series plates, basically faint outlines, coloured and tinted by hand. These are service plates, often used as wall plaques.

193. Miss Doris Lindner working on her plasticine model of the Brahman Bull. See page 125.

194. Pair of limited edition mounted Guards Officers subjects modelled by Doris Lindner. Left, Life Guards, and right, Royal Horse Guards (The Blues), issued in 1961 in an edition of 150. Length of the Royal Horse Guards is $6\frac{3}{4}$ inches and height $9\frac{1}{2}$ inches and the statuettes are on specially designed ebony plinths.

195. Magnificent study of the famous steeplechaser Arkle, owned by Anne, Duchess of Westminster, modelled by Doris Lindner and issued in 1967 in a limited edition of 500, length 11 inches and height $10\frac{1}{4}$ inches, on walnut plinth. The figure has incredible grace and muscle movement and has a matt glaze so that the painted china body resembles the natural skin.
See page 73.

1314   Randolph rose jar and cover
1315   Boy and girl figure lamp
1316   {Tall lamp and container
         {Tall lamp and container without foot
1317   Lobed jardinière
1318   Vase and cover
1319   Low candlestick, as 482
1320   Vase and cover (22 in.)
1321   Pair boy and girl candlesticks, plain foot
1322   Pair boy and girl candlesticks, claw foot
1323   Lobed biscuit box and cover
1324   Pair boy and girl double branch candelabra
1325   Wicker bowl and double figure centre
1326   Bamboo rose jar and cover and also as an ink
1327   Vase (2 sizes)
1328   Fluted piano candlestick
1329   Lamp, lion head handles
1330   Lamp, figure handles
1331   Globular bottle (4 sizes)
1332   Festoon rose jar and cover
1333   Bamboo ewer
1334   Lobed coffee cup, teacup and saucers
1335   Embossed oval festooned flower bowl
1336   Embossed round bowl on claw foot
1337   Flower bowl
1338   Bamboo spill
1339   Japanese tea kettle
1340   Cache pots, set of 3 different sizes and a biscuit box
1341   Bamboo jug
1342   Individual dessert dish, scalloped and fluted
1343   Individual dessert dish, scalloped
1344   Individual dessert dish, triangular
1345   Individual dessert dish, triangular
1346   Individual dessert dish, leaf
1347   Individual dessert dish, oval
1348   Regent dessert plate and high and low comports
1349   Regent dessert plate and high and low comports
1350   Park dessert plate
1351   Hatfield dessert plate
1352   Pair sitting boy and girl figures and branch
1353   Pair standing boy and girl figures and branch
‡1354   The Sower centre (33 in.) and as a lamp
1355   Suspending lamp
1356   Lamp and container
1357   Lamp and container on foot

1889

1358   Vase on fluted pedestal
1359   Tall orchid comport
1360   Low orchid comport
1361   Fluted ewer (2 sizes)
‡1362   Beefeater figure (spear and menu card extra)
1363   Embossed and panelled vase and cover
1364   Pair double figure comports

P

1365	Pair boy and girl figures and baskets
*1366	Mask spout jug (5 sizes)
1367	Oblong celery dish
1368	Embossed vase figure handles
1369	Embossed melon ice jug and a plain shape (2 sizes)
1370	Low candlestick as 1050
1371	Pair male and female figures and baskets
1372	Flowerpot embossed orchids
1373	Square embossed teapot, sugar box and cream
1374	Embossed jardinière
1375	Double toast shell (2 sizes)
1376	Ball jug (5 sizes)
1377	Chamber candlestick, deep bowl
1378	Twist jug (3 sizes)
1379	Jardinière
1380	Fluted biscuit box, cover and stand
1381	Vase and cover
1382	Globe shaped spouted jug (5 sizes) Chocolate jug (2 sizes)
1383	'Health to the King', pair of male and female figures
1384	Vase and cover
‡1385	Lyre clock case, hexagon stand
1386	Lamp with claw feet Lamp without claw feet Lamp as bowl, claw feet, no container
‡1387	Pair figures—innkeeper and female companion
1388	Pair figures, boy and girl with baskets
1389	Sardine tray
1390	Lamp
1391	Lamp
1392	Reservoir lamp
1393	Covered butter pot and drainer
1394	Miniature lamp claw feet
1395	Tall lamp
‡1396	Clock case, head handles
1397	Vase and cover, ram's head handles (3 sizes)
1398	Vase and cover
*1399	Vase and cover (4 sizes) and a miniature (no cover)
1400	Wicker plate pierced edge
1401	Double figure comport (boy and girl and grapes)
1402	Double figure comport (boy and girl and grapes) Double figure comport as pair of 5 light candelabra
1403	Lobed lamp and container (2 sizes)
1404	Shell with handle (2 sizes) Shell, triple luncheon tray
1405	Vase
1406	Long-necked vase and stopper
1407	Vase and cover, head handles (3 sizes)
1408	Vase and cover
1409	Embossed and panel vase and cover
1410	Vase, head handles
1411	Vase, enamelled and scroll (3 sizes)
*1412	Melon cracker jar, cover and stand—middle as a lamp
1413	Toast shell (2 sizes)
*1414	Cabbage leaf (2 sizes)

1415   Star dishes (3 sizes)
1416   Shell plate (5 sizes)
1417   Match stand
1418   Edged oval tray
1419   Round lotus leaf
1420   Preserve shell
1421   3-handled loving cup
1422   Pine mustard pot
1423   Triple luncheon tray, rope handle (2 sizes)
1424   Strawberry plate on shell feet (2 sizes)
1425   Box and cover, embossed blossom
*1426   Empress dessert ware pierced—plates, 2 comports and dishes
1427   Moore dessert ware pierced—plates, 2 comports and dishes
1428   Vase and cover, pierced neck (3 sizes—still made for fruit)

1890

1429   { Pierced vase and cover (Grainger's shape)
         { Pierced vase and cover, plain
1430   Vase and cover, snake handles (4 sizes)
1431   Vase
1432   Vase
1433   Square mustard, pepper and salt
1434   Lobed mustard, pepper and salt
1435   Salad bowl
1436   Small fluted ewer
1437   Jug, shell panels at side (5 sizes)
1438   Jug, cleft top (6 sizes)
1439   Jug, scroll handle
*1440   Male statuette—Satyr (tree trunk added for electric light)
*1441   Female companion—Bacchante with cymbal
1442   Panelled lamp and reservoir
1443   Spiral lamp and reservoir
1444   Vase and cover (2 sizes)
1445   Vase, tall neck, dolphin handles (2 sizes)
1446   Scroll candelabra—5 lights (22 in.)
1447   Cup and saucer
1448   Lamp
1449   Vase (2 sizes)
1450   Spiral lamp with foot, or without foot or as bowl
1451   Biscuit box and cover (2 sizes)
1452   Spiral vase (2 sizes)
1453   Salad bowl
1454   Celery dish
1455   Celery dish
‡1456   Boy and girl on seesaw
1457   Vase and cover
1458   Louis candelabrum, 3 brackets
1459   Jardinière on foot, or low foot or with altered neck
1460   Louis trough
1461   Louis flat dish
1462   Louis lamp on clays and container; ditto no container
1463   Dragon-handled fluted ewer
1464   Lamp on pedestal and container
1465   Lamp and container
1466   Fluted tea set and tray

1467	Fluted jug
1468	Handled lamp and reservoir
‡1469	Floor lamp
1470	Bamboo group—6 straight tubes and 6 crescent tubes
1471	Empress teacup and saucer, coffee and saucer and plate
1472	Oval bowl embossed scrolls
1473	Embossed shell dish
1474	Scroll dish
1475	Crescent dish
1476	2-lobed dish
1477	Embossed dish
1478	Scroll candlestick (2 sizes) single branch
1479	Festooned lamp, tall and squat forms
1480	Pair of sowers—male sower and female companion
1481	Vase and cover (3 sizes and a miniature without cover)
1482	Vase and cover 15 in. and smaller without cover
1483	Scrolled basket (5 sizes)
1484	Lobed cruet
1485	Jardinière on foot, embossed heads; also as lamp
1486	Round scrolled bowl
‡1487	The Violinist
1488	Lamp and reservoir on claw feet
1489	Clayton cruet
1490	Oval jardinière (4 sizes)
1491	Fluted vase (2 sizes)
1492	Figure-handled oval jardinière
1493	Figure-handled ewer (3 sizes)
1494	Elephant-handled lamp and reservoir
1495	Festooned vase and cover (21 in.)
1496	Embossed fluted neck vase and cover
1497	Vase and cover, dolphin feet
1498	Vase and cover
1499	Lamp and reservoir, embossed neck
1500	Louis oval bowl

1891

1501	Vase and cover, embossed heads
1502	Candlestick, high foot
1503	Vase and cover, embossed neck
1504	Vase and cover (22 in.)
1505	Lotus taper
1506	Candlestick—3 feet and cupids
†1507	Coral-handled jug (5 sizes)
1508	Ring-handled vase and cover
1509	Female figure, Roman with basket (23 in.)
1510	Female figure, with vase by fountain
1511	Dessert plate, and round and oval comports
1512	Rococo dessert plate
1513	Tripod jardinière (3 sizes)
1514	Jardinière and cover
1515	Scroll-handled vase and cover (4 sizes)
1516	Jardinière, dolphin head handle
1517	Griffin-handled vase and cover (23 in.)
1518	Embossed vase and cover

1519   Vase and cover, 4-foot pedestal
1520   Vase, 4 claw feet
1521   Oval shell basket (5 sizes)
1522   Salad bowl (4 sizes)
1523   Jardinière (as 1428) (3 sizes)
1524   Oval bowl—griffin handles (17 × 22 in.)
1525   Square embossed vase
1526   Embossed ewer
1527   Festooned vase (as 1332)
1528   Plain vase
1529   Plain vase
1530   Festooned sugar and cream
1531   Vase
1532   Fluted vase, with or without handles
1533   Embossed vase and cover (20 in.)
1534   Italian tea set
1535   Vase
1536   Ewer
1537   Bowl
1538   Vase (2 sizes)
1539   Vase (2 sizes and a miniature)
1540   Vase
1541   Jardinière (2 sizes)
1542   Jardinière, embossed foliage
1543   Jardinière, embossed heads
1544   Vase
1545   Tall vase
*1546   Jug (5 sizes)
1547   Tall electric lamp standard (19 in.)
1548   Tall electric lamp standard (19½ in.)
1549   Electric lamp
1550   Terminal female figure, vase on head
1551   Vase (3 sizes)
1552   Vase (3 sizes)
1553   Vase (4 sizes)
1554   Vase, or as lamp with container
1555   Oval bowl
1556   Flower-holder (3 sizes)
1557   Vase
1558   Candy box and cover (2 sizes)
1559   Candy box and cover, oblong and embossed
1560   Candy box and cover, fan shape and wicker
1561   Candy box and cover, oblong embossed shell
1562   Candy box and cover, tri-lobed
1563   Floor lamp (3 pieces)
1564   Embossed and scroll coffee, tea and chocolate cup and saucer
1565   Shell-embossed plate, teacup and saucer
1566   Embossed potted meat box and cover
*1567   Pair Chinguin Indians, male and female
1568   Basket (4 sizes)
1569   Vase (2 sizes)
1570   Vase
*1571   Dressing table set—tray, candlestick, ring tray, ring pin, puff box, pomade box, ball scent bottle
1572   Vase and cover (2 sizes) [still made for fruit painting]

1892

1573	Vase
1574	Vase
1575	Vase (2 sizes)
1576	Lamp, scroll foot
1577	Rippled dessert plate
1578	Dolphin-handled vase (2 sizes)
1579	Chelsea plate, full-pierced or half-pierced
‡1580	Russian table centre decoration: 5 stumps (13½, 6, 8, 16 and 8 in.), 6 troughs (17½ × 8, 7 × 4½, 15 × 6½, 18 × 7, 15, 17 × 6 in.), lamp, skating boys (1595), sleigh and driver (1597), sleigh and boy pushing (1598), large swan and small swan (1596), punt (1596) and dogs (1597)
1581	Ewer (4 sizes including miniature and toy)
1582	Vase
1583	Small candy dish (Empress)
1584	Dolphin-handled lamp
1585	Dessert plate
1586	Dessert plate, scroll edge
*1587	Empress ewer (2 sizes and a miniature)
1588	Chelsea tea and coffee set
1589	Ribbed tea and coffee set
1590	Lamp, 3 claw feet
1591	Lamp
1592	Richly embossed dessert plate
‡1593	Pair male and female figures, drummer and vivandière
1594	Columbian vase (3 sizes)
‡1595 ‡1596 ‡1597 ‡1598	See Russian centre (1580)
1599	Vase
1600	Vase (3 sizes)
1601	Sporting menu
1602	Tri-luncheon tray
1603	Salad bowl
1604	Figure group, Uncle Tom and Eva (12 × 10 in.)
1605	Dessert plate
1606	Pair Roumanian figures, male and female
1607	Lamp and reservoir (25½ in.)
1608	Strawberry dish
1609	Tea tray (2 sizes)
1610	Ice dish and 3 sizes of plate
1611	Plate
1612	Oyster plate
1613	Tray with chocolate, coffee and tea set
1614	Snake sugar and cream
1615	Claw foot teacup and saucer
1616	Lamp, satyr support (15 in.)
1617	Vase and cover
1618	Vase and cover (2 sizes)
1619	Vase and cover
1620	Jardinière (3 sizes)
1621	Jardinière
1622	Rose jardinière

‡1623   Cupid inkstand—double cupid and two single cupids
1624   Vase and cover
1625   Vase and cover
1626   Vase and cover
1627   Fern pot
1628   Dragon-handled vase and cover
1629   Jardinière (4 sizes)
1630   Tall grass holder (4 sizes, up to 48½ in.)

1893

1631   Vase and cover
1632   Vase and cover
1633   Flower-holder
*1634   Cracker-holder, cover and stand
1635   Embossed salt on foot
1636   Rustic menu
1637   Rustic guest tablet
1638   Daisy coffee cup and saucer
1639   Flower-holder (3 sizes)
1640   Salt
1641   Guest tablet
1642   Stamp box and cover, supported by 2 figures
1643   Tray
1644   Tray
1645   Tray
1646   Jardinière (3 sizes)
1647   Vase
1648   Jardinière (3 sizes)
1649   Scent bottles—Chicago Exhibition commemoration
1650   Lion head handle jardinière
*1651   Cache or flower pot (7 sizes)
*1652   Spiral-fluted jug (5 sizes)
1653   Pair of lamps with boy and girl figures
1654   Vase and cover
1655   Boy and basket
1656   Girl and basket
1657   Boy and basket
1658   Girl and basket
1659   Lamp as 1154 with boy and girl figures
1660   Centre as 1174 with boy and girl figures
1661   Vase (4 sizes)
1662   Cleveland coffee pot, chocolate and hot water jugs
1663   Coral vase, as 1507 jug (5 sizes)
1664   Vase
‡1665   Negro and vase statuette (28½ in.)
‡1666   Negress and vase statuette (28½ in.)
*1667   Fern sugar (3 sizes)
1668   Ewer (2 sizes)
1669   Caddy and cover
1670   Fluted sugar and cream
1671   Panelled vase
1672   Vase and cover
1673   Plain lamp
1674   Griffin-handled vase
1675   Cupid-handled vase

1676	Tripod flower bowl
1677	Pair boy and girl with baskets
1678	Pierced teapot
1679	Double comport, boy and girl with basket
1680	Double comport, boy and girl with basket
1681	Salad set for mounting: bowl, handle, biscuit box, marmalade, butter, sardine, egg cup, jelly, teapot (no cover), sugar, cream, mustard and salt
1682	Cup and saucer
1683	Vase and cover (3 sizes)
1684	Vase and cover (3 sizes)
1685	Tripod vase
1686	Royal vase (2 sizes)
1687	Oblong embossed vase
1688	Flower-holder
1689	Fern bowl
1690	Wide, low vase
*1691	Vase and cover [still made for fruit painting]
*1692	Vase and cover [still made for fruit painting]
1693	Vase
1694	Jardinière
1695	Embossed lamp (27 in.)
1696	Oval fluted dish
1697	Lobed dish
1698	Oval dish
1699	Diamond-shaped dish
1700	Square photo frame
1701	Oval photo frame
1702	Vase and cover
1703	Bamboo candlestick
1704	Bamboo flower holder

1894

1705	Vase
1706	Small star tray
1707	Vase
1708	Bracket
1709	Lamp (26 in.)
1710	Dish and cover
1711	Vase
1712	Vase and cover
1713	Flower bowl
*1714	Lizard jug
1715	Flower-holder
1716	Vase (2 sizes)
1717	Vase
1718	Pair boy and girl with branch for electric light
1719	Pair boy and girl with branch for electric light
1720	Rose jar and cover
1721	Vase and cover (22½ in.)
1722	Vase and cover
1723	Tall lamp (25 in.)
1724	Vase
1725	Figures and basket centre (13 × 16½ in.)
1726	Vase (2 sizes)

1727   Vase (2 sizes)
1728   Vase flower-holder
1729   Tall flower bowl
1730   Embossed vase (2 sizes)
1731   Flower-holder
1732   Vase (2 sizes—22 and 11 in.)
1733   Vase
1734   Vase
1735   Fern pot
1736   Vase
1737   Vase figure handles
1738   Vase
1739   Salad set-server, biscuit, marmalade, sardine, 2 butters, cup and saucer
1740   Pair male and female figures with baskets
1741   Group of figures for electric light
1742   Ewer (4 sizes)
‡1743   Female Moorish slave (24 in. and a small size)
‡1744   Female partner slave (24 in. and a small size)
1745   Ewer
1746   Flower-holder claw feet
1747   Vase
1748   Vase
1749   Vase
1750   Lamp claw feet
1751   Pair boy and girl with basket
‡1752   Low oval jardinière for electric (6 gns. in white, 8 gns. stained ivory)
1753   Jardinière for electric
1754   Lamp spiral foot
1755   Low jardinière
1756   Flower-holder with fixed cover
1757   Spiral vase (3 sizes—small size a Cricklite standard)
1758   Dolphin-handled vase
1759   Head-handled vase
1760   Vase
1761   Vase
1762   Vase (2 sizes)
1763   Fluted vase
1764   Vase and cover (also a miniature without cover)
1765   Candlestick
1766   Vase and cover
1767   Vase
1768   Inkstand
1769   Inkstand
1770   Inkstand
1771   Egg and spoon basket
1772   Spiral vase
1773   Lamp
‡1774   Pair male and female figures—woodman and milkmaid
1775   Fluted vase
1776   3-handled loving cup
1777   Vase
1778   Rococo bracket
1779   Griffin-handled jardinière (6 × 18 × 8½ in.)
1780   Berry bowl (3 sizes), sugar and cream
1781   Candlestick

1782	Lamp
1783	Pair horn brackets
1784	Electrolier bracket, female holding electrolier in left hand
1785	Electrolier bracket, female holding electrolier in right hand
1786	Vase on foot
1787	Loving cup
1788	Fluted vase

1895

1789	Tall lamp (24½ in.)
1790	Flower tube
1791	Fluted vase
1792	Heart-shaped tray (3 sizes)
1793	Pair male and female figures with vase and candlestick
1794	Lamp
1795	Scroll jug (5 sizes)
1796	Biscuit box, cover and stand
1797	Hexagon vase
1798	Spiral vase
1799	Panel vase
1800	Panel vase
1801	Panel vase
1802	Salad set for mounting
1803	Pair figures, boy piper, Strephon, and female companion
1804	Pepper, mustard and salt
1805	Spiral-fluted bowl
1806	Panelled bowl
1807	Bowl on foot (3 sizes)
1808	Rose jar and cover
1809	Panelled rose jar and cover
1810	Navvy and his companion, pair male and female
1811	Panelled vase and cover (3 sizes)
1812	Bowl on foot (2 sizes)
1813	Bowl on foot (2 sizes)
1814	Tall flower-holder
1815	Vase on foot
1816	Heart luncheon tray
1817	Vase and cover
‡1818	Female figure 'Night' (22 in.)
‡1819	Female figure 'Morning' (22 in.)
1820	Heart ice tray and plate
1821	Panel vase and cover
1822	Panel vase
1823	Panel vase and cover
1824	Panel vase
1825	Panel vase
1826	Lotus candlestick
*1827	Female figure 'Dancing'
*1828	Female figure 'Music'
1829	Candlestick
1830	Shell bowl
1831	Handled cake tray
1832	Scroll-handle jug (3 sizes)
1833	Flower bowl

1834   Panel vase
1835   Vase and cover
1836   Panel bowl on foot
1837   Panel bowl
1838   Spiral vase and cover
1839   Vase (2 sizes)
1840   Flower-holder
1841   Heart luncheon tray
1842   Scroll bowl (3 sizes)
1843   Dessert set—plate, centre, high and low comports
1844   Panelled clock case
1845   Flower pot
1846   Plain vase
1847   Plain vase and cover
1848   Panel vase and cover
1849   Panel vase and cover
1850   Panel vase and cover
1851   Vase and cover
1852   Corner bowl
1853   Vase and cover (2 sizes)
1854   Vase and cover (2 sizes)
1855   Vase
1856   Vase and cover
1857   Vase and cover
1858   Vase and cover
1859   Vase
1860   Menu

1896

1861   Small tray
1862   Small tray
1863   Jam pot, salt, pepper and biscuit in form of a potato
1864   Vase and cover
1865   Vase
1866   Vase
1867   Vase
1868   Vase, 19th century Worcester shape
1869   Vase, 19th century Worcester shape
1870   Vase, 19th century Worcester shape
1871   Vase, 19th century Worcester shape
1872   Vase, 19th century Worcester shape, and cover (3 sizes)
1873   Candlestick
*1874   Figure Irish girl
*1875   Pair figures Welsh man and girl
1876   Flower-holder (Rhyton type)
1877   Flower-holder (Rhyton type) (2 sizes)
1878   Flower bowl (2 sizes)
1879   Flower-holder
1880   Handled flower-holder
1881   Wicker sugar and cream
1882   Flower bowl
1883   Bowl on foot
1884   'Potato' cup and saucer
1885   Violet holder

1886	Boy and goat
1887	Girl and goat
1888	Flower-holder
1889	Vase and cover
*1890	Pair figure candlesticks—figures as 1250
1891	Pair figure flower tubes—Joy and Sorrow
1892	Vase and cover
1893	Vase and cover
1894	Vase and cover
1895	Vase and cover
1896	Vase
1897	Vase
1898	Vase
1899	Vase
1900	Crescent trough and straight trough
1901	Pair figure lamps (Satyr figures 1440)
1902	Pair figure flower-holders (Satyr figures 1440)
1903	Vase
1904	Fluted vase and cover
1905	Candlestick
1906	Flower-holder
1907	Violet, with or without foot
1908	Amphora and stand flower-holder

1897

1909	Heart flower-holder
1910	Bowl
1911	Vase and cover (3 sizes and a miniature without cover)
1912	Vase and cover (3 sizes and a miniature without cover)
1913	Vase
1914	Jug, scroll at top (5 sizes)
1915	Pair figure flower-holders (figures as 1250)
1916	Menu flower-holder
1917	Menu flower-holder
1918	Vase
1919	Bowl on foot
1920	Vase
1921	Vase and cover
1922	Vase
1923	Fowl flower-holder
1924	Hexagon biscuit jar for mounting
‡1925	Pedestal and jardinière (49 in., 5 gns. in white, 14 gns. stained ivory, enamelled thistles, £35 b. blue and gilt, exotic birds)
1926	Vase
1927	Rose jar and cover (3 sizes, smallest pierced)
1928	Draped vase
1929	Salad and biscuit for mounting
1930	Vase, with or without swan handles
1931	Tube flower-holder
1932	Vase
1933	Tea set as 1373
1934	Bust of Queen Victoria on small pedestal
1935	Vase
1936	Vase and cover

1937	Vase and cover (4 sizes, smallest can be pierced)
1938	Flower-holder with or without pierced foot
1939	Vase
1940	Pen tray
1941	Vase on pedestal
1942	Vase on pedestal, pierced pedestal
1943	Lotus flower-holder
1944	Ewer (2 sizes)
1945	Monkey and lotus flower-holder
1946	Vase, vine handles (2 sizes)
†1947	Jardinière (4 sizes) and salad pierced or unpierced
1948	Vase on pedestal (2 sizes)
1949	Vase on pierced pedestal (2 sizes)
1950	Vase and cover
1951	Vase
1952	Pair figures on pierced stands
1953	Candlestick
1954	Oval basket
1955	Pair boy and girl figures holding pots
1956	Vase
*1957	Vase and cover on plinth—still made
1958	Vase and cover, plain or pierced
1959	Vase (4 sizes)
1960	Vase (3 sizes)
1961	Vase and cover
1962	Vase and cover
1963	Vase, plain or pierced
1964	Lamp
1965	Shaving mug
1966	Lamp
1967	Vase for acorns
1968	Ewer
*1969	{Vase on pedestal (3 sizes) [still made for fruit] {Vase without pedestal (3 sizes and a miniature)

1898

1970	Vase and cover
‡1971	Figure 'Mercury' (18 in.)
1972	Wicker fern pot
1973	Vase and cover
1974	Vase festoon handle
1975	Pair flower-holders with a cupid and also without cupid
1976	Pedestal jardinière (29½ in.)
1977	Mussel shell
1978	Ivy leaf (4 sizes, number 3 as photo frame with hole in centre)
1979	Tray with mouse, also without mouse (2 sizes)
1980	Mouse tray and grapes
1981	Double mouse tray and acorns, also without mouse
1982	Scroll candy box
1983	Lobed candy box
1984	Diamond candy box
1985	Oval bowl on foot
1986	Oval tray
1987	Leaf tray

1988	Vase
1989	Loving cup and cover
1990	Gadroon tray (6 sizes)
1991	Embossed oval tray
1992	Beaded oval tray (3 sizes and also a tazza)
1993	Fern-embossed tray
1994	Triple luncheon tray
1995	Pot pourri jar
‡1996	Male Bedouin Chief figure (22 in.)
1997	Lamp
1998	Lamp
1999	Lamp
2000	Lamp
2001	Biscuit box for mounting
2002	Tall lamp—Lee Lamp Co. (23 in.)
‡2003	Pair female figures 'Pomona' and 'Flora'
2004	Grass-holder (2 sizes)
2005	Vase and cover
2006	Rococo embossed vase
2007	Vase and cover (23½ in., also smaller)
2008	Female figure 'Sabrina'
2009	Female figure 'Isis'
2010	Vase and cover (25 in. and smaller)
2011	Group 'Anglo American'—John Bull and Uncle Sam shaking hands
‡2012	Male figure 'Sailor'
2013	Boat vase on pedestal
2014	Rococo embossed vase and cover
2015	'Cricklite' standard, 2 cups
*2016	Female figure with cymbals—like 1440 (23½ in. and smaller)
2017	Vase and cover—as 1311
2018	Pair of cupid dishes
2019	'Cricklite' standard and dish (2 sizes)
2020	'Cricklite' Torch, bearer pair of females (2 sizes)
2021	Vase and cover, with or without pedestal
2022	Lamp and container, ring handle
2023	Grass-holder
2024	Lamp and container
2025	Boat vase with or without pedestal
2026	Vase and cover on pedestal and 2 smaller sizes without pedestal
2027	Vase and cover
2028	Pair Bringaree Indian lamps
2029	Flower-holder on feet
2030	Flower-holder (3 sizes)
2031	Vase and cover
2032	Vase and cover
2033	Vase (23½ in.)
2034	Shell and cupid
‡2035	'Cricklite' and figure of 'Student'
2036	Miniature Sèvres vase
2037	Small bowl (Miss Gee)

1899

2038	Pillar
2039	Vase

2040	Vase
2041	Vase and cover
2042	Vase
2043	Vase and cover
2044	Fern dessert set
2045	Wicker dish (4 sizes)
2046	Fern pot (2 sizes)
2047	Jardinière
2048	Rose jar and cover (3 sizes) [small and medium still made for painted fruit]
2049	Vase (9 in. and a miniature)
2050	Vase and cover, griffin handles
2051	Vase and cover
2052	Flower pot
2053	Oval jardinière
2054	Square rose jar and cover
2055	Ewer
2056	Vase
2057	Vase
2058	Vase
2059	Vase
2060	Covered ewer, scaled
2061	Loving cup (3 sizes)
‡2062	Pair of male figures—'Puritan and Cavalier'
2063	Vase (2 sizes)
2064	Vase and cover, wing handles
2065	Tall lamp ($25\frac{1}{2}$ in.)
‡2066	Male statuette 'The Idler'
2067	The Modeller
2068	The Potter
2069	The Decorator
2070	Tall embossed lamp (23 in.)
2071	Pair of Musicians—boy playing lute, girl tambourine
‡2072	Pair of Musicians—seated
2073	Violet embossed
2074	Violet plain
2075	Violet plain
2076	Violet plain
2077	Violet plain
2078	Wicker sugar and cream
2079	Jardinière—as 1310 (2 sizes)
2080	Low Lamp
‡2081	Pair of Musicians—seated
2082	Bowl with or without plinth
2083	Vase and cover
2084	Teapot, sugar and cream embossed scale
2085	Embossed hexagon vase and cover
2086	Vase and cover
2087	Vase and cover
2088	Vase and cover
2089	Box and cover
2090	Vase and cover, griffin handle (2 sizes, 26 in. and a smaller)
2091	Goat head centre ($10\frac{1}{2} \times 22$ in.)
2092	Goat head centre (side rhyton horn)
2093	Fluted bowl on foot (2 sizes)

2094	Pot pourri and cover embossed scale
2095	Vase and cover embossed scale
2096	Vase and cover
2097	Spill vase
2098	Vase, snake handles
2099	Vase, vine handles
2100	Vase, vine handles

1900

‡2101	Figure 'Hebe' (29¼ in., 8 gns. white, 12 gns. coloured)
‡2102	Companion figure 'Psyche' (30 in.)
‡2103	Figure cupid with bow (19¾ in.)
‡2104	Companion with sheath (19¾ in.)
‡2105	Pair figures 'Flemish man and woman'
2106	Boer war soldier—C.I.V. (Imperial Forces)
2107	Boer war soldier—C.I.V. (Imperial Yeoman)
2108	Boer war soldier—C.I.V. (Colonial Trooper)
2109	Boer war soldier—C.I.V. (Black Watch)
2110	Boer war soldier—C.I.V. (Handy Man)
2111	Boer war soldier—C.I.V. (Guardsman)
2112	Vase and cover, griffin handles
2113	Cup, old Worcester shape
2114	Cup, old Worcester shape
2115	Cup, old Worcester shape
2116	Ewer, snake handles
2117	Vase, snake handles
2118	Flower pot, embossed poppies
2119	Vase, plain or with slight piercing
2120	Vase
2121	Vase
2122	Biscuit box and cover as 1366 jug
2123	Loving cup, 3 handles
2124	Vase, pierced globe
2125	Vase and cover
2126	Vase and cover—old Worcester Flight Barr & Barr shape
2127	Spill
2128	Vase and cover
2129	Vase
2130	Bowl—old Worcester shape
2131	Vase and cover, goat heads
2132	Jug (3 sizes)
2133	Lip salve boxes and covers—3 shapes
2134	Handled-tray
2135	Gadroon fern pot

1901

2136	Biscuit box and cover
2137	Vase and cover, embossed scale
2138	Vase and cover, embossed scale
2139	Vase and cover, embossed scale
2140	Vase and cover, embossed scale
2141	Vase
2142	Vase with or without handles

XV. Statuette of a Palomino horse, modelled by Doris Lindner and issued in a Limited Edition in 1971. The superb modelling, sense of movement, making and decorating are an incredible advance upon the figures of 100 years earlier. Length $11\frac{1}{4}$ inches, height without plinth $8\frac{3}{4}$ inches, shape number 3882.

XVI. Nightingale on Honeysuckle, from the English series modelled by Dorothy Doughty, shape 3701, Limited Edition of 500 issued
in 1971. The bird and foliage are naturalistic in size and colouring,
height $9\frac{1}{2}$ inches.

2143	Embossed fern pot
2144	Embossed flower-holder
2145	Embossed flower-holder
2146	Ewer
2147	Spill on foot as 161 (2 sizes)
2148	Beaded vase and cover
2149	Griffin-handled beaded vase and cover
2150	Vase
2151	Vase
2152	Wheatsheaf biscuit box and marmalade
2153	Vine leaf tray
2154	Begonia leaf tray
2155	Dianthus leaf tray
2156	Ewer, griffin handle
*2157	Vase, old Worcester shape (2 sizes, large size with collar as electrolite)
2158	Vase and cover
2159	Vase and cover
2160	Vase and cover
‡2161	Wandering Minstrel, male
‡2162	Wandering Minstrel, female
2163	Ewer
2164	Vase
2165	Vase
2166	Vase
2167	Vase
2168	Vase
2169	Vase
2170	Vase
2171	Vase
2172	Vase and stopper
2173	Ewer
2174	Vase for Sabrina decoration
2175	Vase for Sabrina decoration
2176	Fern pot
2177	Vase
2178	Italian ash tray, on feet or without feet
2179	Basket violet
2180	Octagonal tray
2181	Vase
2182	Candlestick
2183	Curzon ware set: breakfast cup and saucer, tea cup and saucer, flower-holder (5 sizes), candlestick, flower pot (5 sizes), butter and stand, sardine and stand, marmalade and cover, milk jug, cream jug, small size sugar, teapot, egg cup, cruet stand, grass-holder, biscuit and cover, jam jar and cover
2184	Hors d'œuvres tray
2185	Double tray
2186	Vase
2187	Vase
2188	Vase
2189	Biscuit box for mounting
2190	Biscuit box for mounting
2191	Biscuit box for mounting
2192	Vase and cover (2 sizes)
2193	Vase and cover, painted spray flowers by George Cole—stained ivory

Q

2194	Vase and cover (2 sizes)
2195	Vase for Sabrina decoration [shape still made for fruit painting]
2196	Flower-holder for Sabrina decoration
2197	Flower-holder for Sabrina decoration
2198	Flower-holder for Sabrina decoration
2199	Flower-holder for Sabrina decoration
2200	Bowl for Sabrina decoration
2201	Vase for Sabrina decoration
2202	Vase
2203	Tray
2204	Cake plate
2205	Tray
2206	Flower pot for Sabrina-style of decoration
2207	Flower bowl for Sabrina-style of decoration
2208	Flower bowl for Sabrina-style of decoration
2209	Vase and cover

1902

2210	Ewer
2211	Pot pourri vase and cover
2212	Embossed ewer and goblet
‡2213	Figure of Jester
‡2214	Figure of Shepherdess
2215	Pedestal and jardinière (50 in. and smaller)
2216	Vase and cover
2217	Loving cup, 3 handles (2 sizes)
2218	'Broken egg' marmalade pot
‡2219	Imperial Coronation vase (28 in., £30 white, £130 b. blue and coloured)
2220	Fern pot
2221	Biscuit jar and cover for Sabrina-style of decoration
2222	Tobacco jar and cover for Sabrina-style of decoration
2223	Tea caddy and cover for Sabrina-style of decoration
2224	Ink pot and cover for Sabrina-style of decoration
2225	Vase and cover (Adams-style)
2226	Vase
2227	Vase
2228	Vase and as a violet [shape still made for fruit painting]
2229	Caddy and cover
2230	Vase and cover, peacock handles
2231	Vase and cover
2232	Vase and cover
2233	Vase and cover
2234	Vase and cover
2235	Caddy and cover for Sabrina-style of decoration
2236	Vase and cover for Sabrina-style of decoration
2237	Vase and cover for Sabrina-style of decoration
2238	Vase and cover for Sabrina-style of decoration
2239	Vase and cover for Sabrina-style of decoration
2240	Vase and cover for Sabrina-style of decoration
2241	Vase and cover for Sabrina-style of decoration
2241	Vase and cover for Sabrina-style of decoration
2243	Vase and cover for Sabrina-style of decoration
‡2244	Coronation tablet—King and Queen
2245	Ewer

2246	Vase and cover
2247	Vase and cover
2248	Vase
2249	Vase (2 sizes)
2250	Vase (2 sizes)
2251	Scent bottle
2252	Vase and cover for Sabrina
2253	Vase for Sabrina
2254	Jug (4 sizes)
2255	Vase and cover
2256	Vase (3 sizes)
2257	Vase and cover—old Worcester shape
2258	Vase—old Worcester shape (2 sizes)
2259	Ewer
2260	Vase (2 sizes)
2261	Fern pot
2262	Vase (2 sizes)
2263	Fern pot
2264	Vase and cover
2265	Spiral vase for Sabrina-style of decoration (2 sizes)
2266	Spill vase—old Worcester shape
2267	Vase—old Worcester shape

1903

2268	Ink, form of Roman lamp
2269	Vase (2 sizes)
2270	Vase and cover
2271	Vase and cover
2272	Vase and cover (2 sizes)
2273	Vase
2274	Vase and cover
2275	Ewer
2276	Ewer
2277	Vase and cover
2278	Grass-holder
2279	Grass-holder
2280	Grass-holder on tripod
2281	Snake-handled vase
2282	Wing-handled cup
2283	Vase
2284	Lotus taper
2285	Vase and cover (2 sizes)
2286	Grass-holder (3 sizes)
2287	Bowl on foot, low
2288	Bowl on foot, tall
2289	Ewer
2290	Oval jardinière (2 sizes)
2291	Tea caddy and cover
2292	Vase
2293	Vase and cover
2294	Pot pourri and cover, laurel handles
2295	Pot pourri and cover
2296	Vase and cover
2297	Vase and cover

2298	Vase and cover
2299	Vase and cover
2300	Vase and cover
2301	Cup on foot
2302	Striped sugar and cream
2303	Vase and cover
2304	Vase and cover (2 sizes)
2305	Vase and cover
2306	Cup on foot
2307	Vase and cover
2308	Flower-holder
2309	Pierced vase and cover
2310	Pierced vase
2311	Vase and cover
2312	Vase and cover
2313	Fruit centre
2314	Claw spill
2315	Jug and cover
2316	Vase and cover
2317	Vase
2318	Flower-holder
2319	Flower-holder
2320	Violet
2321	Pierced vase and cover

1904

‡2322	Figure of a Beadle
2323	Vase
2324	Pot pourri (2 sizes)
2325	Pot pourri (2 sizes)
2326	Swan-handled vase and cover
2327	Vase
2328	Vase, pierced cover
2329	Vase and cover
2330	Vase and cover (2 sizes)
2331	Vase and cover
2332	Vase
2333	Jug and cover (Dr. Wall shape)
2334	Fluted caddy and cover (Dr. Wall shape)
2335	Square caddy and cover (18th-century shape)
2336	Vase and cover
2337	Vase and cover (as 789 ewer)
2338	Vase and cover
2339	Vase and cover
2340	Vase and cover (2 sizes)
2341	Menu
2342	Pallette menu
2343	Flower-holder, embossed lily
2344	Flower bowl
2345	Oval tray, pierced edge
2346	Serviette ring
2347	Serviette ring, pierced
2348	Match stand
2349	Jug for Sabrina-style of decoration

2350	Pair spills, embossed figures
†2351	Shell flower-holder (2 sizes)
2352	Fruit tray
2353	Vase and cover
2354	Vase and cover
2355	Embossed vase for Sabrina-style of decoration
2356	Embossed vase for Sabrina-style of decoration
2357	Embossed vase for Sabrina-style of decoration
2358	Embossed vase for Sabrina-style of decoration
2359	Flower-holder
2360	Bottle
2361	Flower bowl, embossed vine
2362	Vase and cover
*2363	Vase and cover [still made for fruit painting]
2364	Pot pourri
2365	Wicker basket (3 sizes)
2366	Vase and cover
2367	Dessert set—plate, oval and round dishes, tray, flower pot and fern pot
2368	Vase for Sabrina-style of decoration
2369	Rose bowl, embossed 'gather ye rose buds while ye may' for Sabrina-style of decoration
2370	Rose bowl for Sabrina-style of decoration
2371	Queen Anne fern pot (2 sizes)
2372	Flower-holder, embossed, plain or trough

1905

2373	Small clock case
‡2374	Pair English costume figures
‡2375	Small Greek figure on plinth (6½ in.)
‡2376	Small Greek figure on plinth (6½ in.)
‡2377	Small Greek figure on plinth (6½ in.)
‡2378	Small Greek figure on plinth (6½ in.)
‡2379	Small Greek figure on plinth (6½ in.)
‡2380	Small Greek figure on plinth (6½ in.)
2381	Leathern jug
2382	Round fluted tray
2383	Round tray
2384	Oblong tray
2385	Oblong tray
2386	Heart tray
‡2387	Small figure, baby in dressing gown
‡2388	Figure of a Jockey
‡2389	Pair figures 'early English'
2390	Vase for Sabrina-style of decoration
‡2391	Pair figures 'Music' and 'Song'—man playing lute, woman singing
2392	Ink stand
‡2393	Pair figures 'Pierrots'—male and female
2394	Vase and cover
2395	Vase and cover
2396	Gadroon flower pot
2397	Gadroon flower pot
2398	Vase and cover (2 sizes)
2399	Fern pot
2400	String box in shape of a cockerel

2401	Vase and cover
2402	Vase and cover
2403	Flower-holder (2 sizes)
2404	Match stand—3 pieces
2405	Greek vase
‡2406	Large vase (33 in., £16 in white, £50 green and painted peonies by Roberts)
2407	Pot pourri
2408	Bowl
2409	Ewer
2410	Vase and cover
2411	Vase and cover
2412	Silk box
2413	Caddy
2414	Pot pourri
2415	Tray
2416	Oblong casket
2417	Round casket

1906

2418	Mustard, pepper and salt
2419	Jug for Sabrina-style of decoration
2420	Jug for Sabrina-style of decoration
2421	Vase and cover
2422	Vase and cover
2423	Lavender jar
2424	Pear scent bottle
2425	Vase and cover (3 sizes)
2426	Vase and cover (2 sizes)
2427	Strawberry punnet (3 sizes)
2428	Large bowl
2429	Fern bowl
2430	Vase (3 sizes)
2431	Vase for Sabrina-style of decoration 2 sizes
2432	Vase for Sabrina-style of decoration 2 sizes

1907

2433	Oval bowl (2 sizes)
2434	Pot pourri
2435	Special models for mounting in silver for H. Williamson Ltd., 7 Spencer Street, Birmingham: vase (3 sizes), lobed dish (3 sizes), rose bowl, mustard, pepper and salt, flanged sugar, scuttle sugar, sugar dredger, flanged butter, flat butter, biscuit, marmalade, coffees and sugar, teas and sugar, teapot, sugar and cream
2436	Pot pourri (2 sizes)
2437	Pot pourri (2 sizes)
2438	Shamrock luncheon tray
2439	Basket
2440	Vase (2 sizes)
2441	Ewer (2 sizes)
2442	Low fine pierced jar
2443	Vase and cover
2444	Box and cover

2445	Box and cover
2446	Bowl
†2447	Vase (still made)
2448	Vase and a miniature
2449	Loving cup
2450	Pot pourri
2451	Vase and cover
2452	Vase and cover

1908

2453	Vase and cover
2454	Pot pourri
2455	Perforated fern bowl
2456	Perforated pot pourri
2457	Tazza
2458	Vase and cover
2459	Vase and cover
2460	Vase
2461	Vase and cover
2462	Gadroon ink
2463	Vase
2464	Ewer
2465	Ink (2 sizes)
2466	Scent bottle
2467	Taper
‡2468	Clown's head
2469	Hexagon vase and cover, old Worcester shape
2470	Vase and cover, old Worcester shape
2471	Vase, old Worcester shape
2472	Vase, old Worcester shape
2473	Vase, old Worcester shape
2474	Vase, old Worcester shape
2475	Vase and cover, old Worcester shape
2476	Vase and cover, old Worcester shape

1909

2477	Vase, old Worcester shape
2478	Coffee pot, old Worcester shape
2479	Jug, old Worcester shape
2480	Fine pierced vase and cover
2481	Fine pierced vase and cover
2482	Vase and cover, old Worcester shape
2483	Square caddy
‡2484	Fish ash tray
2485	Vase and cover
2486	Vase and cover
2487	Vase and cover
2488	Flower-holder (2 sizes)
§2489	Extinguisher 'Motorist'
2490	Tazza, no handles
2491	Series of 12 small vases for Sabrina-style of decoration
2492	Vase
2493	Vase

2494   Fine pierced vase and cover
2495   Vase and cover
2496   Bowl (2 sizes)
2497   Flower-holder
2498   Jardinière
2499   Bouillon cup, cover and stand
2500   Fruit bowl
2501   Fruit bowl
2502   Box and cover
2503   Pastille burner (cover and stand)
2504   Photo frame
2505   Ring stand
2506   Sugar and cream
2507   Jardinière

1910

2508   Pierced jardinière
2509   Oval jardinière
*2510   Spill vase (3 sizes)
2511   Daffodil ink as G103—a former Grainger-shape number
2512   Tea caddy
2513   Bonbonnière

1911

‡2514   Brer Rabbit flower-holder
2515   Round salt and pepper
2516   Pot pourri, crown top
‡2517   Duck ring stand
2518   Flower-holder
2519   Vase and cover
‡2520   Coronation scent—George V
2521   Cup and cover
2522   Vase and cover and a miniature
‡2523   Pair male and female figures on rococo scroll base
2524   Box and cover
2525   Pot pourri

1912

2526   Wicker basket (2 sizes)
2527   Bonbonnière
2528   Loving cup, 2 handles
2529   Vase
2530   Pierced flower bowl
2531   Bag lavender jar
2532   Candy box
2533   Vase
2534   Pot pourri
2535   Vase for mounting
†2536   Wicker fern pot—still made (3 sizes)
‡2537   Peacock menu holder
2538   Carboy scent bottle with or without cover
2539   Eventail flower-holder

2540	Flower-holder, embossed or plain
2541	Flower-holder, embossed or plain
2542	Vase and cover
*2543	Extinguisher 'Witch'
2544	Vase
2545	Teapot, sugar and cream
2546	Bowl

1913

2547	Vase and cover
2548	Vase and cover
2549	Vase
2550	Old Worcester cup (3 sizes
2551	Dog of Fo vase and cover
2552	Flower-holder
2553	Vase and cover
2554	Jug (4 sizes)
2555	Box and cover, pear knob
2556	Box and cover, apple knob
2557	Box and cover, plum knob
2558	Flower pot (4 sizes)
2559	Loving cup
2560	Basket
2561	Stamp box
2562	Stamp-holder
2563	Mistletoe pot pourri, pierced or unpierced
2564	Fruit basket
2565	Covered cup, 2 handles

1914

2566	Vase and cover
2567	Fruit dish
*2568	Extinguisher—Chinese Mandarin
2569	Vase and cover
2570	Plain vase
2571	Plain vase
2572	Plain vase
2573	Plain vase
2574	Plain vase
2575	Plain vase
2576	Plain vase
2577	Floating flower bowl (2 sizes)
2578	Bowl
2579	Flower-holder
2580	Melon box and cover
2581	Liqueur bottle
‡2582	French soldier
2583	Box and cover
2584	Box and cover
2585	Octagonal box
2586	Oval box
‡2587	Tomato
‡2588	Territorial soldier

2589	Cream jar
2590	Vase and cover

1915

‡2591	Soldier of the Worcestershire Regiment
*2592	Oval jardinière—still made
2593	Vase
2594	Vase
2595	Vase
2596	Rose bowl
2597	Vase (2 sizes)
2598	Vase
2599	Vase
2600	Vase
2601	Vase
2602	Vase
2603	Bowl

1916

‡2604	Tortoise
‡2605	Snail
‡2606	Cheetah
2607	Rabbit
§2608	Snake
§2609	Cow
2610	Mouse
‡2611	Fish
‡2612	Ape
‡2613	Ram
2614	Figure
‡2615	Group, mother and 2 children
‡2616	Group, 2 ladies
2617	Figure 'Wind'
2618	Boy and Rabbit
‡2619	Crucifix, Christ on the Cross
2620	Crinoline figure with cap
2621	Crinoline figure without cap
§2622	Blackcock
‡2623	Quail
‡2624	Toad
‡2625	Statuette 'The Immaculate'
‡2626	Statuette 'St. Joseph'
2627	Flower-holder for mounting (3 sizes)
2628	Vase and cover
*2629	Figure French Marine Officer (F. Gertner)—still made
2630	Flower-holder (3 sizes)
2631	Rose bowl
‡2632	Figure in evening dress with cigar
‡2633	Figure with cloak and opera hat
*2634	Figure Mary Queen of Scots (F. Gertner)—still made
*2635	Figure Coldstream Guard Officer—still made
‡2636	Double mouse
*2637	Figure King Henry VIII (F. Gertner)—still made
2638	Flower-holder

2639	Flower-holder
2640	Flower-holder
2641	Flower-holder
2642	Flower-holder
*2643	Figure King Edward VII (F. Gertner)—still made
2644	Plant pot
‡2645	Figure of soldier standing, white or khaki
‡2646	Figure of soldier sitting, white or khaki
2647	Flower-holder
*2648	Figure Queen Elizabeth on plinth (F. Gertner)—still made
2649	Female figure with mirror
2650	Female figure with mask
*2651	Figure King Charles I (F. Gertner)—still made
*2652	Figure Queen Anne Boleyn (F. Gertner)
2653	Flower bowl
2654	Figure female dancing
2655	Figure female dancing, companion
2656	Plant pot
*2657	Seaforth Highlander Officer (F. Gertner)—still made
*2658	Artillery Officer (F. Gertner)—still made
2659	Female figure with Lyre
2660	Female figure with Tambourine
*2661	Figure The Admiral (F. Gertner)—still made

1917

2662	Bullfinch on stump
2663	Female paroquet on stump
2664	Male paroquet on stump
2665	Canary on stump
2666	Kingfisher on stump
2667	Goldfinch on stump

(F. Gertner) A few made in crownware but subsequently many made in china after Second World War

*2668	Sir Walter Raleigh (F. Gertner)—still made
2669	Pot pourri
2670	Pot pourri
2671	Pot pourri
*2672	Charles II (F. Gertner)—still made
‡2673	Female figure 'Ball Player' (?F. Gertner)
‡2674	Female figure companion (?F. Gertner)
*2675	Officer of 3rd Dragoons (F. Gertner)—still made
*2676	Officer of Coldstream Guards (F. Gertner)—still made
*2677	Officer of XVII Dragoons (F. Gertner)—still made
2678	Floating flower bowl
‡2679	Columbine
‡2680	Harlequin
‡2681	Columbine
‡2682	Pierrot
2683	Little girl on round plinth
2684	Little boy on round plinth
2685	Standing nude boy
2686	Standing companion
2687	Seated nude boy
‡2688	Nude woman standing
2689	Nude woman sitting
‡2690	Nude woman reclining

1918

2691	Nude female standing
2692	Nude female companion
2693	Nude female sitting
2694	Nude boy
‡2695	Flamingo
‡2696	Flamingo
‡2697	Nude female sitting
‡2698	Nude female kneeling
2699	Plant pot

1919

2700	Vase and Cover
*2701	Vase and Cover (3 sizes, still made, for fruit painting)
2702	Nude boy with fruits
2703	Nude boy with fruits
2704	Nude boy with fruits
2705	Nude boy with fruits
2706	Nude boy with fruits
2707	Nude boy with fruits
2708	Vase and cover (2 sizes)
2709	Vase and cover (2 sizes)
2710	Vase and cover (3 sizes)
2711	Ewer
2712	Vase and cover (2 sizes)
*2713	Vase and cover (3 sizes, still made, for fruit painting)
2714	Vase and cover
2715	Nude girl sitting
2716	Nude girl companion
2717	Nude girl standing
2718	Nude girl companion
2719	Nude girl sitting
2720	Nude girl companion
2721	Vase and cover
2722	Vase and cover (2 sizes)
‡2723	Figure 'Drummer Boy'
‡2724	Companion 'Vivandière'
2725	Figure, boy
2726	Companion, girl
2727	Figure, boy
2728	Companion, girl
2729	Vase and cover (2 sizes)
2730	Vase and cover
2731	Vase and cover (2 sizes)
2732	Figure, standing girl
2733	Figure, standing companion
2734	Figure, standing boy
2735	Figure, standing companion
2736	Vase and cover (2 sizes)
2737	Miniature vase and cover
2738	Miniature vase
2739	Oval vase
2740	Oval vase

2741   Miniature vase
2742   Miniature vase and cover
2743   Miniature vase and cover
2744   Miniature vase and cover
2745   Miniature vase and cover
2746   Miniature vase and cover
2747   Miniature vase and cover
2748   Miniature vase and cover
2749   Miniature vase and cover
2750   Miniature vase

1920

2751   Oval vase
2752   Oval vase and cover
2753   Oval vase
2754   Clock case
2755   Clock case
2756   Clock case
2757   Clock case
2758   Bowl
2759   Bowl
2760   Tablet
2761   Flower pot
2762   Reflector (3 sizes)
2763   Flower bowl with lantern vase and cover
2764   Miniature vase and cover
2765   Vase (2 sizes)
2766   Vase (2 sizes)
2767   Vase (2 sizes)
2768   Vase (2 sizes)
2769   Flower bowl (5 sizes)
2770   Flower bowl (5 sizes)
2771   Vase (2 sizes)
2772   Vase (2 sizes)
2773   Vase (2 sizes)
2774   Vase (2 sizes)
2775   Vase (2 sizes)
2776   Vase (2 sizes)
2777   Vase (2 sizes)
2778   Vase (2 sizes)
2779   Vase (2 sizes)
‡2780   Pair of tigers, couchant
2781   Box and cover (6 sizes)
2782   Vase
2783   Powder puff bowl and cover, kneeling female on cover (made for Dubarry et Cie, 81 Brompton Rd., London)

1921

2784   Candlestick
2785   Flower-holder
2786   Wicker tray
2787   Wicker tray
2788   Wicker tray

2789	Poppy tray
2790	Poppy tray
2791	Marguerite tray
2792	Wicker tray
2793	Flower-holder
2794	Flower-holder
2795	Flower-holder
2796	Ball mustard
2797	Flower bowl on foot
2798	Female figure 'Roses' (modelled by F. Clemincin, Paris)
2799	Female companion 'Grapes' (modelled by F. Clemincin, Paris)
2800	Female companion standing (modelled by F. Clemincin, Paris)
2801	Female companion sitting (modelled by F. Clemincin, Paris)
2802	Pot pourri
2803	Pot pourri
2804	Clock case
‡2805	Nude female figure seated ⎱ (tried with powder bowls but not
‡2806	Nude female companion ⎰ successful)
2807	Double figure powder bowl and cover

1923

2808	Miniature old Worcester hexagonal vase
2809	Miniature old Worcester fluted caddy
2810	Miniature old Worcester mug
2811	Miniature old Worcester coffee pot
2812	Miniature old Worcester teapot
2813	Miniature old Worcester teabowl and saucer
2814	Miniature old Worcester plain caddy
‡2815	Miniature bottle and stopper ⎫
‡2816	Miniature vase and cover ⎬ Cancelled before full production
‡2817	Miniature vase and cover ⎪ started
‡2818	Miniature box and cover ⎭
2819	Dish
2820	Powder puff bowl and cover, lotus on cover (made for Dubarry et Cie)
2821	Powder puff bowl and cover, Kookaburra bird on cover

1924

2822	Oblong Kookaburra ash tray
2823	Round Kookaburra ash tray, or bird on its own

1925

2824	Watch front, round, square or octagonal

1926

2825	Panelled ginger jar
2826	Plain ginger jar
‡2827	Oblong ash tray with mouse
‡2828	Oblong ash tray with mouse

1927

2829	Bowl, (crown ware 307)
2830	Flat bowl (crown ware 308)

2831/2 Toby jug with or without cover (6 in.) also a 3½ and a 1¾ in. size without
       cover and as a pepper and salt with EPNS perforated top
2833   Lamp vase (Khouri)
2834   Lamp vase (Khouri)
2835   Vase (2 sizes, as 2529 altered)
2836   Bowl (also crown ware 259)
2837   Tazza
2838   Tazza
2839   Tazza
2840   Toby jug (crown ware 367)
2841   Mrs. Toby jug and cover, and 2 smaller sizes without cover
‡2842   Rabbit 'Wilfred'
‡2843   Duck
*2844   Figure 'Hush' candle extinguisher

1928

2845   Teapot and cover, old Worcester shape
2846   Teapot and cover, old Worcester shape
2847   Spill old Worcester shape (4 sizes)
2848   Group small Chinese figures
2849   Flower-holder, Warmstry flute

1929

2850   Mephistopheles Toby jug and cover (7 in.) and 2 smaller without cover
2851   Elephant jug, or as mustard, pepper and salt
2852   Cockatoo jug
2853   Pelican jug, or as pepper and salt
2854   Squirrel jug, or as pepper and salt
2855   Dog 'Bonzo' or as pepper and salt
2856   Jester Toby jug and cover
2857   Paddy
‡2858   Brer Rabbit

1930

2859   Embossed flower-holder
2860   Embossed flower-holder
2861   Embossed flower-holder
2862   Embossed flower-holder
2863   Lamp vase—replaced by Polar Bear, as 3062/3 (Doris Lindner)
2864   Lamp vase—(Khouri)

1931

‡2865   Figure 'Cora', with or without plinth (Doris Lindner), very few made
                                (Doris Lindner), very few
‡2866   Pair Book ends Harlequin and Columbine ⎱ made—workmen thought
‡2867   Pair Book ends Pierrot and Columbine   ⎰ they were a waste of
                                              time
‡2868   Figure Harlequin (Doris Lindner)
‡2869   Figure Pierrot (Doris Lindner)
2870   Terrier (Doris Lindner)
2871   Setter (Doris Lindner)

2872   Hound ash tray (Doris Lindner)
2873   Fox ash tray (Doris Lindner)
‡2874   Sleeping doe (Eric Aumonier)
‡2875   Bookend Horseman (Eric Aumonier)
‡2876   Bookend Lion (Eric Aumonier)
‡2877   Young horse (Eric Aumonier) probably only first set of moulds made
2878   Lamp vase (Khouri)
‡2879   Female figure 'Dreaming' (Phoebe Stabler)
‡2880   Female figure 'Flower girl' (Phoebe Stabler)
‡2881   Female figure 'Sauce' (Phoebe Stabler)
‡2882   Boy on boar (Phoebe Stabler)
‡2883   Female figure 'Little dancer' (Phoebe Stabler)
‡2884   Female figure 'Coquette' (Phoebe Stabler)
‡2885   Female figure 'The Mother' (Phoebe Stabler)
‡2886   Female figure 'The old goat woman' (Phoebe Stabler)
‡2887   Female figure 'Pick a back' (Phoebe Stabler)
2888   Vase and cover, as 2368
‡2891   Greyhounds (Stella R. Crofts)
‡2892   Hare (Stella R. Crofts)
‡2893   Pelican ash tray (Stella R. Crofts)
‡2894   Boy with donkey (Stella R. Crofts)
‡2895   Giraffes (Stella R. Crofts)
‡2896   Calf (Stella R. Crofts)
‡2897   Cat eating (Stella R. Crofts)
‡2898   Victorian Musician, female harpist (Ethelwyn Baker)
‡2899   Victorian Musician, male lute player (Ethelwyn Baker)
‡2900   Pair Polar Bear book ends, 'Sam and Barbara' (Ethelwyn Baker)
‡2901   Victorian Musician male flute player (Ethelwyn Baker)
‡2902   Victorian Musician female singer (Ethelwyn Baker)
‡2903   Figure Bluebeard (Sybil V. Williams and Jessamine S. Bray)
‡2904   Figure Fatima (companion)   do.
2905   Female figure 'Noel' (2 sizes)   do.
2906   Female figure 'June' (2 sizes)   do.
‡2907   Figure Indian chief (F. Gertner)
‡2908   Figure Indian brave (F. Gertner)
‡2909   Figure Indian squaw and child on back (F. Gertner)
‡2910   Figure Indian squaw and child on shoulder (F. Gertner)
‡2911   Figure Lady with fan (F. Gertner)
*2912   Figure 'Michael' (F. G. Doughty)
*2913   Figure 'Tommy' (F. G. Doughty)
*2914   Figure 'Mischief' (F. G. Doughty)
*2915   Figure 'Joan' (F. G. Doughty)
‡2916   Figure Girl and mongrel pup (Margaret Cane)
*2917   Figure 'The sea urchin' (Margaret Cane) fairly popular
*2918   Figure 'The sleepy boy' (Margaret Cane) fairly popular
‡2919   Figure 'Tangles' (Anne Acheson)
‡2920   Figure 'Lough Neagh Mary' (Anne Acheson)
2921   Figure 'Dublin flower girl' Went quite well
*2922   Figure 'Dutch girl' (F. Gertner)
*2923   Figure 'Dutch boy' (F. Gertner)
2924   Figure 'Fortune teller' (F. G. Doughty)
2925   Tobacco jar, fox cover (Betzeman)
2926   Tobacco jar, hound cover (Betzeman)
2927   Terrier puff bowl and cover
2928   'Mischief' puff bowl and cover (as 2914) (F. G. Doughty)

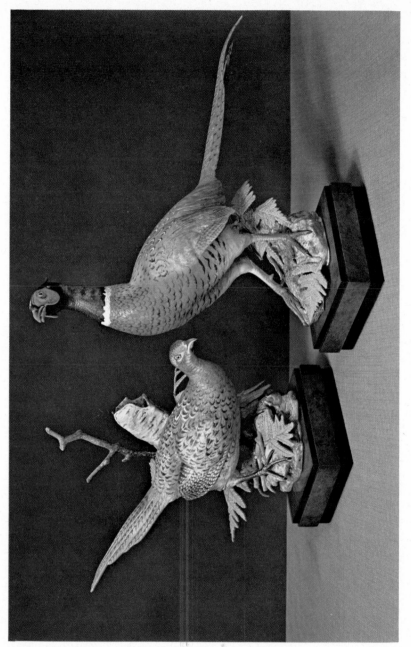

XVII. Pair of American Ring Necked Pheasants, from the American game bird series modelled by Ronald Van Ruyckevelt, shape numbers 3818 and 3819, length of cock bird is 16½ inches, and height 13¾ inches. The breathtakingly beautiful tail feathers and the iridescent sheen on the head of the cock, together with the perfection of firing such an unsupported length of bone-china, would have been thought impossible a few years ago and represent the Company's skill at its finest.

XVIII. Pair from the Victorian and Edwardian series modelled by Ruth Van Ruyckevelt; Elizabeth (shape 3774) carries a feather boa and wears a satin evening gown with embroidered sprays; Madelaine (shape 3775) wears a white taffeta walking gown and carries a walking parasol; both are $8\frac{1}{2}$ inches tall and depict ladies of the 1890's.

2929	Fruit knob puff bowl and cover (Betzeman)
2930	Girl and kitten, 'Buttercup' or 'Betty' (Anne Acheson)
2931	Bull Terrier (2 sizes) (D. Lindner)
2932	Sealyham on stand
2933	Tobacco jar, plain cover (Betzeman)
2934	Sealyham, no stand
2935	Sealyham, ash tray
‡2936	Spanish lady (Anne Acheson)
2937	Girl and Rabbit
2938	'Little dancer' puff bowl (F. G. Doughty)
2939	Peach box (Betzeman)
2940	Apple box (Betzeman)
2941	Toy dog, Pekinese
2942	Toy dog, Terrier and wire-haired terrier
2943	Toy dog, Dandie Dinmont
2944	English Springer Spaniel and as Black Cocker
2945	English Bulldog
2946	Aberdeen Toy Terrier
‡2947	Fox and hound pen tray (D. Lindner)
2948	Flagon (Betzeman)
‡2949	Figure group 'Dancers' (D. Lindner)
2950	Fox on plinth (D. Lindner)
2951	Hound on plinth (D. Lindner)
2952	Setter without stand (D. Lindner)
2953	Menu-holder, fox hound walking
2954	Menu-holder, fox hound running
2955	Menu-holder, fox hound sitting
2956	Menu-holder, fox
2957	Fox brooch
2958	Sealyham brooch
2959	Airedale brooch
2960	Dandie Dinmont brooch
2961	Black Cocker Spaniel brooch
2962	Field Spaniel brooch
2963	Collie brooch
2964	Pekinese brooch
2965	Cairn brooch
2966	Setter brooch
2967	Dachshund brooch
‡2968	Liqueur barrel (Betzeman)
2969	Highland Terrier brooch
2970	Wire Haired Terrier brooch
2971	Alsatian brooch
2972	Scottish Terrier brooch
2973	Foxhound brooch
2974	Chow brooch
2975	Grouse brooch
2976	Snipe brooch
2977	Bullfinch brooch
2978	Sparrow Hawk brooch
2979	Paroquet brooch
2980	Owl brooch
2981	Swallow brooch
2982	Robin brooch
2983	Blackcock brooch

R

2984	Quail brooch
2985	Wild Duck brooch
2986	Wood Pigeon brooch
2987	Kingfisher brooch
2988	Pheasant brooch
2989	Penguin brooch
2990	Woodcock brooch
2991	Jay brooch
2992	Seagull brooch
*2993	Fox for bookend (D. Lindner) still made
*2994	Hound for bookend (D. Lindner) still made
2995	Golden Pheasant brooch
2996	Amherst Pheasant brooch
2997	Straight fox on plinth (Betzeman)
2998	Straight hound on plinth (Betzeman)
‡2999	Figure 'Columbine' (D. Lindner)
‡3000	Fox and Hound calendar (Betzeman)
3001	Puff bowl with 2930 cover
3002	Bull Terrier brooch
3003	Bedlington Terrier brooch
3004	Greyhound brooch
3005	Dalmatian brooch
‡3006	Figure 'Sweet Nell of Old Drury' (Anne Acheson)
3007	Springer Spaniel brooch
*3008	Figure 'Sea Breeze'—girl and seagulls (F. Doughty)
3009	Baby on cushion (F. Gertner)
3010	Figure 'Happy boy'—child lying on back (F. Gertner)
*3011	Figure 'Peter Pan'
*3012	Figure 'Spring' girl and lamb (F. Doughty)
‡3013	Seal
†3014	Figure 'My Favourite', girl with rabbit (F. Doughty)

1933

3015 3016 3017 3018 3019 3020 3021 3022 3023	These numbers do not appear to have been used.
§3024	Fox head (as 2993) (D. Lindner)
§3025	Hound head (as 2994) (D. Lindner)
3026	Airedale, no plinth (D. Lindner)
3027	Wire-haired Terrier no plinth (D. Lindner)
3028	Sealyham Terrier no plinth (D. Lindner)
3029	Scottie Terrier no plinth (D. Lindner)
3030	Naiad figure no plinth (D. Lindner)
‡3031	Salmon
‡3032	Trout
3033	Cocker Spaniel
3034	Peke, sitting
3035	Salmon

3036	Pike
3037	Trout
3038	Roach
3039	Carp
3040	Figure 'The Kiss'
3041	Flower-holder, tall
3042	Flower-holder, low
3043	Bowl
3044	Bowl
3045	Covered jar

1934

3046	Biscuit jar and cover
3047	Embossed candlestick
‡3048	Bottle and cover—(? not made)
3049	Comb tray
3050	Low box and cover
3051	Pin tray
3052	Small low bowl
3053	Round low bowl
3054	Oval low bowl
3055	Flower-holder
3056	Flower-holder
3057	Quart jug
3058	Flower-holder
3059	Flower-holder
3060	Pepper and saltshaker, mustard and cover
3061	Coffee cup and saucer
§3062	Polar bear for bookend, eating (D. Lindner)
§3063	Polar bear for bookend, looking up (D. Lindner)
3064	Ash tray
3065	Small jar or marmalade pot
*3066	'Egypt' figure of girl from Countries of the World (F. Doughty)
*3067	'Italy' figure of girl from Countries of the World (F. Doughty)
†3068	'Burma' figure of girl from Countries of the World (F. Doughty)
*3069	'Greece' figure of girl from Countries of the World (F. Doughty)
*3070	'Spain' figure of girl from Countries of the World (F. Doughty)
†3071	'India' figure of girl from Countries of the World (F. Doughty)
*3072	'Japan' figure of girl from Countries of the World (F. Doughty)
†3073	'China' figure of girl from Countries of the World (F. Doughty)
*3074	'Holland' figure of girl from Countries of the World (F. Doughty)
*3075	'England' figure of girl from Countries of the World (F. Doughty)
3076	'Woodland Dance' figure (F. Doughty)
3077	Vase and cover
3078	Vase and cover
3079	Vase and cover
3080	Dish

1935

†3081	Figure 'Grandmother's Dress' (F. Doughty)
†3082	Figure 'The first cuckoo' (F. Doughty)
*3083	Figure 'Sunshine' (F. Doughty)
*3084	Figure 'The Dandelion' (F. Doughty)

‡3085   Poodle (Champion 'Spriggan Bell') (D. Lindner)
‡3086   Figure Dancing Lady (D. Lindner)
†3087   Figure Boy with Paroquet (F. Doughty)
‡3088   Figure Dance (D. Lindner)
‡3089   Figurine King George V (about 72 made) (G. Parnell)
‡3090   Figurine Queen Mary (about 72 made) (G. Parnell)
 3091   Small bust of King George V (G. Parnell)
 3092   Small bust of Queen Mary (G. Parnell)
‡3093   Penguin with beak up (D. Lindner)
‡3094   Penguin with companion (D. Lindner)
*3095   Cupid kneeling on plinth (G. Parnell)
‡3096   Elephant (E. Evans)
‡3097   Figure 'Lady Bountiful' (G. Parnell)
 3098   Cigarette holder, modelled flowers
‡3099   Figure 'Flower Girl' (Miss Stewart)
‡3100   Lion (E. Evans)
‡3101   Tiger (E. Evans)
‡3102   Elephant (E. Evans)
*3103   'Wales' from Countries of the World (F. Doughty)
*3104   'Scotland' from Countries of the World (F. Doughty)
 3105   Cupid standing 'Hit' (G. Parnell)
‡3106   Figure 'Duchess's Dress' (F. Doughty)
‡3107   Figure 'Applause' (G. Parnell)
‡3108   Figure 'Amaryllis' (G. Parnell)
 3109   Cornucopia
‡3110   Bear
 3111   Figure 'Bal Masqué' (G. Parnell)
‡3112   Doughty Bird Redstart cock (D. Doughty) 66 pairs made
‡3113   Doughty Bird Redstart hen (D. Doughty) 66 pairs made
*3114   'At the Meet' (D. Lindner)
*3115   'Huntsmen and hounds' (D. Lindner)
*3116   'Over the sticks' (D. Lindner)
*3117   'Cantering to the post' (D. Lindner)
‡3118   Group of pekes (D. Lindner)

1936

‡3119   Cigarette box 3 sealyhams on cover (D. Lindner)
‡3120   Dog calender (D. Lindner)
‡3121   Tiger (Guero)
‡3122   Fawn
 3123   Lamb 'Maytime' (D. Lindner)
‡3124   Goat (Bargas)
‡3125   Goat (Bargas)
‡3126   Pierrot puff bowl (Bargas)
‡3127   Baby boy bowl (Bargas)
‡3128   Casket cornucopia knob
‡3129   Casket head knob
‡3130   Group of spaniels (D. Lindner)
‡3131   Group of foxes (D. Lindner)
‡3132   Group of hounds (D. Lindner)
§3133   Group of bull dogs (D. Lindner)
 3134   Doughty Bird Goldfinch cock (D. Doughty) limited edition of 250
 3135   Doughty Bird Goldfinch hen (D. Doughty) limited edition of 250
 3136   Doughty Bird Bluebird hen (D. Doughty) limited edition of 350

3137	Doughty Bird Bluebird cock (D. Doughty) limited edition of 350
‡3138	'The Planter's daughter' (G. Parnell)
‡3139	'Recollections' (G. Parnell)
‡3140	'The pondering mask' (G. Parnell)
‡3141	Group of kittens (D. Lindner)
3142	'The frog' (G. Parnell)
‡3143	'The summit' (G. Parnell)
3144	'Magnolia bud' (G. Parnell)
3145	'Thief' (G. Parnell)
‡3146	Calves (D. Lindner)
3147	Child with lamb (flowers in arms)
3148	Child with lamb in arms
*3149	'The sister' (F. Doughty)
*3150	'Two babies' (F. Doughty)
‡3151	'The Water baby' (F. Doughty)
‡3152	Foals (D. Lindner)
‡3153	Kids at play (D. Lindner)
‡3154	Figure 'The Drummer' (G. Parnell)
‡3155	Sheep (Bargas)
‡3156	Dog Ash tray (as 3033) (D. Lindner)
‡3157	Figure child with 'butterfly' (Anne Acheson)
3158	Flower trough (2 sizes) (F. Gertner)
3159	Flat flower holder
*3160	Figure 'Bubbles' (F. Doughty)
‡3161	Mermaid (Anne Acheson)
‡3162	Cigarette box 3 scottie puppies (D. Lindner)
*3163	Polo player (D. Lindner)
*3164	Hog hunting (D. Lindner)
3165	'Banbury Cross' (Geraldine Blake)
3166	'Highwayman' (Geraldine Blake)
3167	'Yonder he goes' (Geraldine Blake)
3168	Bengal Lancer (Geraldine Blake)
3169	'Young Entry' (Geraldine Blake)
3170	Mare and foal (Geraldine Blake)
‡3171	Figure 'Arita' (Rachel Greaves)
‡3172	Figure 'Tamara' (Rachel Greaves)
‡3173	Figure 'Tatiana' (Rachel Greaves)
‡3174	Figure 'Anna' (Rachel Greaves)
‡3175	Figure 'Alicia' (Rachel Greaves)
‡3176	Figure 'Natasha' (Rachel Greaves)
‡3177	Figure 'Irina' (Rachel Greaves)
*3178	'Ireland' Countries of the World (F. Doughty)

1937

*3179	Group 3 circus horses rearing (D. Lindner)
*3180	3 circus horses in the ring with rider (D. Lindner)
‡3181	Round plaque head of Edward VIII in relief (Mme D. Charol)
*3182	Round plaque head of George VI and Queen Elizabeth (Richard Garbe R.A.)
*3183	Round plaque head of George VI (Richard Garbe)
§3184	Polar bear ash tray, upright (D. Lindner)
§3185	Polar bear ash tray, bending (D. Lindner)
‡3186	Figure ballet dancer (D. Charol)
3187	Foal (G. Blake)
3188	Hound calendar (D. Lindner)

‡3189   Rectangular plaque with head of George VI and Queen Elizabeth
3190   Doughty Bird Cardinal cock (D. Doughty) limited edition of 400 pairs
3191   Doughty Bird Cardinal hen (D. Doughty) limited edition of 400 pairs
‡3192   Figure of ballet dancer (D. Charol)
‡3193   'Queen in the parlour' (Anne Acheson)
‡3194   Male Chinese dancer (G. Parnell)⎫ sold in boxes and intended for
‡3195   Female dancer (G. Parnell)   ⎭ limited editions
3196   Lamp vase (Khouri)
†3197   Robin (small) (Eileen Soper)
†3198   Wren (small) (Eileen Soper)
†3199   Blue tit (small) (Eileen Soper)
†3200   Wood warbler (small) (Eileen Soper)
‡3201   Plaque Rt. Hon. Stanley Baldwin (D. Charol)
‡3202   Pierrot group (D. Charol)
3203   Tall lily vase
3204   Tall lily vase and fern
3205   Low lily and fern
3206   Low lily and fern and leaves
3207   Tray, as 1699, with festoon modelled flowers (Miss Leigh)
3208   Tray as 1420
3209   Round rock bowl
3210   Oval rock bowl
3211   Square rock bowl
†3212   Cornucopia for flowers
3213   Pedestal with vase of modelled flowers
3214   Pedestal with vase of modelled flowers
3215   Tray, modelled festooned flowers
3216   Menu-holder modelled convolvulus (Antonio Vassalo)
3217   Menu-holder modelled primroses (Antonio Vassalo)
3218   Menu-holder modelled roses (Antonio Vassalo)
3219   Menu-holder modelled poppy (Antonio Vassalo)
3220   Menu-holder modelled begonia (Antonio Vassalo)
3221   Menu-holder modelled carnation (Antonio Vassalo)
‡3222   Figure 'The candlestick' (G. Parnell)
§3223   Doughty Bird, 'Indigo Bunting on plum twig' (D. Doughty)

1938

3224   Figure 'The bridesmaid' (F. Doughty)
3225   Figure 'Dancing waves' (F. Doughty)
†3226   Figure 'Only me' (still made) (F. Doughty)
‡3227   Figure 'London cry, delicate cowcumbers' (G. Parnell)
3228   Sporting dog, red setter (D. Lindner)
3229   Sporting dog, pointer (D. Lindner)
3230   Sporting dog, golden retriever (D. Lindner)
3231   Sporting dog, cocker spaniel (D. Lindner)
3232   Sporting dog, clumber spaniel (D. Lindner)
3233   Sporting dog, labrador retriever (D. Lindner)
†3234   Thrush (E. Soper)
†3235   Kingfisher (E. Soper)
†3236   Sparrow (E. Soper)
3237   1293 basket modelled flowers by Mary Leigh
†3238   Bullfinch (E. Soper)
†3239   Goldfinch (E. Soper)
†3240   Chaffinch (E. Soper)

3241	Doughty Bird Chickadee cock (D. Doughty) } limited edition of 325 pairs
3242	Doughty Bird Chickadee hen (D. Doughty)
3243	Welsh Corgi (D. Lindner)
3244	Vase and cover
3245	Low bowl
§3246	Bust of Autumn
§3247	Bust of Spring
†3248	Jay (E. Soper)
†3249	Woodpecker (E. Soper)
‡3250	Figure 'Ripe Asparagus' (G. Parnell)
3251	Vase and cover as 2460
‡3252	Figure 'A merry new song' (G. Parnell)
3253	Lamp (Khouri) as 1957
3254	Lamp (Khouri) as 628
3255	Lamp (Khouri) as 2522
†3256	Figure 'Sunday' (F. Doughty)
†3257	Figure 'Monday' (or 'Susie') (F. Doughty)
†3258	Figure 'Tuesday' (or 'Red Shoes') (F. Doughty)
†3259	Figure 'Wednesday' (F. Doughty)
†3260	Figure 'Thursday' (or 'Smilin' Thro'') (F. Doughty)
†3261	Figure 'Friday' (or 'My Pet') (F. Doughty)
†3262	Figure 'Saturday' (F. Doughty)
‡3263	Zoo babies, leopards (D. Lindner)
‡3264	Zoo babies, lions (D. Lindner)
‡3265	Zoo babies, bears (D. Lindner)
‡3266	Zoo babies, fawns (D. Lindner)
3267	Top hat
3268	Doughty Bird, Baltimore Oriole, cock (D. Doughty)—limited edition of 250 pairs
3269	Doughty Bird, Baltimore Oriole, hen (D. Doughty)
3270	Figure child and dog 'Playmates' (F. Doughty)
‡3271	Figure London cry 'London's gazette here' (G. Parnell)
‡3272	Figure 'Repose' (D. Charol)
‡3273	Zoo babies, Koala cubs (D. Lindner)
‡3274	Zoo babies, Tiger cubs (D. Lindner)
3275	Fluted ash tray

1939

3276	Khouri vase as 2708 with new foot
3277	Khouri vase as 2710/2 with new foot
3278	Khouri vase as 6/129 with new foot
3279	Khouri vase as 1481 no handles
3280	Khouri vase
3281	Khouri vase
3282	Khouri vase
3283	Khouri vase
*3284	Khouri vase
3285	Oval flower vase
3286	Pitcher pot, flowered
3287	Khouri finial as pilaster lamp
‡3288	Figure, girl with beads 'The necklace' (D. Charol)
‡3289	Figure, girl bathing 'Hesitation' (D. Charol)
3290	Miniature tea set
3291	Toy tea set

3292   Miniature sugar and toy cream
3293   Dalmatian (D. Lindner)
3294   Dachshund (D. Lindner)
3295   Alsatian (D. Lindner)
3296   'Hacking in the Park' (D. Lindner)
3297   Oak leaf tray
3298   New oblong tray

1940

‡3299   Figure, London cry—'Fine writing inks' (G. Parnell)
‡3300   Figure, London cry—'Fair cherryes' (G. Parnell)
*3301   Figure 'Miss Muffett' (F. Doughty)
*3302   Figure 'Babes in the wood' (F. Doughty)
†3303   Figure 'Polly put the kettle on' (F. Doughty)
*3304   Figure 'Goosie Gander' (F. Doughty)
*3305   Figure 'Little Jack Horner' (F. Doughty)
*3306   Figure 'Little Boy Blue' (F. Doughty)
§3307   Sporting dog, red setter (D. Lindner)
§3308   Sporting dog, pointer (D. Lindner)
§3309   Sporting dog, golden retriever (D. Lindner)
§3310   Sporting dog, cocker spaniel (D. Lindner)
3311   Sporting dog, clumber spaniel (D. Lindner)
3312   Sporting dog, labrador retriever (D. Lindner)
‡3313   Zoo babies, leopards (D. Lindner)
‡3314   Zoo babies, lions (D. Lindner)
‡3315   Zoo babies, bears (D. Lindner)
‡3316   Zoo babies, fawns (D. Lindner)
‡3317   Zoo babies, koala cubs (D. Lindner
‡3318   Zoo babies, tiger cubs (D. Lindner)
§3319   Dog's head, scottie
§3320   Dog's head, bulldog
§3321   Dog's head, spaniel
§3322   Dog's head, peke
‡3323   Doughty Bird, Bob White Quail cock—limited edition of 22 pairs
‡3324   Doughty Bird, Bob White Quail hen—limited edition of 22 pairs
3325   Cigarette box
3326   Doughty Bird, Mocking Bird cock—limited edition of 500 pairs
3327   Doughty Bird, Mocking Bird hen—limited edition of 500 pairs
3328   Doughty Group, Crab Apple blossom with butterfly—limited edition of 250 pairs
3329   Doughty Group, Crab Apple blossom with butterfly—limited edition of 250 pairs
§3330   'Bogskar'—winner of 1940 Grand National (D. Lindner)
3331   'Toto'—cairn terrier (A. K. Ellis)

1941

3332   Miniature tea set (E. Soper)
†3333   Hedge sparrow (E. Soper)
†3334   Nuthatch (E. Soper)
†3335   Great tit (E. Soper)
†3336   Marsh tit (E. Soper)
†3337   Nightingale (E. Soper)

†3338 Gold crest (E. Soper)
‡3339 'Summer' (G. Parnell)
‡3340 'Winter' (G. Parnell)
‡3341 'Autumn' (G. Parnell)
‡3342 'Spring' (G. Parnell)
3343 Lamp vase (Khouri) as 713
3344 Lamp vase (Khouri) as 972
3345 Lamp vase (Khouri) as 3571
‡3346 Figure 'The rescue' (E. Soper)
‡3347 Figure 'Evacuees' (E. Soper)
3348 Chinoiserie figure (G. Parnell)
3349 Boy and dolphin (F. Gertner)
3350 Cairn terrier 'Rats'
‡3351 Figure 'Take cover' war group (E. Soper)
‡3352 Figure 'Spitfire' war group (E. Soper)
3353 Figure 'Seaweed' (F. Gertner)
3354 Chinoiserie boy (G. Parnell)
3355 West Highland terrier 'Mack' (A. R. Ellis)
3356 Standing hound—'Ranter' (A. R. Ellis)
3357 Doughty Group, 'Apple Blossom and one bee'—limited edition of 250
3358 Doughty Group, 'Apple Blossom and two bees'—limited edition of 250
†3359 Figure 'The Bow' or 'Masquerade' (F. Doughty)
†3360 Figure 'The Curtsey' or 'Masquerade' (F. Doughty)
3361 Sitting spaniel puppy 'Tony' (A. R. Ellis)

1942

3362 Chinoiserie girl (G. Parnell)
†3363 Pied woodpeckers on stump (E. Soper)
†3364 Chaffinches on stump (E. Soper)
†3365 Linnets on stump (E. Soper)
‡3366 Welsh corgi 'Taffy' (A. R. Ellis)
3367 Doughty Bird, Indigo Bunting on blackberry sprays, cock—limited edition of 500 pairs
3368 Doughty Bird, Indigo Bunting on blackberry sprays, hen
‡3369 Figure 'Stowaways' war group (E. Soper)
‡3370 Figure 'Salvage' war group (E. Soper)
3371 Nude boy (F. Gertner)
3372 Nude girl (F. Gertner)
3373 Nude boy with cornucopia (F. Gertner)
3374 Nude girl with cornucopia (F. Gertner)
†3375 Bluetits on stump (E. Soper)
†3376 Coletits on stump (E. Soper)
†3377 Yellow hammers on stump (E. Soper)
3378 Doughty Group, Orange Blossom spray and butterfly—limited edition of 175
3379 Doughty Group, Companion group—limited edition of 175
3380 Sitting child (F. Doughty)
3381 Crawling child (F. Doughty)
‡3382 Figure 'The Letter' War Group (E. Soper)
3383 Bluetit on plinth (D. Lindner)
3384 Goldfinch on plinth (D. Lindner)
3385 Foxhound (A. R. Ellis)
3386 Foxhound (A. R. Ellis)

s

‡3387   Fox (A. R. Ellis)
‡3388   Figure 'Southwind' (Pinder-Davis)

1943-44

3389   Lamp vase (Khouri) as G 923
3390   Lamp vase (Khouri) as G 2469
3391   Lamp vase (Khouri) as G 730
§3392   Doughty Bird, Robin and ivy, not produced in this form
§3393   Doughty Bird, Bluebird and wildrose, not produced in this form

1944-45-46

3394   Doughty Bird, Chaffinch and May Blossom (see 3476), not produced in this form
3395   Doughty Bird, Kingfisher and beach leaves, limited edition of 500
‡3396   Figure 'Westwind' (Pinder-Davis)
‡3397   Male Chinese kneeling (Pinder-Davis)
‡3398   Female Chinese kneeling (Pinder-Davis)
‡3399   Male Chinese standing (Pinder-Davis)
‡3400   Female Chinese standing (Pinder-Davis)
§3401   Doughty Bird, Goldfinch and chicory, not produced
‡3402   Watteau figure, male standing (Pinder-Davis)
‡3403   Watteau figure, female standing (Pinder-Davis)
‡3404   Watteau figure, male sitting (Pinder-Davis)
‡3405   Watteau figure, female sitting (Pinder-Davis)
·3406   Lamp vase (Khouri)
3407   Lamp vase (Khouri)
3409   Lamp vase (Khouri)

1947

‡3410   Orange blossoms (2 sizes and a candlestick) (Mary Leigh)
‡3411   Camellia blossoms (2 sizes and a candlestick) (Mary Leigh)
‡3412   Lapageria blossoms (2 sizes and a candlestick) (Mary Leigh)
‡3414   Regency figure (Pinder-Davis)
‡3415   Regency figure (Pinder-Davis)
†3416   'April' (F. Doughty)
†3417   'October' (F. Doughty)
†3418   'November' (F. Doughty)
3419   Female Chinese, short coat (Pinder-Davis)
3420   Female Chinese, short coat (Pinder-Davis)
§3421   Pigeon, wings crossed (D. Lindner)
§3422   Pigeon, wings crossed (D. Lindner)
3423   Lamp vase
3424   Lamp vase
‡3425   Afghanistan hound (D. Lindner)
‡3426   Borzoi (D. Lindner)
3427   Doughty Group, Orange Spray left hand ⎫ limited edition of 175 pairs
3428   Doughty Group, Orange Spray right hand ⎭
3429   Doughty Bird, Magnolia Warbler, hen ⎫ limited edition of 150 pairs
3430   Doughty Bird, Magnolia Warbler, cock ⎭
3431   Doughty Group, Feijoa ⎫ limited edition of 125 pairs
3432   Doughty Group, Feijoa ⎭
†3433   'Johnnie' (or 'Farmer's Boy') (F. Doughty)

1948

3434	Equestrian statuette, H.R.H. Princess Elizabeth on 'Tommy' (D. Lindner)—limited edition of 100
3435	Figure 'Happy days' (F. Doughty)
3436	Table dessert, rose
3437	Table dessert, syringa

1949

3438	Doughty Bird, Humming Bird, cock—limited edition of 500 pairs
3439	Doughty Bird, Humming Bird, hen—limited edition of 500 pairs
†3440	'July' (F. Doughty)
†3441	'August' (F. Doughty)
‡3442	Double bird (D. Lindner)
‡3443	Double bird (D. Lindner)
‡3444	Double bird (D. Lindner)
‡3445	Double bird (D. Lindner)
3446	Chinese figure (Pinder-Davis)
3447	Chinese figure (Pinder-Davis)
†3452	'January' (F. Doughty)
†3453	'February' (F. Doughty)
†3454	'March' (F. Doughty)
†3455	'May' (F. Doughty)
†3456	'June' (F. Doughty)
†3457	'September' (or 'Snowy') (F. Doughty)
†3458	'December' (F. Doughty)

1950

‡3459	Ducks (D. Lindner)
‡3460	Ducks (D. Lindner)
‡3462	Alsatian (D. Lindner)
‡3463	English setter and Irish Setter (D. Lindner)
3464	Doughty Bird, Yellow headed blackbird cock—limited edition of 350 pairs
3465	Doughty Bird, Yellow headed blackbird hen—limited edition of 350 pairs
3466	Group Wild Horses (D. Lindner)
3467	Doughty Bird, Kinglet Cock single—limited edition of 500
3468	Doughty Bird, Kinglet double—limited edition of 500
3469	Doughty Bird, Vireo cock and azalea—limited edition of 500
3470	Doughty Bird, Vireo hen and azalea—limited edition of 500

1951

3471	Battledore (F. Doughty)
3472	Shuttlecock (F. Doughty)
3473	Balinese Dancer (Pinder-Davis)—limited edition of 25
3474	Siamese Dancer (Pinder-Davis)—limited edition of 25
3475	Angel Fish
3476	Doughty Bird Chaffinch hen (see 3394)

1952

3477	Candlestick lamp embossed
3478	Candlestick lamp plain

3479	Boy with apples (F. Doughty)
3480	Girl with apples (F. Doughty)
3481	Chinese Goddess (Pinder-Davis)
3482	Chinese Goddess (Pinder-Davis)
3483	Jester (Miss Stevens)
3484	Lamp vase (Khouri) 1969 with foot
*3485	Mask jug for Coronation (3 sizes)
3486	Bowl, tall feet (2 sizes)
3487	Bowl, plain (3 sizes)
‡3488	Punch (F. Doughty)
‡3489	Judy (F. Doughty)
3490	Coronation plaque

1953

3491	'Sea scout' (Pinder-Davis)
3492	'Lucky spider' (Pinder-Davis)
3493	'Funny fish' (Pinder-Davis)
3494	'Don't let the cat out of the bag' (Pinder-Davis)
3495	'Slow coach' (Pinder-Davis)
3496	'Joy ride' (Pinder-Davis)
3497	'Apple of your eye' (Pinder-Davis)
3498	'Early bird' (Pinder-Davis)
3499	'Two's company, three's none' (Pinder-Davis)
3500	'Wise as an owl' (Pinder-Davis)
3501	'Hen party' (Pinder-Davis)
3502	'Mad as a hatter' (Pinder-Davis)
3503	Queen's beasts 2 models (F. Gertner)
3504	'Little Rock Temple' (Pinder-Davis)
3505	'Summer house on the hill' (Pinder-Davis)
3506	Doughty Bird, Single gnatcatcher on dogwood—limited edition of 500
3507	Doughty Bird, Double gnatcatcher on dogwood—limited edition of 500

1954

3508	Doughty Bird, Myrtle warbler, cock—limited edition of 500
3509	Doughty Bird, Myrtle warbler, hen—limited edition of 500
‡3510	Red Riding Hood (Miss Stevens)
‡3511	Wolf (Miss Stevens)
3512	Doughty Bird, Bewick Wren, cock—limited edition of 500
3513	Doughty Bird, Bewick Wren, hen—limited edition of 500
‡3514	Foal (D. Lindner)
‡3515	Calves (D. Lindner)
‡3516	Maytime lambs (D. Lindner)
‡3517	Kids at play (D. Lindner)
†3518	'Sunday's child' (F. Doughty)
†3519	'Monday's child' (or 'All mine') (F. Doughty)
†3521	'Wednesday's child' (F. Doughty)
†3522	'Thursday's child' (F. Doughty)
†3523	'Friday's child' (F. Doughty)
†3524	'Saturday's child' (F. Doughty)
3525	Doughty Bird, Scarlet Tanager, cock—limited edition of 500
3526	Doughty Bird, Scarlet Tanager, hen—limited edition of 500
3527	Lying fox (D. Lindner)
3528	Lying hound (D. Lindner)

‡3529   Young spotted deer (D. Lindner)
‡3530   Goat (D. Lindner)
‡3531   Goat (D. Lindner)
3532   Doughty Bird, Oven bird, cock—limited edition of 500
3533   Doughty Bird, Oven bird, hen—limited edition of 500
†3534   'Tuesday's child' (F. Doughty)
*3535   Officer of the 29th Foot (The Worcestershire Reg.) (F. Gertner)
3536   Doughty Bird, Parula Warbler, cock—limited edition of 500
3537   Doughty Bird, Parula Warbler, hen—limited edition of 500

1955

3539   Doughty Bird, Yellow throat, cock—limited edition of 350
3540   Doughty Bird, Yellow throat, hen—limited edition of 350
3541   London cries, 'Rose' (Pinder-Davis)
3542   London cries, 'Violets' (Pinder-Davis)
3543   London cries, 'Heather' (Pinder-Davis)
3544   Lamp column, 3283 cut down
3545   Bermudan shell (Van Ruyckevelt)
3546   'Spring morning' (F. Doughty)
3547   'Summer day' (F. Doughty)
3548   Doughty Bird, Phoebe hen and Flame Vine—limited edition of 500
3549   Doughty Bird, Phoebe cock and Flame Vine—limited edition of 500
3550   Balinese dancer, small size (Pinder-Davis)
3551   Balinese dancer, small size (Pinder-Davis)
‡3552   Brer Fox (Peggy Foy)
‡3553   Brer Rabbit (Peggy Foy)
‡3554   Brer Rabbit (Peggy Foy)
‡3555   Brer Rabbit (Peggy Foy)
‡3556   Brer Rabbit (Peggy Foy)
‡3558   White boy (Peggy Foy)
‡3559   'Piccaninny' (Peggy Foy)
3560   'Daisy' (Pinder Davis)
3561   Chanticleer (D. Lindner)
3562   Gamecock (D. Lindner)
3563   Round cabbage leaf dish
3564   Oval cabbage leaf dish
3565   Cabbage leaf dish
†3566   Round vine leaf dish
*3567   Round vine leaf dish
*3568   Melon dish

1956

3569   Figure 'The seamstress' (F. Doughty)
3570   Lying fox (D. Lindner)
3571   Lying hound (D. Lindner)
†3572   Red Hind (small size) (Van Ruyckevelt)
†3573   Four Eyed Fish (small size) (Van Ruyckevelt)
†3574   Blue Angel Fish (small size) (Van Ruyckevelt)
†3575   Sergeant Major Fish (small size) (Van Ruyckevelt)
†3576   Yellow grunt fish (small size) (Van Ruyckevelt)
3577   Four-eyed fish (large size) (Van Ruyckevelt)—limited edition of 500
3578   Spanish Hogg and Sergeant Major fish (large size) (Van Ruyckevelt)—limited edition of 500

†3579   Spade fish (small size) (Van Ruyckevelt)
3580   Trooper of the Swiss Guard of H.H. the Pope (F. Gertner)—limited edition of 150
3581   Liserion (Azori)
3582   Marguerite (Azori)
3583   Coquelicot (Azori)
3584   Anemone (Azori)
3585   Le Panier (Azori)
3586   La Fleur (Azori)
3587   L'Oiseau (Azori)
3588   La Miroir (Azori)
3589   Privy Chamberlain of the Sword and Cape (F. Gertner)—limited edition of 150
3594   Colonel of the Noble Guard of H.H. the Pope (Neal French)—limited edition of 150
3595   Officer of the Palatine Guard of H.H. the Pope (Neal French)—limited edition of 150
3596   Gendarme of H.H. the Pope (Neal French)—limited edition of 150
3602   Red Hind Fish (large size) (Van Ruyckevelt)—limited edition of 500
3603   Blue Angel Fish (large size) (Van Ruyckevelt)—limited edition of 500
3604   Squirrel Fish (large size) (Van Ruyckevelt)—limited edition of 500
3605   Rock Beauty Fish (large size) (Van Ruyckevelt)—limited edition of 500
3606   Parrot Fish (large size) (Van Ruyckevelt)—not yet produced
‡3607   Clarissa (large size) (Neal French)

1957

§3608   Alice ⎫
§3609   Cheshire Cat ⎪
§3610   Mock Turtle ⎪
§3611   White Rabbit ⎬ (F. Doughty)
§3612   The Duchess ⎪
§3613   The Do Do ⎪
§3614   Father William ⎭
†3615   Long furred cat, Ginger or Grey Persian (F. Doughty)
†3616   Short furred cat, Tortoiseshell or Grey Ginger (F. Doughty)
3617   Doughty Bird, Elf Owl—limited edition of 500
3618   Doughty Bird, Cactus Wren cock—limited edition of 500
3619   Doughty Bird, Cactus Wren hen—limited edition of 500
‡3620   Amanda (Neal French)
3621   Flower vase with or without handle
3622   Officer of the Life Guards, equestrian (D. Lindner)—limited edition of 150
3623   Officer of the Blues, equestrian (D. Lindner)—limited edition of 150
3627   Doughty Bird, Scissor Tailed Flycatcher—limited edition of 250 coloured and 75 white
*3628   Leaf tray (3 sizes)
†3629   'First Dance' (F. Doughty)
†3630   'Sweet Anne' (F. Doughty)
3631   Flower vase candlestick
3632   Doughty Bird, Carolina Paroquet—limited edition of 250 coloured and 75 white
†3634   Flower vase (2 sizes)
3635   Heart-shaped dish (P. Gertner)
3636   Embossed square dish (P. Gertner)

3637   Brooch, plain and embossed (P. Gertner)
†3638   New Wednesday's child

1958

3639   Doughty Bird, Canyon Wren, cock—limited edition of 500
3640   Doughty Bird, Canyon Wren, hen—limited edition of 500
3641   Coffee pot
3642   'Lisette' (Ruth Van Ruyckevelt)—limited edition of 500
3643   'Penelope' (Ruth Van Ruyckevelt)—limited edition of 500
3644   Leaf tray
†3645   Cardinal small
†3646   Jay
†3647   American Robin
†3648   Waxwing
†3649   Bluebird
†3650   Western Tanager
3651   Doughty Bird, Lazuli Bunting, cock—limited edition of 500
3652   Doughty Bird, Lazuli Bunting, hen—limited edition of 500
3653   Tropical flower
3654   'Spanish Beauty'
3655   'Surprise' (F. Doughty)
§3656   'Mayflower' (and see 3679) (F. Doughty)
3657   Doughty Bird, Vermilion flycatcher—limited edition of 500
3658   Doughty Bird, Vermilion flycatcher—limited edition of 500
3659   Doughty Bird, Cerulean warbler—limited edition of 500
3660   Doughty Bird, Cerulean warbler—limited edition of 500
3661   Shadow candlestick
3662   Nursing Sister of London Hospital (Ruth Van Ruyckevelt)—limited edition of 500
3663   Nursing Sister of St. Thomas's Hospital (Ruth Van Ruyckevelt)—limited edition of 500
3664   Passion Flower (Van Ruyckevelt)—limited edition of 500
3665   Doughty Bird, Mountain Blue Bird—limited edition of 500
3666   Doughty Bird, Mountain Blue Bird—limited edition of 500

1959

§3667   'The Winner' with jockey and stable boy, cancelled (D. Lindner)
3668   Hereford Bull (D. Lindner)—limited edition of 1,000 from 'Vern Inspiration' owned by Capt. R. S. de Quincey
3669   Doughty Bird, Audubon Warbler, cock—limited edition of 500
3670   Doughty Bird, Audubon Warbler, hen—limited edition of 500
*3671   'The Winner' (grey or brown horse) (D. Lindner)
3672   Oval spoon tray
3673   Gentiana Acaulis, alpine—not made (D. Doughty)
3674   Pitcher plant
*3675   Coldstream Guards Officer (F. Gertner)
3676   Lamp
*3677   Scots Guards Officer (F. Gertner)
3678   Capt. Harry Llewellyn on 'Foxhunter' (D. Lindner)—limited edition—400 unsigned, 100 signed
§3679   'Falconer' made to go with 3656 (F. Doughty)
3680   Shell Tray
3681   'Beatrice' (Ruth Van Ruyckevelt)—limited edition of 500

3682	'Caroline' (Ruth Van Ruyckevelt)—limited edition of 500
3683	Holly Plate—not produced (F. Doughty)
3684	One circus horse (D. Lindner)
3686	Doughty Bird, Lark Sparrow on Gila Flower—limited edition of 500
3687	'Rebecca' (Ruth Van Ruyckevelt)—limited edition of 500
3688	'Louisa' (Ruth Van Ruyckevelt)—limited edition of 500
3689	Jersey Cow (D. Lindner)—limited edition of 500
3690	Doughty Bird, Wagtail, cock—limited edition of 500
3691	Doughty Bird, Wagtail, hen—limited edition of 500
3692	Doughty Bird, Redstart on Gorse, cock—limited edition of 500
3693	Doughty Bird, Redstart on Gorse, hen—limited edition of 500
3694	Doughty Bird, Whitethroat, cock—limited edition of 500
3695	Doughty Bird, Whitethroat, hen—limited edition of 500
3696	Doughty Bird, Wren—limited edition of 500
3697	Aberdeen Angus (D. Lindner)—limited edition of 500

1960

3698	'Invitation' (F. Doughty)
3699	'Red Ribbons' (F. Doughty)
3700	Tea Party group (Ruth Van Ruyckevelt)—limited edition of 250
3701	Doughty Bird, Nightingale—limited edition
3702	Santa Gertrudis bull (D. Lindner)—limited edition of 500
3703	Doughty Bird, Goldcrest, cock, not yet started—limited edition of 500
3704	Doughty Bird, Goldcrest, hen, not yet started—limited edition of 500
3705	Oval spoon tray
3706	3 partition tray

1961

3707	Doughty Bird, Robin in autumn woods—limited edition of 500
3708	Doughty Bird, Blue Tit, cock—limited edition of 500
3709	Doughty Bird, Blue Tit, hen—limited edition of 500
3710	Hibiscus (Van Ruyckevelt)—limited edition of 500
3711	Tall bon bon (P. Gertner)
3712	Doughty Bird, Bullfinch—limited edition, not yet started
3713	Doughty Bird, Meadow Pipit—limited edition, not yet started
3714	Siamese cat (F. Doughty)
3715	Water lily
3716	Triple tray, gadroon edge
3717	Triple tray, fluted panels
3718	Tray for Tiffany's
3719	Arab Stallion (D. Lindner)—limited edition of 500
3720	'Will you, won't you?' (F. Doughty)
3721	Sail fish (Van Ruyckevelt)—limited edition of 500
3722	Flying fish (Van Ruyckevelt)—limited edition of 500
3723	Doughty Bird, Chiffchaff on Hogweed—limited edition of 500
3724	Rose and blackberry ring candlestick
3725	Rose candlestick
3726	Doughty Bird, Moorhen on Water lily pads—limited edition of 500
3727	Doughty Bird, Wren hen on Burnet rose—limited edition of 500

1962

‡3728	Modelled fruit (Neal French)
‡3729	Right hand (Neal French)

210. Two of the set of 12 Fontainebleau figures modelled by Neal French, made in hard porcelain and intended for table decoration in the eighteenth-century Meissen style; there are 6 different figures each with 2 forms of decoration. See page 74.

208. Mallard, from the American gamebird series, modelled by Ronald van Ruyckevelt, issued in a limited edition of 500 in 1968, height 12 inches, length $12\frac{1}{2}$ inches. See page 72.

209. Day and Night, pair modelled by Arnold Machin, made in a limited edition of 250 pairs in glazed hard porcelain, height $10\frac{1}{2}$ inches without plinth. See page 74.

206. A tropical fish series study of blue angel fish, issued in 1958 in a edition of 500, modelled by Ronald van Ruyckevelt, height 12 inches, length 6¾ inches. See page 72.

207. Sailfish from the sporting fish series, modelled by Ronald van Ruyckevelt and issued in a limited edition of 500, height 8¾ inches, length 11 inches.

204. Sister of the London Hospital, modelled by Ruth van Ruyckevelt and issued in 1963 in a limited edition of 500, height 6¾ inches.

205. Ronald van Ruyckevelt working on the model of the Pintail in the American Game Bird series. See page 72.

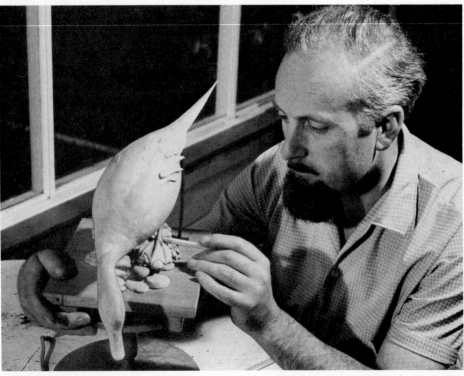

203.   Charlotte and Jane, dressed in the styles of 1896, modelled by
Ruth van Ruyckevelt and issued in 1968 in a limited edition of 500,
height $6\frac{1}{2}$ inches, width $5\frac{1}{2}$ inches.

202. Exquisite group of 'The Tea Party' modelled by Ruth van Ruyckevelt and issued as a limited edition of 250 in 1964, height 8 inches, width 7½ inches. See page 72.

200. Study of a Charolais Bull, modelled by Doris Lindner, from Vaillant, the 1967 champion of the Concours Général Agricole de Paris, owned by M. Paul Pacaud, Viry, near Charolles. A limited edition of 500, issued in 1968, height 8 inches, length 11 inches.

201. The plaster moulds that form the separate parts that are built up into the Santa Gertrudis Bull, with the cast pieces of raw china body awaiting sticking up.

199. Companion statuette of H.R.H. Duke of Edinburgh on his polo pony. Modelled by Doris Lindner and issued in 1968 in a limited edition of 750, height 15¾ inches, length 12½ inches.

198. Equestrian statuette of H.M. the Queen (when Princess
Elizabeth) in the uniform of Colonel-in-Chief of the Grenadier Guards on
the occasion of the Trooping of the Colour in 1947, on Tommy, the
police horse, modelled by Doris Lindner. A limited edition of 100,
height 15 inches, length 11 inches. See page 63.

196. A remarkable action study of an Arab stallion, modelled by Doris Lindner from Indian Magic, winner of many prizes. A limited edition of 500, issued in 1962, height 10 inches, length 11½ inches, on a walnut plinth. See page 73.

197. Equestrian study of Marian Coakes on Stroller, the international show jumper, a limited edition subject issued in 1970. See page 73.

211. Dramatic study of Napoleon crossing the Alps, modelled by Bernard Winskill, bone china body, decorated in strong red, black and gold. The first of a military commanders series, issued in 1969 in a limited edition of 750; height $16\frac{1}{4}$ inches, length $14\frac{3}{4}$ inches, rosewood plinth with ormolu base and frieze. See page 73.

212. Typical Scottie Wilson designs in black, on crownware body, the mark having the name 'Scottie Wilson' and 'Royal Worcester Crown Ware England'. See page 72.

213. Lithograph colour prints can be of fine quality, as illustrated by this beautiful pattern called 'Royal Garden', first made in 1970. The pink and white roses, different toned green leaves and effective gilding are noteworthy examples of modern printing on well-designed china shapes. See page xxviii.

214. Example of the fine quality of the transfer printing still produced by the Company. A limited edition bowl commemorating the 350th Anniversary of the Sailing of the Mayflower, printed in black. See page xxviii.

215. Attractive small china vessels, modelled by Paul Gertner, some based on early Worcester shapes, painted with 'Imari' designs. Above, left to right, 3849, 3862, 3863, 3847. Centre, 3854, 3851, 3866, 3850. Below, 3853, RA2, 3858 and 3855.

216. Examples of lustre ware, made with either gold or silver lustre on 'Severn' shape. See page 74.

217. Examples of bold and colourful litho transfers on the hard porcelain body, capable of being used in the oven.

218. Cats. Left, short-haired shape 3613; right, long-haired shape 3615, in current production and made in different colours.

219. The frontage of the fine new porcelain factory extension built on the banks of the River Severn within a few hundred yards of the existing factory. Production in the new factory started in 1970. See page 74.

220. The Men Painters and some of the paintresses, taken in the summer of 1970 in the same position as the 1928 group. From left to right: back row, Richard Lewis, Christopher Smith, David Buckle, Alan Telford and Michael Tandy; second row, Malcolm Johnson, Melvyn Holloway, Frank Higgins, Anthony Thompson, David Peplow, Ray Poole, Nigel Creed, Carole Hughes, Christine Erdman and Dorothy Sparks; third row, Fay Stevens, Pat Rigby, Angela Taylor, Judy Vickers, Gillian Moody, Vyonne Evans, Judy Owen, Lorraine Smith, Wyn Harris, Marie Millward, Lybbe Griffiths, Mona McHarg and Eveline Sedgley; front row, Freda Griffiths, John Smith, Arthur Badham, John Freeman, Edward Townsend, Harry Ayrton, Derek Jones, Peter Platt and Daisy Rea.

‡3730   Left hand (Neal French)
§3731   Red Admiral butterfly on Clematis (Peter Ewence)
3732   Small gadroon candlestick
3733   Quarter horse (D. Lindner)—limited edition of 500
3734   Doughty Bird, Kingfisher cock and Autumn beech—limited edition of 500
3735   Doughty Bird, Long Tailed Tit, not yet produced
3736   Lamp with roses as 3725
3737   Lamp without roses as 3725
3738   Vase as 3685 without handles
3739   As 6/161 (3)
3740   As 2354 lamp, larger base
3741   As 3424 lamp, larger base
3742   Clog
3743   Loving cup
3744   Wine cooler
3745   Captain Raimondo d'Inzeo on Merano (D. Lindner)—limited edition of 500
3746   British Friesian bull (D. Lindner)—limited edition of 500
‡3747   'Young England' (Neal French)
‡3748   'Treasure Trove' (Neal French)
3749   'Melanie' (Ruth Van Ruyckevelt)—limited edition of 500
3750   'Rosalind' (Ruth Van Ruyckevelt)—limited edition of 500
3751   Tarpon (Van Ruyckevelt)—limited edition of 500
3752   Barracuda, not yet produced (Van Ruyckevelt)
3753   Dolphin (Van Ruyckevelt)—limited edition of 500
‡3754   'Poupée' (Neal French)
‡3755   'Master Mariner' (Neal French)
‡3756   'First Aid' (Neal French)
‡3757   'Sheriff'

1963

3758   Hyperion (D. Lindner)—limited edition of 500
3759   Shire Horse (D. Lindner)—limited edition of 500
†3760   'Fantail' ('November' but without bird on boy's foot)
§3761   Mayflower—see 3685 (F. Doughty) simplified version without hat or telescope
3762   As 3676 lamp with 1481 base
3763   1346 enlarged
3764   Similar to 2847, smaller
3765   Salt and pepper grinders (D. Reeves)
3766   Show slab

1964

3767   Square vase (Neal French)
3768   Cherry blossom on rock (Van Ruyckevelt)
3769   Square candlestick (Neal French)
3770   Cigar tray
3771   Nursing sister, University College Hospital (Ruth van Ruyckevelt)—limited edition of 500
3772   Bougainvillea (Van Ruyckevelt)—limited edition of 500
3773   Rectangular cigarette box
3774   'Elizabeth' (Ruth Van Ruyckevelt)—limited edition of 500
3775   'Madelaine' (Ruth Van Ruyckevelt)—limited edition of 500

3776	Jersey bull (D. Lindner)—limited edition of 500
3777	Cricket bowl, Elizabethan
3778	Blue marlin (Van Ruyckevelt)—limited edition of 500
3779	Embossed tray
3780	Tray
3781	Dairy Shorthorn bull (D. Lindner)—limited edition of 500
3782	Cache pot (3 sizes) (P. Gertner)
3783	Tea caddy

1965

3784	Flower-holder (P. Gertner)
3785	Powder box
3786	Percheron horse (D. Lindner)—limited edition of 500
3787	Bluefin Tuna (Van Ruyckevelt)—limited edition of 500
3788	Swordfish (Van Ruyckevelt)—limited edition of 500
3791	Oblong flower-holder (P. Gertner)
3792	Pierced ashtray (P. Gertner)
3793	Rope and ring flower-holder (P. Gertner)
3794	Chinese Pagoda mustard (P. Gertner)
3795	Chinese Pagoda pepper (P. Gertner)
3796	Chinese Pagoda salt (P. Gertner)
3797	Spill 6/161 type foot (P. Gertner)
3798	3-footed flower-holder (P. Gertner)
3799	Deeply scalloped punch bowl (P. Gertner)
3800	Acanthus vase (P. Gertner)
3801	Large round fluted ashtray (P. Gertner)
3802	Welsh Mountain Pony (D. Lindner)—limited edition of 500
3803	'Marion' (Van Ruyckevelt)—limited edition of 500
3804	'Charlotte and Jane' group (Van Ruyckevelt)—limited edition of 500
3805	Canadian Mountie (D. Lindner)—limited edition of 500

1966

3806	Chinese pagoda marmalade (P. Gertner)
3807	Chinese pagoda candlestick (P. Gertner)
3808	Not yet produced
3813	Mallard cock (Van Ruyckevelt)—limited edition of 500
3814	Mallard hen (Van Ruyckevelt)—limited edition of 500
3817	Arkle, racehorse (D. Lindner)—limited edition of 500
3818	Pheasant cock (ringneck) (Van Ruyckevelt)—limited edition of 500
3819	Pheasant hen (ringneck) (Van Ruyckevelt)—limited edition of 500

1967

3821	Brahman bull (D. Lindner)—limited edition of 500
3822	Bulldog 'Mack' (D. Lindner)—limited edition of 500
3823	Oleander (Van Ruyckevelt)—limited edition of 500
3824	Charolais bull (D. Lindner)—limited edition of 500
3825	Suffolk stallion (D. Lindner)—limited edition of 500
‡3826	Vennier (P. Gertner)
3827	Bob white quail, cock (Van Ruyckevelt)—limited edition of 500
3828	Bob white quail, hen (Van Ruyckevelt)—limited edition of 500
3833	Pintail drake (Van Ruyckevelt)—limited edition of 500
3834	Pintail drake (Van Ruyckevelt)—limited edition of 500

3836   Green winged teal (Van Ruyckevelt)—limited edition of 500
3841   'Emily' (Van Ruyckevelt)—limited edition of 500
3842   'Bridget' (Van Ruyckevelt)—limited edition of 500
3843   Cache pot, wire design (3 sizes)

1968

3846   H.R.H. The Duke of Edinburgh on polo pony (D. Lindner)—limited edition of 750
3847   Trinket scent bottle and cover (P. Gertner)
3848   4-sided trinket box and cover ((P. Gertner)
3849   Clover shape box and cover (P. Gertner)
3850   Moulded lid box and cover (P. Gertner)
3851   Moulded lid, 8-sided (P. Gertner) not made
3852   Moulded lid (P. Gertner)
3853   Moulded lid, oval (P. Gertner)
3854   Moulded lid, 6-sided (P. Gertner)
3855   Moulded lid, fluted front (P. Gertner)
3856   Moulded lid, trunk shape (P. Gertner) not made
3857   Moulded lid, trunk shape (P. Gertner) not made
3858   Trinket tray, heart shape (P. Gertner)
3859   Fluted scallop not made
3860   Napoleon, equestrian (Bernard Winskill)—limited edition of 750
3861   Red Cross V.A.D. Member (Van Ruyckevelt)—limited edition of 500
3862   Spill vase (P. Gertner)
3863   6-sided covered vase (P. Gertner)
3864   Cigar store Indian, for Rothman's (P. Ewence)—limited edition of 500
3866   Trinket box (P. Gertner)
3869   Appaloosa horse (D. Lindner)—limited edition of 500

1969 et seq.

3870   Wellington equestrian (B. Winskill)—limited edition of 750
3871   Mare and foal (D. Lindner)—limited edition of 750 coloured and 250 white
3872   Marian Coakes and 'Stroller' (D. Lindner)—limited edition of 750
3877   Elaine with guitar (Van Ruyckevelt)—limited edition of 750
3878   Felicity with dog (Van Ruyckevelt)—limited edition of 750
3880   Saddle Horse (D. Lindner)—limited edition of 750
3882   Palomino (D. Lindner)—limited edition of 750
3887   Alice on swing (Van Ruyckevelt)—limited edition of 750
3892   Cecilia in tree (Van Ruyckevelt)—limited editon of 750
3893   Nijinsky the racehorse (D. Lindner)—limited edition of 500
3912   H.R.H. Princess Anne on Doublet (D. Lindner)—limited edition of 750
3913   Silver Wedding Doves (Van Ruyckevelt)—limited edition of 25

Appendix II

Factory, Trade, and Year, Marks

A large number of factory trade marks have been used at Worcester since 1862 and the principal ones are shown in the following fifteen drawings. A number of variations can occur, such as additions of names or symbols of the dealers through whom the wares were sold. The principal mark from 1862 to 1875 was number 1, which can be found either impressed or printed, but rarer marks of this period are numbers 2, 3 and 4, the latter only found impressed. Another variation in this period occasionally found is the words 'Royal Porcelain Works Worcester' enclosed in an oval. The crown of mark number 1 is very different from that of mark 5, which took over in the year 1876, and mark 6 followed in 1891, having a different crown which sits down tight upon the circle and there is an addition of the word 'England'. There has been hardly any change in the mark on bone china since then, exceptions being number 7 found on Vitreous Ware and 9 on hard porcelain.

Numbers 10, 11 and 12 are the main marks on Grainger and are referred to in the special section in Chapter II, as are the marks for Hadley's factory—numbers 13 to 15. The outside factory of Locke & Company used a mark of a Globe with associated words. Some other firms have used marks that sometimes cause confusion; such as the firm of Wileman and Co. whose mark was a C across a W, under a crown; George Jones & Sons, whose mark was a J G monogram inside a Turkish looking crescent; a mark of RW, which was used by the New York Rudolstat Pottery Company of Thuringia, who made a considerable quantity of Worcester-style stained ivory wares; another Continental mark was a crown above the word ROYAL to be found on similar Worcester-styled wares.

With most of the Worcester printed marks since 1862 an elaborate system of year mark codes is used and a knowledge of these will lead to a great understanding of the wares.

Mark 1 is either found with a small capital letter directly underneath the circle or the last two numbers of the year; for example the drawing of the mark shows the number '73', which stands for the year 1873. These year numbers can be found from 1862 up to about 1877, but very few year marks before 1867 have been noticed. An alternative way of noting the year of finishing the piece was the use of small letters, such as are shown under mark 5 and these are shown in the following list, together with the 'clay' mark, found impressed in the wares and which also indicate the year of making of the piece. It will be appreciated that the year indicated by the clay mark (the year in which the vessel was fashioned) may be a year or two before the printed code mark (indicating the year in which the piece was decorated).

In the year 1891 there is no letter under the circle but the word 'England' is added. From 1892 until 1915 a system of dots is used, one dot per year, beginning with the first dot shown to the left of the crown as is seen in the drawing of mark 6, which also shows the very large letter C to indicate a piece prepared for the Chicago World Fair and not to be confused with the little letter C under the circle, which would indicate the year 1869 and would be associated with mark 1. In the following year, 1893, a second dot is added to the right of the crown, in 1894 another dot to the left of the crown, and so on until there are six dots each side of the crown, making a total of twelve dots, which indicate the year 1903. In 1904 a thirteenth dot is added under the circle and an extra dot is added for each year, until a total of twenty-four dots is reached in the year 1915. Sometimes twenty-five or twenty-six dots are found, which meant that the dot system was continued on a particular copper plate to avoid planishing it and replacing the copper.

But the main system changed in 1916, the dots being dropped as they had become too complicated. In 1916 the code is a * under the circle, each subsequent year having an extra dot put each side of the * until eleven dots are reached by 1927. In the next few years a different geometric symbol for each year is used; in 1932 there are three interlaced circles which have a dot added on alternate sides for each subsequent year.

In 1949 a letter V appears and in 1950 a letter W, to which is added a system of dots for each year, superseded by letter R in 1956. Letter W could continue if produced from an old copper, and a dot for each year added, but from 1963 the year of introduction of a shape or pattern is added and a system of a code for the actual year of production is no longer used.

The system is summed up as follows:

YEAR	CLAY MARK	PRINTED MARK	
1867	A	A	(or 67 for 1867)
8	B	B	
9	C	C	
70	D	D	
1	E	E	
2	G	G	
3	H	H	
4	I	I	
5	K	K	
6	L	L	(different crown)
7	M	M	
8	N	N	
9	P	P	
80	R	R	
1	S	S	
2	T	T	
3	U	U	
4	V	V	
5	W	W	
6	X	X	
7	Y	Y	
8	Z	Z	
9	O	O	
90	a	a	
1	b		(New crown and word England)
2	c	.	1 dot to left of crown
3	d	..	2 dots, one each side of crown
4	e		3 dots
5	f		4 dots
6	g		5 dots

YEAR	CLAY MARK	PRINTED MARK
7	h	6 dots
8	i	7 dots
9	k	8 dots
1900	m	9 dots
1	n	10 dots
2	p	11 dots
3	A	12 dots
4	B	13 dots
5	C	14 dots
6	D	15 dots
7	E	16 dots
8	G	17 dots
9	H	18 dots
10	K	19 dots
1	L	20 dots
2	M	21 dots
3	N	22 dots
4	O	23 dots
5	P	24 dots
6	Q	* under the circle (dots could continue)
7	R	.* and 1 dot
8	S	.*. and 2 dots
9	T	* and 3 dots
20	U	* and 4 dots
1	V	* and 5 dots
2	X	* and 6 dots
3	Y	* and 7 dots
4	Z	* and 8 dots
5	𝖆	* and 9 dots
6	𝖇	* and 10 dots
7	𝖈	* and 11 dots
8	𝖉	□
9	𝖊	◇
30	𝖌	÷
1	𝖍	OO
2	𝖐	OOO
3	𝖑	OOO. and 1 dot
4	𝖒	.OOO. and 2 dots
5	𝖓	and 3 dots
6	𝖔	and 4 dots
7	𝖕	and 5 dots
8	𝖖	and 6 dots
9		and 7 dots
40		and 8 dots
1		and 9 dots
1948	A	
9	B	V
50	C	W
1	D	W.
2	E	.W.
3	F	.W. and 3 dots
4	G	W and 4 dots
5	H	W and 5 dots
6	I	and 6 dots (or W and 6 dots etc.)

YEAR	CLAY MARK	PRINTED MARK
7	K	and 7 dots
8	L	and 8 dots
9	M	and 9 dots
60	N	and 10 dots
1	O	and 11 dots
2	P	and 12 dots
3	Q	and 13 dots

After the year 1963 the year of introduction of shape or pattern will be noted, except on transfer printed patterns which will continue the W and dot system until there are twenty dots (year 1970) and thereafter a circle will be put around a dot for each subsequent year; i.e. twenty dots with five of them ringed will equal 1975.

The Grainger factory used a code letter system from 1891 to 1902. A letter was added under the word England, below the Shield Mark, as follows:

A	1891	E	1895	I	1899
B	1892	F	1896	J	1900
C	1893	G	1897	K	1901
D	1894	H	1898	L	1902

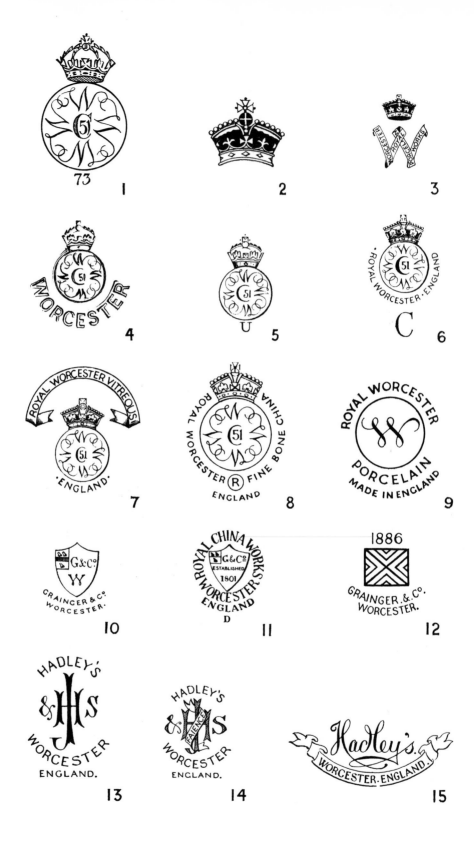

Extracts from the Diary of Henry Baldwyn

This diary kept by Henry Baldwyn, the Worcester piano tuner and harpist, father of C. H. C. Baldwyn, the Worcester painter, has been made available by Rodney C. Baldwyn, grandson of C. H. C. (Charley) Baldwyn.

There was an interesting mixture of painting and music in the life of Charley, musician friends often coming to their little house in the Arboretum to enjoy musical evenings. Arboretum Road was the road built where the driveway to the factory, shown in Plate 25, would have been. Out of the many thousands of entries, the few quoted here give an interesting picture of a dedicated, hard-working painter from a musical family, who would walk miles in the surrounding countryside to study birds, frequently buying or borrowing them to study. They also give a vivid impression of the social life of the factory and town at the time. Notes in square brackets are editorial, parentheses are those of the diarist.

1885

4th Feb.	Charley went to tea with W. Hawkins. Charley paid cheque of one guinea prize for best Christmas card.
15th Apr.	The China Works Tricycle Club met at Mr. Evans house, Barbourne Bank for a run.
21st May	Tuned at Mr. Albert Gyngell, Waverley Terrace, paid 3/6.
5th Jun.	Edgar had his violin lesson at Elgar's. [Edgar was another son.]
14th Sep.	Charley bought plates cups and saucers at his works (paid 4/9).
31st Dec.	Charley went sketching by Hawford (G. Johnson along).

1886

1st Jan.	Drawing of Charley's returned (from Magazine of Music, London). Message sent from Mr. Evans (China Works) for Charley's attendance (to do some work for him).
23rd Jan.	Cheque sent Charley £1.1.0 (prize from Magazine of Music, London).
24th Apr.	(Good Friday) Charley went out sketching with Buckingham and Johnson.
27th Sep.	Mr. T. Bott here at work at china painting.
30th Sep.	Box of tiles brought here for Charley's painting.
2nd Nov.	Charley went to Surveyor of Taxes and gave his income as £140.
6th Nov.	Mr. Bott paid Charley £5 for work done (painting tiles).

1887

5th Jan.	Charley went to Dr. Bates (for pain in the head). Charley paid him 5/–.
14th Mar.	Charley took picture to Masons.
23rd Apr.	This morning the postman brought the news (by card) that Charley's picture (Study on Teazles) was accepted by the Royal Academy.
26th Apr.	Maud and Charley went to the Public Hall (Presentation to Mr. E. P. Evans of the Royal Porcelain Works, Diglis).
28th Apr.	A reporter called from the Journal Office, High Street, about Charley's picture in the Royal Academy, London—I went down to the China Works to see Charley about it. Charley called himself at the Journal Office.

[The following report appeared in Berrow's Worcester Journal, on Saturday 30th April 1887, 'Mr. C. H. C. Baldwyn's success in connection with the Royal Academy Exhibition is notable. . . . The large water-colour drawing which is now at the Royal Academy Exhibition is a study from nature of teazles, birds and foliage. It is the first picture he had submitted to the Royal Academy committee; in fact, the first he has sent anywhere for exhibition, excepting the porcelain picture. It is, I imagine, a long time since an artist engaged as Mr. Baldwyn is has been fortunate enough to get a first painting hung at Burlington House. There can be no idea of influence or prepossession. It is a case of sheer merit, and I trust Mr. Baldwyn will go on adding to the reputations of local art.' This picture is shown in Plate 124.]

2nd Aug.	This morning I took two vases for Charley to Padmore's (Sidbury) to be fired (paid to man 3/– owing to bottle of liquid gold). [Probably refers to vases decorated privately by Charley.]
3rd Oct.	Church brought Charley's china painting—'Garfield's death'—from Underhills (I paid him 6d for it).

1888

9th Jul.	Charley went with W. Hawkins to London (to the Royal Academy of Painting).
4th Sep.	Barrel of ale brought from Ind Coope. Charley's picture fell down (Teazles).
16th Sep.	Present of an owl sent for Charley (from Hughes, Shaw Street). [Charley was later to marry John Hughes' daughter.]
2nd Dec.	Emily Hughes called to bring a dead bird (a Jay).

1889

19th Mar.	Charley took his first lesson in perspective drawing of W. Ricketts.

1890

6th Feb.	I rode for the first time in the New Omnibus from the Cherry Orchard to the Cross (paid 2d).
26th Apr.	This morning Charley received notice that two of his pictures were accepted by the Royal Academy.
13th May	Charley went to the first meeting of the Worcester Art Club (held at Mr. Firkins, Barbourne).
22nd Jun.	Charley bought three thrushes for 1/6 in Severn Street.
23rd Jun.	Letter came for Charley about his picture being accepted by the Royal Society of British Artists.

3rd Aug.	This morning someone unknown sent Charley fifteen pounds for his picture 'Study of Teazles', letter dated London, Aug. 2nd 1890. [Now in possession of Charley's grandson Rodney Baldwyn, see Plate 124.]
8th Nov.	Charley paid 10/6 at H. Day's office, 5 Foregate Street (Subscription for the Art Club). Mr. Richardson brought 2 pairs of new trousers made (paid him 19/– for it) at night.

1891

3rd Mar.	Charley received letter from Royal Institute of Water Colours.
3rd Jul.	Charley borrowed a young magpie from Mr. Elvin (Saddler) Sidbury for painting. Charley had his club money 15/6.

1892

16th Jan.	George Johnson's sister-in-law called here for his money—3/– wages, 19/8 club money (George being ill).
3rd Mar.	Cheque for £5.17.0 sent for Charley for sale of picture 'Magpies' to Mr. Caldicott.
23rd Apr.	Notice of acceptance of Charley's picture sent from Royal Academy London (two sent, one kept).
30th May	Charley sold Mr. Wood (Tobacconist, Broad Street) a picture (birds) for three guineas. Charley took Mr. C. Williams a bottle of whiskey commission on sale of picture.

1893

15th Feb.	Charley sent two pictures for exhibition at the Royal Institute of Painters in Watercolours, Piccadilly, London. Charley gave Miss Thomas her first lesson in china painting at 9 Britannia Square.
1st Mar.	This morning notice was received that Charley's two pictures were for exhibition at the Royal Institute of Water Colours, London.
13th Mar.	Mr. Mackay from Bristol called to see Charley and left forty-eight cards for him to paint.

1894

30th Jan.	Charley went to the Theatre. The play 'Charley's Aunt'.
3rd Apr.	Visit of the Duke of York to Worcester (laid the stone at the Victoria Institute). Charley went with Jarman to Great Bridge for the day—to paint.

1895

1st Jan.	This day Charley called upon John Hughes (Shaw Street) to see him about Emily Hughes. The engagement entered upon.
18th Feb.	Charley sent a vase to the Potteries to be fired (Mr. Plant, Stoke on Trent).
3rd Aug.	Charley sent two pictures to Jackson of Liverpool for exhibition at the Walker Art Gallery.
26th Aug.	Charley went to Warndon to let our young owl fly away. (Emily Hughes along).

1897

15th Mar.   This morning my son, Charles Henry Clifford Baldwyn was married
             at the Baptist Chapel, Sansome Walk to Miss Emily Hughes, adopted
             daughter of the late Mr. John Hughes, Builder of Shaw St. Worcester.
             Best man Mr. W. Hawkins.

1900

9th May   Charley called this morning to say that his little daughter Stella died
             at 19 minutes to one last night (from meningitis). Buried 11th May—
             age one year eleven months.
18th May   Yapp brought the two birds from Charley—cockatoo and young crow.
20th Oct.   Yapp brought the cockatoo from Charley's ('Stokesay'). [The paintings
             of cockatoos date from this period.]

1901

8th Aug.   Charley & Edgar went to flower show (Madresfield Court)—Frank
             Elgar's band.

1905

27th Jan.   Charley sent Musical design to Sir Edward Elgar.
31st Jan.   Letter sent to Charley from Sir Edward Elgar (from 'Plas Gwyn'
             Hereford) in return for musical design sent on Friday last. [Design
             now lost.]
16th May   Charley, George Johnson and the two Stintons from the China Works
             —went to Stourbridge to see exhibition of pictures.

1907

4th Jan.   Charley's infant, Bernard, died, aged one year.

1909

9th Jan.   Mr. Booth [Walter R.] called for Charley in Motor Car and went to
             Martley to see Mr. Buckingham.

Bibliographical Note

There have only been two major published books dealing exclusively with the productions of the Worcester Royal Porcelain Company. These were *Worcester China, a record of the work of forty five years 1852–1897*, by R. W. Binns, published by Quaritch in 1897, and *The American Birds of Dorothy Doughty*, a critical appreciation by George Savage, published in a limited edition of 1500 copies by The Worcester Royal Porcelain Company Limited in 1962. The former book was Mr. Binns' follow-up to his monumental *Century of Potting in the City of Worcester*, which dealt with the first hundred years of the history, and although *Worcester China* tends to be a bit rambling and to concentrate on laudatory newspaper reports, it illuminates the great love of the factory, its products and craftsmen that Mr. Binns had. Mr. Savage's book is a magnificently produced and printed detailed account of the Doughty Birds, their modeller and methods of production, illustrates all the birds of the American series in colour and is full of Miss Doughty's anecdotes about the finding and modelling of each bird.

A number of published books have included sections devoted to this period of Worcester, the most useful being *Victorian Porcelain* by Geoffrey A. Godden, published by Herbert Jenkins, 1961, and *Worcester Porcelain* by Stanley W. Fisher, published by Ward Lock & Co. Ltd. 1968.

The Company has also issued a number of small booklets that provide a lot of interesting information. The most important of these were the booklets variously entitled in such ways as *A Guide Through the Royal Porcelain Works Worcester* which were given to visitors to the factory from the Kerr & Binns period onwards, the charge for the tour and the booklet being sixpence in the nineteenth century. Engravings by the Callowhills and others were used, an example being shown in Plate 26 of this book. Other publications of interest are *Report on Proceedings at a Luncheon to the Directors* printed by the Worcestershire Newspapers & General Printing Company, Worcester in 1884; *The Shakespeare Service* reprinted from *Worcester China* by R. W. Binns, printed by George W. Jones, Fleet Street, London in 1897; *The Story of Royal Worcester China* by John Drinkwater, published by Asprey & Co. Ltd. in the 1920s; *The Perrins Museum of Royal Worcester Porcelain*, a reprint of a *Pottery Gazette* article of August, September and October, 1956; catalogue of a selection of Early Worcester Porcelain and a series of Doughty Birds, held at Worcester House, 30 Curzon Street, London in 1960; handbook of a Summer Exhibition of Worcester Victorian Porcelain held at Curzon Street in 1961, written by Geoffrey Godden, and a catalogue of the same Exhibition; *British Birds in Porcelain by Dorothy Doughty*, issued in conjunction with an Exhibition at Curzon Street in 1962; *The Story of Royal Worcester and the Dyson Perrins Museum* by George Savage, published by Pitkin Pictorials Limited in 1968; *The Ceramic Birds and Flowers of Dorothy Doughty* by Joan Bamford, reprinted from *Antiques and Investing*, August 1969; *Royal Worcester Models of Ronald Van Ruyckevelt* reprinted from *World of Antiques*, published by Antique Dealer and Collectors

Guide; *The Ceramic Sculpture of Doris Lindner*, by Joan Bamford, published by The Dyson Perrins Museum, Worcester 1970 and *The Collectors' Handbook of Royal Worcester Models*, published by Worcester Royal Porcelain Company Limited 1970. Copies of the last five publications may be obtained from the Dyson Perrins Museum, Worcester.

Index